AF623957

GLOBAL HISTORY OF PHILOSOPHY

Global History of Philosophy

VOLUME II

The Han-Hellenistic-Bactrian Period

JOHN C. PLOTT

with

James Michael Dolin

Russell E. Hatton

Paul D. Mays

MOTILAL BANARSIDASS

Delhi Varanasi Patna

Bangalore Madras

First Edition: Delhi, 1979
Reprinted: Delhi, 1989

MOTILAL BANARSIDASS
Bungalow Road, Jawahar Nagar, Delhi 110 007

Branches
Chowk, Varanasi 221 001
Ashok Rajpath, Patna 800 004
24 Race Course Road, Bangalore 560 001
120 Royapettah High Road, Mylapore, Madras 600 004

© 1989 by Motilal Banarsidass. All rights Reserved.

ISBN: 81-208-0456-2

PRINTED IN INDIA
BY JAINENDRA PRAKASH JAIN AT SHRI JAINENDRA PRESS, A-45 NARAINA INDUSTRIAL AREA, PHASE I, NEW DELHI 110 028 AND PUBLISHED BY NARENDRA PRAKASH JAIN FOR MOTILAL BANARSIDASS, DELHI 110 007.

CONTENTS

FOREWORD

A Global History of Philosophy is bound to be a hazardous venture in Comparative Philosophy. It requires not merely stupendous scholarship but discernment in selection, judgment and appraisal of ideas. Professor John Plott has, in a fair measure, succeeded in this attempt.

The present Volume (which is the Second Volume of the *Global History of Philosophy*) is concerned with the period from the 3rd Century B.C. to the end of the 3rd Century A.D.—a span of nearly six hundred years in the history of human thought. The area covered is where religious and philosophical activities were cultivated, in China, India, Greece, Rome and Persia. The author calls this the Han-Hellenistic-Bactrian Period. The seminal ideas which were sown in the Axial Period (dealt with in the First Volume) are elaborated, explained, systematised, synthesized and syncreticized by the thinkers during this period.

The Chinese philosophers like, Tung Chung, Ma Jung, Wang Fu, Hsun Yueh, Ko-Hung, Wang Ch'ung and some others, were concerned with interpretations, modifications and sophisticated applications to social conditions in various permutations and combinations of Confucianism, Taoism and Neo-Taoism. Buddhism had just begun to appear; its influence was marginal, but was distinctly growing.

In the Indian context, the *Bhagavadgītā* (assuming that it took final shape in the 3rd or 2nd Century B.C.) is first taken up for comment and discussion. This is followed by the Rise of Mahāyāna, the Mādhyamika (Nāgārjuna) and Yogācāra (Asaṅga-Vasubandhu) and by the Jaina system of Kundakundācārya and Umāsvāti, etc.

In the West, we have an impressive array of philosophers to consider: from the Sceptics of Academy like Pyrrho, Carneades, followed later on by Sextus Empiricus; Seneca, Plutarch and the widespread and influential Stoics like Epictetus and Marcus Aurelius; Lucretius; Philo the Jew and Plotinus; and the Rise of Christianity.

It must not be thought that Professor Plott deals with the philosophers of different regions piecemeal and in isolation, separately as it were. If at all, they are integrated together, and their points of view are shown to emerge and clash, from an understandable norm. Parochialisms are strictly ruled out; the 'mysterious East' and the 'militant West' are not sundered; their interaction is already pre-supposed. I would like to draw the attention of the serious reader especially to Professor Plott's treatment of Nāgārjuna and Philo (pp. 84-95) and Plotinus and Vasubandhu (pp. 127-164). These constitute some of the brilliant spots of the whole book.

What has Nāgārjuna's Dialectic, his Śūnyavāda, in common with Philo's allegorical interpretation of the *Septuagint*, his gnosticism and above all his passionate attachment to God and theism? Probably, the *via negotiva*, their conception of *Sophia* and *prajñā* and the distinction of levels of truth might have suggested the comparison. As against this, there are vital differences. Nāgārjuna's dialectic is destructive; all points of view must be given up as empty and meaningless. This is brought home by *reductio ad absurdum* arguments. The 'No-Position', 'no-metaphysics' is Śūnyatā or Prajñā; this itself cannot be construed as constituting another position. Nāgārjuna should have been, in my opinion, studied with Sextus Empiricus; they have a good deal in common.

The comparative study of Vasubandhu with Plotinus is more apt, fruitful and sustained. "In outline, Plotinus' cosmological scheme is as follows: from the One proceeds Intelligence (*nous*), from Intelligence proceeds the Soul, from the Soul proceed the souls, and through the agency of the Soul and souls comes the sensible world. Matter is the final term in this hierarchical procession. In outline, Vasubandhu's cosmological scheme is as follows: *Vijñaptimātra* gives rise to the *Ālayavijñāna* or simply the *Ālaya*, the *Ālaya* gives rise to *Manas*, and from *Manas* we proceed to the egos and then to subject-object duality we call the sensible world." (Actually, from the *manas*, there are the rising of six content-consciousness (ṣaṭ-pravṛtti-vijñāna)). "The final term in this hierarchical scheme is, in a negative sense, non-substance, i.e. there is not posited any kind of matter out of which the world is made." (p.131). After noting the similarities and differences,

Plott concludes the comparison by saying: "Perhaps the greatest comparison between Plotinus and Vasubandhu is not between any of the doctrines we have presented but in the spirit of philosophy as found in them. To follow one rather than the other may mean a difference in method, but their views of the nature, destiny, and dignity of man are virtually the same," (p. 164).

(Professor Plott's use of the term *Yogācārin* in a number of places is incorrect Sanskrit; probably, he has taken it from Conze. The term *Yogācāra* stands both for the system as well as for the advocates of the system).

One other unique feature of the book is the absence of biased or partisan attitude. Although a westerner, Professor Plott is completely free from any trace of superciliousness in dealing with non-western philosophy or religion. One may differ from him in his interpretation or judgment of certain philosophers or systems. What Professor Plott writes is quite free from prejudice, bias or favouritism. I am tempted to quote to show this objectivity in his attitude and judgment. Regarding the *Bhagavadgītā*, he says:

> "Among the world's scriptures, the *Gītā* remains perhaps the most intensely philosophical in that it contains, as well as keen aesthetic appeal, a full panoply of problems in epistemology, religious *ascesis*, ethical obligations in a problematic setting, in addition to hints and nuances in everything from cosmology to philosophy of history. In other words, it does belong explicitly to the history of philosophy as well as to the history of religion in a way that is not true of the Judaeo-Christian scriptures or even the Sūtra literature of the Mahāyāna.
>
> The *Gītā* may yet, even after all these centuries, have a major role to play in formulation of souls disciplined in relation to Self, humble and ready to be of service to others, purifying the world by renunciation of the things and values that hinder righteousness and salvation from all that is gross and unworthy of man, whose essential nature is, if only ignorance and delusion are removed, divine." (p. 26).

Similarly with regard to Nāgārjuna, he says this:

> Nāgārjuna's *Kārikās* represent perhaps the most stringent statement of a systematic position that speaks 'from beyond system that the world has so far witnessed. Nāgārjuna's greatness cannot be denied; he stands alone at the pinnacle of Hindu-Buddhist dialectics. Philo, on the other hand, is not so uniquely great in his own right but is immeasurably important as the transmitter of the synthesis-in-suspension (a sort of colloidal amalgam) between the Hebraic, the Egyptian, and the Graeco-Roman elements that are still the foundations of European culture. With Philo, faith becomes technically important to philosophy in the European tradition." (p. 95)

The specialist is likely to miss detail and the emphasis of his particular field. Condensation and picking up of salient features are to be expected of such a general and broad study as this. The work is balanced, reasonable, and engaging and presented in good style. Such studies as the present one bring out clearly the distinct contributions made by different cultures, their interaction and above all their deep underlying common humanity.

T.R.V. Murti
Professor Emeritus, Philosophy.
Banaras Hindu University.

INTRODUCTORY NOTE

Professor John C. Plott, one of the greatest synoptic thinkers of the twentieth century, has undertaken the formidable task of writing the *Global History of Philosophy* which is expected to be completed in several volumes. It seems to be the most rational approach to write a history of philosophy from the global point of view. No writer has made such an attempt prior to Professor Plott. A few scholars have made preliminary attempts to write comparative philosophy in which they have compared the Eastern and the Western philosophical systems. However, their attempts to compare the philosophical thought-structures of the Eastern and the Western philosophical systems have remained so far very inadequate and superficial. Professor Plott's point of view is a pioneering attempt in writing history of philosophy from our planetary point of view. His unique endeavor is expected to dovelop a synoptic point of view in his readers and enable them to discover intelligible meanings in the thought-patterns of philosophers down the ages.

In ancient Greece Plato enunciated the doctrine that empirical phenomena are the imperfect copies of perfect ideas which are eternal. Several centuries later Alfred North Whitehead enunciated a similar philosophical doctrine and maintained that eternal objects ingress into the actual entities which are incessantly in the process of creative advance. Among the other possible interpretations of the author's work is the attempt to trace the drama of this ingression in the context of the general history of civilization, such as Toynbee and others have presented, but with specific focus on the emergence of philosophical systems and traditions in their historic milieux.

This ingression of the ideas or the eternal objects must be understood as the manifestation of the cosmic play (*līlā*) of the ultimate reality in its manifold diversity of philosophical systems and traditions, as well as political ideologies, scientific theories, cultural norms and sociological structurings of societies in their various encounters with each other. Necessarily, due to human limitations in our all-too-finite worlds, in which we seldom emerge from our native situations-in-the-world, these ingressions, this cosmic *lilā*, is only dimly discerned even by the greatest minds. Nevertheless the challenge remains for every generation both to deepen and to broaden the perspectives within which this drama, this cosmic play, has been and continues to be staged. As instanced by the present volume, the author attempts such a multidimensional understanding of participation in this drama.

Not only the Vedic *ṛṣis*, Plato, Aristotle, Śaṅkara, Rāmānuja, Confucius, Lao-tzu, Chu Hsi, Spinoza, Kant, Whitehead and other best known thinkers in the history of mankind but also the philosophers included in this present volume are best understood as participating in this cosmic *lilā*, struggling to bridge the gaps between the seminal ideas (as the Stoics called them), the eternal truths, and their adequate manifestation and expression in forms. Their *weltanschauungen* therefore do not fade but retain their seminal qualities across the ages and also across cultural boundaries. In a transcultural-perspective such as Professor Plott has developed, cultural values and philosophical concepts must be treated in their perennial relevance, both in their transcendence of particular circumstances and in their concretion in historical time and geographical space. The present work attempts to highlight the relevance of these values and concepts for our own time through an impartial, detached presentation of their occurrences in this continuing drama or *lilā* of history-in-the-making.

Human thought-forms are usually found on two distinct planes which may be metaphorically called 'the horizontal plane' and 'the vertical plane'. The thought-patterns on the horizontal plane are empirical ideas and conceptual thought-forms which are embedded within the framework of empirical space-time. These empirical ideas and thought-forms are culture-relative. They are influenced by historical development of ideas. They usually have a very short-lasting importance. Metaphysical doctrines, political ideologies and scientific theories constitute checkered thought-patterns on the horizontal plane, i.e., empirical plane which is bounded by empirical space and time.

The seminal ideas on the vertical plane tend to transcend the sequential time. These ideas do not pertain to any specific region of empirical space and time, rather, they belong to the plane of transempirical space and time. It is impossible to comprehend these seminal ideas with the aid merely of logic and the scientific method. The seminal ideas which transcend empirical space and time can be comprehended by intuitive consciousness. Yoga, *sādhanā*, and mystic experience are the methods by which individuals may get emancipated from the firm grip of empirical space-time, and ascend to the plane of dimensionless space and time in which the past, the present, the future and the distant can be intuitively comprehended in an instant. These are the methods of attaining partial omniscience. Even scientists, poets, painters, musicians and metaphysicians can have intuitive glimpses of seminal ideas which transcend the framework of empirical space-time.

The seminal ideas on the horizontal plane of empirical space-time and the vertical plane of transempirical space-time constitute the warp and woof of human cognition. Analogous thought-patterns are usually found to occur synchronously on the wide canvas of human cognition.

Professor Plott has taken immense pains to show how that both on this horizontal and the vertical plane analogous thought-patterns have emerged, often simultaneously in the various historical epochs on the global scale. He has shown how religious and ethical ideas as well as scientific concepts are intimately related, historically, to metaphysical ideas.

Necessarily any thinker who deals in global dimensions must have a very comprehensive perspective. In order to arrive at such comprehensiveness, especially in dealing historically with systems of perennial value, he must undergo very intensive *sādhanā* and arrive at such detachment (*niṣkāma karma*) that he does not "play favorites" with any particular system or tradition or *darśana*. At the same time he must deal with them all empathetically so that he does not neglect the *tattvas* of each philosophy in its own merit and role in the historic drama of the unfolding of reality. A global thinker tries to rise from the plane of empirical space and time. He is a *draṣṭā* (visionary) who has *darśana* (intuitive vision) of the play theme of reality.

In the present volume the author has clarified his position regarding his approach to the problem of periodization in writing the global history of philosophy. He has written most aptly that "the old periodization of history in terms of ancient, medieval and modern, even when applied only to the history of the West, is awkward; and frequent attempts at forcing other civilizations into the traditional framework of the history of Europe have caused many distortions in the entire picture of the history of cultures and civilizations. Even the division of 'East' and 'West' does not fit the facts at all."

Professor Plott and his young collaborators, in their broad but not superficial humanist concern for world peace and social justice on an international scale, express the hope that the global approach to the history of philosophy will "deliver future generations from the provincialisms, cultural fanaticisms, and ethnocentricities which have plagued mankind thus far." Furthermore they issue a serious challenge to all mankind that "nationalism is often condemned, and rightly so, for it has become a disease of divisiveness, the chief inhibition to the global community. For the *myth of national sovereignty* has become successor to the older ideology of the Divine Right of Kings."

I first met Professor Plott at Vrindābana in 1956 when he had just finished his PhD studies at Benaras Hindu University in India and I mine at the University of Illinois, U.S.A. I found him to be a very austere ascetic and a devout Vaiṣṇava according to the Viśiṣṭādvaita interpretation. On several occasions he and I sat on the solitary banks of the river Jamuna at Vrindābana and meditated for hours. I found him to be extremely humane, humble, and a lover of mankind.

I met Professor Plott for the second time in Marshall University, Huntington, U.S.A., in 1975. I found him to be an ascetic living as a solitary pedestrian in an affluent country. His pristine simplicity, unassuming modesty, and sincere love for mankind charmed me very profoundly. I found that he was constantly searching for deep meaning in every human behaviour, every social episode and every pattern of thought.

The author's delineation of the parallel philosophical Ideas of different geographical regions and cultural epochs is both a challenging and an exhilarating experience for the reader. Posterity will remain grateful to Professor Plott and his collaborators for giving a new direction to mankind for viewing all episodes of life and thought-patterns of human beings clearly and rationally. Professor Plott can be counted among those who will guide mankind closer to universal justice, harmonious community and lasting planetary peace, while we explore, no longer in imagination but in historical actuality, the cosmic perspectives that have become our heritage.

A.K. Sinha
Professor of Philosophy
University of Kurukshetra

ACKNOWLEDGMENTS

Through the years the work on this volume has involved so many teachers, gurus, assistants, associates, colleagues and counsellors that it is impossible to name them all specifically. Nevertheless, there are those who have had the most indispensable and directly instrumental roles in getting this particular volume into publishable shape and form.

First, the reference librarians at Marshall University and the University of Michigan are to be commended for their patience and efficiency in searching out difficult-to-locate materials and managing a host of interlibrary loan arrangements. In a similar way, acknowledgments must be made to Randy Miller for design of the dust cover. It was his conception that the same essential design should be used for all volumes in the series. Special mention is due likewise to Paul Salstrom for preparing the index and glossary, as well as assistance with proofreading. Robert Henry Staley-Mays deserves credit for initial editing of the first draft of "The Problem of Periodization" in the appendix, and also as a friend who has given encouragement in a personal way that is imponderable but very essential. Also, thanks must be given to the many work-study students who, in a behind the scenes role, have done the typing and other essential tasks of seeing the type-script through the many drafts before publication.

But most of all, both personally and professionally, words fail to express my profound appreciation to Paul D. Mays, James M. Dolin and Russell E. Hatton, who have worked sacrificially with selfless dedication on this and the preceding volume. Without their contribution, these volumes would have remained in the original unpublishable draft. In short, they have put together what once was a virtual jig-saw puzzle of scrambled explorations and researches into the new perspectives which we hope will become—as the late Professor of Tufts University once said—a complete revolution in the teaching of philosophy in many countries. In fine, I am very grateful to Prof. T.R.V. Murti and Prof. A.K. Sinha for their kind words in appreciation of my humble work.

INTRODUCTION

Our previous volume covered what is commonly known as The Axial Age, in which the dominating theme was the emergence of systematic philosophy out of mythological consciousness and the establishment of the different basic types of philosophical systems in China, India, and Greece. The time span presented no major problem since from around 500 B.C. to about 250 B.C. essentially the same characteristic is true of all three civilizations, and also to a very great extent of Zoroastrian Iranian civilization.

But the problem of periodization* is always with us and generally is the most difficult in any field of historiography. In philosophy it is doubly confounded by the fact that very often ideas seem to appear out of nowhere and then are gone only to reappear unpredictably later, apparently with no causal connection. We intend to superimpose no new counter-stereotypes on those already distortingly current, but for the present we shall designate the time from the expedition of Alexander to about 50 A.D. as the Earlier Han-Hellenistic-Bactrian Period. This cut off date is not arbitrary, for in China that roughly divides the Former Han Dynasty from the Later Han, and at the same time it marks approximately the transition from Republican Rome to Imperial Rome; also, in India the Śaka Era officially begins only a little later (78 A.D.). Then from 50 A.D. to about 325 A.D. shall be designated as the Later Han-Hellenistic-Bactrian Period. Although at first it may appear that the choice of 325 as the ending of the Han-Hellenistic-Bactrian Period is prejudiced by the Council of Nicaea and the accession of Constantine, nevertheless it roughly coincides with the beginnings of Sassanian Dynasty in Persia, the Gupta Dynasty in India, and the fall of Loyang and the beginning of the Eastern Chin in China.

As we now move into what we have provisionally called the Han-Hellenistic-Bactrian Period, we continue to explore patterns

* See Appendix.

of historical development. This is not the study of individual systems and their internal consistency and/or comprehensiveness and/or intensity of technical expertise. For far too long historians have neglected philosophy, and historians of philosophy have too often written in oblivion of the global historical milieux in which the systems emerge, not asking questions about the causes and consequences of the development of philosophical traditions and their interaction on each other.

During the Han-Hellenistic-Bactrian Period the channels of communication throughout Eurasia are known to have been open, the peoples of Central Asia begin to be on the move, and we find the concomitant emergence of Mahāyāna Buddhism, Manichaeanism, and Christianity. These things cannot be lightly passed over. That they have much to do with the philosophical systems and traditions emerging and developing should be obvious; for philosophy, no less than science, art, religion, politics, and economic systems, does not occur in a vacuum — although too often it is interpreted as though that were the case.

As one begins to seriously reassess the total situation in Eurasia, one begins to realize that the current division of East-West has been very wrongly superimposed. In Bactria, Sogdiana, and the Parthian realms intensively, and to a surprising degree also in Babylon, Edessa and Baghdad, in Alexandria, in Taxila, and even in Chang-An and Loyang, there was mingling and commingling of goods and ideas from all over Eurasia. Geographically, then, our unit of inquiry is Eurasia. We discard the old East-West distinction except where that is necessary for clarity and convenience. Eventually even geographical distinctions should be disregarded and the whole of world history treated as an integral process.

We need no longer posit after the manner of Hegel and the German Idealists, who have thus far fairly dominated the fields of the history of philosophy and comparative studies, any *Weltgeist* or Absolute mysteriously moving the world through some cosmic dance of Śiva. Ideas indeed do have causal power, but they are not the products of ghosts. They live and move in human heads and hearts and on human feet — or as the case may be, those astride the feet of horses, camels and elephants.

It is a fact that Apollonius of Tyana did travel to Taxila in India and to Persia and was well-received by the kings. This being the case, who could possibly claim that there was no influence from India on the Roman Empire? We must insist, using such evidence as Apollonius, that intercultural communication between India and Rome was not uncommon and that that is one major reason why we find common trends throughout this Han-Hellenistic-Bactrian Period. Indeed, we shall be finding a wealth of varieties of philosophies everywhere and in virtually every century, and the hypothesis suggests itself that where there is the maximum of intercultural communication there will also be greatest richness and variety of types of philosophies. There is also the question of whether and to what extent there are sufficient correlations in each period to hypothesize that there may be more differences between the philosophizing of different historical periods in Eurasia than there are differences between contemporary philosophers of the various cultures. But this hypothesis may be more apposite for future centuries since during this period it is probably better to conceptualize India and Greece as in rather close intercommunication and together in a fairly parallel development, with China as the "other" world not yet in complete contact.

We shall study the process of development out of the basic statements of the Axial Age through eclecticism/syncretism, scepticism, and mysticism/magic/esoterics as the three civilizations go through the cycle of arising, strengthening, spreading, over-extending, hierarchization, alienation of the masses, urbanization, along with corruption and even degeneracy of the aristocracy (who nevertheless still hold power), until things are so rotten that it takes salvation religions to pull them out of the mire.

In general it appears that this period has been slighted, even where it has not been ignored, for the simple reason that as far as philosophy is concerned there is very little that is really new. However, in the history of religion, as distinct from the history of philosophy, Christianity and Mahāyāna emerge at the apogee of the period; and it might be asserted that Vaiṣṇavism and Śaivism likewise take on definitive form, replacing the older more strictly Vedic forms. One might also stress the fact that within this period Confucian philosophy becomes the state religion and the Taoist Church emerges. What is new, then, is the emergence of the Faiths, of religion in the sense that it has continued through the centuries. Perhaps philosophy in the classical sense did go into decline and decadence, or descend or even degenerate into religion; but what less-than-omniscient human finite mind is capable, short of hybris, to judge whether or in what sense there was some sort of Revelation whose mission was to transform 'philosophy' from rational and not-so-rational *speculation* into a Way of Life ?

What cannot be ignored withal is that the period from about 250 B.C. to about 325 A.D. is quite a long expanse. Thus Plotinus is chronologically as far removed from Plato as, say, Whitehead from Ficino, Liang Ch'i-ch'ao from Wang Yang Ming, or Śrī Aurobindo from Madhusūdana Sarasvatī. If one observed strict proportionality only in terms of time, histories of European philosophy from Theophrastus to Augustine would take up at least five times the space usually devoted to Socrates, Plato and Aristotle alone; and correspondingly, the long list of thinkers down to, say, Bodhidharma are given no more pages than those given to Confucius alone. And in India Nāgārjuna and Vasubandhu, for example, are too often treated as though they did not belong to any solar system, much less to a definitive period of integral Eurasian history.

The similarities between now and then is another salient reason for giving the Han-Hellenistic-Bactrian Period our serious reconsideration. In the political, social and economic worlds, then as now, things had become too big and too corrupt for human remedy, with the result that some sought supernatural salvation while others took the "grin and bear it" attitude, hoping for some ultimate (if at present unseen) harmony and justice. Others escaped into dilettantish aestheticism, cultivating their gardens, bamboo groves or mango orchards as the case might be. Still others, not unlike an increasing number of people today, turned to astrology, magic, drugs, and other esoterica in an effort to transform both nature and human nature by one or two or at most three manageable formulae. Also, the masses were emerging, as now, and became increasingly the agents of change, while the elites held on to tradition even where that had become meaningless ritual. Not only Epictetus, but quite a few Chinese sages and not infrequently a Buddhist monk, experienced considerable social mobility. Did the military forces commit the same errors then as are being repeated now? Is bureaucracy now as inevitable as it was then, and ithw the same results? And should philosophy remain immune from these mundane affairs? The answers to these questions in Rome, China and India were as varied then as they are now.

The question of historical patterns is there and we must ask, whether we answer or not. Our basic purpose should be kept constantly in mind: to develop a capacity for seeing the world, including the world of ideas in history, multi-dimensionally. In this work we must risk impressionistic characterizations and suggestive generalizations in the spirit of exploration. We are exploring, breaking a path which others, it is hoped, will enlarge until it becomes a passable highway. We are seeking to integrate, or to reintegrate, what ethnocentricities have artificially separated.

ONE

I. ECLECTICISM/SYNCRETISM
(250 B. C.-100 A. D.)

A. Rome and India

(The *Gitā* in the Han-Hellenistic-Bactrian Setting)

Introduction

The dates for any period have to be rather rough and approximate. Concerning the beginning of the Han-Hellenistic-Bactrian Period, we might note these events in world history: Alexander dies at Babylon, 323 B.C.; Aśoka in India, d. 226 B.C.; Tsin Dynasty in China, 226 B.C.; Former Han begins, 206 B.C.; revolt of the Maccabees, 167 B.C.; Menander (Milinda) in Bactria, d. cir. 150 B.C.; Macedonia and Greece under Roman rule, cir. 146 B.C. Generally, then, we consider the beginning of the Han-Hellenistic-Bactrian Period to be somewhere between the death of Alexander and the rise of the Han. We more or less associate the ending of the period with these events: Later Han ends, 220 A. D.; Roman Empire divided, 314 A.D.; rise of Gupta Dynasty in North India, cir. 320 A.D.; Council of Nicea, 325 A.D.; death of Constantine, 337 A.D.

The *Bhagavadgitā* is the document *par excellence* which characterizes the early Han-Hellenistic-Bactrian Period. The basic characteristic of the early part of the period, and a current continuing throughout the entire period, is that of eclecticism, and it is in part by virtue of this characteristic of the *Gitā* that we now place it at the forefront. We characterize the early Han-Hellenistic-Bactrian Period as eclectic and syncretistic because it seems that a basic dynamic was at work then. In the Classical or Axial Age in all three civilizations there had been the seminal insights and the setting forth of the different types of systems to deal with those basic problems which we have reviewed in Volume One. In all three civilizations in our present period, as communications increased between them — for this is the new feature — there were very few genuinely new developments so that those who demand such things of philosophy still neglect this period almost completely. But historically speaking, this is a serious mistake, especially since this period seems to hold many suggestive analogies to our own modern era. The philosophers of the Han-Hellenistic-Bactrian Period were well aware of the stature of their predecessors in the Axial Age; therefore, no premium was placed on originality. The emphasis was on putting theory and practice together or trying new combinations of old ideas. Also, there was a tendency to renounce civilization and its discontents. There were attempts (although usually not too successful) to get back to the Original Source of things, or else, bowing to the inevitable, to ride the tide as life became so complex that nothing could be done except to hope for a personal salvation from the mess in another world or an eventual *parousia*, or at least for a social revolution by which justice and goodness would finally be established on earth.

Our reconstruction of the period must include China and India, therefore we hyphenate: Han-Hellenistic-Bactrian. If there is any one that characterizes the whole we should prefer to call it the Bactrian Period since here all of the civilizations overtly coalesced, even though there had been intercultural contacts before then. In Bactria at the cross-roads between Persian, Hellenistic, Chinese, and Indian civilizations, there was not only a "meeting of East and West" but a complete interfusion, a cultural synthesis, which has seldom, if ever, been equalled. Taxila in particular excelled in medicine, and the sculpture of Gandhara incorporates all the technical excellence of classical Greek sculpture as well as the brevity of line of Chinese art and the deep contemplative repose of the Indian genius. It is noteworthy, by the way, that here for the first time the Buddha was depicted in art. At the political level there seems to have been a genuine rule of enlightenment, uniting Scythians, Parthians, Greeks, Tartars, Indians and Chinese in a peaceful regime where the higher ideational products of culture as well as merchandise could be exchanged freely. In short, Bactria seems to have been a cross-roads through which all sorts of ideas wandered in human heads from various places to almost the whole of Eurasia.

It should prove an interesting exercise in exegesis to see if there is anything in the *Gītā* that is really unique from the global perspective. We shall avoid one issue, however, which usually confounds scholars and has been the "open-sesame" to commentators down through the centuries: the reconciliation of all possible discrepancies within the *Gītā*. There is no reason for not taking it, as most spiritual scriptures are traditionally taken, as an unsystematic, inspired work, eclectic even if it is woven around a central thesis. It is certainly no more inconsistent than, say, the *New Testament*; *Qur'an*, or the *Tao Teh Ching*. It appears to be a *neo*-orthodox text presenting traditional philosophical views in a supremely religious inspiration. The literature surrounding the *Gītā* is very vast indeed, comprising enough for a lifetime study. The commentaries of Śaṅkara and Rāmānuja are the best known, although the commentary of Madhusūdana Sarasvatī (unfortunately unavailable in English) is generally considered by most Indian scholars to be the best.

The earliest Sceptics (Pyrrho, 365-275 B.C. and Carneades, 219-129 B.C.) and the Jainas historically are the most likely connecting links between India/Bactria and the Mediterranean. It is definitely known that Pyrrho went with Alexander's expedition and returned; and Carneades' use of the snake and rope metaphor, common among Advaitins later on but derived from the early *Upaniṣads*, and never found in Greek philosophy before him, as well as his other epistemological discussions which very closely resemble what is found in both Theravāda Buddhism and Jainism, strongly indicate that the Sceptics were influenced by Indian thought. Like the Buddhists, Carneades stressed a rather rigorous theory of universal causation and, like them, found in this a basis for optimism since new causes can be introduced into the causal nexus which can give man some measure of freedom. However, it seems he did not countenance the possibility of emerging from the causal realm. We shall be continually returning to the theme of inter-cultural contacts during this period. For now we shall simply mention a fairly recent study by R.A. Jairazbhoy under the title *Foreign Influence in India* which presents much evidence of intercommunication and the real possibility of mutual influence.

It will be especially difficult not to get bogged down in

controversies, for there are many matters, including chronology, upon which scholars specializing in the various philosophical traditions which we seek to integrate are not agreed. One major difficulty is the proper dating of the beginnings of the Mahāyāna, for some scholars put it back almost contemporaneous with the beginnings of the Hīnayāna. Another difficulty is the extremely vexing problem of dating the *Bhagavadgītā*. Some would take the traditional view quite seriously that it is an integral part of the *Mahābhārata* which is traditionally thought to be at least as early as the Homeric era. Others, such as Holzmann and Garbe, would interpret it as it now stands as an accretion around an original nucleus that may have been part of the *Mahābhārata* but which comes to its established form much later. At any rate, somewhere between 200 B.C. and 200 A.D. it takes its final form.

Deity

In the *Gītā*, Kṛṣṇa is not just another participant in the battle but a God Incarnate. This strictly theistic orientation towards God the Supreme Person is not found in either the Stoics or Epicureans or in any of the post-Aristotelian schools in the Mediterranean or in the Chinese schools. There is nothing in them comparable to Kṛṣṇa's authoritative imparting of the Way by personal instruction to a particular person — a teaching which is, nevertheless, valid for all. The Stoics had a definite doctrine of God, though a God of impersonal Reason conforming more to the concept of the highest Universal Law. Such Law is at once the laws that govern nature and the laws that should govern the conduct of man, who must conform to the way of this Universal Principle if he is to find salvation. The Epicureans were atheistic, although not quite in the sense that some might think, for to them atheism did not mean an abandonment of right living. Theirs was a way of retirement, a sort of monastic life wherein to calculate and pursue the greatest pleasure, not in terms of gross sensual indulgence, but in terms of the contemplative life that would lead to the greatest enlightenment for man. Epicurus himself (341-271 B.C.), like the more sophisticated Cārvākas in India, was not a crass hedonist or crude materialist. He was opposed to superstition and almost more than the cultivation of pleasure, even intellectual pleasure, he taught the avoidance of pain — a teaching superficially reminding us of the Buddha's Fourfold Noble Truths. We have no evidence of direct influence even though, of course, the possibility of indirect influence cannot easily be ruled out since the influence from India on the Sceptics is highly probable.

Most of the schools of this period were no longer systems of philosophy in the sense of mere formulations of a body of doctrine. The doctrines were cultivated and followed as ways of enlightenment/salvation from a world that had grown corrupt and degenerate. Although under Tung Chung-shu (179-104 B.C.) an eclectic Confucianism became a religion, and the established church at that, the concern of the Han Confucianists was still for the right relation between the basically impersonal Will of Heaven — more comparable to the Stoic Universal Reason than to Kṛṣṇa's revelation of his cosmic aspect as Restorer of *Dharma*, as Unifying Principle of Nature, in the *Viśvarūpa* vision — and the ordering of the empire by a correct balancing of the *yin* and *yang*. Philosophy in all of Eurasia for the most part had taken the place of the older mythological religions, at least among the intellectuals. Hence, even when philosophy was atheistic, as with Epicureanism, it was embraced with considerable religious zeal.

Although it is difficult indeed to squeeze any philosophy out of the Maccabees, still the question should be asked whether there was anything elsewhere like the concept of God in the Maccabeean tradition — a completely transcendent Deity who operates through the voice of the prophets. In almost all of the *Old Testament Apocrypha*, whatever the degree of syncretism or of fanaticism, the transcendence of the Deity is uppermost and is much more radical than the transcendence found in the *Gītā*. It is rather difficult to find in the *Gītā* the doctrine of *nirguṇa* Brahman such as Śaṅkara later tries to read into it, and not too successfully. Though transcendence is included as a characteristic attribute, the adjectives with which Brahman is described there indicate a basic orientation toward the doctrine of the avatār, the incarnation of God. In Yang Hsiung's (53 B.C.-18 A.D.) poem on "The Great Mystery," although there is acknowledgement of the changefulness and instability of the phenomenal world, the Mystery is quite as transcendent as *Yahwe*, governs all, and is beyond grasping by ordinary human effort of intellection; and, above all, it is beyond the functioning of the opposites of *yin* and *yang*. There is, of course, no Deity, much less a transcendent one, in Theravāda tradition nor in the *Questions of Milinda*; in fact, there is really no "theology" there at all. But by the time we get to the *Lotus Sūtra* of the Mahāyāna Buddhist tradition, we already find a complete theology of Buddhahood in the *trikāya* doctrine, which includes transcendence as well as incarnation.

Soul/Immortality

In regard to the soul of man, the Stoics designated three levels. The corporeal soul (*psyche*) is the vital principle governing everything. The *pneuma* joins the somatic with the intellective functions, since it is obvious that *nous* (mind in the strict sense) is not merely physical even though illness or malfunction of the body (*soma*) may hinder its adequate operation. Thus far the Stoic designations are almost Aristotle's. But what the Stoics add that is of supreme significance historically is emphasis on the importance of the will. The Stoics are, in the systematic sense, voluntarists, whereas the Aristotelians are intellectualists—a polarity like that between the Taoists and the Confucianists in China, or like the later Augustinians and Thomists in the Latin Christian heritage, or the Averroists and the followers of Al-Ghazali in the Islamic world. As a result of their concern with the will, the Stoics were deeply involved in problems of destiny, fate, free will, and—something relatively new in the history of human thought in the global as well as in the Western arena — the doctrine of Providence as a sort of modulation between the extremes of rigorous determinism and unlimited libertarianism.

The distinction between *psyche* and *pneuma* among the Stoics parallels the distinction between *jiva* and *ātman* so basic to virtually all Hindu systems. Though it might be argued philologically that *pneuma* is more like *prāṇa*, in actual use *pneuma* is more comparable to *ātman*. This distinction is also what is essentially involved in Lucretius' distinction between spirit and mind, except that Lucretius is keenly critical of those who try to interpret the distinction idealistically. The triad of body, soul, and spirit is preserved; but mind or soul is a harmony that observes all that is going on in the psycho-physical organism as well as being active in the epistemological acts of perception and conception. Lucretius denies its immortality.

According to Lucretius (99-54 B.C.), it is impossible to extricate the soul from the body without destroying the body since just as without body there can be no mind or soul, so without soul as animating principle there can be no body. Since it is Brahman as Kṛṣṇa who is the 'real' animator, we therefore cannot construe the *Gītā* in the materialist sense that we find Lucretius proposing. Just as matter is real in the *Gītā*, so is spirit, soul, mind, and all the rest. *Māyā* is scarcely mentioned at all, and even when it is, it is in a very carefully qualified positive sense such that one can build very little upon it.

The *Gītā*'s attitude toward death and immortality is summed up when Kṛṣṇa says (II, 27):

> For one that is born death is certain,
> And birth is certain for one that has died;
> Therefore the thing being unavoidable,
> Thou shouldst not mourn.

The Han Confucianists seemed not so much concerned with personal immortality as with the cult of the ancestors. Wang Ch'ung's (27-107) views on death resemble those of Lucretius more than those of the *Gītā* or the Stoics: "To assert that a man after death is still conscious is like saying that an extinguished flame may again have light." Many Taoists beginning in this period tried too much to attain longevity on earth instead of following more the metaphysical implications of their classics. The metempsychosis concept was evidently not known in China until after the introduction of Buddhism. The Epicureans boldly denied immortality of the soul. The Stoics affirmed a qualified if not full doctrine of immortality, although some were vague about it, reflecting "philosophically" that this life, being radically incomplete, must be only the preparation for a better one. But already by Seneca's (4-65 A.D.) time there is a definite doctrine of purgatory and of ultimate resolution into the Primary Substance, the Divine Being, since the individual soul is considered only a part of the World Soul. There was, however, some dispute among the Stoics, Cleanthes (310-230 B.C.) and Chrysippus (280-209 B.C.) for example, as to whether all souls would survive or only the souls of the wise. This theory occupies the middle ground between the purely cultural "immortality" of the sophisticated Confucianists and the metempsychosis of Plato and the Hindus which later Origen affirmed but Augustine denied. Augustine added the dimension of the supranatural to what had been the supremely and all-inclusively naturalistic view of the universe and perforce of human nature also on the part of virtually all of the Stoic philosophers.

Fatalism/Grace

Though Wang Ch'ung's concept of destiny is similar to some Stoic interpretations of the concept of fate, he is actually less fatalistic than Lucretius or Seneca. Instead of finding consolation in the hope for an eventual balancing out of good and ill fortune, he sees in the variability of good and ill fortune a margin of indeterminacy such as should afford to men a correspondingly variable margin of control over destiny provided that they do not violently try to bend nature to selfish ends or disrupt its harmony. Wang does not consider that things happen in a strictly predetermined way. Neither chaos nor strict determinism conform to the universal human condition. Both Seneca and Wang Ch'ung speak freely of fate and destiny, but more or less metaphorically and not always with complete consistency. For both, the concepts of fate and destiny should not relieve us of moral responsibility and duty to truth.

Chrysippus had achieved something of Wang's balance between mere fatalist resignation to one's lot — that often entailed suicide as a duty, not as an escape, lest one's honor be compromised — and involvement in public affairs to the extent that one had to lose integrity or allow ends and means to get reversed. By the time of Seneca, however, there seems to have been a "failure of nerve", the development of an almost pseudo-philosophy that merely seeks some consolation against the sorrows of mortal existence and the collapse of the politico-economic order. Although the *sva-dharma* of the *Gītā* implies acceptance, the acceptance is a positive surrender (*śaraṇagati*) which should be viewed in the context of the theology of grace in the *Gītā*. It is not merely fortitude against misfortune.

Although in most orthodox Hindu traditions, especially Mīmāṁsā, karma is described as beginningless and inexorable, in the *Gītā* surrender to Kṛṣṇa affords a way of deliverance from the inexorability of karma that is no less dramatic than that offered by the *Lotus Sūtra* and upon which is built in later Vaiṣṇava tradition a whole theology of grace at least as fully as in the Franciscan or the Amida traditions. It is an easy inference that since practicing virtue as a sage (i.e., being a sage) is a possibility, therefore the hindrances to the practice of that virtue (chief of which hindrances is bondage to past karma) must be removable. In this sense, then, fate is annullable.

There is, however, no guarantee that one can become a *jivan-mukta* without the possibility of backsliding. But the emphasis is not on this possibility but on the spontaneous faith in and dependence on the Lord which leads the Lord to promise not only deliverance from the normal hindrances to salvation or *mokṣa* but even some degree of sharing His nature with His devotees. The "victory" promised carries the sense of victory over fate since it entails, according to the best tradition, sharing in the Freedom of the Lord. If pride holds one back, then one will be subjected to the laws of material existence, including the fluctuations of fortune. But if the *śaraṇagati* is complete and sincere, then all unfailing good is promised. The *ānanda* is completely contingent on the absoluteness and sincerity of the *bhakti* and *śaraṇagati* to the Lord. If that lapses, then everything else lapses. Normally it should not happen, but the fact that it could happen only emphasizes, according to tradition, the necessity of total dependence. If *ānanda* were guaranteed, as it were, by some eternal law, then the intimacy of the theism would be compromised.

Fatalism is as much a part of the Western as of the Oriental tradition, as is, for that matter, the opposite end of the psychological spectrum. Indeed, the *Gitā*, *Lotus Sūtra*, and Wang

Ch'ung on the whole manifest less fatalism than many of their Stoic and Epicurean contemporaries.

Vicarious Purgation

Neither the *Gitā* nor the Stoics and Epicureans conceived of the possibility of vicarious elimination of evil. That is reserved for the Christian doctrine of *agapé* and the Mahāyāna doctrine of *mahākaruṇā* (great compassion). The basic spirit of Mahāyāna literature, the sūtras in particular, is exemplified by the exercise of *mahākaruṇā* wherein the *Bodhisattva*, in contemplating the sufferings of all living things, is profoundly moved to compassion and by psychic supra-normal powers diffuses Good in the world such as will overpower the lesser good that fluctuates in the opposition between good and evil. The *Bodhisattva* can exercise *mahākaruṇā* not only for the sake of all of humanity but for the sake of all living creatures and eventually for the whole universe as well. We find the vicarious elimination of evil in early Greek Christianity (though it is a bit high-flown for the Latin tradition), in Hassidic Jewry, and in the Zurvan and Manichaean traditions in Zoroastrianism. At the most, it is found only germinally in the *Gitā*.

As to how the vicarious level of *agapé* and *mahākaruṇā* works, one had better ask a saint rather than a philosopher or a theologian, for according to tradition it is not a matter for speculation or of definition but a matter of use for the good of all. The whole concept of the Mass, or rather the theology that has accrued around the liturgy, is built on the idea that Christ bore our (all mankind's) sins for us; and in the Mahāyāna literature — chiefly in the *Lotus Sūtra* — the Buddha is virtually assigned the same role such that any and all can become a Buddha. One may speculate that what does happen in vicarious atonement is that psychic power is generated and we benefit just as, analogically we bathe in the salubrious sunlight "all free" as far as nature is concerned. The saint or *Bodhisattva* is like a clear glass window where there was not one before, letting the light shine in; or, as Saint Bonaventura later develops the metaphor, the saint's mirror is without blemish and allows not only light but the full image of perfection to shine forth.

Renunciation

Arjuna's dilemma is not a small one. His "pacificism" is of a mixed nature for he is torn between filial piety and Stoic fortitude on the one hand and the pursuit of a life of contemplation and spiritual sensitivity (compassion) in retirement on the other. Kṛṣṇa's counsel is rather surprising to some, for He urges Arjuna on to battle in a Stoicism that is stronger than that of the Mediterranean philosophers. Herein the "battle" is shifted immediately to a different plane. Out of Arjuna's dilemma comes almost the full gamut of possible metaphysical as well as moral speculations. The battle, in other words, becomes allegorically the battle of human existence with all of its temptations to the extremes and all of its little triumphs, its razor's edge balance between Being and Becoming, its pseudo-conflicts between knowing and doing, between evolution and involution, and all the dialectical oscillations between all the opposites.

The Han Confucianists remained, on the personal level, primarily concerned with the right ordering of the family as the basis of a sound sociological and political system, whereas the Epicureans join the *Gītā* in extolling the abandonment of all worldly engagements, preferring the higher values attainable by renunciation to the settled course of normal existence or the pursuit of name and fame.

The Stoics renounced the pleasures of the non-virtuous life but they did not renounce all worldly engagement. Philosophy was pursued as the best way to attain participation in the Universal Reason that is above the passions and governs all things. The Epicureans sought freedom from the cares of worldly entanglement by renouncing all worldly engagement. The higher pleasures of philosophy and the contemplative life were to be cultivated in a life of retirement.

Because of its doctrine of detachment, it is popularly charged that the *Gītā* teaches primarily only a Stoic doctrine, but an examination of the texts will scarcely support this. In the first place, nothing short of perfection is enjoined therein, whereas the Stoics, bent on consolation against the decadence of the days in which they lived, cultivated the virtues as an exercise in *proper measure*. The virtues are primarily those which are conducive to the maximum personal peace of mind, good taste, serenity, and repose. As such, the Stoics are not so greatly different after all from the Epicureans. They both appealed to reason as the ultimate guide, although the Stoics considered reason as a universal principle whereas the Epicureans considered it as a mere function of the mind. But neither quite approaches the profound *challenge to transcendence* which the *Gītā* holds out.

Though Buddhist renunciation is not quite so rigorous as that which the *Gītā* is usually interpreted as enjoining, at least for those who are ready for the *sannyāsa āśrama*, the fourth stage in the complete Hindu life, the importance of the *saṁgha*, the community of monks who carried the *Dharma* and the best of Indian culture with it throughout Southeast Asia and into China, Japan, and Central Asia (Bactria), cannot be over-estimated. Practicing compassion, they became a hidden leaven to society — a fact as yet unrecognized by most secular historians — which no doubt contributed very greatly to making this period universally, and not only within the bounds of the Roman Empire, one of the most peaceful in the history of humanity. Indeed, it would seem that in our own day a revival of the vitality of the Buddhist *saṁgha*, especially as the different sects and subsects become reunited, could be a very powerful force to offset the trends toward increasing violence in public affairs in almost all countries and cultures. The conquest of external political-economic regimes, though more spectacular, is of far less intrinsic value and productive of fewer enduring results than a movement that deals with ideas and the virtues of purity, compassion and non-violence.

Human Nature

It might be argued that there is no specific concept of human nature in the *Gītā*. We find nothing closely corresponding to the Confucian, Taoist, or Legalist concepts of *ming* and *hsing*, nor yet their close parallels in Stoicism where man is viewed as superior to the other animals by virtue of his having the capacity to understand both Cosmic Reason and rational argument about his own conduct and nature. However, the eclectic or even syncretistic version of Sāṃkhya-Yoga psychology and Nyāya-Vaiśeṣika metaphysics and epistemology in the *Gītā* allows the following propositions to be derived from its teachings: (1) human nature is essentially good and is realized as such when *sādhana* is undertaken to render the law of karma of no more effect. Considering karma, it might even be argued that man's nature is neutral, at least in the ideal, since the fruition of both good and evil karma is to be treated with the utmost detachment. (2) Human nature is transformable by the practice of yoga and, whether by *bhakti*, *karma*, *jñāna*, or any combination of these, it is man's duty to transform his nature and strive toward the *jivanmukta* ideal until ultimately, although to what extent has been a matter of great controversy in the commentaries through the centuries, there is *theosis* or identification with Deity or the transcendental Reality which is without doubt or illusion (*māyā*). (3) As in the Stoic and Confucian traditions, the moral aspect of human nature dominates in the *Gītā*. In all three, virtue is taken to be its own reward and considerations of actions from the standpoint of their results are subordinated to disciplined detachment and conformity to principles of virtue regardless of results. The *Gītā* is so versatile that other positions than these are derivable; but if one takes all possible interpretations, the above should come out somewhere near the center.

Not all Stoics were completely of the same mind concerning human nature. Since Zeno (340-265 B.C.) himself, like most seminal founders of traditions, did not explicate or systematize his basic and original insights, we may take Chrysippus as the most typical and as the most influential historically. He disagreed with the Cynics about human nature, the Cynics having radical doubts about the supposed superiority of human beings over the other animals. Both schools affirmed the slogan *biozēn kata physin* "to live according to nature", but the Cynics took that to mean that man should literally, in a crude way, return to nature. In some Neo-Taoists we have a more sophisticated parallel to the Cynics. The Stoics, however, affirmed that man was naturally reasonable, that man was not truly man unless he lived, not like a beast, but in conformity with the *Logos*, in harmony with the great things of the Cosmic Order. To them nature was orderly, law-governed, and therefore anything that was irregular, disorderly, or slovenly, was not according to human nature but simply perverse. In short, they were humanists *par excellence*, actually coming closer to the Han Confucian ideal than to any Hindu or Buddhist ideals.

One should consider the cultural and historical situation in which the slogan "to live according to nature" was affirmed by the Cynics. Athens had become over-sophisticated and corrupt, as sooner or later all civilizations do after their apogée. The cry of "back to nature" as the romantic reaction to this phenomenon is almost too well known to mention. Rousseau in the eighteenth century exemplifies the positive side of this reaction in his insistence upon the *return to* nature. In Suni Islam the Sufi mystics, and in Christian Rome the desert hermits like Saint Jerome and Saint Anthony, exemplify the negative side of this reaction in their desire to *escape from* civilization. Evidence suggests that even the Mayas, Aztecs, and Incas had similar "counter-culture" clusters. These romantic reactions are, of course, always very un-Confucian and un-*Gītā* like positions and very un-Stoic attitudes as well.

The world had grown much grander than the small world of the Greek city-state. All the sciences had made some advances. Commerce and communications were open over a much vaster area, more so in China than in Europe, but still much more than in the world of the Pre-Socratics or even of Plato and Aristotle. Hence for the Stoics, nature, including human nature, must be conceived as a grandiose affair, something inspiring awe and wonder, not merely an object of scientific curiosity. Man, by nature, through his participation in the same Universal Reason (*Logos*) that governs all things, has a natural place of great dignity in the total scheme of things. He is the knower, the investigator, the orderer, not the object of investigation or the ordered as the Peripatetics seem to have affirmed as they continued their work of classifying everything.

Tung Chung-shu's (179-104 B.C.) rather eclectic view of human nature includes elements from Mencius, Hsün Tzu, and the Taoists. The epithet "Cicero of China" seems to fit him well since in both cases there is a lack of profundity and originality and both were really eclectics. Not that this is a demerit in itself, for there is a real need for intelligent eclecticism after a period of intellectual ground-breaking before a synthesis can be derived by more original minds from their collectings. Cicero and

Tung Chung-shu are the chief channels through which the classical heritages have come down to us. Between these two there are many parallels in spite of minor differences.

Tung Chung-shu teaches both a personal and a societal harmony with, rather than a transcendence of, or an aloofness from, the realm of nature. The Stoics considered the four elements to be an integral part of the composition of man. Although non-material reason could govern the relative balance of the elements within the soul, neither the Stoics nor the Han Confucianists (e.g., Tung Chung-shu) seem to have countenanced the possibility of man's becoming completely freed from their operation, Thus, when Kṛṣṇa urges complete self-possession, he is setting a higher ideal than that taught by either the Stoics or the Han Confucianists. However, the ideal of harmony as compared with transcendence may be attainable by a greater mass of the population and may be more practical in ordering the affairs of society.

The Stoics considered the happiness of the virtuous man to be more negative than positive. The emotions are deterrents from the true good; one must not depend on external aids of fortune; one must be self-reliant, indifferent to everything that does not conform with the moral life as rationally conceived and formulated. Desire (*hormé*) and aversion (*aphormé*) are equally to be disregarded. Irrational impulses which govern the greater part of mankind are the source of evil, and self-control is to be gained by making right choices.

Some of the Neo-Taoists may be interpreted as a retraction from the rigors of the Dialecticians of the previous era. Instead of teaching that the sage should be devoid of emotions or immune to them, Wang Pi and other Neo-Taoists taught, citing Confucius' being grieved at times or quietly playing the flute at other times as the model, that the sage cannot be devoid of emotions for they are an integral part of human nature. Nevertheless, the sage, as different from the ordinary man, though he reacts to things emotionally, is not ensnared by them. They also appealed to Chuang Tzu, who teaches that "the Perfect Man employs his mind like a mirror. It grasps nothing; it refuses nothing; it receives but does not keep. Thus he can triumph over things without injury to himself."

Although the Epicureans are remembered more for their doctrine of pleasure, the emphasis, especially in Lucretius, is on intelligence. Intelligence (*nous*, but with a different connotation than the *nous* of Democritus, Aristotle, and the other Greeks preceding Epicurus and Lucretius) is the link between the virtuous life and the processes of nature, and it is the principle whereby man is liberated from the necessity to which the Stoics taught resignation. It is by intelligence, in other words, that man may govern the passions and become liberated from them; it is by intelligence that man may calculate that wherein lies his highest good, which is inherently pleasurable; it is by intelligence that man is delivered from bondage to the mythological consciousness; and although the Epicureans do not teach immortality of the soul, it is again by intelligence that man may find the greatest and most enduring values whereby life may be governed. Nature, in other words, makes ample provision for the happiness of man, and it is by intelligence that man thankfully receives these goods, exercises compassion toward those who have fewer of them, and quietly pursues the virtuous life, abiding in that *ānanda* above the fluctuations of pleasure and pain, or abiding even in the Tao in detachment from the fluctuations of *yin* and *yang*.

To Lucretius as much as to any other Hellenistic thinker, reason (*ratio*) is the judge, for reason is also the guarantor of the uniformity of nature or the "laws" of nature. Though nothing is completely fixed or stable, nevertheless, things are basically orderly. Lucretius states his almost axiomatic dictum that it is by the laws of nature that things become differentiated and are resolved again into nature's nexus. The idea of "laws of nature" is not so explicit in the *Gītā* as one might wish; but it is easy to infer them from the passages incorporating Sāṃkhya into the text.

Reason to the Stoics is ontological and not a matter of human, or at least merely human, experience since it is the metaphysical principle *par excellence* whereby Order in the universe may be echoed in the microcosm or at least the principle where by one may live in harmony with the universe. This conception of the *Logos* resembles the Hindu — not the Buddhist — concept of *Dharma* implicit in the *Gītā* context.

Dharma here is not just what individual people are bound to do in obedience to command from the *śruti* but almost "Law" in the metaphysical sense, the power or dynamism behind the cycles of civilization and culture if not of the universe itself. For Theravāda, reason remains merely human reasonableness, not a cosmic principle governing the realm of the gods, the world, and the state of human affairs. Nor can the Stoic Reason be equated with the concept of *buddhi* (reason) in the *Gītā*. *Buddhi* is the level of mind still concerned with discursive thought. It is neither a cosmic principle nor the Divine Mind but the faculty in man by which he may come to discern all things natural, human, and divine to be what they truly are.

Tung Chung-shu's wisdom (*chih*) is more equatable with the *prajñā* of the Patañjali *Sūtras* and the *Gītā* than with the wisdom (*sōphrosynē*) of his Mediterranean contemporaries. *sōphrosynē* as a concept inherited directly from Aristotle was a matter of rational, calculated judgment rather than a principle of the unity of all virtues, a unity which is more or less intuitive, super-rational, and really a matter of the will. Although the rational calculations of right and wrong are included in each of the concepts of wisdom, i.e., in *chih*, *prajñā* and *sōphrosynē*, in all three cases the exercise of virtue and the cultivation of wisdom have close associations with metaphysical concepts of human destiny. Both human virtue and human wisdom are considered to be varieties of conformity with the cosmic order of things; but again — and here is perhaps a difference in all three from the previous period — the emphasis is almost completely ethical rather than scientific or intellectualistic. Humanism has, therefore, it might be said, gained the ascendency over value-free curiosity about nature.

The chief function of mind/intelligence in any dimension for the whole Hellenistic context is no longer mere knowledge about things. It becomes very closely linked with the will and with ethical matters. In order to make rational judgments in affairs emotionally charged, and in order to get beyond blind impulse which can only lead to pain and suffering, the faculty of judgment must reach an area of neutrality above the fluctuating duality of pain and pleasure or *yin* and *yang*. Just as it is by reason that we humans can govern ourselves in conformity with nature, so there must be in nature something like reason, if not that same reason itself, that makes this possible, reason being the principle of orderliness and regularity. Nevertheless, in contrast with the Stoics, who pushed this idea to the utmost and made it the basis of their teleological concept of Nature as well as their justification for the doctrines of Providence and fate, Lucretius and the other Epicureans stopped short of affirming that all of nature is geared to human advantage.

Nature

Lucretius does not have any concept so definite as the *Gītā* version of Brahman; nevertheless, his concept of Nature is almost as all-embracing. A double meaning is involved in the word '*Natura*': the *n*ature of things (as in the title of his great poem) and *N*ature which is the all-embracing concept of reality, anything "supernatural" being rejected. The word in this latter sense comes very close to the term "Brahman", at least where that is not used in the technical sense that the later commentators on the *Brahmasūtras* use it. Both Brahman and Nature are probably best translated not as "the Absolute" but as "Reality as such", or perhaps both are best simply left untranslated in their convenient ambiguity.

Lucretius' *Materia* is very close if not the exact equivalent of "matter" in English. Matter in both Lucretius and the *Gītā* is a concept embracing everything that has actual existence. However, the closer parallel is between Lucretius and Vaiśeṣika — even though the *prakṛti* of the *Gītā* is sometimes translated as Nature, especially in the context of Sāṁkhya, it is better translated as matter — since Matter and Nature are almost equatable in the all-inclusive sense in both of them.

There is no explicit doctrine of atoms as such in the *Gītā* in the sense that there is in the Hindu systems and in Lucretius. The *Gītā* follows Sāṃkhya more than Vaiśeṣika and thus the three *guṇas* come to the fore rather than atoms as the basic constituents of *prakṛti*. Lucretius' poem, like the *Gītā*, is rather syncretistic, fusing at the cost of exactitude all of the previous concepts of Nature and its components (atoms especially) or evolutes, just as one finds in the *Gītā* the concept of Brahman on the one hand but the concept of *prakṛti* on the other. The difference, at any rate, between Lucretius and the *Gītā* is rather plain: Lucretius does not retain the Sāṃkhya-like dualism between *prakṛti* and *puruṣa* such as we find in the *Gītā*, his materialism being rather complete and thorough.

Lucretius gets his concept of the Void (*vacuum*) from the Pre-Socratics, and it has been retained in Europe as a basic concept. The temptation is very strong to equate Lucretius' Void with the Buddhist (and Hindu mathematical) concept of *śunya*, zero, "emptiness", sometimes actually rendered as the "Void". But this might be deceptive since the Hindu concept is more strictly mathematical than philosophical and in the Buddhist context the concept is not so much a matter af physics as of logic and epistemology. *Ākāśa*, rather, serves essentially the same function in the Hindu scheme of things as does the concept *vacuum*, "vacuum" being the Latin translation of the Greek *tò kénon*. *Ākāśa*, *vacuum*, and *tò kénon* are all three infinite in the sense of being undefinable as well as the "that within which all things take material form" while themselves remaining essentially formless. Of course there is not a one-to-one correspondence as though one were merely a translation of the other; nevertheless, we may find these parallel structures: *Natura*—Brahman : all-inclusiveness; *Materia*—*prakṛti* : what all things are made of; Void—*ākāśa* : that within which all things take manifest form.

Lucretius and the other Epicureans held to the position that the only *a priori*, purely rational principle that could not be doubted is that "out of nothing, nothing can be made" (*ex nihilo nihil fit*); therefore, the world, including matter, is eternal Although the doctrine of *nihil ex nihilo* is not explicit in the *Gītā*, the Sāṃkhya doctrine of the eternity of *prakṛti* and *puruṣa* is continued without dilution. Thus, if the world is eternal and "uncreated", the idea of the world being created *ex nihilo* (out of nothing) cannot possibly be asserted. And in XIII, 26 and 27, we find the compensating doctrine that things do not really perish even though they appear to do so (*nihil ad nihilo*). This may be compared with Lucretius' doctrine that when things appear to perish, the imperishable "first beginnings" (atoms) of which they are composed have simply dispersed.

In the commentaries on the *Gitā* we find a reiteration and further development of the old controversy about the relation of cause and effect, i.e., whether the effect pre-exists in its material cause (*satkāryavāda*) or is truly a new creation (*asatkārya-vāda*). The basic problem of coming-to-be and change/perishing has a focal place in the Buddhist *Questions of Milinda*, which disagrees with Lucretius by holding that nothing is permanent or has lasting endurance; however, it agrees with Lucretius that everything must have a cause, i.e., *nihil ex nihilo*. Perpetual flux is as much Lucretius' as it is the Buddhist view because, even though Lucretius posits eternal atoms, these atoms are eternally changing their configurations and thus no "thing" is ever permanent and everything is in flux.

Although Yang Hsiung (53 B.C.-18 A.D.) speaks of the Great Void (*Hsüan*) out of which has emanated the multitude of things by the interaction of *yin* and *yang*, it is not the same sort of "nothing" indicated in an *ex nihilo* doctrine. It is rather — as we also find in Lucretius and in Hindu descriptions of *pralaya* — the undifferentiated mass out of which diversified forms evolve by emanation. There is thus no question of creation *ex nihilo* by some external agency such as a deity. Indeed, from the various versions of the *nihil ex nihilo* the conclusion may be drawn that the concept that there is always something, however undifferentiated, rather than "nothing" seems to have been the prevailing view throughout Eurasia during the period.

Politics/Society

Though the Stoics had many followers among prominent administrators of the Roman Empire, it is difficult to see that they had any complete social philosophy. The Epicureans, on the other hand, were not interested in good government and usually, along with the Cynics and Cyrenaics, declined to accept responsibility for the running of society. Tung Chung-shu, however, carried on with a full philosophy, not retiring from the responsibility of and toward society, thus coming up to the measure of Kṛṣṇa's challenge to Arjuna not to become weak and cease from the struggle. Ideally, out of duty a Confucian scholar, as a normal, rational, humanistic matter, humbly (that degenerated into mere ceremonial pretense of humility) accepted public office (that degenerated into all sorts of intrigues and rivalries). Given the tendency towards corruption in public life in all three civilizations, it took more than ordinary virtue to clean up the mess. According to Tung Chung-shu, for those who can assert a superior measure of virtue, accept responsibility with selfless detachment, and retain integrity in spite of all decadence, serving in government is a worthy pursuit.

It might even be said that in Tung Chung-shu we find the beginnings of scientific sociology. His prediction of the decline of the glories of the Han Dynasty was not a matter of direct revelation from the Almighty but was based on a calculation of the waxing and waning of all things according to the balance of *yin* and *yang*. He seems in all to have struck a happy middle between the Jewish theocratic and the Roman autocratic systems, in both of which the ruler takes on a divine institutional charisma without adequate regard for his personal character, whereas the Chinese emperor, according to Tung, has the duty and office of "opening" Heaven in a role of comprehensive humility that is rare in utopian systems.

One of the chief points wherein the *Gitā* is criticized is that it does not offer any social philosophy explicitly; however, it should be pointed out that the *Gitā*, as all basic works of Hindu philosophy, presupposes Manu and Kauṭilya for the covering of this field. Also of relevance to social philosophy in the *Gitā* is the discussion of *sva-dharma*, the selfless doing of one's duty. The *sva-dharma* of XVIII, 45, has been variously interpreted by Western commentators, the variations ranging from a Fichtean philosophy of the Will to the simple naive American "mind your own business". But what is really intended, aside from the injunctions that each should conduct his life according to his duties of family, caste, society-at-large, God, and the cultivation of the life of meditation and establishment in unaltering spiritual reality — besides these, there is a profound sense of vocation which each soul should find if his cultivation of self and his devotion to God are adequate. It is by no means a way of consolation, a world-denying ethos, that is enjoined but a positive way first of self-purification, then of grounding in the eternality of Being, then of triumph over all that is gross, harsh, cruel and self-centered, and then of perseverance in normal duties with selfless detachment. Indeed, from the perspective which the *Gitā* gives may we not charge the Stoics and Epicureans alike of being too self-centered, too much concerned with appropriation of what good may be eked out of a miserable life in a crumbling Empire?

The social implications of *sva-dharma* should be obvious. If everyone does his duty then all will go well since society is organically integrated according to the natural hierarchy of caste functions — a notion not too far from the Confucian ideal in the form it takes at the hands of Wàng Ch'ung as the middle way between Legalist rigorism and Taoist spontaneity. Actually, it is probably in Wang Ch'ung rather than in India or the Mediterranean that we find, in spite of his syncretistic mixture of materialism, magic, statecraft, and all the rest, the best discernment of the basics of cultural dynamics or cultural anthropology. His very mature consideration of the relation of individual and society is coupled with a basic emphasis on the concept of destiny (*ming-yi*). Since it appears that one's circumstances are not completely controlled by Heaven, nor are they completely in one's own control, one should live according to the norm of one's lot in life, not ambitiously striving at all odds for success nor yet slothfully or despondently conforming to the fatalism of the common man. One should selflessly and desirelessly do one's duty in that state of life in which one happens to be. Truth and duty are as inseparable in Wang Ch'ung as in the *Gitā*; and in both cases, he who lives according to either or both will be living according to his destiny, his *dharma*, his *sva-dharma*, his own *li* and *i*.

For the Stoics, Wang Ch'ung, and the *Gitā*, duty as conformity with the order of things is natural. Even when disorder prevails one does one's duty to restore order as rationally as possible. Not meddling in others' affairs but doing one's own duty regardless of consequences is completely rational. Virtue is thus its own reward since duty is not a matter of advantage for oneself or even for others but simply a manifestation of devotion to truth. Even though this focuses ethics into a dramatically personal thing, it has very far reaching implications for society which is considered, in all three cases, to be a part of the Rational Order of Things In conforming to destiny or fate or *sva-dharma*, one has some measure of freedom; certainly one has more freedom than if one vainly tried to oppose or confront this Order in a spirit of pride or in any spirit other than one of humility. Thus, there are in all three cases metaphysical over-tones to the concept of duty since that entails sensitivity to cultural dynamics which in turn echoes the cosmic order, whether it *seems* good, absurd, or worse.

It is difficult to find concrete evidence that the Buddha himself ever, after his own renunciation, envisaged a reform that would have political and social repercussions. But, when the *Dharma* becomes a concern of a whole country, the external order is bound to become affected; and thus it is not surprising to find an ideal Buddha's City of Righteousness being depicted in the *Miliñda Pañha*, and that at some length, with the whole range of occupations properly set in place.

Tung Chung-shu developed a philosophy of history that is more complete than that of Herodotus or Thucydides since it countenances the cessation of old dynasties and the renovation of the empire by the giving of the Mandate of Heaven to a new dynasty. This, by the way, is not completely foreign to the *Gitā*, although the *Gitā* has no explicit philosophy of history in the same sense that we find in almost all of the Chinese philosophers — not to mention the historians Pan Ku and Ssu'ma Chien — and supremely in Tung Chung-shu. According to traditional interpretations of the *Gitā*, however, this much is held in common with Tung Chung-shu, that it is not just human manipulation of things that makes history; rather, there is some element of the divine. The Stoics had a philosophy of Providence, but whether this is comparable to the Mandate of Heaven is doubtful. The Stoic doctrine was linked with a doctrine of necessity, completely Greek, and thus much more fatalistic than the Chinese concept. Reason is divine, governing and permeating all; Providence therefore governs *totally*, and thus for the Stoics the giving or withholding of a Mandate is not dependent on human affairs.

Considering such concepts as covenants, mandates, and Providence, the Israelites were not so unique. The idea of being a "chosen people" was rather universal. We may look at this as a strange psychological necessity for people everywhere to think that there is something unique and/or superior about themselves; or we might consider it a manifestation of man's primordial realization of his own inadequacy in managing his affairs without divine assistance. This latter is usually coupled with a sense of ultimate justice : if the just are unrewarded in the present, surely in some other dimension of existence things will ultimately be levelled out. The common denominator between the Covenant and the Chinese Mandate of Heaven is that if it is violated on the human side, God or Heaven (*T'ien*) will withdraw mercy and see that things are rectified by bringing down the proud and exalting the humble. The drama of this levelling aspect of the Mandate is vividly presented in Ssu'ma Chien and in the Book of Kings in the *Old Testament*. Some might claim that there was nothing like this in the Indic tradition, whether Hindu, Buddhist or Jaina. But in story after story in both the *Mahābhārata* and *Rāmāyaṇa*, not to mention the *Purāṇas*, there is a great abundance of themes of the same character. In the Theravâda Buddhist and Jaina contexts, however, there was no covenant concept. Being radical humanists, they discarded all appeals to the supernatural, existentially insisting that man must accept responsibility for his own destiny since man creates his own merit and demerit.

With the Maccabees we find the beginnings of the cult of martyrdom. What are you going to do with a fanaticism that cannot, for life or death, think except in terms of either/or and invariably thinks that "I" am on God's side and God is on "my" side fighting my battles for "me" ? Better, perhaps, is Arjuna's hesitance ! The Maccabees (175-164 B.C.) are a contrast to the more tolerant and non-martyrdom trends in Buddhism, Confucianism and Taoism. As a paradigm case of "Zealotism" as the polar opposite of, or reaction to "Herodianism" or syncretism, as well as a transition to Philo, the Maccabees stand as a type that should give us more understanding of today's situation of "withdrawal from encounter" such as seems to have happened also in the eighteenth century. Again and again one extreme breeds its opposite : Alexandria was chaotically syncretistic — the wisdom literature of the *Old Testament Apocrypha* represents extreme Alexandrian syncretism which is, in a watered-down sense, quite philosophical — Jerusalem was valiantly anti-syncretistic. Zealots and Herodians ! How can we do any comparative philosophy, let alone understand the dynamics of world history of philosophy, without being aware of this variety of *yin* and *yang* response to encounters between traditions ?

Intolerant reactions to syncretism (which we may designate as *yang*) are generally characterized by a tendency toward a transcendental personal Deity or Undifferentiated Absolute in metaphysics. Such rather intolerant reactions may be found in Maccabeean Zealotism, post-Buddhist theistic Hinduism (especially Śaivism), "theistic" Confucianism heavily weighted with Legalism, the Orthodox Zoroastrian church-state, "Old Roman Puritans" like the stricter Stoics and even the strictest Cynics (yogi types), and later in the Latin papacy. Those with a more tolerant attitude towards syncretism (*yin*) tend to be syncretistic (or eclectic) themselves, having an emphasis on immanence in theology or pluralism in metaphysics (even polytheistic), trends towards hedonism and cultivation of the arts, generally a non-rigorous ethics, and a relativism and curiosity about the ways of others ("let's try it at least once" attitude). Such tolerant and syncretistic approaches may be found in Mahāyāna Buddhism following after the *Questions of Milinda*, Alexandrian Jewry (Herodians completely Hellenized), the *Gītā* as opposed to stricter Sāṃkhya or Mīmāṁsā, Neo-Taoism, Greek (not Roman) Epicureanism and Cyrenaics, Manichaean Zoroastrianism, and later in the Greek Church.

Conclusion

It is difficult not to return to the *Gītā* as the focal point for this period. It may be that on the larger historical scale the Mahāyāna becomes much more important in the periods to follow; but until the setting down of the *Brahmasūtra*s of Bādarāyana and, in the wider perspective, until Philo (30 B.C.-50 A.D.) and the Judeo-Hellenistic (Alexandrian) synthesis, the *Gītā* stands alone and unassailed in its excellence. The reason its great spiritual force did not spread far and wide long before the modern period is that it is deeply rooted in the specifically Hindu soil, with the caste system as undeniably one of the tap roots that has at once given it its undecaying tenacity, its wide range of ideas, and its failure ever to inspire a missionary religion. It is remarkable that Christianity and Buddhism, especially in its Mahāyāna forms, became missionary religions about the same time. This is a new thing in the history of mankind since all the older traditions were ethnically rooted.

In reply to the possible objection that the *Gītā* will always remain so rigorously Hindu that it can have little application outside of India because of its roots in the caste system, it must first be noted that this is a very modern — even an anachronous — criticism. We too easily overlook the fact (or easily forget it) that Plato's *Republic* advocates something very much resembling the Hindu caste system; that in the Iranian and Israelitic traditions there was certainly no completely egalitarian model or tradition; that in China the Mohist gesture towards egalitarianism did not succeed. The empirical fact that the *Gītā* has been gaining in popularity globally for the last century or so and that its popularity is still growing is itself sufficient rebuttal to the notion that it is not applicable outside its native habitat.

Among the world's scriptures, the *Gītā* remains perhaps the most intensely philosophical in that it contains, as well as keen aesthetic appeal, a full panoply of problems in epistemology, religious *ascesis*, ethical obligations in a problematic setting, in addition to hints and nuances in everything from cosmology to philosophy of history. In other words, it does belong explicitly to the history of philosophy as well as to the history of religion in a way that is not true of the Judeo-Christian scriptures or even the Sūtra literature of the Mahāyāna.

The *Gītā* may yet, even after all these centuries, have a major role to play in formulation of souls disciplined in relation to Self, humble and ready to be of service to others, purifying the world by renunciation of the things and values that hinder righteousness and salvation from all that is gross and unworthy of man, whose essential nature is, if only ignorance and delusion are removed, divine.

B. Rome and China

Introduction

Since the dominant characteristic of the Han-Hellenistic-Bactrian Period is eclecticism, it follows that we shall be confronted with a welter of minor figures. This is especially true when we attempt to deal with the developments of philosophy in Rome and China. Though minor figures, many of them deserve mention because of their influence at the time or in later tradition, because they exemplify the trends of the time, and/or because of their profound though non-comprehensive insights. Their being minor figures has necessitated a change in our foremat since no one of them is of such calibre as to serve as the focus for an entire chapter (the exceptions to this being Tung Chung-shu and perhaps Mani, who are in many ways quite major figures). These are not the only minor figures treated in this volume. Others have been dealt with in conjunction with major figures where this was deemed appropriate. Although it is true that there does seem to be the pattern of change from eclecticism to scepticism to interiority through this period, these figures represent the constant underlying current of eclecticism which seems to serve as the basis of philosophizing throughout the period.

Eclecticism implies a looking toward, and reverence for, the past. This often takes the form of commentaries on the great works or sometimes a dislike of commentaries and a return to the great works themselves. In either case, truth has been discovered and recorded in the past, and it only remains for man to rediscover it in the works of the great thinkers. Thus originality is subordinated to exegetical insight.

The eclectic philosophers represented in this chapter show a weakness in metaphysics because they have relied on the metaphysics of their predecessors. Their focus was primarily on the present and the application of the teachings of the ancients. Though they attempted to remain faithful to the original teachings, still these underwent some minor modifications in their hands, and their practice usually remained more notable than their justifications of it. Many of these Roman and Chinese characters were Renaissance men before their time, and philosophy (as we generally think of such today) was only one aspect of their many concerns and approaches. Actually, to view them only as philosophers is not to do them justice.

Rather than extensive speculation (again, with a qualification for Tung Chung-shu), these men usually emphasized the practical side of philosophy. Their greatest achievements came in their considerations of the individual in relation to other individuals, to society, and to government. In short, ethics and political philosophy were their greatest concerns. Though their ethical theories tended to degenerate into moralizings, still they often offered existential insights and profound comments on the nature of the Good. And though virtually all of these thinkers may be considered as failures in terms of what they had hoped to accomplish politically and socially, still their lives can serve as models of integrity and high ideals. In this they exemplify one of their first principles: to do the right action regardless of consequences.

Consolation and destiny are two major themes of this period and for these thinkers. A modern philosopher may be, for example, a theist or a naturalist and yet may find such a position to be mostly irrelevant to what he does *qua* philosopher (one may think of some linguistic analysts). But such a situation was not the case for a philosopher of the Han-Hellenistic-Bactrian Period. How one should *live* is the theme, and that question could only be answered by determining human destiny. Of course the answers covered the entire spectrum of possibilities, but the question of destiny was always seriously encountered and deeply explored.

The philosophies of the Han-Hellenistic-Bactrian Period are often so much like religions because of this concern with human destiny. Seldom in history has a period been more characterized by that existential quality which we know so well today than is this period. If we may generalize to suggest a point, the Axial Age — Plato/Aristotle, Confucius, Buddha — conveys a tone of cool rationality, impersonality, calmness, order, community, deliberateness, in short, *yang*. But with the Han-Hellenistic-Bactrian Period it is almost as though a strong sense of individuality had developed historically so that the individual saw himself against the background of the infinite in a new, more dramatic, way. Often he felt overwhelmed, recognized his dependency, and sought consolation. Or he felt commensurate with the infinite and sought to actualize his potential mystically. Whatever the responses — and they included everything from the highly refined to the frenzied — the point is that his individual relation to the cosmos, his destiny, became the dominant theme for philosophizing, even though the resultant theory may even entail the loss of *individual* destiny. The more impersonal attitude of knowledge for its own sake, the scientific attitude, more or less lay dormant for several centuries yet. Many students who find contemporary philosophy irrelevant would appreciate the quality or tone (when not the content) of the philosophizings of this period, for it is supremely relevant, focused on the individual, his life in the world, and his highest destiny.

Consolation characterizes one of the responses to the question of human destiny and is the response most common to the philosophers in this section. Philosophy as consolation does not necessarily mean that life is somehow negative, but there is a recognition of man's limitations such that he had best come to terms with the cosmos rather than attempt to identify mystically with it or even transcend it, so to speak. Philosophies of consolation may be contrasted with such other positions as the Jaina quest for omniscience and Tīrthaṅkarahood (cf. Kundakundācārya and Umāsvāti); with the Buddhist quest for *prajañā* and Buddhahood (cf. Nāgārjuna and Vasubandhu); with those varieties of Taoism which virtually equate *teh*, the Tao as manifested, e.g., in man, with the eternal Tao (cf. Wang Pi); with the various doctrines of apotheosis (cf. Origen in the Christian context). These understadings of the question of human destiny present man as virtually limitless in potential. Because it is through self-reliance and hard (spiritual) work that his highest destiny is to be attained, in these views man hardly needs consolation so much as exhortation.

Philosophies of consolation tend to view man as essentially finite and often at the mercy of forces beyond his comprehension, let alone control (cf. Philo's *Yahwe* and Stoic *Logos*). Thus rather than *prajñā* a Stoic is enjoined to develop *apatheia*, and most Confucianists enjoin harmony with or submission to the

Will of Heaven rather than a lifting of the will, mind or spirit of man to a level commensurate with the Will of Heaven. The less mystical forms of Taoism emphasize more man's conforming himself to "the reversals of the Tao" than man's actually lifting himself above the interplay of *yin* and *yang* and thus transcending rather than conforming to the play of opposites. In general, philosophies of consolation tend to emphasize conformation rather than transformation, harmony rather than transcendence, at least in this life.

Concerning human destiny we may note three basic positions vis-á-vis consolation. At one extreme we have the view that man is essentially limitless and will realize his limitlessness when he becomes enlightened. Such enlightenment is within his own power and thus his destiny is more or less within his own hands. Consolation is not needed. In the middle we have the view of man as essentially or potentially destined for some ideal but presently laboring under unmovable limitations. Such states as omniscience and Buddhahood not being possibilities in this life, man needs a philosophy of consolation, a perspective by which to live righteously in the world while yet living in accord with his higher destiny. At the other extreme we find those views which deny that man has a transcendental destiny. From such views a philosophy of consolation may result (Epicureans) or some kind of cynical and/or hedonistic philosophy (Cyrenaics, Cārvākas).

The philosopher's role in this period is to discern and relate "the way things are" and how man can best adapt himself to his situation, socially, personally, religio-metaphysically. Considering the spectrum we have outlined above, those adherents of the two extremes tend to abandon the world as useless, or even as a positive hindrance, to the attainment of one's highest potential, or at the lower extreme they use the world for purely selfish purposes. We recall the mystic-recluse and the Cārvāka. But those who hold the middle position tend to be concerned with government, social welfare, community, posterity, and the things at hand generally since it is an integral part of their destiny that they live with and through them. In short, if one cannot hope to attain one's highest destiny now, but if one still admits to having a destiny beyond the now, then one usually attempts to transform the world as best one can. The philosophers in this section tend to belong to the middle of the spectrum.

Tung Chung-shu (179-104 B.C.)

Being a Confucian, and indeed a Confucian *par excellence*, Tung Chung-shu is at present out of favor with the regime in Peking, for he could scarcely be called a revolutionary and he taught an hierarchical ordering of society. Within a century after his death Wang Ch'ung was already making fun of his ceremonialisms, labeling them as empty hypocrisy. As the founder of the New Text School Tung is generally rated as conservative even by other Chinese thinkers within our Han-Hellenistic-Bactrian Period. Because of his historical importance in moulding Confucian philosophy into a state cult, if not indeed making it into an established religion, and because of his philosophy of history as based not on intuitive prophecy or revelation, as was the case with the Old Testament's prophets, but on empirical observations of the patterns of the past and careful projections of those into the future, and also because of his proto-scientific correlations between microcosm and macrocosm, he not only cannot be neglected but should be considered as one of the more important thinkers in Han China.

The epithet "the Cicero of China", though revealing a buried ethnocentric bias, seems to describe him pretty well. Both Cicero and Tung held priestly offices presiding over official state ceremonies which had become only empty ritual, even though they were survivals from primitive cults bordering on magic and superstition; both were orators and literary men of the first rank, having been educated by the best minds in every field, both being complete polymaths; and both not only influenced the development of the governmental bureaucracy of their respective Empires (both of which badly needed reform), but also virtually established the canon of literature, eclectically selecting from vast accumulations of the past and setting the style for formal writing and oratory for many hundreds of years and even down to the late nineteenth century to a great extent.

That Tung Chung-shu made a theology out of Confucian humanist philosophy cannot be denied, but whether or not this was a good thing is a matter of judgment. This was typical of the basic trend throughout Eurasia during this period, especially-among the Stoics and Buddhists. The Buddhists had begun to fructify into a large number of sects many of whom held very controversial views on the nature of the Buddha and the *Dharma*, which in historical perspective now seem equally to have compromised the original humanist anti-metaphysical, anti-theological reform of the Buddha.

In origin the New Text School was simply the result of the Burning of the Books, an effort to break with the past, to modernize China, under the great Ch'in Emperor, the Unifier of China, at the advice of his chief minister, Li Ssu. Actually, not all the books were burned however, since in addition to secret copies concealed in walls of private houses there were official copies kept in the Imperial Library, plus some apocryphal commentaries which ascribed virtual if not actual divinity to Confucius. Thus, when Tung Chung-shu came into power as chief adviser, to preserve and enhance the unification that had been achieved, justified in his own eyes by some expositions on the Principle of Unity or Unification, he had new texts of the Confucian classics issued, in a new script. And so he became the founder of this New Text School, which remained much more speculative (if not more esoteric, in keeping with the tendency of the times) than any which had preceded it, and established Confucianism as the state religion, with proper rites and ceremonies. While Tung set the idealistic trend of the New Text School, the Old Text School, based on some of the books that had escaped the purge and in opposition to this following of Tung, became increasingly realistic in orientation.

One word that might be used as a key term to typify Tung's philosophy is "correlations". Others have referred to these correlations as cosmology. Basically they follow the *yin-yang* dialectic as applied to the five elements. That would not be anything unusual however, since such were traditional in all three civilizations, the only basic difference being that the Chinese included wood along with earth, water, fire and air, while some of the Indian systems listed *chidākāsh* as the fifth.

But Tung was not content to stop here. He wanted *everything* classified systematically and correspondingly interrelated, not only with the five elements, but also with the five colors, the four directions (including the center), the five notes of the pentatonic scale, the seasons, the twelve months of the year, the twelve pitch pipes, and so on.

In the Axial Age the *yin-yang* dialectic was mostly associated with Taoism and not with Confucianism. But during the Han Dynasty there was a constantly increasing syncretism between the Taoists and the Confucianists such that in some instances it is not easy to tell the difference; and it might be said that Tung Chung-shu is one of the first to set this trend in motion in his endeavor to be as all-inclusive in his world-view as possible.

In his interpretation of the correlations, Needham stresses that this was more of an organicist type of philosophizing, almost a Whiteheadian process philosophy indeed, rather than a crude mechanist manner of fitting loose parts together.

> The key-word in Chinese thought is *Order* and above all *Pattern* (and, if I may whisper it for the first time, *Organism*). The symbolic correlations or correspondences all formed part of one colossal pattern. Things behaved in particular ways not necessarily because of prior actions or impulsions of other things, but because their position in the ever-moving cyclical universe was such that they were endowed with intrinsic natures which made that behaviour inevitable for them. If they did not behave in those particular ways they would lose their relational positions in the whole (which made them what they were), and turn into something other than themselves. They were thus parts in existential dependence upon the whole world-organism. And they reacted upon one another not so much by mechanical impulsion or causation as by a kind of mysterious resonance.[1]

After quoting Tung Chung-shu, whom, he says, best exemplifies such conceptions, Needham remarks about Tung's discussion of sound-waves:

> To those who could know nothing of sound-waves it must have been very convincing, and it proved his point that

> things in the universe which belonged to the same classes (e.g. east, wood, green, wind, wheat) resonated with, or energised, each other. This was not mere primitive undifferentiatedness, in which anything could affect anything else; it was part of a very closely knit universe in which only things of certain classes would affect other things of the same class.[2]

Neo-Pythagoreanism should make a good comparison with the Confucianism of Tung Chung-shu, for in both cases science and what was virtually magic were still not distinctly separated so that music, physics, mathematics, biology and religion were all intertwined organically in a mystical discipline designed to promote harmony of inner and outer human life, and harmony of both with the pre-established harmony of the universe. As a matter of fact, by comparison with his contemporaries in both India and Europe, Tung stands on relatively high ground, no longer merely rejecting or imitating antiquity, but interpreting, or re-interpreting it, with the best tools available.

Incidentally, Chan's remark that the elements with Tung are *hierarchically* considered in a linear order rather than in a cyclic order is an arresting point. But how much emphasis we may rightly put on this in our wider perspective is difficult to measure. One could argue that this increasing sense of hierarchy is, along with eclecticism and syncretism, another characteristic of the Han-Hellenistic-Bactrian Period, whereas dialectic more generally characterizes the Axial Age, just as in the "renaissance" periods dialectic re-emerges out of the hierarchies of the "medieval" periods. Certainly both the Han and the Roman Empires became increasingly hierarchical in social structure, as perhaps any civilization does as it becomes more widespread and reaches its zenith of achievement, until the stratification becomes pathological and revolution or evolution ensues. However, about all we can do is to offer this as a point of speculation.

The next field of inquiry in terms of correlations to which we now turn in regard to Tung Chung-shu's system is his philosophy of the human body. Of the influences of *yin-yang* on the body, and of the many correlations between the microcosmic body and the macrocosm, we shall note only a few. Tung says :

> The agreement of heaven and earth and the correspondence between yin and yang are ever found complete in the human body. The body is like heaven. Its numerical categories and those of heaven are mutually interwoven, and therefore their lives are interlocked. Heaven completes the human body with the number of days in a full year. Consequently the body's 366 lesser joints correspond to the number of days in a year, and the twelve larger joints correspond to the number of months. Internally the body has the five viscera, which correspond to the number of the Five Agents. Externally there are the four limbs, which correspond to the four seasons. The alternating of opening and closing of the eyes corresponds to day and night. The alternating of strength and weakness corresponds to winter and summer. And the alternating of sorrow and joy corresponds to yin and yang. . . . In what may be numbered, there is correspondence in number. In what may not be numbered, there is correspondence in kind. They are all identical and correspond to Heaven. Thus [Heaven and man] are one.[3]

There is nothing unique, really, about this little meditation. One finds such thoughts in Latin medieval texts (Saint Bonaventura, for example), in Pico della Mirandola, in Buddhist and Hindu Tantric texts, and in both Taoist and Neo-Confucianist literature down through the centuries. No doubt if we looked long enough it would be possible to find parallel passages in Tung's contemporaries, Panoetius of Rhodes or Carneades, for example, or even in the *Questions of Milinda*. Basically Tung is here voicing a rather universal concept, although certainly he tries to carry it into detail too exactingly to be convincing for all times.

But one reflection — besides that submitted by Chan that the effort towards mathematizing everything was laudable even though not very successful — that might go unobserved is that we here have a psycho-physical concept of embodiment rather than a Cartesian, Platonic or Zoroastrian dualism of body and soul in conflict with each other. Another reflection that easily comes to mind is that Tung is not giving a merely factual, static view. For although these correlations are, according to him, perfectly natural, nevertheless they are not absolutely fixed and unalterable. Over and over again in other contexts he counsels refinement of the *ch'i*, the breaths or vital force, as the chief discipline required of all human beings, and especially of those in government lest they lose their internal integrity and harmony and project their own personal disorders on to the public affairs for which they are responsible.

In Tung's philosophizing about the Source(*yüan*) he says that it is the same as the One from which the many emanate. But once again, this pro-mystical thinking is not especially "oriental", for we find essentially the same concept in Greece and Rome from Parmenides to Plotinus and beyond. Nevertheless, historically it must be conceded that in the Han-Hellenistic-Bactrian Period this sort of thinking such as we find in Neo-Platonism, Neo Taoism, and which also affected the emergence of the Mahāyāna schools through such as the *Lotus Sūtra* and the *Laṅkāvatāra Sūtra*, does increase and become more and more esoteric. As a matter of fact, Tung's expression of it, which is scarcely more than an acknowledgment rather than an exposition, is relatively reserved, for he is more interested in the demand for precision in his correlations than he is in cultivating the mystical origin of all things. Still, in his bid to be comprehensive, he cannot ignore this essentially Taoist sentiment.

On the question of human nature, Tung Chung-shu attempts to reconcile the extremes by his method of correlations. It will be remembered that Mencius, interpreting Confucius, believed that human nature was basically good but capable of being corrupted by circumstances, whereas Hsün Tzu believed that it was basically bad but could be rectified by education. Succinctly, Tung believes that human nature is really neutral and can become either corrupted or enlightened by circumstances and/or by education. Later on we shall see that his contribution to this discussion did not by any means settle the matter. Some went back to one of the original positions, while others, like Wang Ch'ung, believed that it is wrong to overgeneralize since some are good and some are bad; and still others, like Yang Hsiang, believed that human nature is a mixture. Thus the Han Confucianists explored and virtually exhausted the possible positions on this point.

Concerning the emotions, Tung finds that they are so universal in human affairs that it is foolish to try to ignore them in the name of objectivity (*yang*), just as it is dangerous to yield to them completely since that would be allowing too much prevalence of *yin*. In harmonizing the *yin* and *yang*, the Confucian middle path should be observed. Tung linked *hsing* (human nature) very closely with *ming* (destiny), and through his system of correlations could not think of man apart from Heaven and earth, the three comprising the *pantôs pan*, the Whole of wholes.

In his political and social philosophy Tung claims that the Emperor's mere emotions may be the cause or cure of ills and omens, feasts and famines, of life and death, throughout the Empire. This virtual attribution of divine powers not only to Confucius but also to the Emperor led to every sort of corruption, which even the usurpation of the radical reformer-dictator Wang Mang could not rectify. Within Tung's own century and in the centuries soon following, this sort of thinking was considered too much. Huan T'an and Wang Ch'ung, for example, rebelled and debunked, appealing to a more common sense empirical, if not outright sceptical, philosophy of natural causation.

This is not the place to go into minute detail about the crucial importance of music in the history of Chinese civilization, and it should not be necessary to recapitulate the comparison of Confucius and Plato on the importance of music for philosophers especially, although we suggest a fresh reinvestigation into the theory of music and its importance for both the Stoics (as part of the Universal Harmony) and the Epicureans (as affording the highest pleasure and giving direction to the emotions); likewise, it is premature, in view of the scanty materials available, to speculate on the status of music and musical theory in India during the second century B.C., nothing being very clear until the emergence of the Tamil Sangham in the first century A.D. But this much is clear: aesthetics is no matter of mere sensuous entertainment but a matter of harmonics, a matter of getting into sympathetic vibration with the universe itself. Perhaps Tung Chung-shu did make some blunders in his attempt at harmonics of correlations, but surely it cannot be denied that he was on a right path. For it is in the aesthetics such as he encouraged at court that one could, if internally in tune, come into harmony with Being and Becoming, and then, and perhaps only then, there would be harmony between microcosm and macrocosm.

Huan T'an (33 B. C.-39 A. D.)

Huan T'an is a partisan of the Old Text School, a chief point to be remembered being that the New Text School became fascinated with magic and the occult whereas the Old Text School, even though it may have been based on forgeries (as was claimed many centuries later by Chinese scholars themselves), nevertheless was more definitely if not radically humanist in orientation and even rather naturalistic in its outlook. The followers of the New Text School included Tung Chung-shu, who had tried to make Confucian philosophy into a state religion, while the Old Text School included such thinkers as Liu Hsin, Yang Hsiung, Wang Ch'ung and others, who were moderate rational reformers and not mere traditionalists. Instead of arguing about the authenticity of their scriptures, the controversy between these two schools became definitely philosophical, involving fundamental issues in regard to nature and man. Huan T'an's commitment to this Old Text tradition punctuates our tentative interpretation that the key to understanding him is epitomized in the word "discretion". For instance, he chides those who are so excessive in their filial piety that they completely impoverish themselves and their families by elaborate funerals. Huan T'an says that just because the Yellow River is muddy does not mean that it is no good for irrigation, the inference being that sometimes you have to make do with a little apparent evil in order to retain the greater good, whereas to eliminate the little evil may be to risk allowing an even greater one.

Although Huan T'an was an adherent to the Old Text School, one should not infer from this that he had merely a pious and uncritical attitude towards the Confucian classics. He was not willing to discard the classics but, on the other hand, he felt that they should not be venerated to the extent that they become only a ritualistic burden and an object of superstitious worship, both extremes evidently being present during his time. The classics are the depository of the invaluable experience and wisdom of the sages, but there should be no hindrances to freedom and the responsibility of intelligent interpretation which will make them relevant to the present condition of man.

According to Pokora, "... Huan T'an attacked politely but at the same time vigorously the ideological monopoly of Confucianism while proposing that the teachings of Taoism become also part of the spiritual life of Huan T'an's period. This was courageous in a period when the Confucian ideological control reached its climax."[4] Huan T'an was very much an iconoclast since, over against the virtual deification of Confucius under Tung Chung-shu, he was bold enough to say that Confucius was not a sage for all time but for his own time only. There is some indication that Nâgârjuna also disapproved of the tendency to deify the Buddha which was current in Mahâyāna literature.

Huan T'an is noted for having been ousted from court (7 B.C.) because he introduced "scandalous modern" music into the court ceremonies, music which was judged as being "lewd". Along with his passionate interest in music he acquired considerable expertise in astronomy and meteorology, and as minister of works during a period when the Yellow River was giving a lot of trouble he had to learn quite a bit about engineering also. In addition to being concerned about public affairs, Huan T'an, like Benjamin Franklin in another age, but scarcely paralleled in Rome except perhaps by Seneca, also was much concerned to keep up with the latest developments in the sciences of his day. He also wrote on economic problems, made ridicule of many of the practices of the magicians and sorcerers, and made some contributions to epistemology. Thus we can readily see him as a very versatile man, as all literati of his time and throughout the history of China were expected to be. He is now most remembered for his book the *Hsin lun* or *New Treatise*, although this survives only in fragments.

Huan T'an engaged in many discussions with well-known contemporaries, discussions which were mostly concerned with his somewhat heretical views, which were further developed by Wang Ch'ung. He appears to have been one of those seminal thinkers whose influence was such that those who developed his ideas became better known.

Huan T'an remarks that he too is, of course, interested in antiquity, but he is much more realistically concerned about good government and economics in the present time. There is a misconception of this Chinese tendency to "look backwards." After all, history can be an empirical science to a very high degree; and for management of current affairs there is an obvious value in critically examining records of the past, filtering out the factors that are relevant to the present and that will hopefully afford some projections or extrapolations towards the future and upon which new models can be devised for planning. This is what Marx attempted in the nineteenth century, what many generations of Chinese philosophers had done before him, and what present day social scientists are attempting. In this light surely Huan T'an's attitude toward history deserves closer attention, at least as much as has been given to Aristotle and Augustine in the recent past.

Huan T'an records that scepticism has gone very far in his own time, so far that people even try to doubt that "an oyster is not a bivalve or that two times five makes ten!" Thus for Huan T'an the greater part of wisdom lies in eclecticism instead of scepticism. True enough, there is a lot of nonsense in Chuang Tzu and there are a lot of virtually meaningless platitudes in Confucius; but this does not mean that they are all bad. One must pick and choose what is useful.

In general, Huan T'an attempts to find some happy medium between Legalism and Cofucianism. Good counsellors are absolutely essential to a ruler. Age makes little difference in such men, although of course it is normal for those of ripe old years to be wiser and they should be respected. Speaking on the theme of securing adequate ministers Huan T'an uses the universal metaphor of a physician healing a patient: just as the doctor himself does not have to do everything for every patient but may and must depend on assistants, so the state does not need an omnipotent and omniscient doctor but a capable and wise person who can be aided by capable and reliable assistants. Concerning the selection of governmental personnel, those must be selected who understand and respect the proper observance of the five relationships in society according to the Confucian hierarchical scheme. From this we infer that by this time the

Confucian canon had gained such standing that even iconoclasts as Huan T'an and Wang Ch'ung did not dare to question all of it. It seems that Mohist egalitarianism was not even taken into consideration as a possible ideal. Finally, advisers should have both integrity and learning. Without learning a man of integrity will be able to operate only in a very small domain; but without integrity, the great man's learning is all in vain. Huan T'an may have been defective in metaphysics such as one finds in his Mahāyāna contemporaries, but certainly one cannot say that he was sociologically naive.

Huan T'an ridiculed the superstitions which had become unquestioned rituals, such as consulting the oracle-bones, the tortoise shell, the straws and other means of prognostication. In these things he anticipates much that Wang Ch'ung capitalized on. His debunking is pointedly at Wang Mang who was at least as superstitious as Nero in Rome. Neither Seneca nor Huan T'an were very influential with their philosophies in these matters. Huan T'an is pragmatic about the whole affair, simply pointing out realistically that such practices failed to produce any results. Failure of nerve and withdrawal from the struggle simply because it is too much for us is not going to solve the problems — such seems to have been Huan T'an's attitude against the Neo-Taoists and others who were resorting to supernatural, esoteric and religious remedies.

It is strange to observe how widespread and deep-seated is the desire of human beings everywhere and everywhen to get in touch with departed souls, spirits, ghosts, demons, etc., as well as by magic or otherwise to get control of the forces of nature. And one cannot but marvel at the antics, some amusing, some downright heroic, of those who tried to achieve spiritualization of their whole being. In this context there is a story, very much like those of yogis in the *Purāṇas* in India and not unlike some of the stories of the Desert Fathers of early Christian asceticism, of a semi-legendary Taoist sage named Wang Chung-tu who could withstand both heat and cold of such intensity that others would perish therein. Another typical story is of a magician by the name of Tung Chung-chun who, having been put in prison, still remained uncannily alive even after his body began to stink like a corpse with maggots in it. To say the least,

Apollonius of Tyana was no unique phenomenon of his time. Eurasia was full of such yogis at the turn of the first century A.D.

A blind musician of the age of 180 years was received by the emperor who asked about his diet and other ways he had achieved such a long life. His reply politely denied any Taoist practices. At this Huan T'an seemed quietly delighted, remarking only that this marvelous person had lived long because he had taken advantage of his blindness to cultivate his inner vision. Now this is quite important since one can too easily exaggerate the sceptical tendencies in Huan T'an and Wang Ch'ung, ignoring the fact that their debunking of magic, sorcery, and superstition did not entail an insistence that there was no need of interior discipline at all. Although they avoided the foolish extremes of the esoteric cults and even ridiculed them, nevertheless, retaining their integrity and detachment in the midst of all the corruption must have required tremendous self-discipline and dedication to the inner vision which he praised in this man.

Huan T'an said, "Moreover, if those who establish laws and prohibitions are unable to stem entirely the wickedness of the world, they should at least agree with the wishes of the masses."[5] Here we have a very sharp contrast with India and Rome where, in spite of attempts at reform, the intellectual and administrative elites — seldom did they coalesce except in China — still considered the masses as there only to provide their basic needs, not as fellow humans to be served. Huan T'an's attitude towards responsibility for the welfare of the people, and therefore for social reform, is rather traditional but no less enlightened for that. He submitted a memorial to the emperor on these things suggesting that resorting to magicians and sorcerers would not do the work of social reform for the benefit of the masses but will only make things worse: "In my foolish opinion the only reason why plans should be judged to be of benefit to government policy is because they are in harmony with the mind of the people and have grasped the real state of affairs. . . . "[6]

Huan T'an implicitly condemns the Han bureaucracy when he says that the first and last duty of a good administrator is to clean up the corruption which has become so habitual that no one considers it as such. To separate politics from ethics has been one of the major fallacies of political economists in the modern world. Maybe a strong dose of Confucian re-establishment of ethical norms in public circles would still do the world a lot of good.

It is one of those queer twirks of fate that Huan T'an's works have been better preserved in Japan than in China. Nevertheless, he was frequently quoted by major thinkers all through the history of Chinese thought. Tentatively our judgment is that he is at least as important as Seneca, whom he resembles considerably. Huan T'an had to confront problems and situations which were quite similar to those which Seneca and Cicero had to confront, and their solutions are not really much different. But once again, we boast no conclusions even though emphatically we hope to open discussion.

Seneca (4 B.C.-65 A.D.)

Seneca was the world citizen *par excellence*, the perfect embodiment of the Stoic or even Confucian ideal of the universal man whose influence extends everywhere, not by exercise of political cleverness, but simply by virtue of his detached conformity to rational tolerance, human dignity, and level-headedness. It might be said of Seneca that he was to Rome what John Dewey was to the United States: he embodied the spirit of his civilization and brought it to conscious awareness.

Like many of his contemporary intellectuals in the Roman Empire, Seneca was a Spaniard. He spent quite a bit of time in Alexandria and of course made his visits to Athens, Rhodes, and other places noted for philosophy and letters. Seneca's book on India in imitation of Arrian's *Tá Indika* and the one on Egyptian religions are both now lost. Most traditional histories of philosophy completely overlook these works. If they had survived, we might view Seneca in an entirely different light. They might have been quite an eye-opening experience to those who have not yet become acquainted with the perspective whereby, during the apogée of the Roman Empire, India and the Mediterranean were so closely linked that those histories which try to lump India and China together as though they were in a completely different world are really not faithful to the facts. China, having been the "other world", now comes into full communication. Is there any possibility, then, of influence one way or the other, or mutually (as seems most likely), between the various cultural contexts which produced Mahāyāna Buddhism, the compilation of the *Gitā*, the development of Han Confucianism and Neo-Taoism, Seneca's Stoicism, Philo's Alexandrian syncretistic Judaism, and Christianity? Certainly a strong possibility. It will take a long time to prove or disprove the theses of influences; but the increasing evidence is certainly positive, contrary to opinions and attitudes inherited largely from Hegel, if not from Augustine. Still, each civilization, even when there is inter-communication between them, seems to have its own rhythms. Stoicism was an old philosophy. Mahāyāna was new. Stoicism was capable of cross-fertilization and receiving hybrid vigor, and then it became, after Seneca, Christianity. Stoicism did not affirm change. Mahāyāna and Christianity did; indeed, they affirmed not only change but total transformation of everything natural, human, and divine. Later this was true of Neo-Taoism also, perhaps through the influence of Mahāyāna Buddhism.

Rome to Seneca was the Empire of Universal Man. China to the Chinese was the Central Kingdom, i.e., the civilized country, all others being barbarian. Since Rome to Seneca meant the Empire that embraced all men and all things human, demonic, and divine, tolerance was a primary virtue, though one must not let that degenerate into fascination with the latest fads or sensational promises of instant salvation which the proliferating cults from the Orient offered. Popular religion with its extremes held no appeal for him, but he had a profound reverence for the manifestation of Cosmic Reason within nature. And to Seneca the Roman Empire was a part of that manifestation rather than a part of the manifestation of the uninhibited mythological imagination. To live in harmony with the whole — one has to look to China to find thinkers comparable to Seneca; perhaps no single Confucianist would be comparable, though Yang Hsiung might come closest.

Seneca was a vegetarian. It was not just the temptations of the flesh that he resisted, but the luxury and display of the aristocracy in the face of the poverty and suffering of the masses, though he did belong by heritage to the Roman aristocracy. Seneca's ideal would have been Plato's philosopher king. Stoic *ataxaria* forbade ambition. Ambition had ruined Caesar; passion had been Anthony's downfall; and dishonesty, intrigue, graft, and corruption had become almost endemic in government circles. Without action, contemplation may be mere escape from reality; but without contemplation, action may only increase confusion and lead to greater woe. Better to remain a philosopher, an advisor, a power not of this world to whom those in it could come for counsel and fortification of their spiritual stamina.

Cicero and Lucretius had pioneered, and Seneca continues, philosophizing in the vernacular. Is that not a revolution in itself, not incomparable to the abandonment in turn of Latin for modern European vernaculars or of Sanskrit for modern Indian vernaculars ?

In spite of his cynicism in other matters, even Wang Ch'ung constantly counselled altruism in treating even the barbarians at the borders. It is sometimes a shock to naive Christians to find out that *agapé* is not necessarily or exclusively Christian after all. But one must also say further that neither Seneca nor the Roman Empire was unique in claiming this as the highest virtue nor unique in failing miserably to practice it. Seneca is very sensitive to the facts of evil and irrationality. Indeed, his philosophy is almost entirely an attempt at answering the perpetual questions derived from these; still, he neglects almost entirely the sciences and positive investigation of things. Concerning suicide, we would like to say only this : in both Rome and China the dominant view was that one's destiny and one's honor could not possibly be separated except by death in disgrace instead of death at one's own hands.

In conclusion we might ask what is not to be found in Seneca. He is weak in metaphysics, especially ontology, by comparison with his Mahāyāna contemporaries. He clings too much to permanency and allows too little room for change by Christian, Mahāyāna, and Neo-Taoist standards. Historically, philosophy with Seneca becomes rather like the popular sense of the word today : not a technical matter including sophisticated techniques of symbolic logic or linguistic analysis, but simply a way of life, almost a semi-secular religion. Some interpreters seem to worry about Seneca's pantheism, while others rejoice that he humanized Stoicism and made it a livable doctrine whereas before him it had been too cold, too austere, too rational. In Seneca philosophy becomes mostly moralizings and consolations, nothing revolutionary but at least a stabilizing force in troubled times. Within the first century A.D. Seneca stands out as the shaper of tradition, if not as the form-giver to Roman civilization and to its successor, the Latin West.

We might here mention Musonius Rufus, the teacher of Epictetus, as an interesting contrast to Seneca. More like the Cynics or Wang Fu than the Stoics, he takes philosophy as a more rigorously monastic vocation for which family ties, marriage, wealth, fortune, ambition, and all the worldly bourgeois values are to be left behind. The philosopher's kingdom, like Jesus's, is not of this world. He reminds us that in every civilization these vocations of renunciation have been a natural phenomenon and that when civilizations have tried to get along without them, they have tried to do the unnatural thing. Monastic life, in all its forms, is a human universal, and those societies that try to prohibit it are doing so at their own peril. Of course we are reminded of Hindu yogis and Jaina and Buddhist monks. We are also reminded of the *Gītā*'s teaching of *sva-dharma* when we find that Musonius Rufus decried the degeneration of the family in Rome. For the philosopher there is one set of duties, but for the householder, and especially for the public administrator, there is quite another set of duties. Philosophy for those of his persuasion is not for everyone for its pursuit requires total commitment.

Plutarch (50-125 A.D.)

Plutarch of Chaeronea, in spite of his great influence in the Roman Empire, wrote in Greek. He was Greek and complains of the difficulty of learning Latin even after being in Rome. He was a popularizer, a good one, reminding us of Will Durant in our own time. But was he a philosopher ? We usually do not think so; nevertheless, it not only can but must be said of him that he is a Platonist with a complete philosophy behind his biographies, moral essays, and dialogues. Eclectic ? But who was not so in the first century A.D. ?

Through acquaintance with the younger Pliny and others, Plutarch could not have been completely ignorant of India or even of China. One of his intimate friends had been to England at the other end of the Empire. He definitely registers knowledge of Zoroaster and even associates demonology with that source, and he records other knowledge of Persia. Still, these things do not seem to have had any great influence on him.

Plutarch's *Symposia* — actual "table talk" reported almost verbatim after parties at which intellectuals gathered to engage in light conversation — reminds us all too readily of the "Seven Sages of the Bamboo Grove" sort of thing which was going on in China under similar circumstances. Not that there could have been any influence one way or the other very easily; rather, socio-economic and cultural conditions were similar. Trade and slavery made for leisure among the aristocracy, who had to do something to keep from being bored.

Plutarch is not concerned with or bothered by the plight of the masses. He was an elitist and even in political matters he wrote for his fellow elitists. It is the right and duty of the aristocrats to rule. Realizing their common lot against the constant threat of mob violence and public disturbance, the aristocrats must preserve concord among themselves such that the masses would be infused with their example, enspirited by their integrity, and ennobled by their virtue. Again, there are clear parallels with the Confucian *geist*, in theory if not in practice also. While the Stoics and Confucians accepted public responsibility, the Epicureans and the Neo-Taoists claimed the right to abstain, as did the Cynics and the pioneer Buddhist and Jaina monks who denounced what they had renounced. As the successor to the Cynics in Roman society, Christianity played a parallel role : a total embarrassment to the establishment and a concern with kingdoms not of this world. Buddhism and Christianity were soon to have very similar roles in China and Europe, but who could have foretold that ? Yang Hsiung and even Wang Ch'ung seem as oblivious of Buddhism as Plutarch is of the Christians.

Plutarch's deliberate choice to write biography instead of history as such reminds us of Dilthey's insistence on the "quality of life" being manifested in the lived-through situations of individual people rather than in the abstract universal, classifiable trends superimposed on the living realities. In the contemporary world Plutarch would probably be called a personalist if not indeed an existentialist, even though he still had a lot of Greek rationality and at a time when that was becoming unpopular. Though philosophy in Rome tended to become anti-intellectual moralizing, nevertheless philosophers were banned by Hadrian in 94 A.D. as corruptors of the faith and morals of the people. We may find parallels in China as we approach the dictatorship of Wang Mang. However, Plutarch did have a philosophy of history, and one not much different from that of the Stoics. His philosophy of history was essentially a dialectic, it seems, between the doctrine of Providence and that of individual fate or destiny.

As a teacher Plutarch does manifest considerable ability to discourse on the classical problems of chaos and order, problems in which a non-anthropomorphic rational theology plays a prominent part. In philosophy of religion Plutarch makes a sharp distinction between higher philosophic rational thought and the superstitions and excesses of the popular religious cults prevalent and even proliferating beneath his sophisticated nose. He disagrees with the Epicureans who tended to dismiss all religion and theology as mere stupidity and shere emotion. Plutarch, needless to say, is not ignorant of the Jewish faith, although it would be difficult to assert that he knew of Philo and it is definite that he makes no mention of Christianity as a guiding force in history.

Plutarch's philosophical writings are not really very Hellenic after all but are very Hellenistic in tone: eclectic in method, with such copious quotations that original thought is virtually stifled; moralistic spirit predominating over genuine speculation; an attempt at making sense of the accumulated past rather than exploring into the future, and therein something not too different from the Han Chinese trend in the same century.

Plutarch's consolations and *euthymia* appear to be much more like the Han Confucianists' cultivation of serenity than the Mahāyāna varieties of the same thing, for they carry with them very little if any neo-mythologizing or yoga or necessary metaphysical rigor. Likewise there is nothing in Plutarch of the transformation of human nature as will soon come to the fore in Mahāyāna and Christianity. It is not yet transcendence, as with Plotinus later, but serenity as making the most of one's lot. In spite of his opposition to Stoicism, Plutarch is after all quite Stoical himself.

Plutarch was a country gentleman who had no financial worries to speak of; a man of leisure, happily married; an elitist to the core, very much like his Chinese literati contemporarises. Humanist *par excellence,* he would not have approved of the extremes and oddities even of Apollonius, for they would not be conducive to serenity. Indeed, Plutarch and Seneca are not far apart in spirit even though they came from opposite ends of the Mediterranean, wrote in different languages, and had different positions in the world. *Euthemia* was no magic key to immortality or to other worlds or to cosmic consciousness. It was rather a matter of practical or applied psychology and ethics.

In a small brilliant community like Athens of the previous centuries, serenity and consolation were not necessarily virtues. But when one has to deal with a much larger and more incomprehensible world, such as the world of Rome or Han China in the first century A.D., or the United States and elsewhere today, a world wherein secularization has left a vacuum formerly filled by religion, what is left to restore men to their senses unless it be philosophy? Actually it might be said that there is a greater watershed between Plato and Plutarch (even though he thinks he is a faithful interpreter of Plato) than there is between Plutarch and Boethius or between Boethius and the concept of philosophy in home-town America today where one is proverbially advised to "take it philosophically". In order to know who we are and whence our subconscious sentiments come, Plutarch is very important indeed. And the Americas need consolation in a "way of life" since the Marxist challenge to revolution is falling on deaf ears while the proletarians are becoming more religious than ever in a pentacostal way, and the bourgeoisie are taking philosophy along with golf as a relief from boredom and as a possible alternative to almost continuous television.

Plutarch associates poetry very closely with philosophy in accordance with his preference for Plato, whereas among the Peripatetics then as now among the analytic school, there were those who would prefer to see philosophy dominated by such intellectual curiosities as the chicken-and-egg problem. So philosophy was no longer a system into which the sciences could be properly fitted together. But as an illustration of the attitude toward science we may note that in both Han China and in Rome animals were no longer a subject for scientific investigation as they had been with Aristotle and Theophrastus. They were only another good subject for literati to write about, a matter of entertainment and a subject for casual reading, not to be taken too seriously. In one's (assumed) comfort and security, it was a pleasant pastime to 'philosophize' about the relation between man and the beasts. Plutarch discusses the question of whether land or sea animals are more intelligent, and the question soon gets him involved in everything from teleology to Aesop's fables. One's civilized job was to know and to record, to select and to correlate, the accumulated wisdom of the ages, but not to be bothered by the infinity of miscellaneous, meaningless facts of science. After all, cannot Homer tell us more about the pigs of Beoetia than the Beoetians themselves ?

Why the perpetual gap between theory and practice in all countries and in all ages ? This was Plutarch's question and it is still ours. Are our possible worlds only perpetually possible ? Plutarch's answer is in the positive. After all the miscellanea are sifted and the essence extracted from his eclecticism, there is really Platonism at the core after all, and dualistic Platonism at that. We are citizens of both worlds, and only rarely, as in moments of musical ecstacy, do they become harmonized. As with Zoroastrian dualism, there is perpetual struggle and no single utopian scheme will bring us to finality even after many messiahs, *avatārs*, and *Bodhisattvas* have appeared in the flesh and dwelt among us.

Ma Jung (79-166)

The first years which followed the restoration of the Han Dynasty (after the dictatorship under Wang Mang) were a time of stabilizing the new power. There was a need for philosophical justification of the new dynasty, hence the literati were reinstated in full, at least those who were willing to interpret the ancient classics to fit the ideological needs of the restored regime. Needless to say, the literati could not all agree as to what really did constitute true unadulterated orthodoxy, and there was a polarization between two contending parties, the dominant of these being under the leadership of, or at least typified by, Ma Jung and his disciple Tcheng Hiuan.

Balazs speaks of Ma Jung as the "grand patrician . . . who was the first to write a commentary on the entire classical canon."[7] He gave up hope of reforming the court from within and returned to his own estate to do his scholarly work in retirement. His editing and commenting on the classics set the pace for several centuries; indeed, there were very few until the time of Chu Hsi who worked more comprehensively than he.

It is his work on loyalty, *Tschung Tching* (*Classic of Loyalty*), which is most significant. It is loyalty to the truth as such that is at the heart of the matter, not just external conformity to institutions without consideration of whether or not they are worthy of loyalty. In public affairs as well as in personal life there is always both the inner and the outer aspect of human existence. The aristocrat, the literatus, should be able to provide the inner wisdom while those in society who are not of the aristocracy furnish the outer active aspect of truth. But preserving these inner distinctions does not, or certainly should not, compromise the Unity of Truth, which must be a Large and Generous Idea, which must perforce be inclusive of everything.

Although in all the historical materials we have there are many stories of martyrdom for a cause, this was never overtly exalted as an integral part of any philosophy until Ma Jung gives it sanction. He is not sentimental about it, but he feels that this capacity of man to die for a cause is closely linked with the goodness in human nature. But much more radically it raises a new issue which traditional dealers in Chinese philosophy may have overlooked : is there finally beginning to emerge in Ma Jung a new ethic out of the weak and often decadent syncretism of the period, a new *geist*, a completely different interpretation of Confucian integrity as a vital adherence to principle regardless of consequences—something like the Gandhian interpretation of the *Gita*—and no longer merely the strict adherence to empty ceremonial formulae ?

Typical of his period Ma Jung's Confucianism is syncretistically infused with Taoism also. However, syncretism had become sufficiently advanced so that Ma Jung did not strictly associate himself with any particular school but was seeking to combine them all, or even to transcend them all after having ingested them all, for transcendence without comprehensiveness may lead to meaningless vacuity, just as comprehensiveness without transcendence will result only in meaningless pedantry. This reminds us of Nicholas Berdyaev's comment that although hereditary aristocracies based only on biological pedigree, economic inheritance and social robbery constitute in any civilization a great evil, if not a vice of a parasitic nature, nevertheless some sort of cultural aristocracy is necessary if democracy is not to degenerate into sheer banality and ultimate suicide of excellence in everything from etiquette to architecture.

Ma Jung appeals as often to Chuang Tzu and Lao Tzu as to Confucius and wrote commentaries on the *Lao Tzu* and the *Huai Nan-tzu.* Indeed, Ma Jung's voluminous works are, significantly, almost all commentaries, and from now on for many centuries, in China as well as in India and in both Greek and Latin Europe, we will have little else. And let us not condemn him prematurely for not being "original"; originality was simply not demanded of his epoch, and anyone who had not exhausted the resources of his time could not dare to attempt originality.

Ma Jung might be called the Plutarch of Han China. Extremely eclectic, voracious reader, aristocratic individualist who preserves his integrity in and out of officialdom, even idealist of a sort in spite of the signs of decay and disorder all around. Although he made no sensational innovations and established no radically new tradition, he embodies everything that had been achieved up to his own time, and that was no small achievement.

Wang Fu (90-165)

What was the role of the philosophers in all of the chaos, corruption, anarchy and confusion of the times? Hsün Yüeh brought out the Confucian classics, trying, like Plotinus shortly later and Marcus Aurelius his contemporary, to effect a restoration of the old older, but probably did not find much of an audience. The Seven Sages of the Bamboo Grove decided to return to nature, abandoned books, got drunk and congratulated themselves on becoming enlightened. The Legalists, who formerly had been unofficially rather successful in keeping things in running order beneath the cloak of Confucian formalities, could not pull things together again. Ma Jung simply went into premature retirement, no longer attempting to restore order; Epicurean-like, he literally cultivated his garden while writing compendious commentaries on the classics with only some slender hope that they might be of use to future generations. Life had become cheap and hope was virtually gone, and some had even resorted to cannibalism in order to survive. Who could blame Wang Fu for becoming a hermit ? Buddhism was soon to fill the vacuum, but that is another story. That similar conditions prevailed in Rome is well known, and Christianity was to fill the vacuum there.

Wang Fu was not effective within his century, although perhaps tragically prophetic. Dilettantism was the rule among intellectuals as in other periods of decadence in other civilizations, but Wang Fu saw through it and issued a strong rebuke. By example in action as well as in writing he registered his protest, searching for authenticity. In particular Wang Fu railed against the corruption of the civil service system, which, when operative, is one of the best of the world's institutions for guaranteeing that intelligence will be put to work for the good of all. If brain power is not so employed, it may either be wasted entirely, or work for alien forces, or else be turned to crime and the disruption of society.

What is perhaps most significant about Wang Fu is that he gives the lie to the stereotypic conception of the Confucian philosopher as merely a mouther of platitudes and a preserver of the status quo, placing all his energies on good manners and proper decorum, unruffled even when the whole world is crashing down on his shoulders. Rather, Wang Fu may be characterized as the prophetic type of philosopher, without the fanaticism of a Tertullian but with the moral fervor of Jerome or Anthony the Hermit (who were to come a few years later in a different part of the world).

In all of his writings Wang Fu made a strong appeal to return to the root (*pen*) and to suppress the secondary (*mo*, the branches). This is significant historically since it is relatively new among Confucianists, although it became quite common for Taoists in this and future centuries. He carried this distinction between *pen* and *mo* through all the fields of human endeavor from agriculture through commerce, art, research, and writing, not to mention government and public affairs.

Wang Fu had gone back to the original texts of the Confucian classics, paying no heed to the accumulated commentaries, and had attempted with some success to restore their unity. Still, his Confucianism was far from pure since it manifested some Taoist influences. Wang Fu's is not the Confucianist concept of Tao but that strange sort of semi-materialist mystical Source (if one may put it that paradoxically) of all dynamism. Not only the spiritual things but also the material aspects of the universe "live and move and have their being" in the Tao. Although as all-pervading and transcending every finitude his Tao is indeed mysterious, nevertheless it operates through the *chih*, that term so vexing which means fluid or breath or vital principle or even moving force in all of reality.

With Wang Fu, the parallelism of *yin-yang* is carried about as far as possible, for just as Heaven and earth are *yin* and *yang*, so man's nature is both spiritual and material and it is thus that his destiny is explained. And with this concept of human nature and destiny (*hsing* and *ming*; they are never separated), astrology and the other esoteric means of determining one's destiny come again into the picture, including an assertion that one's sacrificial prayers are ineffectual if hindered by the demons but good fortune follows if they are accepted or furthered by the good spirits. All of this seems to confirm our general impression that in the later stages of the Han-Hellenistic-Bactrian Period there was everywhere a degeneration from the earlier classical norms, and after eclecticism and syncretism, fascination with the esoteric as in our own times. But we must be cautious since we do not have access to the full texts or to very much about the decline and fall of Han China.

"Heaven is the grounding of the state," Wang Fu says almost categorically. But were there many serious thinkers anywhere in Eurasia in the second century A.D. who did not think this or hold some view very close to it? We are reminded of Marcus Aurelius, or perhaps of his teacher, Epictetus; but Wang Fu's Mahāyāna and Jaina contemporaries were less apt to put their philosophy into political application, and we are still relatively in the dark as to the political views of their Hindu contemporaries except to assume that they were still following Kauṭilya, even though Milinda and perhaps even Kanishka did have Greek counsellors as well as Indian assistants. Under the formalities of his semi-Confucianism, it is difficult to discern whether there was anything in Wang Fu distinct from the usual Confucian norm of the Mandate of Heaven being given only to those who hold the needs of the people of primary concern. There is a note of pessimism emerging from the actual conditions of his time as he attempts to find out why there had been a decline and degeneration from the excellence of the past. We might note that even though Mohism as an officially recognized philosophy was no longer functional, Wang Fu seems to have been impressed by its relevance for his own time.

Wang Fu disagreed even with Hsün Yüeh on rigorous enforcement of the criminal law code, arguing that the kings of old did not enforce it so strictly but simply strengthened the good and tried to eliminate rather than punish the evil in the people. He says very explicitly that crime is the result of actual needs, poverty and misery; therefore, instead of trying to make the laws stricter, one should straighten out the economic situation in the Empire.

For reasons that are not easy to discern, although Wang Fu had the theory he did not have the power and ability to put it into practice. We have to wait more than a hundred years after his death before a new dynasty, the Wei, attempts some of the far-reaching reforms he had proposed.

Epictetus (50-125) *and Marcus Aurelius* (121-180)

Our traditional histories of philosophy may have done us an injustice by neglecting these Stoic thinkers whose thoughts have, like those of Cicero and Augustine, become virtually household adages. Their universality challenges us still to transcend our provincialities, and closer re-examination should reveal an unexpected amount of knowledge of the non-Western world. By neglecting to give a critical re-appraisal of their contributions, traditional histories have failed to give us a lever for understanding ourselves; for they were, whether we like it or not, what we have become.

Since nothing should be alien to man, philosophy also should seek for universality. It could not become, and therefore should not try to become, anything less than the all-embracing discipline as such, by no means simply a specialization in disputation as had become the situation among the Academics and the Sceptics. And it should not become merely an intellectual pleasure as it had become with the Epicureans and with what was left of the Cyrenaics (they had burned themselves out pretty fast). Although Epictetus and Marcus Aurelius affirmed, along with the Cynics, the maximum of detachment as concerns external affairs, this did not necessarily entail complete renunciation. As for Oriental religions, the cults of the mysteries, the fascination with magic and the occult arts, since these are part of the total picture one should neither ignore them nor loose perspective concerning them. One should rather rationally avoid the extremes, be aware of his proper role and destiny, and not meddle in others' business. Such is the way to live. To live ! That is the issue. Salvation had become important.

The great Pax Romana and the at least equally great Pax Sinica, both of them bought at the very high price of the dictatorships of Caesar and Wang Mang respectively, were almost simultaneous. It was during this period that the Mediterranean, Chinese, and Indic civilizations experienced a maximum of contact and intercommunication. Marcus Aurelius at the top of the social scale and Epictetus at the bottom probably had some knowledge of India and China even if they had not read (though no doubt they had) Arrian's *Tá Indika* and Seneca's now lost book on India. Flavius Arrian who records Epictetus' immortal discourses — Epictetus himself, like Socrates and many more of the world's wise men, having written nothing — was the same Flavius Arrian who wrote the *Tá Indika,* which remains to this day one of our most reliable sources of information about India from the time of Alexander to the days of Epictetus and Marcus Aurelius themselves. How historians of philosophy could ignore such an obvious thing is difficult to comprehend. We have only begun to put the world back together as it really was, in place of the fanciful distortions bequested to us by Hegel and others.

Epictetus makes a sharp distinction between different states of consciousness or awareness, especially the difference between sleep, dream, and waking states. Certainly here we can only conjecture, as we did formerly with Carneades' snake and rope metaphor, that it might be further evidence of influence from India. What is omitted in Epictetus' case, however, is very important, for in India this division is really only a metaphor to illustrate the difference between true philosophical wisdom (*prajñā, sophia*) and knowledge (*jñāna, gnosis*), for there is the same difference between waking and wisdom states as there is between dream and waking states.

Along with the Buddha, Socrates, Bodhidharma, Honen, Shinran, Nanak, Kabir, or Tukaram, Epictetus remains one of the most charismatic philosophers of all times and all places. We should note that Marcus Aurelius was not just his friend but an outright disciple. Epictetus exerted influence on, among others, Celsus, Galen, John Chrysostom, Gregory Nazianzen, Origen and Augustine, not to mention his repute during the Italian Renaissance and on down to Pascal and the present.

Epictetus' philosophy is almost exclusively ethical, almost to the complete neglect of both physics and metaphysics. The Sceptics went further and regarded all philosophy, logic and metaphysics in particular, as maladies and even proposed treatment techniques *pace* Nāgārjuna and Wittgenstein. Sextus Empiricus regarded Scepticism itself not as just another philosophy but as a kind of 'laxative' which expells itself at the same time as it cleanses the mind. Epictetus' philosophy is also profoundly religious, even devout, so much so that it has been used by Christian monks as a *vade mecum* for centuries. And it is supremely personal in spite of the fact that for the most part Stoicism is reported to be a very pantheistic, impersonal philosophy.

The problems of freedom vs. destiny, of providence, of fate and/or fortune vis-à-vis evident cruelty and dereliction in the world — suffering, in short, is recognized by Epictetus (as by the Buddhists) as that condition from which we should *begin* to philosophize, not that with which we end. Other themes which he takes up are the problems of duty vs. pleasure, mental discipline vs. the natural inclinations of impulse and emotion, and, of course, after the rest of the catalogue is spelled out, the problem of death and immortality and the conquest of fear. There is nothing distinctively Western here since these problems are universal; and it seems that all of these were being treated in a very similar manner by Epictetus' contemporaries in other parts of the world. So rather than Epictetus furnishing an exceptions to our characterization of the age as eclectic and syncretistic, he represents the quintessence of the Hellenistic and Bactrian (if not Han also) civilizations.

From various sources we make passing note that the word "diatribe", which was one title given to his manual or his *Discourses*, has changed its meaning considerably. Originally it simply meant the gentle exercise of dialectics in order to eliminate false notions, whereas now it has come to mean something much more damaging, if not an almost violent attack. The *Enchiridion* or "little manual" was also compiled by Arrian. It remains intact although part of the *Diatribes* is lost.

Epictetus believed in the inherent goodness of man, and there are even adumbrations at times of the philosophy of the transformation of human nature into something god-like, a view which will dominate Eurasia in future centuries. Although there are traces of Cynic tradition in his intellectual and spiritual heritage — the strong bent towards renunciation comes in there — the Stoic belief in rational moderation prevails for the most part. The *ascesis* is there, although the stages of spiritual progress are not so elaborately put forth as among the Buddhists and Jainas of his century or of that previous to him. Still, they are rather definite, namely, (1) control of the emotions; (2) selfless performance of duty (we may read *niśkāma karma* from the *Gitā* here) ; (3) good moral judgment even in the face of uncertainty (here we might even read *prajñā* (wisdom) as above *jñāna* (knowledge).

Another point is that Epictetus counsels us to live in the 'timeless' perspective, neither regretting the past nor putting false hope in foolish plans for the future, but remaining aware that the present is only a fleeting moment (he had a great reverence for Heraclitus). Once again, influence or no influence one way or the other, this is a common theme for the period and is just another instance of the climate of opinion in Eurasia as a whole.

Epictetus' attitude toward the problem of self-knowledge is derived from Socrates as well as from a sincere and almost devout reverence for Diogenes and his utter simplicity and spirit of renunciation. Iason Xenakis says that the problem of self-knowledge was treated as sufficiently important as virtually to crowd out any interest in exterior things. He then goes on to explain that even this self-knowledge for Epictetus, for which all the rest of philosophy is only at best a propaedeutic, is basically if not completely ethical and is not a matter of introspective auto-psychoanalysis.[8]

Epictetus taught that we should never blunt our aesthetic sense, our capacity for wonder and awe, our capacity for contemplation. This is salutary counsel for those who are so morally 'good' that they become virtually ugly people, unresponsive to spontaneous activity and often missing wonderful opportunities because they are so duty bound to the routine of their system. But one must, on the other hand, be careful lest spontaneity become impulsiveness and irresponsibility. Again, perhaps for each individual his own *sva-dharma.*

What constitutes the difference between Epictetus' Stoicism and Scepticism? Are they not equally anti-intellectual and more inclined toward voluntarism? Epictetus thought that Scepticism is self-refuting. To hold that nothing is worth believing is already to assert something; and the Sceptic is all too prone to wax verbose instead of residing in the silence to which his 'logic' should lead him. Besides, such attitudes usually come from perverse motives of obstinacy — a moral issue, not a logical one at all — and therefore should be, as the Buddhists and the Jainas also taught, rectified by ethical considerations most of all. Such views are wrong simply because they lead to greater suffering and ignorance.

There was an ongoing dialogue between the Sceptics and the Stoics as to whether to argue that the senses deceive us is in vain since it is only by the senses that we can check up on them. According to Epictetus, it is neither denial of the senses nor enslavement to them that is the proper way. He seems to agree with Nāgārjuna that *saṃsāra* is *nirvāṇa* and *nirvāṇa* is *saṃsāra,* if one has acquired the art of awareness. With practice one can learn to use the senses at will, to turn them off or turn them on; and eventually one can use the mind in the same way. Turning off thoughts or turning them on implies that they are not ultimate but that they are useful. Indeed, as with the *Gitā* and Nāgārjuna, Epictetus had reached the stage of renunciation of renunciation, of detachment from detachment, and a conscious but deliberate return to the natural way without being enslaved to it.

Strange philosophy that could at once and in one century give guidance and — let us not forget, for this is a new role for philosophy, not only among Buddhists, Taoists and Christians — *consolation* to both slave and emperor, though one wonders how often Marcus Aurelius really envied Epictetus. Externals meant virtually nothing, perverse though this doctrine could be in justifying what was impossible to correct; but in the inner world all men are equal just as they all are born in the same naked way, and just as they all die sooner or later. Differences are only temporary and are not ultimately real.

Even more than Seneca, and more consciously also, Marcus Aurelius was not just a citizen of Rome but a citizen of the world. But Emperor of the Universe, as the title offered to him even in his youth? Preposterous! Rome was not everything, but it had a little bit of everything in it. To Marcus Aurelius the whole world, not to mention Rome, was only a tiny droplet in a very vast universe. Therefore his job was not so much expansion as consolidation, harmonizing all in accordance with the *Logos*, the Rational Order of the universe. He did not want the job; but selflessly, as selflessly as possible, he accepted the responsibility and bore the burden nobly. His profound faith in Providence allowed him to be somewhat detached (*apatheia*) about it all.

Marcus Aurelius wanted to restore Rome to its former purity and strength of character and customs — a sort of neo-Puritanism, one might say. But he also wanted to be a philosopher. He was, as Romain puts it *Empereur malgré lui*. Indeed, at a time when it had become the custom for a Roman in government to be clean shaven, he broke all protocol and grew a beard, thereby declaring himself to be a philosopher! For to be a philosopher in Hellenistic Rome was very nearly the equivalent of joining a monastic order or joining the Buddhist *saṁgha* anddonningthe yellow robe. He wanted to be like Epictetus, but could not, so he chose the most rational middle ground possible and did his duty, trying to live his philosophy without any gap between theory and practice.

Marcus Aurelius' persecution of the Christians, especially the martyrs of Lyons, marked the end of antiquity. After him the triumph of Christianity was assured, and that meant a new era of human history for the Latin West. His attempts at restoration of the old Roman spirit and stamina were a complete failure. He wanted only to hold the Empire together, any more than that being an ambition unnecessary and unworthy of a Stoic philosopher. But doing his duty and doing it valiantly could not prevent the eventual fall. In spite of him, Rome was no longer Rome, Empire, or *res publicae*. It became barbarized from within while he was trying to keep it from shrinking on the periphery. Tradition was very important in both Rome and China. China without Confucius — who could ever have imagined such a thing? But it happened! China became

Buddhized, accepted the religion of the Western barbarians. And so, after Marcus Aurelius, it happened; the barbarians, the 'godless' ones, triumphed. Rome never fell; it was Christianized.

Stoicism, like Confucianism, looked back to the past; but Christianity, like Mahâyâna Buddhism, had a teaching for the present and for the masses, not for the cultured elite. Moreover, at least in theory, they were both humanistic, antisuperstitious, even making fun of the old gods and mythology, and claiming historic persons as their founders, saviors, and teachers. By analogy, one wonders to what philosophy we may look. I dare say, none! Philosophical systems in times of cultural decadence also partake of the same blindness as the decadence they try to remedy. It will probably be some unpretentious world-sweeping, mass-convincing Faith that will give vitality to humanity again and probably not philosophy at all, although that Faith will later develop many philosophies as it becomes, also, decadent.

In leaving Marcus Aurelius we may question whether a philosophy which primarily gives consolation but which issues few challenges is really worthy of being called a philosophy at all. Given the increasing secularization of all cultures today, it is hoped that those involved in the current disputes about what philosophy really is and/or should be will not be unaware of that dimension of experience and reality which may be found in Epictetus, even though it must proceed, evidently, from disciplines other than those presently taught in our world's universities. After all, philosophy is a vocation, as it was with Epictetus and his contemporaries, not a bourgeois business or trade.

Hsün Yüeh (148-209)

Hsün Yüeh for the most part continues in the tradition of Tung Chung-shu, but of course times had changed. There had been the revolution of Wang Mang followed by the restoration of the traditional (reactionary) order, the domination of the eunuchs while "petticoat government" prevailed at court under a series of dowager-empresses, which provoked the abortive rebellion of the Taoist Yellow Turbans in 184, and many other circumstances of a disturbing nature such as are portrayed in the famous *Romance of the Three Kingdoms.* The Later Han Dynasty Period in China is not unlike that of the Pax Romana in the Mediterranean. Philosophy was not popular, nor were philosophers very free to contribute their criticism or seek rectification of what they knew to be wrong. In short, the second century in China was, no less than in the Mediterranean and in India, essentially a time of decadence. The marvel is that there were any thinkers of weight whose philosophizing has survived in written record.

Hsün Yüeh and Hsü Kan (171-218) are important historically because it was on the basis of their work that, after the Buddhist-Taoist interlude during the period of anarchy and disruption of the external order called the Period of the Three Kingdoms, the Neo-Confucian revival took place at the hands of Han Yü and Li Ao and others in the late eighth and early ninth centuries (which we will be considering in a future volume as parallel with other neo-orthodoxies in Eurasia).

According to Busch, Hsün Yüeh in character and type of thought is usually classified along with Wang Ch'ung and Huan T'an as a sceptical rationalist.[9] But this does not mean that he does not remain in the Confucian tradition, especially in regard to his philosophy of human nature and destiny, and in his philosophy of ruling by virtue more than by strict law. As to matters concerning death and the relation between Heaven and earth, he remains considerably more orthodox than Wang Ch'ung, staying close to the classics; although when it came to actual practice, he resorted to astrology and esoteric practices.

Opinions about Hsün Yüeh must be cautiously put forth since resources in European languages are very scanty. His major work, *Shen-chien Chien*, is primarily a political treatise containing sharp criticisms of the Taoists whom he blamed for the degeneracy of the age. His first attempts were in historical writing, and then he turned (with good cause) to ethics. It seems he wrote rather extensively on the theory of the good, seeking critically to incorporate the thinking of those who had preceded him. Thus we should not be surprised to find a large measure of syncretism in his own thought.

Like his Mediterranean contemporaries it no doubt seemed to him that everything had already been accomplished in the past, and it was up to each generation to learn as much of this past as possible. Integration had taken precedence over discovery.

Hsün Yüeh approached his problems in a rational spirit, profiting somewhat from the debunking of superstitions by Wang Ch'ung although not necessarily daring to be an iconoclast or innovator like him. Thus Hsün Yüeh discourses in a rather traditional fashion on the classic themes of *yin-yang*, human nature, Tao, the Will of Heaven and human destiny, nature and natural law, body and spirit, both of which are considered to be natural and not supernatural. Indeed, he did not consider the Tao as transcendental but rather as the immanent world-ordering Principle. One soon gets the impression that his entire outlook was basically humanist and naturalist.

In dealing with the perennial problem of human nature, Hsün Yüeh opted for its neutrality. Also he says that just as "over" and "under" are essentially subjective ways of conceptualizing our perceptions since we are in the "middle" of these polar opposites, so it is with good and evil : they depend on our position in society as well as our situation in nature. There's nothing supernatural or metaphysical about good and evil. To the little beasts the big beasts seem evil, and why should human affairs be otherwise ? Though human nature is essentially neutral, Hsün Yüeh felt that men in action left without any outside motivation would gravitate toward the evil end of the spectrum. Although perhaps a little less harsh than the full-fledged Legalists, he did approve of punishment as a complement to education, law and education being equally emphasized.

In Hsün Yüeh we find still further development of the idea of harmonizing the vital spirits in accordance with *yin* and *yang* of Taoist heritage. For as with most of the later Han Confucianists, he was not exclusively a Confucianist but syncretistically was a mixture of all that had accumulated before him. As with the Aristotelians, it is not enough, according to Hsün Yüeh, just to live; one must live well. And evidently that means something like what we found in the *Gitā* under the heading of *sva-dharma*, that one should conduct himself in accordance with his own nature and not bother too much about others' duties.

Hsün Yüeh, like almost all of his contemporaries, was interested in alchemy, although not to the same extent as his contemporary Wei Po-yang who is generally credited with being the founder of Chinese alchemy as a distinct discipline on a 'scientific' basis. There was a prevalent desire, especially among the Taoists, for immortality through the transformation of one's nature. But Hsün Yüeh denied any possibility of this. He regarded immortality as entirely unnatural and therefore something which would not be good even if it were artificially possible, as it would not be good for a man to be transformed into a woman, or vice versa. Man's life is like the seasons; here he is a true Confucianist. It is in vain and vanity to strive against this natural pattern.

But it was Hsün's political philosophy that was almost always uppermost, as might be expected of any Confucianist of his era. Whether or not it is a valid judgment that both the Confucianists and the Taoists failed to hold the Empire together before the advent of the barbarians and of Buddhism, the fact remains that such men as Hsün Yüeh certainly did do their best to prevent further disruption and, where possible, according to their own lights, to put things in working order again. But the real question is to what extent any man has the power to do this since cycles in political affairs are to be expected just as cycles in all of the rest of nature. To try to alter the Ways of Heaven and earth is perhaps a bit presumptuous on the part of man.

Hsun Yüeh was aligned with the Ku-wen party or the Old Text School, the "radical" party, the New Text School being historically the conservative wing of Han Confucianism. Perhaps his chief merit was in the practical application of the classics to individual personal situations, his delving in speculations about the nature and destiny of man being motivated only by the necessity of making them meaningful.

On the relation between Heaven and man, Hsün held the rather prevalent view that there is a Way of Heaven, a way of earth, and a way of man; and all is well as long as each remains harmoniously in its proper orbit. If one transgresses the laws or Way of Heaven, then one should expect frustration in return. And if one transgresses the norms of earth, then earth likewise will repay in kind. Therefore one should learn to remain in harmony with things as much as possible. Hsün Yüeh comes much closer to his Stoic contemporaries than to the Neo-Platonists (Numenius, for example) or to his Mahāyāna contemporaries like Vasubandhu or Nāgārjuna.

This immanent way of self-rectification on the part of nature excluded both strict determinism and complete unhindered freedom. In this respect there is a radical difference between the almost cynical fatalism of Wang Ch'ung and the views of Hsün Yüeh on human destiny, as there was also between the Sceptics and the Stoics in Rome. It is natural for nature to be both spontaneous and orderly, and man partakes (at least ideally) of this same pattern. Though things may seem chaotic at times, sooner or later one may see how all fits into the total pattern, including the fact that internally nature is full of dynamisms of self-transformations. Accordingly, it should not be disconcerting to us to observe that there are some men who are naturally free and others who right from infancy seem to be plagued with all sorts of troubles. Here we find something which the Mīmāṁsā tradition would explain by referring us to the doctrine of *karma* inherited from previous lives; but the Confucianists never accepted that "foreign" notion of reincarnation whether in Hindu or Buddhist form. Rather, conceding quite a bit to the Taoists, the Han Confucianists explained the same phenomena by the omnipresent operation of *yin* and *yang*.

Just as the orbits of the sun and moon cannot be altered by our prayers, so there is not much we can do about good and bad luck since nature includes contingency and chance as well as order and pattern. The folk saying has a lot of truth in it: "Heaven gives no rest." Man's management of things opens no new possible courses, but Heaven leaves large room for man's management *within* destiny.

Hsün Yüeh emphasizes the distinction of classes as a part of destiny. In the Roman Empire there was little explicitly stated in this regard, but of course the teachings of Plato and Aristotle were still there, neither of them sanctioning complete equality among the classes. Saint Paul's insistence that all are equal in Christ may have made some challenge to the status quo, but even he made all sorts of compromises, advising slaves to be obedient to their masters. We might remember that the only thing that impressed Marcus Aurelius about the Christians was that because of their integrity and high moral standards they made good soldiers. Likewise in India, as far as we know, there was little alteration in the caste system in spite of the insistence of the *Lotus Sūtra* that everyone could equally achieve Buddhahood; and even after seven hundred years or so the Buddhist Reformation had failed to bring very much equalization of castes. In Parthia (Persia) likewise, even the Zoroastrian priesthood reflected rigid hierarchy, not democracy. Thus, although one might be tempted by the hypothesis that differentiation of class structures and the development of class consciousness among the proletariats is a typical sign of decadence of a civilization, still one must remember that nowhere in the world in the second century A.D. was complete social equality put forth even as an ideal. In so far as Wang Mang had tried to level down some of the corrupt elite and give the commoners a chance, he failed; and it might well be that Hsün Yüeh is simply writing against his abortive egalitarian reforms.

Hsün Yüeh's chief historical importance is that his philosophy of life which was completely dominated by his Confucian affirmation of the concept of the Will of Heaven and the physical-spiritual parallelism all the way through will later become the foundation for Chu Hsi's Neo-Confucianist refutation of Buddhism during the Śung Dynasty. Sensitivity to self-criticism within and strength of character without are his constant norms, for inner character is worth far more than brilliant talent or intellect and inner intergrity worth far more than external rulership of a vast empire. The noble man is always aware of his shortcomings and constantly seeks to improve, not his reputation, but his authenticity, his genuineness, and hence he never swerves from truth and friendship with rectitude. These are platitudes, of course, but they were just as much needed then as now, for without these simple, common principles, society will lose cohesiveness and men will cease to be truly and fully human.

Once again, this is very much like Marcus Aurelius and Epictetus. Platitudes may sometimes turn out to be one of the most essential things after all; and no matter how nearly perfect the constitution or the economic system, there must be men of integrity to run it.

Hsün Yüeh urged that the impersonal nature of the state be preserved lest personality clashes and intrigues despoil everything. In true Confucian style he idealized the past, moralizing all the while, fully believing that the welfare of the people depended on the proper use of ceremonies and symbols at court. Neither radical nor conservative, he simply wanted (like Marcus Aurelius) to keep things on an even keel even when the Empire began to reel wildly between military over-expansion and the Neo-Taoist retreat into irresponsible hedonism, magic and superstition.

Ko Hung (253-333)

Studying everything available and without teachers to guide him, Ko Hung acquired the necessary mastery of the classics on his own. Although he is usually regarded as a Neo-Taoist, he necessarily represents himself in good Confucian style, calling himself stupid and ignorant in spite of his heroic efforts to get access to everything written. In his preface to the *Nei P'ieu*, his magnum opus, after some ritualistic Confucian professions of humility, he mentions that he has examined not a few books in order that his opinions will be well based on sound information and not merely on hearsay; nevertheless, it appears that Ko Hung gives us nothing essentially new. Ethics, for example, while not neglected, is more or less a presupposition for him.

We cannot say that Ko Hung is as anti-superstitious as Wang Ch'ung. He uses sophisticated arguments to insist that the existence of supernatural creatures cannot be disproved, and since the majority of mankind do believe in them there must be something really there. He appeals to experience withal, somewhat as William James used to do, arguing that just because one has not had an experience of supernatural beings does not mean that they do not exist. Others claim that they have had such experiences, and that should be taken as substantial evidence. In a similar vein Ko Hung accepts the records of previous alchemists. He studied the subject exhaustively, so much so that he became one of the world's greatest in this field of proto-scientific chemistry.

By no means is alchemy in Ko Hung's hands merely a matter of superstition. Here he is anti-superstitious, an empirical investigator to a very high degree, and often a clever inventor. Alchemy really should be regarded as a proto-science, not as pre-science. It was not just a tinkering with elements to produce gold artificially, but a whole philosophy-in-application in that it is based on the metaphysics of transformation as opposed to the metaphysics of permanency. The controversy between these had already had a long history all over Eurasia by Ko Hung's time, and the controversy continued throughout Eurasia. It might be said that whereas Wang Ch'ung marvelled at the credulity of the masses (and even of some intellectuals) in regard to superstitions, Ko Hung reverses the coin and marvels at the incredulity of those who will not believe in the marvels of science.

Concerning metaphysics and cosmology, Ko Hung simply presents the old *yin-yang* philosophy with some concrete illustrations from nature. He stresses the inexhaustibility of the Tao, which at once remains the Source of all of nature and also the principle of differentiation therein. Tao is vast, ultimate, beyond finite comprehension; but the man who cultivates the Tao in all things becomes almost an incarnation of it. Thus, whereas so often in Taoist art man is depicted as a very tiny creature in a vast, vast universe (or like a louse in a man's pants' leg), Ko Hung puts in a bid for the Confucian dignity of man.

In Ko Hung we find the usual things associated with the concept of the Tao as all-embracing while transcendent in the sense of being beyond comprehension, i.e., "Oriental mysticism" in the classical sense. And herein we are again confronted with the perennial problem of how to know the Unknowable, a problem which will increasingly demand attention for the next several centuries all over Eurasia. It seems that Ko Hung like so many others is more adept at the *via negativa* than he is at indicating the virtue and positive attributes of the spiritual man or sage. Must we infer, then, that spirit is known only (or at least best) by dialectics ? We know that things are not right; we must condemn what is wrong. And since we know no more than did Ko Hung, we also must affirm the opposite of the squalid mess we are in as both the ideal and the goal, whatever methods are to be used to reach it.

It could be said that Ko Hung is not so clear as are some of his Buddhist contemporaries, like Vasubandhu, or even as explicit as Plotinus or Origen, as to the positive steps to be taken and the path to be followed on the way to wisdom; but his denunciations of the wrong ways are certainly no less vivid than theirs. The ascetic strain in his thought closely resembles that of his contemporaries, all of whom are beginning to manifest a different *zeitgeist* than we found in previous centuries. They have had enough of dilettantism and eclecticism; the times are more demanding now. It is time to clean up the debris left from the past and, striving again for purification, if not for transformation of their all-too-human nature, reach afresh into the unknown rather than merely mulling over the vast accumulations of the learning of the past. We should not search for something unique or sensational in Ko Hung. That is just what he does not want; China had had enough of sensational things. Evidently he thought that a return to the essentials would be the simplest and most effective remedy both personally and societally.

Ko Hung reiterates the microcosm-macrocosm point of view with the usual confusion — as it seems to us in the modern world — between cause and effect, e.g., if the Emperor directs everything according to the Tao, then even natural calamaties do not occur and all is in harmony; and when this is not the case, then nature is upset and calamities occur, at first as warnings and then as punishments. Here we see that for Ko Hung, as for many of his contemporaries, science is not necessarily associated with materialism. Though he made many contributions to the development not only of alchemy but to other sciences as well, he still affirmed the existence of the spiritual realm in an almost panentheistic spirit, or at least a panpsychism like that of Plotinus.

In his chapter entitled "Truth On Earth", Ko Hung states (we substitute "Tao" for "God" in Ware's translation): "Tao arises from Unity and is honored without peer. Everything dwelling in Unity thereby becomes the image of heaven, earth, and man; whence our expression 'triune'. Heaven, gets its purity from Unity; earth, its tranquility; man, his existence; and the gods their powers."[10] He then considers the methods of preserving this Unity. He makes a distinction between what Ware translates as "Mystery-Unity" and "Truth-Unity", noting that the preservation of the former is easier. He gives the methods in remarkable detail, and a careful comparison of them with the methods described in the Patañjali *Yoga Sūtras* and the Neo-Pythagoreans should eventually be made. There are also some similarities in the more esoteric Mahāyāna sūtras like the *Vajracchedika*, but the basic trend of classical Theravāda was away from the esoteric. At any rate, the methods include fasting, breath control and intensive concentration on the object, condition or psycho-physical state to be attained. Real yoga is for filling human needs, not for attaining super-human powers, and this basic purpose of the discipline should take precedence over all the rest : "Only through intelligence and great wisdom and through the use of world-regulating and people-saving capacity can one be sure of success when working at this matter. Even with the best will and love, ordinary people of shallow experience cannot carry it through to the end."[11] Let that word to the wise be sufficient, for it is the universal counsel in every culture and has been so all through the history of mankind, and no doubt will remain so even if it is observed more in the breach than in truth and fidelity.

Ko Hung's references to the stolid ignorance of the masses who have little if any understanding of such sublime things raises a real problem: how is it that the philosophy which supposedly is ultimately the most valid must necessarily be elitist ? Why can't the attitudes of the masses be trusted ? Why must the enlightened few inevitably carry with them this *contemptus mundi* and *contemptus populi* ? Certainly Ko Hụng, who studied humility so assiduously, has allowed his class consciousness to show. Nevertheless, is it not true that the notion of looking at things through the lense of class consciousness belongs to the late nineteenth century so that we are really committing an anachronism in asking that question, though it may be a good one in other regards? For who in Eurasia was asking such a question then? And who has not complained about or at least discoursed on the difference between the *Natur Mensch*, the natural man, animal that he is, and the saved or enlightened saint or sage? At least for this period the hierarchy of being presupposes the transformability of human nature.

We might appropriately conclude this discussion of Ko Hung by taking up the theme of corruption and degeneracy in society, a major theme throughout our treatment of Rome and China. In this context Ko Hung is generally less optimistic by comparison with some of his predecessors in previous centuries, like Tung Chung-shu. When asked why so many wise men had forsaken the world and gone into retirement as hermits, he replies that although Tao is everywhere still those who want to cultivate Tao "are obliged to enter mountains and forests because they must get away from the fats and biles of society and enjoy the purity of these places."[12] Then as now there was far too much hustle and bustle, too much noise and confusion, too much moral and physical filth. There is a limit to any man's power to resist the influences of environment; but if he cannot change it he still has the option of leaving it. Purity being the chief object, the highest value, one must find a place where purification is possible. Every age and every climate and every civilization will sooner or later produce its own renunciates; such seems to be a law of history. But admittedly the late third and early fourth centuries, whether cause or cure we are not sure, certainly exceeded its quota.

According to Ko Hung the reason for most of the world's trouble is the struggle for power. The remedy, obviously enough, is to find a good teacher who can help one to awaken or reawaken the latent powers within oneself. Honor and respect for the teacher, the guru, is just as important (if not more so) as respect and honor for parents. Ko Hung warns that one must be wary of pseudo-teachers: "They sometimes give themselves highsounding titles, claim to have been alive for generations, sometimes three or four hundred years, but of course under different names. They impose upon others by claiming to be sages, and many people follow them."[13]

In the Neo-Taoism of Ko Hung and others of his generation,

there was a revulsion against the degenerate debauchery and art of self delusion that had become all too characteristic of the affluent aristocracy. Like Plotinus, Ko Hung attempted to institute a neo-Puritanism; and like Plotinus, his efforts proved to be only patch work on the old order, whereas almost outside his window the new order in the shape of Buddhist monasticism was already beginning to profoundly influence China.

Mani (215-276)

Mani, though neither Chinese nor Roman, is included in this section because he stands almost alone as the arch-syncretist of all time. His attempt at synthesis is the high point of the basic eclectic/syncretistic tendencies of our period. Few in world history have overtly attempted to put so much from so many civilizations and religious and philosophical backgrounds together into a single mould. Ort punctuates the comprehensiveness of Mani's teachings, and although Ort still calls it religion, we submit that it is by virtue of this comprehensiveness that Mani can and should be rated as a philosopher also; for his teachings were not limited to ethics, ritual, meditation, or preaching but encompassed "cosmology, eschatology, anthropology, liturgy, cosmogony, theology (i.e., the doctrine with relation to the divine principles), ethics and the ecclesiological structure of the Manichaean communities."[14] This latter might be read as sociology. This covers the ground just about as completely as had been done by anyone up to that time.

Elsewhere we have made the speculation that the Buddha was a philosopher in the fullest sense of the word but that his philosophy tended to degenerate into a popular religion. Jesus and Muhammad probably should be classified as prophets whose teachings later had to become adjusted to Greek philoso phy and Roman law. But Mani seems to have been both a philosopher and a prophet.

In treating Mani we must reflect that during the first few centuries of the Christian Era there was not the sharp division between religion, science and philosophy that there is today. The Stoics, Epicureans, and even the Sceptics, not to mention the Neo-Pythagoreans and Neo-Platonists, all had a sense of religious vocation about their mission and role in society. In

China Confucianism, which was beginning its defence of the old order against the degeneracy of the late Han and the beginnings of Buddhism, had long since become the state religion in spite of its humanist outlook on the world. Thus even aside from the adjustment of the Christians and Jews to Greek philosophy, it is false to force the separation now made.

Of course Mani was not a "Manichaean" any more than Marx was a "Marxist" or Jesus was a "Christian" or the Buddha was a "Zen" master bopping disciples over the head with bamboo poles. The inevitable modifications (or perversions) of the teachings of any great man in any field cannot but arouse our attention frequently as a real problem for both the philosophy of history and the philosophy of religion. And that it also happens in the history of philosophy itself cannot be ignored. Plato was not a "Platonist" nor was Aquinas a "Thomist".

Before attempting to place Mani in the global perspective it might be well to ask ourselves what had been transpiring in philosophy in Persia/Iran between the time of Zoroaster and Mani, a stretch of history as long as that between, say, Madhva and Radhakrishnan, or Aquinas and Maritain, or Chu Hsi and Chairman Mao, or al Ghazâli and Iqbal. Unfortunately, as far as systematic philosophy in the stricter sense is concerned, the answer is not too encouraging. Following the fragmentation of Alexander's short-lived empire, Persia as such almost went into eclipse, with the Parthians and Bactrians and others dominating the scene until the rise of the Arsacid and Sassanid Dynasties. Though the area remained a cultural and commercial crossroads where one would expect to find quite a bit of philosophizing, actually there seems to be no literary trace of any distinctively Zoroastrian philosophizing in this period.

Nevertheless, the Zoroastrian *religion* did survive in very vital form with a rigid orthodoxy at the core. There were also many sectarian heresies, often equally vital and, as might be expected, usually syncretistic and not infrequently spreading far beyond the boundaries of their origin. Thus even in the case of the Gnostics there is still the controversy as to the degree of their Iranian origin; and the Mandaneans likewise certainly must have been influenced to a great extent by some sort of Zoroastrianism. Then too there was Mithraism, sometimes spoken of as Christianity's greatest rival during this period; and of course Manichaeanism, thanks to Augustine, is still a word that is anathema even today in some orthodox Christian circles. But Zurvanism, as Zaehner puts it even in the title of his book,[15] is a "dilemma", a puzzle historically as well as doctrinally and, as we may well add, philosophically because of its philosophy of Time as virtually the Prime Source-and-End of everything.

Even the specialists admit that the picture is still very confusing, especially as to which were really Zoroastrian heresies and which were simply syncretistic cults with many roots and sources. The cult of Zurvan and perhaps at least in origin the cult of Mani were only typical of the general trend. It is still difficult indeed to discern the real relation between them since the sources of information available now are all extremely biased against them both.

The cult of Zurvan, according to Zaehner and others, was an attempt in the face of the prevailing stricter monotheism to overlay the radical spiritual dualism of original Zoroastrianism with a higher monotheism by the most natural process of henotheistic selection of one of the symbolic deities from the pantheon, namely Time, and to claim that He had primacy over the Twin Spirits of Good and Evil, Light and Darkness. Of course time implies change, flux, process; and knowing historically that the Buddhist *kṣaṇavāda* had been around for a long time, we might speculate that the Zurvanites could have been influenced by Buddhism, though we should also remember that the Śūnyavāda and Vijñānavāda emerging at the time of Mani were increasingly denying, over against Vaiśeṣika and Mīmāṁsā, the ultimate reality of time. Adding external likelihood to internal evidence, we know that Buddhism of some sort or other was already long since included in the list of Persian religions of Mani's time. Thus the probability of both Mani and the Zurvanites having been influenced by Buddhism is very great.

What is generally considered today as Oriental mysticism is really Eurasian philosophical religion of the later Han-Hellenistic-Bactrian Period. And Mani and Zurvanism are very near the core of this, along with Gnosticism and hundreds of other "isms" that stretched from China to Spain and from England to Indonesia. But if they were so similar, why was there so much rivalry, even to the point of violent persecutions, purges, and martyrdoms? The answer to that is perhaps easier than might be expected: if there is too much difference there will be no rivalry but simply choice. There must be some common ground before rivalry can become active, and such seems to have been the case very critically during Mani's time, especially in Persia.

As with Socrates, Jesus, Saint Francis and many other charismatic figures in world history, it is often Mani's life almost more than his teachings which impress us. According to Jackson[16] the following seems to be relatively reliable. Mani was Persian by birth, and the family seems to have moved to Babylon early in Mani's life. During this epoch Babylonia's fame as a center of learning and culture far outshone its reputation as a symbol of corruption as presented in the Apocalypse of the New Testament. Even more than Alexandria it was a completely cosmopolitan multi-national, multi-cultural center. Even in his childhood Mani probably was influenced by people from many realms. He was an aristocrat by birth; however, this does not seem to have influenced his teachings, for neither in practice nor in doctrine does he seem to show any signs of elitism based on caste. Mani was a physician. It should be remembered that this was also the case with Galen, Sextus Empiricus, many Taoist contemporaries, and many others who are ranked as philosophers both before Mani's time and well on through the medieval period. The modern world has fragmented wisdom too much.

Mani's father was already inclined to eclecticism in religion; and we might well infer that being an educated person of aristocratic heritage, he was probably not ignorant of many basic texts and commentaries that now are termed philosophical. By the age of twenty Mani was declared a prophet. King Shāhpuhr (Sapor) I seems to have been favorably disposed toward him, but the Zoroastrian theocratic Church was very rigid and dominated everything and could not tolerate his tolerant views and 'radical' doctrines. Hence Shâhpuhr had to banish Mani. During his exile Mani had dialogues with Buddhists and others in northern India, Tibet, Turkistan and Khurâsân. We may infer that Mani most probably encountered some variety of Mahâyâna as well as perhaps some Jainas. Our present sources indicate that he declared himself as a prophet who is equally the successor of the Buddha, Zoroaster and Jesus whereas no mention is made of Kṛṣṇa, Râma, Śiva or any other Hindu deity or avatar.

Mani returned to Persia about 273 and was executed by Shâhpuhr's successor, Bahrâm I. Needless to say, his martyrdom only increased the zeal of his followers who, along with the Nestorian Christians, could soon be found from the interior of China to the shores of Spain — no less an expanse than that of Islam a little less than four centuries later, but made without violence. Given the spirit of the age wherein there was a strong proclivity towards magic and marvels mixed in with all the syncretistic amalgam of traditions, it is not surprising that the cult which followed Mani virtually deified him.

Jackson acknowledges the extremely eclectic nature of Mani's teachings but also claims that he did achieve "distinctly and designedly a synthesis". He is even more explicit about Mani's attitude toward Zoroaster, the Buddha and Jesus:

> He accounted Zoroaster's dualistic doctrine of the fundamental struggle between light and darkness, soul and matter, to be at basis the solution of the problem of good and evil. He found in the teachings of the gentle Buddha certain lessons for the conduct of life to be accepted everywhere by mankind. He recognized in Jesus a verified ideal and claimed to be the Paraclete promised by Christ and for whom the world was seeking.[17]

Jackson immediately adds that ancient Babylonian as well as Hellenistic Gnostic elements had also been incorporated into Mani's world-view. Acknowledging, as others also do, that the sect which followed after Mani adapted itself to local conditions, Jackson nevertheless puts primary stress on Mani's Zoroastrianism with the radical dualism, not just a dualism of spirit and matter as was the tendency among Neo-Pythagoreans and Neo-Platonists and Sāṃkhya, but a dualism between two opposing *spiritual* forces of Light and Darkness, Good and Evil.

The interaction of these two opposing Principles is also the generating source of Mani's elaborate hierarchy, not only of spiritual beings but of cosmic principles or natural laws as we would call them in a less imaginative frame of reference. The Good Ruler of the Realm of Light has, for example, four (not three as in the Christian, Mahâyâna and Hindu worlds) aspects as Deity, Light, Power and Wisdom, five Realms or Aeons, and twelve personified abstractions, Majesties or Sovereignties. And of course there are countless minor divinities and celestial angels, all as a manifestation of Light; but all of these are also paralleled with beings of the Realm of Darkness. We may note here that light had become a universal symbol of intellect and spirituality. In the coming centuries we may be able to observe how much is built upon such a symbol, and not unjustifiably. However, for our present purpose it is enough to note that in Mani's own time in all of the Taoist, Buddhist, Neo-Pythagorean, Neo-Platonic and Christian worlds light was already a primary subject for meditation and played a basic role in ritual and liturgy.

Mani's conception of the Celestial Hierarchy is at least as elaborate as that of Dionysius the pseudo-Areopagite or the Amida cult of Chinese Mahāyāna which, as a matter of fact, may have been influenced by his followers. Whether Mani himself believed in it literally, or whether it was rather a symbolic system for the less educated of his followers, it is difficult to say. But we do know that at Baghdad, Edessa and Babylon the art of allegorizing had reached an even higher level of sophistication than at Alexandria. Still, the point at issue here is not whether literalism or symbolism prevailed with Mani himself but that elaboration of hierarchies was already becoming a universal phenomenon in Eurasia during his time. Mani's Celestial Hierarchy is intimately related to his epistemology since it is against these cosmic forces that man must struggle before he can attain knowledge, much less wisdom.

It appears that Mani basically follows an emanational

scheme, possibly being influenced by Neo-Platonism or Neo-Pythagoreanism. He nevertheless does retain something of a creation doctrine, mostly inherited, of course, from the Biblical tradition. But there is also the possibility of influence by the views of creation that were beginning to infiltrate into Vaiṣṇavism and Śaivism in India or those found even in the Taoist writings of this time. Even in Mou Tzu, the Chinese apologist for Mahâyāna Buddhism, one finds speculations about a First Cause and meditations as to how existence came out of the Void.

By both friends and foes of Mani and the Manichaeans considerable emphasis has been put on the fact that the evil principle of Darkness or realm of Darkness is virtually identified with matter or material existences. Looked at from a distance in a different age, this is usually regarded as an extreme view and especially as one not in consonance with the Christian doctrine of the Incarnation. Both Plotinus and Mani associate evil with matter, but with different results. For Plotinus it is the essential negativity of matter which emphasizes its unreality, while for Mani Darkness (matter) is not so much the *absence* of Light as the *opposite* of Light. Mani not only believed in the reality of Evil and of Darkness, but believed also that the powers inhabiting these realms had the power to invade the Realm of Light and to do harm there. The radical difference between Light and Darkness can easily be oversimplified, for each of these extends infinitely into the other.

The struggle between these forces evidently was conceived to be the cause of the generation of time. Like the great majority of those dealing with philosophy of history, Mani periodizes in a Grand Triad. First is the period before the Great Conflict began. The description of the period of the Great Conflict in which we ourselves continue to struggle (except in Southern California) very much resembles that of the Kali Yuga in Hindu mythology. In the period of the Final Triumph, as in the Kalki Yuga in Hinduism, and after the Coming of the Messiah, as in many (if not most) varieties of Judaism, and after the Second Coming of Christ, as in some interpretations of Christianity, and after the coming of the Mahdi, as in Islam, all will be rectified and the Light and the Good will triumph in timeless Time or Eternity.

Eschatologically, Mani taught that there would be a General Conflagration, a matter which may seem rather fanciful to the twentieth century reader. But once again, we must not read history backwards. After all, the Stoics, Christians, Gnostics and Neo-Pythagoreans had a similar eschatology, and popular Mahāyāna Buddhism by Mani's time had already taken on a lot of neo-mythological dimensions, especially in the way of furthering hope in future redemption for all rather than mere enlightenment for the few.

Once the Two Principles come into conflict, the Primal Mother and the Primal Man appear also as emanations, not as creations strictly speaking for they are respectively embodiments of their principles. Perhaps here we find something of Neo-Taoism. Woman is considered to be the Darkness principle (shades of Taoism) and man the Light principle. The fact that Chinese records are one major source of information about Mani raises the question as to how much he knew about such basic Chinese concepts as *yin* and *yang*, *ming* and *hsing*, Tao and the Will of Heaven. We should remind ourselves that much the same view of the primordiality of the Two Parents was equally prevalent in Hindu, Greek and Roman mythologies. This is just one more expression by Mani of the universal and evident principle of polarization.

In spite of his desire for comprehensiveness, Mani was no more successful than Augustine in finding a place for sex in his grand scheme. He tended to view it as a necessary evil for the begetting of children. And did not Origen, not content with mere ascetic discipline, castrate himself? Of course some of the Seven Sages of the Bamboo Grove in China went to the other extreme, with wine and all that goes with it, as did some of the Gnostics and some enthusiasts of the Orphic mysteries in the Mediterranean, not to mention some Tantric cults in India and Tibet. To say the least, the times beget extremes in almost all of Eurasia.

Though much in Mani may sound rather fanciful to the modern reader, especially the notion that the stars were formed out of the remnants of light left after the slaying of the demonic forces and were set in motion as an effort at rescuing these remnants, still such a judgment is historically naive, for during Mani's century there was no theory any more 'scientific' than his. Actually his view manifests the rather universal trend in almost all mythologies that incorporate a basic perspective of cosmic evolution from primordial principles down through all the astronomical realm, until we finally get to man, the confused animal *par excellence*, the microcosm in the middle. The temptation is all too strong as far as cosmology is concerned to judge this whole period anachronously, glorifying the Greek achievements in the previous period but sliding over most of the developments not only in India and China, not to mention Persia, but the other parts of the Mediterranean as well. Cosmological speculations were still not divorced from mythology and would not be until the seventeenth century.

Mani's views of Jesus were basically if not exclusively docetic, resembling very much the extreme Mahâyâna views of the Eternal Buddha who only appeared in mortal form to "turn the Wheel of the *Dharma*," or, to use the Christian metaphor, to inaugurate a New Dispensation, or, to use a reference to the *Gītā*, to renovate *Dharma*. Mani, like some sufis in later centuries in the same geographical region (Al Ḥallaj, for example), thought of himself as sharing the divinity of Jesus.

Jackson notes that Mani's doctrine of metempsychosis was very important in the tradition. Again, Confucianists would be puzzled by this, and many Neo-Taoists would marvel that longevity of any sort would be delayed until after death since they were after immortality in this life, not immortality in some other world. We might here recall that Origen believed in metempsychosis, following Plato and Pythagoras therein, who in turn could have been and probably were influenced by views from Hinduism, Buddhism and/or Jainism. In European civilization and even in the Christian synthesis of Hellenic and Hebraic traditions the doctrine of the immortality of the soul comes more through Plato's Socrates than from the Bible as such, and therefore in many circles it is still regarded as a philosophical rather than a merely religious problem.

Though Mani was a pacifist, it is another of those strange paradoxes of history that, like the early Christians and later Franciscans, and many centuries later the Sikhs, and to some extent the followers of Mo Tzu, the disciples of Mani were to be found in armies of Rome and elsewhere. Pacifism has been it seems too often the ideal without becoming the actual.

Mani's influence spread eastward to China as well as westward to France and Spain in a way that has scarcely ever been rivalled in world history except perhaps by the spread of Islam a few centuries later, or perhaps by the work of the Jesuits in the sixteenth and seventeenth centuries. Augustine never completely overcame his first conversion to Manichaeanism, and thus it may be claimed that the indirect influence of Mani even in the Latin West was perhaps as great as that of any one man from the time of Jesus to the time of the Jesuits. His influence in Central Asia and, indeed, throughout Eurasia is only recently coming to light. Along with the Nestorians, Manichaeanism had quite a sizable following in China also. In fact it has been suggested that Amida even as Buddhist *Bodhisattva* might originally have been Mani, though there is no proof as yet for or against such a speculation. At any rate, no doubt his indirect influence in Central and East Asia was greater than is generally acknowledged, even as his being influenced not only by Christianity but also by Hinduism, Buddhism, Zoroastrianism, and possibly Jainism puts him at the center ideologically as well as geographically not only for the third century but for several centuries to come.

It is indeed highly ironical that such an influence should lapse into such relative oblivion. Perhaps Mani's Way was so all-inclusive that each could find his own in it, and indeed that seems to have happened to such an extent that the old ethnocentricities that Mani had hoped to overcome actually reemerged in his name. Mere unification of traditions may not be enough ; there must be some fresh challenge for all, some supra-national cause to embrace, or there will be no cohesiveness to the new movement. There must also be new creativity, new inspiration, a new revelation, a new *Dharma*, a new *li*. Meanwhile, one wonders : will the nineteenth and twentieth century attempts at similar synthesis — Soka Gakki, Cao Dai, the Ramakrishna Mission, or Baha'i, to name only a few of the best known candidates which have come on the scene since the Theosophical Movement made its attempts at syncretizing all the faiths — succeed any more than Mani himself did ?

TWO

SCEPTICISM (100-200)

A. Philo and Nāgārjuna

Ever since the Maccabees there had been considerable differences between the Alexandrian community and Jewry in Jerusalem, the Alexandrian community having lost the Hebrew language and having become very syncretistic, assimilating themes not only from the Egyptian and Greek heritages but also from the international community of commerce and trade. The philosophy of Philo (20 B.C.-50 A.D.) is quite a different thing from the antiphilosophical tradition of the Maccabees a couple of centuries before and in a different locale. Whether he knew the Hebrew language or had to depend on the *Septuagint* is uncertain, but his Greek is polished, precise, clear, natural and unforced. And he is just as much at home in the history of Greek philosophy as he is in *Old Testament* lore.

Allegorical interpretation of the *Old Testament* no doubt had been going on for a long time before Philo. But Philo is historically very significant since much of his allegorizing was adopted, assimilated or adapted by the Christian Fathers and further elaborated upon during the medieval period. There are many who object to the allegorical method of interpretation of any scripture, and their arguments against it are to be respected, especially if they offer verified historical facts. Still, allegory is not the *alternative* to historical fact but is rather an aesthetic embellishment of historical fact, making it meaningful to all-and-sundry. It is an art, not a science. The criterion should be how well or how meaningfully for the present generation the allegorizing has been done. Allegory is like a growing vine: if one trims it too much, it dies; but without pruning, it will be prone to bear many leaves and little fruit. Dogmas and fixed doctrines can never be derived from it. Dogmas are like the roots of the vine : without the leaves above, the roots below will perish; but without the roots below, the leaves will wither away.

Concerning Philo's Neo-Platonism, the *Logos* doctrine is perhaps the most obvious aspect of his inheritance from Greek philosophy. His frequent references to *Sophia* (wisdom) instead of *philo-sophia* might make one suspect some Gnostic influence or sympathies were it not true that here he is leaning heavily on the *Old Testament Apocrypha,* the Wisdom Literature. But one wonders also whether in the background there might be some knowledge of the Mahāyāna *prajñā* (wisdom) lore. Though this must remain a matter of speculation, the fact that the *Prajñāpāramitā* ("perfection of wisdom") literature was already blossoming, and the fact that communications were open, establish the possibility that the parallel is significant. Philo's Platonism or Neo-Platonism is quite obvious when he distinguishes quite sharply between the lower realm of opinion and the transcendental level of Wisdom or of Truth (with a capital T), between the *vyavahārika* and the *pāramārthika* levels. Again, the *prajñā* of the *Prajñāpāramitā* literature is virtually identical with Philo's *Sophia.* Yet Philo was perhaps as much a Neo-Pythagorean as a Neo-Platonist. This entailed a rather rigorous sort of 'yoga' discipline, vegetarianism, esoteric numerology and investigation into musical theory and more or less scientific mathematics. Neo-Platonist or not, Philo is syncretistic, almost more so than anyone else in Europe before or after him.

In Philo the *via negativa* begins to take form. Epistemologically this negative dialectic or reductionist logic is used to trim away all non-essentials until supposedly only essence is left, stripped of attributes. According to Philo we can, and must of necessity, admit that God exists, but we cannot and dare not try to say what He is. We can, however, say what God is not. This is another of those basic trends in philosophy that uncannily crops up everywhere about the same time in virtually all of Eurasia. One is sometimes tempted — unless he is more factually aware of the conditions of transportation and communications — to posit some sort of Hegelian *Weltgeist* moving through history. That is hardly necessary if taken in the completely idealistic or mystical sense, however, since material means of dissemination of ideas is almost a priori necessary, howsoever spiritual the content.

Admittedly, it may not be ultimately important who was the

first to affirm new ideas, since that gives no test of their validity or value, Nevertheless, it does appear highly probable that this idea of *via negativa* is an example of permeation into Alexandria of *Upaniṣadic* thought or perhaps of Buddhist thought of the type represented by Nāgārjuna. It will be remembered that the *neti neti* (not this, not that) motif in the *Upaniṣads* is very strong, and that these most likely are pre-Buddhistic, or at least pre-Aśokan. Nāgārjuna's *Kārikās*, all negative in form whether positive in content or not, are a fresh echo of the same theme. Therefore, although we suggest this only very tentatively, the inference might be made that, directly or indirectly, and to some extent, Philo may have been indebted to Mahāyāna and *Upaniṣadic* lore. As to his being familiar with the concept of Tao, it is possible but not as probable, since communication with China was not yet as open as it was with India.

Another note which might too easily be overlooked is Philo's concern for social justice. He accepted the responsibility of representing the Jewish minority of Alexandria at the Roman court during a time when anti-Semitism was rather widespread. The fact that Philo was in a definite, even in a classical, sense a philosophical mystic by no means excludes him from concern for economic and social equality and political freedom from oppression, a concern naturally inherited from the rather revolutionary code in *Deuteronomy* and from the later Prophets.

It is perhaps surprising that Philo historically had more influence in the Christian than in the later Jewish world; and that, with very few alterations or modifications, Clement of Alexandria and Origen adopted his allegorizations of the *Old Testament* without the least censure.

On first examination no two philosophers could be further apart than Philo and Nāgārjuna (c. 100 A.D.). The former is first and foremost — and will be grossly misunderstood if taken otherwise — a Jew : that is, foremost in zeal for God's righteous protection of his Chosen People and jealous vengeance against the unrighteous, who, of course, are mostly among the Gentiles. But Philo, in addition, lived in Alexandria during the Hellenistic Period, during which one could very easily find every unthinkable vice as well as every virtue and every sort of theory about anything that had to do with the soul of man. So at first reading one is impressed not so much by the Neo-Platonism of Philo as by the almost holier-than-thou moral rigorism stemming from his in-group attitude and from the ritualistic armor with which the Jewish community in Alexandria had to surround itself in order to prevent pollution. The preservation of Jewish heritage through extremely close family ties, for example, exceeds anything any Confucianist ever imagined. Even the little tract *On the Unchangeableness of God* turns out to be more concerned with God's dealings with and through Moses and Noah, and more concerned with what, primarily for the sake of the Israelites, God *did* than with what He *is*.

In short, although Philo does take in Plato and Aristotle — the Ideas and the Four Causes, for example — to illuminate his elaborations on the *Septuagint*, he never departs from the strictly Jewish tradition as his *locus operandi*. God remains primarily the uncreated Creator, almost anthropomorphic, who has the freedom and right to do with his creation just what he will. The distinctly Greek elements in his philosophy — if indeed they may clearly be said to be that, for he does not seem primarily concerned with a conscious synthesis but with an allegorical interpretation of the Law and the Prophets that will square up with the current theories of his day — are taken in more by way of the construction of an apologetic to those who did not know Jewish tradition so clearly. Indeed, here he is really closer to Josephus and the Maccabees than to the later Neo-Platonists, Christian and neo-classic, who were not so much trying to preserve an old tradition as to establish a valid *via contemplationis* that would survive and rise above, serenely and securely, the crumbling of the external political framework of the Roman Empire. It is in this frame of reference that Philo remains supremely a theist throughout, and a very devout one at that, who is interested in dialectics only secondarily.

Nāgārjuna, on the other hand, belonged to the relatively new community of Buddhists in South India. He never resorts to allegorizing, uses a minimum of metaphors, and is one of the most ruthless dialecticians in the whole world's history of philosophy. He is not impious or rebellious by any means, for he is no reformer or counter-reformer. He can hardly be classed as a theist, although he incorporates most of the Mahāyāna Buddhology for the practical benefit of those who still need a god to worship. Nāgārjuna goes a step further in the anti-dogmatic Buddhist discipline of non-clinging to the insistence that for philosophizing the view-of-no-views is the only possible adequate orientation. Here he almost anticipates al-Ghazali in his method of the sceptical 'escape' : all viewpoints must be given up as empty and meaningless from the ultimate and all-encompassing perspective of the standpoint-of-no-standpoint. Nāgārjuna seems to be doggedly out to negate every possible metaphysical position, thus leaving one no point to stand on. His *Kārikās* boldly plow through the opponents' views on relations, entities, attributes, etc., and leave one wondering just what *prajñā* might be. Through all of this Śūnyavāda is also Mādhyamika, the Way of Emptiness is also the Middle Way.

For Philo there is no essential connection of wisdom with dialectics ; indeed he seems, through his excess of piety, almost unaware of the near-contradictions into which he allows himself sometimes to be led. But these difficulties are slight for him. Philo only presents an apologetic for what to him is an unquestioning faith in the Wisdom, Justice, and Providence of God. He finds it difficult to understand why others should have any difficulty, and he cannot see why the philosophers indulge in such blind sophistries or logomachies over what they cannot understand anyway because of the dissoluteness of their lives. Argumentation may even take one further away from the living truth, which resides, not in human cleverness, but in the Wisdom and the *Logos* of the Most High. Arguments *qua* arguments are not so important as attitudes; and if the attitude of profound humility and reverence is lost, then nothing of real understanding can be gained. Therefore man should not be overtly troubled about puzzles and paradoxes but conduct his life as peacefully and rationally and as passionlessly as possible.

In a sense Nāgārjuna is neo-orthodox no less than Philo : the Buddhist tradition had to start philosophizing, in spite of its original anti-metaphysical bias, in order to defend itself against the persistence of Hindu orthodoxy. And if Philo is zealous against the corruption of the Jewish faith by the ontologisms of the Greeks, so is Nāgārjuna zealous against the permanencies, the ontologisms, of the Hindu philosophers, as well as against the re-entrance of the Hindu pantheon into cultic practice and the re-substitution of ritual for adequate meditation and study on the part of the *bikkhus*.

In a double sense Nāgārjuna's *śūnya* turns out to be not so dissimilar from Philo's God after all. Until Philo, theologizing had been inadequately done because the concept of God was still too closely associated with the previous cultic gods and tribal deities, while the generalized philosophical concept of God had been left too vague on the one hand and too rational (demanding no authoritative *faith*) on the other. The concept of Yahwe is seen by Philo to fill in this gap in the Greek tradition without being in the least compromised but rather exalted out of the range of human attribution. Essentially inconceivable, Philo's God, in spite of the ritualistic overlay and recounting of the marvellous things that He has done, is a sort of *śūnya*, inapproachable, beyond the range of merely human speculation or argumentation, not just transcendent but unquestionable, beyond the reach even of *ananke*, Necessity. Because of this, his problem is essentially the same as that of Nāgārjuna : having gained some understanding of the Relationless, how can he relate the relative and pseudo-substantial hierarchical structure of the world to It ?

The impersonal deity of the Stoics, as well as the atheism of the Epicureans and the agnosticism of the Sceptics or the 'Academicians', high-light the background, the philosophical milieu, in which Philo was working. This should be emphasized since the outcome is certainly much more than the hodge-podge eclecticism which we find so often in this period. Indeed, Philo is important. precisely because he could take in so much and do it harmoniously. An emphasis on Philo's background also spotlights his relative uniqueness as a bridge between two entirely different civilizations, the Hebraic and the Hellenistic. Of course, at this time the Indic and Hellenistic civilizations were really much more alike than the Hellenistic and Hebraic. For the first time in the history of Western Civilization, Philo makes the linkage of the Greek concept of Being and the Hebraic concept of

God. True, one can find a sense in which God and Being had been identified in Parmenides, Plato, Aristotle, and even some other 'gentiles', but that had been incomplete and left rather vague.

Philo's doctrine of Providence is almost absolute. Only God and God only, according to His own unquestionable Will, is the dispenser and withholder of all good and evil — in some ways Philo almost anticipates orthodox Islam in this point. And though it be strict, it is out of condescension to our weakness that He has given the Law. No doubt the Stoic doctrine of Providence is in the background of Philo's particular doctrine of Providence.

Theism in the technical sense, though vaguely adopted by the Stoics, becomes a major focus for the Mediterranean and Mesopotamian regions with Philo, and for the first time in the global history of philosophy the absolute *Thou* becomes the basic orientation philosophically. Still more important, in Philo theology emerges out of philosophy in a serious way and really begins to take its place.

Although a personal God remains no more than optional for the Mādhyamika, Philo, as a theist, saw a personal God as the necessary capping stone of the pyramid of rational relativism built up by the post-Aristotelians before him. With the possible exception of Cleanthes' *Hymn to Zeus*, the prayerful approach to God had been neglected except as empty traditional observances in the temples. Aristotle's Unmoved Mover and even Plato's Demiurge were not, from the standpoint of later Christian thought, and really from the standpoint of Philo, complete.

The equation of the yawning abyss between God and the world almost with hell itself is part of Philo's Jewish heritage. From the human point of view there can be absolutely no relation between God and the world. God is too high, too exalted, even to be named except indirectly by the high priest in the most solemn ceremony. Parenthetically, this was one reason why Jesus got in trouble : God *here* ! Blasphemy ! And that beyond all others was the unpardonable sin. Since Philo tends to retain the radical transcendence of Yahwe, his personalism remains problematic. However, in addition to this strain from the

Old Testament heritage, there was already evolving the concept of the "God of Mercy". Indeed, there was emerging within the Jewish heritage, from whatever sources, a concept of immanence that was already bridging the 'gap'. This was quite different from the pantheistic tendencies of the Stoics, for whom there was no 'gap' between the divine and the earthly, the entire universe being an orderly and rational harmony.

As to whether the ethical systems of Philo and Nāgārjuna are at all comparable, the answer, in general, is largely negative. Philo is still emphasizing the negative prohibitions of the Mosaic Code rather than establishing a rigorous pattern of *ascesis*; Nāgārjuna is throughout a monk, philosophizing on the basis of what may be available to the enlightened ascetic.

The three levels in Philo's *Logos* suggest an equation with Nāgārjuna's treatment of the *Trikāya* doctrine. Nāgārjuna does not depart from, but rather may be the original propounder or at least clarifier of, this cardinal Mahāyāna doctrine. On the one hand, while he poetically praises it, Nāgārjuna 'allows' the *Trikāya* only as a sort of functional and deliberate "as if", knowing full well aside from the absolutely transcendental (*pāramārthika*) perspective, from which everything is seen as subject to negation, process, elimination and dissolution, everything has only quasi-reality and may be treated in complete detachment, as though it were as not-true as it is true or as not-real as it is real. Thus he avoids the problem that bothers post-Aristotelian Platonists : he does not posit existent and manipulatable ideal structures; neither does he insist that all mental constructions must be demonstrable; nor does he add predicates to Being. He theologizes largely for the purpose of inciting devotion from the less-initiated. His position is suggestive of that of Santayana, which was once summarized by one of his students as "There is no god and He was born of Mary".

Philo's development of the concept of "embodiments" of the One is a half-compromise with the previous absolutistic orientation. Such a development seems a universal trend, a concession rightly or wrongly — for it indicates a greater psychic expansion, even though it may compromise the purity of the conception of the Ultimate by bringing It into relatedness — to the less visionary fiber of the Bactrian *Weltgeist* which, devoid of any original seminal insights, did rather well at bringing the classic trends-to-transcendence within comprehensibility.

One can almost distinguish a Trinity in Philo composed of God in his holy exaltedness, God as mediated by the *Logos*, and God as operative through this mediation in the field of *Nous* (intelligence) wherein the seminal ideas, the archtypes of creation, are immanently governing the patterning of things and leading man back to Wisdom. This does appear to roughly resemble Nāgārjuna's unity of the *Dharmakāya*, the *Sambhogakāya*, and the *Nirmāṇakāya*, although one must be cautious in drawing the analogy too closely. For in Philo this Trinity is geared very closely to the doctrine of God as Creator (which is not true of Nāgārjuna), whereas it can be said that Nāgārjuna (but not Philo) sees nature as one great epiphenomenon without any real foundation and as a snare to the unenlightened.

What Nāgārjuna says of the soul is even more true of creation. It is no creation of any Creator; rather it is an endless process, a weaving without warp or woof, and under the possibility of going "poof!" at any time. At best it is only a sort of congealing of a cosmic Idea which could be dissolved or is being more or less gradually dissolved anyway. As 'appearance' — and it is not legitimate to ask the answerless question, "Appearance of what ?" — the world and ourselves in it go on; but there is absolutely nothing to be found in the way of a definable Ultimate or Absolute either within or around or above it. 'Nothingness' is *nirvāṇa*, the realization of which may take years of rigorous psychic (not merely mental) discipline, although the final stage is the casting away of even this discipline lest it be a matter of clinging again. It is by the Buddha's Great Compassion, and through the mediative role of the Bodhisattvas, who take the Great Vow not to enter final *nirvāṇa* until all are redeemed, that eventually all are enlightened about 'Nothingness' (*śūnya*).

Philo is desperately determined not to compromise the ontological validity of his God, nor to reduce His transcendental nature to any approachability; at the same time, he must give an account of the actuality of the realm of Reason in its own right. These must be somehow related without admitting any doctrine of illusoriness or of absolutistic transitoriness. The *Logos* is, therefore, pluralized in its function almost without his being aware of it. Nature is the direct manifestation of God's creatorship, but the order found in Nature is intrinsic, and it is not necessary to assume that God is behind the scenes making it go. If the order of nature were totally or even partially dependent on God, then obviously it would not be intrinsic. The principle of order would really reside in His nature, with matter and all the rest being otherwise in a state of chaos or formlessness. Thus we would have a contrast with the Stoics, for whom Reason or Law permeated all things, itself being divine. In making his apologetic, Philo did not wish to alienate the Stoics, but neither did he want to surrender the exaltedness of God, who is supremely One and indivisible above and beyond corruption in matter. Therefore, interpretations of Philo vary according to the emphasis placed on the immanential tendency of his Neo-Platonism as opposed to the extreme monotheism and transcendental tendencies from Jewish heritage. The success with which Philo reconciles these opposing tendencies is open to question.

There is a problem of mediation in Philo's system, a problem which evidently does not arise for Nāgārjuna, though *prajñā* is sometimes interpreted as bridging the gap between *śūnya* and the practical necessities of everyday struggles in and with *māyā*. Having established the utter and complete transcendence of God to such an extent that his Yahwe is virtually the equivalent of Nāgārjuna's *śūnya* — both Philo and Nāgārjuna consider the world as "vanity, vanity, all is vanity" or literally as nothing — Philo still has to reconcile this with the concept of immanence from both the Stoic and the *Old Testament* sources. And Philo does it with allegory rather than with dialectics.

Nāgārjuna conceives of the highest attainment and the deepest possible enlargement of consciousness (*prajñāpāramitā*, perfect wisdom) as primarily a result of dialectical effort and the use of proper method in contemplation. Perfect wisdom is all-embracing, bridging the gap between subjective and objective, recipient and giver, and any further possible dialectical or hierarchical distinctions. Whereas Nāgārjuna, who is not a theist and therefore must depend on human wit to manage his metaphysical anti-metaphysics, thinks of *prajāñā* as merely the fruit of detachment such that the burden of figuring things out still rests on man, for Philo there is not the necessity of figuring things out, but the understanding (wisdom, *sōphrosyné*) follows easily after confidence in Providence is restored. For Philo, holiness is integral to wisdom. The holy in Nāgārjuna is taken as a sort of prerequisite for the other deeper expansions of consciousness; but for Philo it is the Supreme Itself, even in reference to God.

In both Philo and Nāgārjuna Wisdom is exalted as an almost self-existent power mediating the realm of the Divine and human achievement. This link with the *Logos* in Philo is not so much unlike the link between *prajñā* and the *Trikāya* in Nāgārjuna. *Prajñā* is not only that by which the three-in-one relationality of the *Trikāya* is discerned, but in a profound sense also that by which one achieves a certain identity with it. *Prajñā*, in short, is not just a faculty exercised by separate individuals, but a manifestation of Buddhahood, which is synonymous with a supreme enlightenment experience. Two of the more interesting characteristics of this enlightenment experience are "to know in detail the thoughts of all beings" and "to restrain (vicariously) the passions of all beings". This near-approach to omniscience is, of course, almost completely foreign to Philo. He projects it rather into his *Logos*. But this much is common; the hiatus between the transcendental Yahwe and the all-too-rarified *śūnya* on the one hand, and the world on the other, needs mediation of some sort !

That mediation is attempted is a new feature in the history of human thought distinctive of this Han-Hellenistic-Bactrian Period. It emerges out of the sceptical, eclectic and syncretistic trends that characterize this period. However, whereas for Nāgārjuna mediation is merely the providing of a way through what is clearly seen to be a phenomenal façade of existence, in Philo the mediation is ontologically grounded and is quite 'real' to him. However, Philo puts these incorporeal mediating powers — of which the *Logos* is one and the chief, and yet is almost inseparable from the Being of God Himself — into a context of relatedness which is rather difficult to follow. Although their distinctness he seems to discern very clearly, their immateriality we are too much accustomed to push into a field of vagueness. What we have lost since this age when these purely spiritual realms were distinguished as clearly as most of us distinguish between elements in the periodic table is evidently immeasurable. It is only as these radical insights are recovered that we shall gain any adequate concept of holiness.

Nāgārjuna's *Kārikās* represent perhaps the most stringent statement of a systematic position that speaks from beyond system that the world has so far witnessed. Nāgārjuna's greatness cannot be denied; he stands alone at the pinnacle of Hindu-Buddhist dialectics. Philo, on the other hand, is not so uniquely great in his own right but is immeasurably important as the transmitter of the synthesis-in-suspension (a sort of colloidal amalgam) between the Hebraic, the Egyptian, and the Graeco-Roman elements that are still the foundations of European culture. With Philo, faith becomes technically important to philosophy in the European tradition.

B. Sextus Empiricus

Pyrrho and Anaxarchus returned from "mystical" India, whither they had gone with Alexander's expedition, not infused with Oriental mysticism but rather as sceptics. The probabilities are that in his travels Pyrrho encountered Theravāda Buddhists and perhaps even Jaina relativists, and no doubt some Cārvākas.

It is often forgotten that the Sceptics held sway mostly in Plato's Academy, and that thence we get the popular expression "merely academic" as indicating juggling of arguments for arguments' sake and having no relevance to the world of practical affairs. This gives us a clue as to what aspect of Plato's teaching survived among his first and second generation interpreters. These teachings were something quite different from the mysticism of the Neo-Platonic Plato, which was the only Plato known in Europe from the time of Ficino until critical scholarship of the nineteenth century recovered the Plato of such astute dialectical skill who challenges us to think for ourselves and to derive our own right opinions (*ortha doxa*) after reasoning things out as best we can in spite of the lack of any promise of certainty.

Léon Robin in his book *Pyrrhon et le Scepticisme Grec* calls the thought of Aenesidemus (80-130) and his successors, such as Agrippa, Neo-Scepticism. What distinguishes the original variety from the "neo" variety ? This question intrigues us because one aspect of the typical pattern we have been tracing all through the Han-Hellenistic-Bactrian Period is the trend toward neo-isms, right along with or perhaps as alternatives to the challenge presented by the eclecticisms and syncretisms that seem to be so typical of the era. Thus, not only Neo-Platonism and Neo-Aristotelianism, but also Neo-Taoism, Neo-Scepticism and perhaps even already a sort of Neo-Mīmāṁsā, constituting the difference between Jaimini and Śabara. Of course, these have been so named only in recent years when essentially the same phenomena are transpiring in another cycle of civilization.

It might be argued that neo-this or neo-that is already synthesis, having had the original inspiration as thesis, with alienation or challenge from other traditions and/or cultures constituting the antithesis, to which concessions are made in nonessential matters while the core philosophy is retained. As we shall see in the future centuries, this is actually what often happens historically. Nevertheless, such neo-istic "syntheses" do not seem to remain very stable for very long. They too readily lapse back into the orthodox tradition with only the slightest influence on that tradition. The tradition is shocked into action by another encounter, another "neo", or else simply disappears in due course from sheer lack of energy and vitalily. This last seems to be what happened to Hellenistic Scepticism. Or perhaps it simply argued itself out business, digging its own grave, so to speak, leaving only the fossilized bones as evidence of what was once a thriving and noble enterprise, which bones, even, were neglected until the French Enlightenment.

The followers of the New Academy were accused by the Sceptics of actually *affirming* some things instead of retaining their complete neutrality, whereas the Academics made the counter-accusation that in trying to retain neutrality the Sceptics had fallen into the opposite extreme of sheer negativism. Neither one, it seems, was rescued by Saint Augustine, although they both had a common enemy during their common journey, namely, dogmatism. In actual practice the Sceptics were not devastating critics going around carping at everything and everybody as being stupid; rather they were very gentle and genteel, tolerant of all and sundry, neither condemning nor condoning anyone.

The term "scepticism" has a different meaning and function than the popular notion of being sceptical about this or that as a general attitude of denigration or disapproving doubtfulness. Classical Scepticism was rather only a hope that by further refinement and wider application of 'scientific' method, we might, in the face of the extreme difficulty at arriving at Certainty. attain to a higher probability or approximation of the truth of actual situations. In this sense there was little concern with lack of religious faith and agnosticism now associated with popular notions of scepticism; in fact, the question of religious agnosticism was really no issue, or no major issue, even though that might be a possible consequence.

By the time of Sextus Empiricus (c. 200-250) the Roman Empire had already begun to shrink back from its eastern frontier. Even though the Parthians were making the shipment of goods and the travel of man an expensive thing, trade between China, Rome and India had virtually become commonplace. Silk and spices, and occasionally a monk or a philosopher, as well as diseases and ideas, all travelled the silk routes.

In Sextus we find relativism of ethical and moral codes: it is a matter of consensus, of custom, rather than a matter of divine revelation or commandment or other form of sacred law. This represents the agony of secularization which every civilization goes through before it reaches the stage of decadence and collapse and/or renewal from below. We find essentially the same thing in the Han and Wei Dynasties in China, for from Wang Ch'ung (if not earlier) to Ko Hung there had been a progressive decline of confidence, if not a failure of faith, in the traditional ways. This failure is epitomized by the Seven Sages of the Bamboo Grove, where we see a complete collapse of the traditional mores and a rather desperate attempt to fill the vacuum. Both Rome and China had exhausted creativity long ago. All that they could do was compile encyclopedic collections and commentaries (like Ma Jung, for example) and compendia of past perfections.

We are pointedly puzzled that Plotinus, Sextus Empiricus, Origen, and Tertullian, not only contemporaries but all at one time or other having had at least a sojourn to Rome, could have written without reference to one another. It is a bit strange that Sextus has exerted so little influence, by comparison with Plotinus for example, on the history of philosophy, particularly British. The notable exception is his rediscovery by and influence on the French Enlightenment, especially Montaigne and Montesquieu. As a matter of fact, when we come to that many centuries and a few volumes later, we will be reminded that much of Descartes' philosophizing was an effort at refuting this scepticism. Thus his indirect influence on modern philosophy is not to be neglected, even though it has become virtually imperceptible, although John Stuart Mill's thinking does, as Copleston reminds us, resemble Sextus rather remarkably. Another line of influence that is also far too easily and too often overlooked is that on Husserl, who takes much of his terminology (*epoché*, *noesis*, *noema*, etc.,) directly from Sextus. Ervin Laszlo even treats Husserl as a modern Sceptic.

As to Sextus Empiricus himself, the thing that catches the eye first is his association as a medic. Scepticism as therapy : what a remedy ! But is it much different after all from the Buddhist schools in this respect ? As with Nāgārjuna, Sextus uses philosophy to refute itself, as it were, by presenting argument and counter-argument in antinomies so that one argument is always cancelled out by an equally tenable counter-argument. Nāgārjuna had been dead at least seventy-five or one hundred years before Sextus was born; but he did leave disciples behind, so we may once again suspect influence in some form or other, probably more from India than on India. In addition to the sceptical influence of Mādhyamika, we suspect too that some Jaina relativism might have come across the oceans and/or deserts, for "maybe" is a key word with Sextus.

If we must insist on placing him in some category or other, even though this is the last thing he would consent to, we might call him, like some of his semi-sceptical Confucian contemporaries, a humanist. But one wonders : would Sextus have welcomed some of his Neo-Taoist contemporaries ? He might have outwitted (or out-talked) them in disputation, but they might have shrugged their shoulders and said, "Why all the bother ? We never made any judgments to suspend !" We shall say tentatively that in the end, in principle, Sextus is more like the more serious Neo-Taoists, but in method much more akin to the Mahāyāna, especially Mādhyamika.

Sextus' current of thinking follows essentially the same pattern of attack and counter-attack as Wittgenstein and Nāgārjuna. He takes a rather mature anthropological approach to the history of religions as he knew them in the Graeco-Roman past as an exercise, as it were, in scientific study of comparative mythology. He comes rather quickly to the view that none of them is absolutely true. All views are only relative and therefore to be neither accepted nor rejected but treated with a sort of phenomenological method, descriptively bracketing each belief or practice examined but not allowing it to master one, remaining open to further inquiry. As ever he seems primarily concerned to avoid dogmatism. It is his perpetual openness to inquiry, we may infer, which brings together his philosophy and his religious motivations. Certainly after Sextus no dogmatism should ever have survived. Perhaps that is why he almost did not survive.

Can empirical method be applied to the study of philosophies and yield something when some of those philosophies deny the validity of empirical method except in non-philosophical or scientific matters? Michel[1] hints that this is what Sextus is really out to do, not just formulate an eclectic amalgam of views of the past; nor is he involved in a mere *jeu dès systèmes*, for philosophy is no game but a serious matter of finding one's way between birth and death, of surviving as a person. Perhaps Sextus did start out empirically to study systems of philosophy as historical phenomena and then, by playing one against the other, to eliminate the false and to find out which were more universal in their affirmations, which were in the minority, and which were completely deviant and mostly sensational. Still, philosophy has become for Sextus a sort of scholasticism, brilliant but not very applicable. However, the philosopher should not be required to supply a religion for the masses any more than he should be required to make tools for the engineers and scientists or to paint pictures or be a composer in order to gain the right to philosophize about art and beauty. Sextus, in short, is the philosopher's philosopher and not just a wise old man who can give consolation, as later Boethius is called on to do.

It is the history of the theories which are available to him that is his chief source. He does not point to any patterns of development in history so much as he seems to show that patterns of development also cancel each other out. The idealistic geometers against the empiricist or Epicurean materialists, for example, get a thorough treatment whatever the topic, whether the argument be from whole and part — here amazingly like what we find in the dialogue between the

Vaiṣeśikas and the Buddhists — or whether in terms of the "logic of tensing" whereby, sophistically perhaps, he gives virtually the same analysis of time as that given by Dignāga and his predecessors, namely that nothing "happens" in the present tense, for as soon as we say it is happening it has already happened. One might claim that the judgment of history was more final than Sextus' own suspended judgment, and that actually he was, almost in anticipation of Kant, using intellect only to eliminate the tyranny of intellect and thereby, unwittingly, making room for faith.

To say the least, Sextus does not classify philosophies according to any impossible geographical division like East-West or such other divisions like Greek-Roman-Hebraic or Proletarian-Elitist, although indeed, given the conditions in his environment, he well could have done so. What he does say is very plain, and perhaps interpreters have overlooked the profundity of his deliberate simplicity. If empirical chronicling of other matters yields intelligible results, why should not historical treatment of philosophies yield similar results ? For certainly before any systematic synthesis of systems or of traditions can be made they should be gathered intelligibly together. Of course the ultimate ambition may not be realizable, namely, to let them cancel each other out by their own momentum or in dialectical play to reveal universal truth as the residuum after such self-cancelling is finished.

In his refutation of Aenesidemus, Sextus puts considerable emphasis on the unreliability of the argument from common consent which Aenesidemus had stressed, since phenomena could be universally subject to mistaken interpretation (as, we might interpose, was the case with the geocentric theory of the universe). But if consensus is reduced to nil, there is not much left. Scepticism becomes the inevitable consequence of any truly consistent empiricism, and if that in turn is linked with a reductionist logic, not only scepticism but a sort of 'nihilism' is almost inevitable. But then, so what ? Rather than ending up in a solipsistic impasse, if we look at this scepticism through Mādhyamika eyes what we should experience is a deliverance from all possible dogmatism as well as from the tyranny of the senses and animal appetites. Holding everything in detached perspective, we should then have the positive freedom to play one ideology or philosophy off against the others. Here Sextus may be closer to the pre-Vijñānavāda period of Sarvāstivāda — we can acknowledge that although no one philosophy has the whole truth, there is always some truth in each.

What emerges in Stough's treatment[2] is really empiricism in the modern sense even more than the "scepticism" we might expect. First she traces his treatment of the universal pattern of the progressive evolution of concepts from raw sense impressions to perceptions into which consciousness enters and from which, in turn, by abstraction and other commonplace epistemological processes, concepts are derived. Instead of trying to find Hume in Sextus, perhaps we should reexamine him. It might be that he is really nearer to Locke. At least Stough seems to find something very close to the distinction between primary and secondary qualities and many other similarities.

However, the structure of Sextus' procedure is not so much that of derivation of conceptualization out of sense impressions as it is a reductionist method wherein the arguments *per-impossibile* seem to prevail over the method of abstraction. Hence it is not so much the difficulty of coming to the idea that something is really there in a perceptual situation as it is a matter of the difficulty — we might almost say of communication, but more precisely in the classical sense which continues in use at least down to Ockham — of demonstration. For example, I want to demonstrate my hypothesis that a certain athelete had religious motives for his extraordinary exertions; but all that I can verify is a whole complex pattern of bodily movements, facial expressions, and other discernibles of an external nature. If I ask him outright I still have the option of screening his response through a filter of awareness that his reply might be excessively modest. Thus, without some very risky indirect inferences, I cannot demonstrate the truth or the falsity of my hypothesis. If (and this *if* is rather crucial) I do not wish to indulge in illicit speculation, I am left with a suspended judgment. Sextus, however, does not seem to have intended to reject induction or deduction entirely, or one in favor of the other.[3] He simply rejected the extremes of Aenesidemus and Carneades.

According to Stough, Sextus "links truth with the criterion by which we judge existence and not with the criterion for the conduct of life." What emerges is that neutrality is of more value in his perspective than affirmation or negation. Stough continues:

> Sextus' conservatism with respect to the concept of truth is partly responsible for his skepticism. His position ends by barring the notion of truth from any application. He is forced to conclude, therefore, that nothing is true. Had Sextus not followed the tradition of assimilating the true to the real, a domain he believed to be unknowable in principle, he could have reclaimed the concept of truth by applying it to sense statements, which refer to phenomenal objects and hence are verifiable. The unknowable real object would thus have become quite superfluous. But Sextus rejects such a phenomenalistic position.[4]

Otherwise he might have ended in Advaita's unknowability of unknowability and consequent failure to achieve a negation of negation except through a 'leap' from *māyā* to Brahman. We mention this because it might be argued (perhaps more vividly than accurately) that without a similar 'leap' (the flight of the alone to the Alone) Plotinus would have been in the same boat with Sextus Empiricus.

Stough continues:

> The real object, as he has argued, exists independently of what we experience, whereas the phenomenal object is affected by the conditions and circumstances of perception. The idea of an object, therefore, is not exhausted by its phenomenal appearances. It is just this separation of external object and phenomenon, along with the association of truth with the real, which makes Sextus a skeptic instead of a phenomenalist.[5]

Having come to the traditional impasse of scepticism viewed in the narrower sense — that if one cannot affirm any position because none is really true, then can one affirm one's own scepticism ? — Sextus replies :

> And again, just as it is not impossible for a man who has

> climbed up to a high place by a ladder to overturn the ladder with his foot after his ascent, so too it is not unreasonable that the Skeptic, after he has proceeded, as it were by a kind of ladder, to construct the above argument proving that there is no true thing as demonstration, would then also do away with this very argument.[6]

In India today this is still the most popular metaphor used by Advaitins for the 'leap' from the self-refutation (as they conceive of it) of *māyā* to the self-subsisting, qualityless, undemonstrable, indescribable, completely transcendental *nirguṇa* Brahman. That Śaṅkara and everyone since him no doubt got this metaphor ultimately from Śūnyavāda almost goes without saying. It will be remembered that Śaṅkara was called (and still is in many circles) a crypto-Buddhist for just such reasons — the dividing line between Śūnyavāda and Advaita is very thin indeed!

From this perspective the dividing line between Sextus Empiricus and Plotinus is not very wide either, contrary to our usual textbook interpretations. Plotinus leaps from the alone to the Alone. Sextus leaps from Nothing to Everything (since there's not much difference between these after all, both being infinites). Nāgārjuna leaps from Emptiness to Freedom, at the price of Total Detachment from Everything. Ko Hung and Wang Pi — whither did they leap, or did they leap at all? By comparison with their Indo-European contemporaries they retained much more humanist commonsense and interest in actual scientific endeavor, inspite of a certain esoteric trend. But that the Seven Sages of the Bamboo Grove did leap "back to nature" cannot be denied. Yes, they did use drugs and wine, but what were they after? Was it not, in every case, whether in mysticism or in scepticism, in science or in inebriation, by asceticism or by orgiastic indulgence, an attempt to gain a loss of self in a Larger World?

Sextus takes the Stoics to task on their handling of the problem of opposites. For, he says in effect, it depends on which you start with as to which is the "opposite". Language is certainly deceptive. Is the spiritual the opposite of the material or the material the opposite of the spiritual? In either case we can use the negative : non-spiritual equals material, and non-material equals spiritual. We really do not know either without the other, and yet neither can be the beginning of our knowing. How can we know both together when we know neither separately ?

In almost all logics the disjunctive syllogism remains a convenient tool but gives no reason for positing which member of the disjunction is the major and which the minor. Sextus seems to think, therefore, that every disjunction is really hypothetical at the foundation, and hypotheticals give us only a form of truth, not truth itself. Pretty soon we find that we ourselves as logicians are trapped by our own tools in the "net of Indra", the infinite spider web of interlocking hypotheses such that none can really be proved until the others are. Since there is no beginning or end of these things, in the end nothing is proved at all.

Sextus' treatment of the problem of absolute and relative pivots on the statement that "relatives are apprehended together", reminding us that this is a matter of signs or of communication rather than a matter of essence. Communication is a matter of degree since sometimes we fail almost completely, but never quite, just as likewise we never succeed completely but only to a high degree. Therefore, once again, suspended judgment gives, shall we say, the Tao, the answer that is no-answer, or the no-answer that is the open-answer, or the *prajñā* of the Middle (Socratic or Buddhist) Way. Proof is also only a sign and not ever a "conclusion". Philosophy is the endless vocation. Again, his pattern turns out to be, it seems, very much like the *syādvāda* of his Jaina contemporaries.

In dealing with cause and effect, many of the arguments frequently used sound strangely similar to many standard arguments in most Indian philosophies, but especially in the Buddhist systems. His treatment of cause and effect in relation to motion, and motion in relation to the relation between the corporeal and the bodiless — if indeed that may be said to exist without considerable dialectical mental gymnastics — is not at all dissimilar to the treatment of the same problem by Dignāga, if not to others before him. But, of course, no conclusion is reached; and the philosopher is rendered incapable of helping the scientist any more than he could help or hinder the theologian. Advancement of science to Sextus would also probably be a matter for dialectical scrutiny and might be shown to be as detrimental in some aspects as beneficial in others. Therefore, suspended judgment once again. For Sextus the purpose of philosophy is not to help or to hinder any other aspect of life but simply to understand, as much as possible, what is transpiring both at the extremes and also in the middle.

It is Sextus' treatment of *genesis* and *phthora* that fascinates us the most since, as was previously the case with Aristotle, this seems to afford the greatest possibilities of comparison with similar ideas in India and China. What he does is essentially the further application of his technique of reduction to the absurd, marshalling his arguments systematically and then, as though he were playing a game of tin soldiers, having also marshalled his counter-arguments, he engages them in combat until they exterminate each other. He seems not so much concerned with the reality behind the arguments but fully engaged in the argumentation techniques as such, so that after mutual cancelling out he remains free to treat any position with detachment, being bound by none.

Plato's name figures rather prominently in this context; but one may well ask, which Plato ? When the English translation reads, "It is also possible for us, as doubters, to argue directly. . . .", the word translated as "doubters" is *aporountas*, which is a rather obvious reference to the *aporia* in Plato's earlier dialogues (and even in the later ones sometimes) wherein it is found that the chief thing is the openness of dialectic and not the arriving at any 'conclusions'. Our minds being finite, we cannot find any conclusions. All we can do is balance arguments against each other, make tentative judgments, and go on as best we can on the basis of right opinion (*orthé doxa*). Thus the typification of Sextus as a Sceptic may be misleading for the modern world. He may be more Socratic than appears on the surface.

The same reasons gathered against becoming (*genesis*) are used against passing-away (*phthora*). In a way similar to the method of Zeno the Eleatic, we run into the difficulty of locating the time when becoming, existing or perishing "happens" since we can never locate the moment when present becomes past or when future becomes present or, to put it the other way, when the past becomes present or the present becomes future; therefore (so the argument runs) there can be neither perishing nor becoming. There Sextus leaves us dangling, as it were, *in vacuo*. One might criticize him for not providing something other than these destructions of destructions to hold on to; but, as is the proper discipline with Buddhist traditions in general, he intentionally leaves us nothing to cling to, except 'nothing'. To those accustomed to the Aristotelian system, or to the Nyāya-Vaiśeṣika with their respective realist orientations, or even to the Jaina views of substance, this may seem strange; to those nurtured in Buddhist traditions such detachment toward all particular views was the norm. According to Śūnyavāda especially, what the Buddha taught — if he really taught anything at all — was the "view of no view".

As we move from the above considerations concerning physics or matters of nature to ethical considerations, it might be expected that, as many centuries later with Kant, as well as with some Buddhist thinkers of Sextus' own era, where the physical or natural world yielded no certainty we might yet hope to find something more real or at least more reliable in ethical realm. Does Sextus also "remove reason with reason in order to make room for faith" ? Not only because he still uses essentially the same method, but also — or so might claim (and perhaps they actually do) some Christian apologists like Augustine — because he remained a pagan, the light of faith did not dawn on him. As a matter of fact, what Sextus finds is less certainty rather than more.

Over and over again in the cycles of civilization we may observe that when a culture or civilization is in fresh vitality, with a strong *dharma*, relativism is scarcely a problem. The common code is the cohesive force that keeps the culture alive and creative, optimistic and confident in its powers both in matters of investigating and using nature and also in advance and expansion in the political and economic spheres. But as it grows older, more complex, encountering other peoples, other faiths, other traditions, other *dharmas*, and as corruption creeps in, especially in high places, there begins to be a questioning, but a questioning which is not always fruitful philosophically, and instead becomes inward-directed in the wrong way. Scepticism (in the popular sense of the word) easily degenerates into cynicism; and then, having lost interest in the external world, the people tend in turn to lose interest in themselves. Counter-cultures spring up, romantic gestures at return to nature, often coupled with a fresh fascination, not with religion, but with magic, astrology, miracles and all the rest of the range of esoterica which is usually considered far beyond the pale of philosophy.

Such was the environment in which Sextus lived and worked. He was indeed a critic of it — critic, but not reformer; that would be asking too much. For one thing, quite unlike Plotinus, who certainly failed in that role as much as he would like to have played it well. Sextus probably had a keen realist sense of his limitations as well as his talents.

Sextus is a scholarly critic, not just a carping one, much less a sermonizing one. He is always careful not just to quote his sources faithfully, but to dig into the historical roots of almost every custom that comes within his scrutiny. If he still does not posit any positive new ethical code — as almost within his lifetime Justinian did in the field of law — nevertheless, he certainly intends and succeeds in a high degree to deliver his readers from inadequate codes of the past.

Sextus examines what became almost standard problems in most ethics textbooks after his time and remain so pretty much today : theories of the good as pleasure, the good as utility, intention vs actual results of action, accidental or incidental vs intrinsic good, as well as considerations as to the interrelations between the Platonic Ideas and their actualization in the here and now, not to mention the distinction between happiness, pleasure and the good. Sextus treats all of these almost simultaneously, but actually in an order of hierarchical series, hinting that the highest is the intrinsic but not insisting on that any more than on any other possible definition or view.

Sextus mentions the Ethiopians alongside the Persians as illustrative of the fact that tastes are quite relative and therefore should be dissociated from the notion of absolute good as perfectly embodied in any one code or custom. Soon after some illustrations of this point, which is now so familiar in our world even as it was in the Roman world, he presents the proposal that it is not necessarily true that everything is either good or bad since some things and actions can be indifferent. He examines in detail the arguments about whether things are good or bad by nature (and we might add) or by custom. Here we could well draw some comparisons with Wang Ch'ung and his successors in China who under similar circumstances had begun to argue against the older conservative Confucianists and conservative Taoists in a similar vein.

It must be noted withall that Sextus does not say that there does not exist good anywhere or that good is a false notion. He has only finally constructed a proof that nothing is good *by nature* or naturally good. For the sake of argument Sextus assumes that there are things that are inherently good by nature. Given this, would it then be possible, desirable or reasonable for the Sceptics to abandon their suspended judgment ? Would the dogmatists have any advantage if such a concession were made ? What emerges in this context seems to be on a slightly different level. The terms *epistémé* and *phronésis* begin to appear with increasing frequency, here translated as science (of life) and wisdom respectively. This seems rather significant to us in our broader context since according to traditional interpretations both Śūnyavāda and Vijñānavāda go through a similar sort of therapeutics of dialectical elimination of false and inadequate views, as do some of the Neo-Taoists also. But in their cases supposedly this is only a propaedeutic to the gaining of intuitive insight or inspiration, wisdom, *prajñā* or Tao, after the rational ways have been exhausted. And it may well be that Sextus hopes that the same might be true in his own case.

But there seems to be a rather radical difference, and here he may be closer to the Confucianists than to the Buddhists and Taoists. For *phronésis* is not *sophia*, even though both words are translated as "wisdom". Sextus never explicitly mentions the Gnostics, but one doubts very seriously whether they would have fared any better at his hands than the Stoics, Epicureans or the dogmatists, for *phronēsis* is really the 'wisdom' of right judgment after rational deliberation and has no intuitive overtones at all. As a matter of fact, his use of *epistēmē* and *phronēsis* in close conjunction is reminiscent of Plato — the Plato of dialectics, not the Neo-Platonist Plato of the *Timaeus* and the myths which Plotinus takes to be the "real" Plato. Sextus is no dobut assuming that his readers will already be familiar with these things which may seem like pedantic niceties now but were commonplaces then among the educated elite.

Phronēsis is not a suspension of suspended judgment but rather the rational outcome of its continued exercise. Deontology is essential if one is to follow a distinctly human, not to say humanistic, ethics. For it is still only reason that can keep us unperturbed in the midst of all the disturbances of the external world and the impulses of our lower selves. The *epochē*, the suspension of judgment, is only a slight further extension of the Greek — but also Buddhist as distinct from Hindu—view of keeping to the middle path, avoiding such extremes as fanaticism on the one hand and sheer apathy, idleness, and insensitivity on the other. It might also be seen as a further extension of the Stoic ideal of *apatheia*, which we have already compared with the *niṣkāma karma* of the *Gitā*. However, these things come into play only incidentally at Sextus' hands, for his chief purpose still is the further extension of his exposition disproving that anything is good or evil by nature.

Incidentally, it will be noted in this context that just as in the Hindu and Jaina views both good and evil *karma* must equally be eliminated, so here, in order to keep equanimity, one must not be over-enfatuated with the good nor over-inflamed against the evil. What a contrast with the Manichaean view of things!

As in Mādhyamika, the view of no views gives the philosopher freedom not only to live in detached freedom himself, but to administer to others such opinions as will give them balance and harmony, or at least deliverance from inadequate or false views, each in his own proper measure. Not everybody is ready for every philosophy at every given time and place. *Epoché*, suspension of judgment, at least allows for a wide measure of pluralism without violating the wider and broader unitive field in which that pluralism can and must be operative. Sextus is not legislating for anyone in particular or for any one religion or community. Citizen of the world, he must at least be tolerant of all while becoming subjected to none. Such is the secret of true freedom even though it may entail the price of voluntary alienation from any and all particularities.

Socrates was simply using arguments derived directly from dialogues with other living people or out of his own bald pate, whereas Sextus is still able, right to the end, to juxtapose actual historical positions in such a way that they cancel each other out of their own momentum, and the results appear to be rather devastating. Thus, paradoxically, we must learn from him, if not from the Seven Sages of the Bamboo Grove also, that we can learn nothing from him, since Sceptical doubt precludes certainty, which is essential to communication, and without communication, no information.

But the argument does not stop there. Still using his technique of the destructive dilemma, he pushes his *epoché* almost to the breaking point by bringing us to the brink of admitting that if a man is wise he cannot teach the unwise, but if he cannot do that, then he is not truly wise. Wisdom seems all wrapped up in itself solipsistically in some other dimension that cannot be experienced, if indeed it exists at all. Suspended judgment to those who would like to cling to something is no doubt very uncomfortable; and to some others who nevertheless would not mind "throwing in the sponge", it might seem that Sextus has been playing parlor games and could not really be serious about his — art!

Sextus seems not to be interested in arguments but in the (history of) controversies as such; and this is what leads us to relate him to the discipline of cultural dynamics. There are some questions he does not answer which did arise among some of his Chinese contemporaries, at least implicitly, namely under what social and economic conditions do which sorts of controversies arise in philosophy ? Indeed, this is a rather cogent question to ask of Sextus himself. True enough, his expertise in handling his materials is remarkable and not infrequently brilliant. But sometimes one wonders what it is that provokes him deep down underneath it all. The search for truth, even if he does not find it, of course. However, even that, being terribly amorphous and so all-encompassing, can be reduced, as he has apparently done, to a self-defeating enterprise. But then is truth something to be searched for as though it were "out there," as though it were a thing, rather than the living milieu within which the search is made ? Here is where Vasubandhu, if not Plotinus, can perhaps be said to have "succeeded" where Sextus "failed".

Sextus is constantly exhausting the past, not projecting any hope, not to say faith, into the future. He fails to see that to some extent truth is a matter of creativity, of commitment, of living through situations, and not merely a matter of analysis of the achievements and failures of others. If history be the judge, he left a vacuum. And that vacuum, like that of his fellow sceptics in China, was filled by the new religions of (Athanasian) Christianity and (Mahāyāna) Buddhism. Whether these were answers or escapes or solutions to the problem of truth can be argued endlessly.

Rome had over-extended itself until, having embraced all things, it ceased to be anything in itself. Did Sextus, likewise dealing exhaustively with everything, achieve, howsoever gloriously, nothing in the end ? Perhaps, knowing full well that no answer to any question can be final for finite human understanding, he is simply trying to be as all-inclusive as possible, exhaustive of all possibilities, and impossibilities too. What else can one do, without jumping out of human finitude and becoming a god, or very much like God ? Ironically that is just what Plotinus and Origen do, or attempt to do, or pretend to do. But not Sextus and Tertullian. They remain in human finitude, unpretentiously but honestly struggling on through, the one claiming faith the other not, but otherwise very much alike in spirit.

Was not Sextus in about the same relation to the cultural climate of his time that Wittgenstein has been to our own ?

Then, if that be true, may we expect post-Wittgensteinian philosophy to follow the same or similar trends as that which followed after Sextus, namely a sort of further failure of nerve and/or acceptance of a revelation and/or the development of mysticism after some futile experimenting with esoterics and other nostrums promising instant enlightenment? The trend appears to be already in that direction.

C. Wang Ch'ung

What we would suggest basically is that Wang Ch'ung (27-c. 100 A.D.) held to the doctrine and practice of suspended judgment characteristic of the Sceptics. If anything, Wang Ch'ung was too sceptical and distrusting of traditional opinions. He did propose several radically new theories, but sometimes they now appear to be a little naive. He might be accused of being merely a sceptical "thinker" without any connections with theory sufficient to call his observations science at all, much less philosophy. But this is not the case. He consciously held a general philosophy which he proposed as an alternative to all those that had preceded him, even though, of course, he had to pay lip service to the syncretistic Confucianism which had become the "official" philosophy. His philosophy was basically that of cyclic variation of the *yin-yang* in all things or the principle of polarization as a general phenomenon of nature without reference to any praeternatural or supernatural force beyond it.

Wang Ch'ung overtly rejected a cardinal aspect of traditional Confucianism, namely, the relations between natural and supernatural phenomena and good or bad government. To him just as much as to many of his Greek and Roman contemporaries, there was no causal connection. Thus we find that iconoclasm, not to say scepticism or naturalism, is a chief motive for his writing the *Lun Heng*. This work was often doubted as authentic by many scholars throughout the history of China since it was so inconceivable to many that anyone of Wang Ch'ung's stature and social station could say such nasty things against their avatar. Nevertheless, the evidence is quite convincing that he did write these things, or at least the evidence to the contrary is sufficiently weak to merit our overlooking it.

Coming from the middle upper class and having experienced social mobility himself, Wang seems nevertheless to have retained a certain earthiness in his character. He would taunt the superintellectuals for their exaggerated speculations which were not humanly practical. Although he retained some private superstitions (which then were not acknowledged as such), most of the traditional superstitions he rejected outright. Indeed, his interpretation of Heaven and earth, the traditional Confucian cosmology, bordered on an almost naive materialism. He just could not conceive of any purely non-material substance. It must be quickly added, of course, that much depends on the reporter, different critics condemning him for the very things which others maintain he lacks. He is sufficiently versatile that all parties will find ample points to quarrel about.

Wang attacks Tung Chung-shu, who was the establisher of the cult that by that time had accumulated around Confucius even as such cults had gathered in the same period around many such avatars from Socrates himself and Moses to Alexander the Great, Kṛṣṇa, the Buddha and Lao Tzu. Even Confucius himself did not escape Wang's criticism, nor did Mencius, Han Fei Tzu and many aspects of Taoism. Concerning Taoists 'untruths', Wang Ch'ung seems even bemused by the stories about emperors and sages who were supposed to have gone up to heaven bodily. Of course mythology in general is easy enough to attack; but Wang goes much farther than that. He sceptically taunts us to be sensible about it and not to get caught up in embarrassing contradictions. This basic attitude seems to underlie almost all that is justifiably attributed to him. There is plenty of evidence to support our adding the word "rationalistic" to our list of epithets.

It seems that such characters as Wang Ch'ung can be found in almost every civilization as it reaches maturity and before it lapses into decadence. One may criticize him for being too "negative", perhaps as one might also criticize some of the Pre-Socratics or some contemporaries of Wang in the Roman Empire, such as Anesidemus; but the purging of superstition and meaningless accretions of sheer empty tradition actually leaves the emphasis very open, and very positive at that, for a rational humanism without which scientific attitudes could not develop. Only after mankind is freed from the encumbrances of myths and superstitions which arise out of fear can man, individually and socially, take control and actually do something about natural phenomena instead of feeling helpless and fatalistic in the face of them.

Although we cannot assert that Wang anticipated any Copernican revolution in his naturalistic cosmology, at least he rejected most superstitious explanations. Heaven to him was inconceivable except as embodied in something material. Concerning spirits, he debunked the Mohists and Taoists even more firmly than Confucius himself had done, so that much opposition was aroused on the part of those pseudo-Confucianists who had become so syncretistic as to forget Confucius' own humanism. In these matters Wang was perhaps even more outspoken than most of his European contemporaries, and certainly more so than his Hindu and Mahâyâna Buddhist contemporaries, Nâgârjuna included.

It is on his doctrine of human nature, including his denial of immortality of the soul, that the emphasis ought to weigh most heavily. Here he remains more traditional than at first may appear since he always reviews the views of others in the past before he asserts any view of his own. His method seems very close to the predecessors of Sextus Empiricus and to Nâgârjuna in so far as by playing one view against the others he himself finally gains deliverance from dogmatism. It is above all to be emphasized that, after considering virtually all the possible positions concerning the goodness or evilness of human nature, he ends on a note of open-mindedness : "This teaching alone does not exhaust human nature." Scarcely in any other literature of this or any other age could we ask for a more complete listing of the possibilities, except perhaps in Plutarch, although even then one would have to put several scattered passages together.

There is one aspect of Wang's presentation here which is not quite so obvious. He presupposes a sort of radical humanism which is a basic undercurrent of virtually all Chinese thought. This carries with it a sort of down-to-earthness which is quite the opposite of the heavily metaphysical trend in much of Hinduism and Indian Mahâyâna of the same period, not to mention the mystical or at least speculative trends in Philo and other European philosophers. Or perhaps we should schematize the situation still differently, pointing to the parallel differences between Wang Ch'ung and his Taoist (or already Neo-Taoist) contemporaries, and those between Neo-Platonism and Scepticism in the Mediterranean area, and again between Mahâyâna and Hīnayâna in India. At any rate, even though Wang does certainly highlight that trend toward humanistic clear-headedness perhaps more than anyone before Chang Tsai's ridicule of Buddha bones and other relics and cultic objects, he could be considered as just another example of our favorite theme : particular types of philosophies and a wide variety of types of philosophies can be found in virtually every geographical region.

But rather than meta-historical considerations, let us turn to Needham[7] as a guide through the basic themes in the *Lun Hêng*. Wang had had predecessors, such as Hsün Tzu, who had his sceptical moments and was not very credulous about the efficacy of prayers for rain. Huan T'an likewise is not immune from this naturalistic and anti-superstitious attitude which aptly Needham calls "scepticism". Forke[8] in his copious introduction makes much more capital out of the possible comparison with Lucretius. Wang Ch'ung is akin to Lucretius in his interest in natural phenomena; in fact, he was active in the investigation of nature, not content with merely writing poetry about other people's findings and theories as was the case with Lucretius.

Needham considers the matter of what he calls Centrifugal Cosmology which, it has been suggested, may have eventually influenced Descartes' concept of cosmic vortices. This view was sufficiently common that it would have been remarkable if Wang Ch'ung had opposed it, even though one might debate whether or not he attempted to improve on it. It is easy to exaggerate the sophistication, or lack of it, of any Eurasian cosmology during our Han-Hellenistic-Bactrian Period; but Wang did reject the anthropocentric view of the universe. Citing Wang's famous metaphor that the universe will pay heed to man no more than man would to the song of a flea, Needham claims that with such statements "was swept away the whole basis of the systems of divination" which had always, as in Rome, been part and parcel of the state religion as well as of the everyday course of individual life and conduct.

And such systems of divination had become especially extreme in the later days of the Han and Roman Empires. It would be an exaggeration to attribute to Wang Ch'ung anything like a prophetic spirit. He was not preaching, but he was rather humanistically taunting his contemporaries into realizing the stupidities which still prevailed unconsciously simply because they were a part of hallowed tradition.

Needham reviews what he calls Wang's attack on the phenomenalists or the "change-and-reversion school" which had gained considerable inroads into politics via the ignorant and superstitious ladies in the harem. It seems that not only the famous Tung Chung-shu but also many other relatively famous philosophers connected with the "establishment" belonged. Indeed, it was evidently considered to be the orthodox school no less than Stoicism, for example, became the orthodox school in Rome. Contrary to its original humanistic initiation, it had been able to give full support to the sacrificial rites of the state religion. The basic tenet of this type of cult from the strictly anthropological point of view was that the running well-being of the universe itself depended on the sacrifices performed by human beings. Other schools rebelled from such things, such as reformed Hinduism and Buddhism and the Christian "reform" (or heresy) of Judaism, and centuries later Islam, and still later the Sikh faith and the Bahai. Wang Ch'ung also could not stop with renouncing them; he had to denounce them.

At first it may be difficult to understand how scepticism such as Wang's could constitute such a scandal or almost a revolution in the Chinese Empire. But one has only to reflect briefly to remember that doubt in the divine right of kings used to entail excommunication from the Church; and was it not virtually the same issue, the state cult of the emperor as divine Caesar, that caused all the stir about Christian martyrdom ? Chinese tolerance, however, was greater, at least in Wang's case. He did not have to become a martyr, even though some martyrs might have been more effective in changing the public rites and ceremonies.

We need not be reminded that the interrelations between human nature and human destiny had constituted a major topic for virtually every Chinese thinker since long before Confucius, and that the views expressed ranged very widely from complete, almost mechanistic, determinism to romantic espousals of individual liberties and even downright cultivation of eccentricity. Given what we already have gathered about Wang Ch'ung's views and character, we should not be surprised that he gives large room for sheer chance without design to natural events like floods and other calamities; but, on the other hand, he is quite aware that in the normal course of events, most developments are the result of normal causational patterns of nature. Although Needham claims that Wang was more of a determinist than Hsün Tzu, neither were strict determinists for then education would be futile. It seems that even Wang had a sense of destiny that could not be accounted for by a completely random or by a completely determined universe and human nature. We might say that he held a 'judicial' astrology in a strong deterministic interpretation.

Wang's selfless devotion to truth regardless of consequences comes out pretty well in the chapters "On Intelligence" and "The Real Nature of Knowledge".[9] From these we may take note of the following. As usual with vivid metaphors, usually of a down-to-earth sort, he warns us that rich people are not necessarily — indeed, are very seldom — the most intelligent. For which would be the greater treasure, a fancy camphor wood chest full of silks and jewels, or a plain wooden box full of books? Many people in such matters are like blind people who can't see the difference, or they are even like wooden or clay images or dummies which have ears and eyes quite complete and yet are insensible. After a criticism of those who become obsessed with only one classic or only one philosophy, Wang also criticizes the opposite type who have a dilettantish knowledge of everything in a superficial scattered way, flippantly making a show of their erudition. He advocates both a wide range of learning and depth of understanding with intensive specialization in some field, balancing that with open-mindedness and comprehensive range of operation. Wang reminds us that it would be foolish to expect a fast race horse to do the same work as a big strong ox, or vice versa; and so with intellectuals. Some are slow, strong and heavy, while others are swift, light and subtle. It is not reasonable to expect all qualities in everyone or anyone.

Toynbee noted that nearly every generation in every country thinks its own generation, or the younger generation more commonly, is "going to the dogs". Wang Ch'ung is certainly no exception. Along with those in Rome of his own time, there were plenty of reasons to justify his complaint. Otherwise Wang Mang's dictatorship would never have been needed, or even if it had come about, it would have been far more successful in giving social justice and equal distribution of the empire's prosperity. Both the Roman and Han Empires had become so corrupt that even the good dictators with the best of intentions often became the victims of the very corruption they were trying to purge. One might understand, even where one could not easily condone, resorts to violence; but one can hardly understand the extent to which lust, gluttony, bribery, cunning and craftiness in court intrigue, etc., were cultivated in their extreme forms almost as though they were fine arts. Concerning such things, Wang Ch'ung has only indignation, for certainly intelligence cannot live very long in such an atmosphere. His struggle against such typical behavior on the part of most of those he had to associate with may well explain why his philosophizing so often appears to be negative and condemnatory rather than positive and constructive.

The chapter under the title "The Real Nature of Knowledge" deserves our special attention for its iconoclasm as far as what came to be considered as learning. This, like most of Wang Ch'ung, is probably best understood in terms of his social, political and cultural milieu. Is it not true that in times of decadence one may expect to have a lot of pseudo-savants constituting a class of authorities whose opinion becomes the last word on everything from trivialities about food and dress to conduct of wars and investigation of the universe itself, but who are really culture-bound and blinded by their own importance ? How much original and even revolutionary materials, how many ideas that would have benefitted civilization, got politely ignored by such cliques we have no way of knowing.

What Wang Ch'ung says about the authority of the written

records of the hoary and therefore unquestionable past is about as caustic as one might expect from people like Voltaire. Everything had become a matter of deliberate obscurity as a key to demonstrating how advanced one was in scholarly enterprise. Here his satire is as salient as it might be effective even today were it better known.

Not unlike what happens among proletarian Americans who find "prophecy" in anything that is not easily understood, such as the pyramids of Egypt, the *Book of Daniel* and the *Book of Revelations* — and in the Medieval Latin world even Virgil and Ovid were brought in as "prophecies" among the literate clergy — so Wang Ch'ung indicates that according to superstitious tradition even Confucius had been invested with the capacity of seeing into the future and making prophecies about it. Thus the masses used his writings in a magical way expecting them to perform miracles (which in the social sphere indeed they would) and to reveal the future. Though researches are still incomplete, it appears that the concept of "revealed scriptures" does not come into full effect until the *Qur'an* gets into circulation all across Eurasia; but it did have some expressions long before then, perhaps by 100 A.D. in some areas. Several passaged in Wang Ch'ung indicate that he was not convinced that Tung Chung-shu had done the right thing in canonizing the Confucian classics and setting Confucius up as a worshipful deity. Rather, he criticizes him at almost any and every opportunity because he was quite aware, as K'ang Yu-wei became aware in the last of the nineteenth century, that Confucius himself was a humanist who rejected superstition quite openly.

Omniscience of all the avatars and prophets up to that time is one of the ideas that somehow "gets around" all over Eurasia and affects public attitudes for several centuries. Controversies about the omniscience of Jesus began soon after Saint Paul's preachings and the syncretistic adaptations of the life and teachings of Jesus to Hellenistic conditions, not only virgin birth but omniscience being a requisite attribute of deified people. In the Buddhist world the concept of the Eternal Buddha also involved the omniscience of the human Śākyamuni Buddha; and long since we have seen how the

Jainas claimed omniscience for their *Tirthaṅkaras*. Hence it should not be surprising to learn that both Confucius and Lao Tzu, having been deified and made the center of cultic religions, should also have omniscience attributed to them. Wang Ch'ung, however, debunks the notion altogether.

There are some things that cannot be known, whether by Taoist intuition or by reward from the spirits for proper observance of magical rites or by Confucianist pursuit of learning. In this concept of the radically unknowable a newcomer for most of Eurasia by this time, or is it another older idea resurfacing? We suspect, without means of proof or disproof, that this is just another echo of the *via negativa* that has already almost completely dominated philosophizing everywhere by this time, but especially in reference to God, Ultimate Reality, or the Absolute, as well as ascetic discipline, all of which Wang thought was unnecessary. According to him knowledge of the truth does not depend on prescience of a superhuman kind such as Confucius and the pre-Confucian Sage Kings were supposed to have had. Truth, in short, is the fruit of hard work, not of idle speculation or indulgence in magic and superstition. There are no short cuts. Perspiration is more important than inspiration or revelation; otherwise exasperation and you end up nowhere!

Wang is really not interested in proofs as such; rather, by appeals to common sense and by using vivid metaphors, he seeks only to awaken his fellow men to reasonableness in all things. Thus, while he is unsparing in ridicule of certain excesses, especially those of superstitions and deadening empty tradition, he does admire unreservedly those whose scholarship is thorough and done with a sincere purpose. But again experience and erudition are equally important. Wang is not an extremist. He wants to avoid useless pedantry but at the same time he does not sanction depending on spontaneity and one's own ideas alone, for it is not the rational way, not the truly human way. Experience and eloquence joined to learning are still not enough. Practicality, comprehensiveness, coherence, and sincerity of feeling are also required, for Wang is not a heartless rationalist but a true well-rounded humanist withal.

Intellectuals, poets, historians, essayists, and scholars all have a responsibility to society, and even though many if not most Taoists preferred contemplation in the beautiful mountain solitudes to service to the emperor, Wang Ch'ung remained true to the best of Confucian humanist tradition in insisting that they were in the wrong and that one's efforts are due to the state. When anything goes wrong, it is their duty to attempt to set it right. The popular preference for antiquity may be one of the reasons why the Mediterranean also ceased to be fruitful of new things during the same centuries; but according to Wang, the past and the present are of equal value, and if anything the present offers a living challenge which the past does not.

In most contexts we have stressed, and perhaps even overstressed, the decadence of the later years of both the Former and the Later Han, and we can still hold to this reading of the total situation. Indeed, it fits nicely with the basic Chinese philosophy of history in which the cyclic view of rise and decline of dynasties is affirmed and studied rather carefully. However, we do not wish to be misunderstood. Simply because there was decadence at the end of each cycle of the Former and Later Han Dynasty we must not infer that both cycles were dominated by decadence all the way through. Quite the contrary, there were many brilliant achievements during these centuries such that many have seldom been excelled since.

If Wang Ch'ung could have met some of his global contemporaries, what sort of *entretiens* would it have been ? Would the mystical Philo have been shocked at Wang's iconoclastic spirit? Would Wang have rejected Philo's mysticism as sheer superstition and bunk, a waste of human effort to allegorize obsolete scriptures, just as he had disparaged the cults of Confucius, Lao Tzu and other worthies of his own geographical area ? Would Nāgārjuna have shared Wang's scepticism, at least with some detachment, even if without appreciating his levity or his tinkering with "scientific toys" instead of struggling over logical puzzles and meditation on—Nothing? How unfortunate that Plutarch could not have included Wang in his biographical anthology, although there were, we must remember,

Chinese biographers who would have relished Plutarch's own story. Apollonius of Tyana would probably have been more impressed with some of Wang's (uninvited) Taoist guests, necromancers, magicians, and miracle-mongers, anxious to see which could out do the others in controlling the supernatural. Seneca, very polite, dignified and reserved, listening more than talking, no doubt would have invited Wang to come back to Rome with him, outwardly showing no elation at having met — an honest man. And if Wang met some disciple of the Sceptic Aenesidemus, such as Agrippa, there would have been such an animated exchange of *bons mots* between them that one would have hesitated to interrupt.

Hopefully our survey has shown that excellent though Forke's comparison of Wang Ch'ung with Lucretius, it might be still more apposite to compare him with some of the Sceptics, but probably best to put him into sharp contrast also with those with definitely mystical tendencies. Once again we have found, not a mystical West and a materialist East — that may belong to the fourth quarter of the twentieth century — nor a mystical East and a materialist West, but a very mixed up West and also a very mixed up (Chinese) East, both in very similar economic, social and political straits and producing a very wide range of types of philosophies and philosophers.

Finally for Wang Ch'ung, we would avoid both extremes of interpretation of romantic espousal as a revolutionary and condemnation as just another old fuddy Confucianist after all. Even though he had his brighter moments, in his fatalism he left little room for hope, and in spite of his ridicule of some superstitions, he still had quite a few himself. But he does exemplify the doubting spirit of nonconclusiveness and openness — though in Wang more as a social debunker than as a theologian, metaphysician, or historian — that is also found in Philo, Nāgārjuna, and Sextus Empiricus.

III. Interiority (200-325)

Introduction

Interiority, mysticism and esoterics became dominant characteristics throughout Eurasia from about the second century A.D. Was this because of a failure of nerve, as Nietzsche puts it, in regard to the external natural world available through the scientific method, and failure also — as may happen again in our own time — to come to grips or even to comprehend the social and political realities of the time, coupled with retreat into individualism and searching for the meaning of life, a meaning which could not be found with reference to this world only? Or was it that, having included all of these to a very high degree, the capstone of the arch was still needed to make the structure firm, i.e., mysticism at the apex of the whole architectonic? Or was it that having exhausted (at least in their own perspectives) other resources, philosophers concentrated on these interior aspects of human existence and explored realms not within the reach of externalized modern life? Probably the truth lies somewhere within these extremes. On the one hand, interiority can be just as scientifically explored as exteriority once the observer-consciousness is identified as pivotal for both — and this was one of the great contributions of Vijñānavāda, although one finds presages of it everywhere even before Vasubandhu, Plotinus, and Wang Pi — but, on the other hand, this is easily confused with the seductive practices of magic and may finally degenerate into outright superstition (and this is true even for today). Such pursuits should not be an escape from acceptance of public responsibility, for which reason we continue to admire Seneca, Marcus Aurelius, Ma Jung, Pan Ku, Hsü Kan and the other Han Confucianists considerably more than those of their contemporaries who spent so much time and energy on alchemy astrology, numerology, rites of mystery cults, and even black magic.

Along with the other trends, is monotheism emerging? With Philo and Numenius and most of the Stoics, yes, to a remarkable degree; but not among the Epicureans, and certainly not among the Sceptics. In India, it would be difficult to call Nāgārjuna a monotheist, although there might be and actually were monotheistic interpretations of later Vijñānavāda with the cult of Mañjuśrī and the other *Bodhisattvas,* especially Amida. Also, the *Gītā* tradition and even the Śaiva tradition tended from henotheism towards monotheism. But with both the Han Confucianists and the Neo-Taoists, the issue is not so sharply defined. They would find a theism difficult to accept which asserts that what cannot be done within the natural harmony of the things of nature (Heaven, earth, man) can and is done by God. Having no Hellenic or Hebraic resentment against necessity, virtually all Chinese philosophers of the later Han, including Hsün Yüeh and Wang Ch'ung, needed nothing beyond it since ultimately how could there be any conflict between harmony and necessity either in natural phenomena or in human conduct ? Eccentricity was easily tolerated, but that which is contrary to nature is very strange and even punishably wrong.

What may be observed is that out of the long and variegated mixtures of cynicism, eclectism, syncretism and resort to esoterics there is the slow emergence of monistic trends. Even though this trend is strong in Numenius, it was already in Philo; but it will not emerge as completely dominate until Scotus Erigena. Likewise in India and China there is a long history from the *Questions of Milinda* to Śaṅkara, and from Yang Hsiung to Han Yu and Li Ao.

A. Plotinus and Vasubandhu

Introduction

In considering Neo-Platonism before Plotinus, we may especially note Numenius of Apameia (c. 175). Virtually everything that Numenius contributed Plotinus adopted, so much so indeed that Plotinus was accused of plagiarizing from him. Numenius also exemplifies the age in that his syncretism is scarcely less than that of the Gnostics.

Numenius traced the history of the Platonists and accused them of having wrongly become sceptics, completely at odds with the true Plato. Perhaps as a result of his indebtedness to Diogenes Laertius and/or Plutarch, Numenius' monism and mysticism are not anti-historical. Rather he strives to place himself in the stream of history by reviewing the development of Neo-Platonism and giving critical accounts of the transition from Plato through Carneades and the "schism" of Philo of Larissa.

In his work *On the Good* Numenius says he is going to discuss not only Pythagoras and Plato, but also "the doctrines of famous nations which agree with Plato, especially those of Brahmans, Jews, Magi, and Egyptians." It seems that it was rather the rule than the exception for philosophers in the Roman Empire to include views reputedly if not actually from "points further East". However, there was a shift since the time of Pyrrho's Scepticism from the anti-metaphysical tendencies of Theravāda to the extreme idealism of Vijñānavāda. Numenius had such a favorable opinion of these "nations" because they believed in an incorporeal God. If by Orientalism we mean knowledge of or sympathy for Oriental wisdom — Sāṃkhya, Yoga, Vaiśeṣika, Nyāya, Jainism, Theravāda, Śūnyavāda, Vijñānavāda, Gītā, etc.: we do wish that those of antiquity as well as modern writers would be more specific ! — then Numenius was an Orientalist. If, however, we mean by Orientalism being influenced by Oriental doctrines to such an extent as to try to incorporate them into Greek philosophy or interpret Greek philosophy in relation to them, then there are only a few traces of Orientalism in either Numenius or Plotinus.

Numenius stressed Plato's "Second Letter" as pivotal to right interpretation even though the doctrine of the three Gods therein is ascribed to Socrates and not to Plato himself. This is also the Socrates-Plato which Plotinus adopts and from which he derives his three hypostases which, of course, influenced the development of the Christian Trinitarian doctrine profoundly. Thus Numenius, if for no other reason, is a very important link in the chain of history.

Numenius' First God roughly corresponds to the *nirguṇa* Brahman concept or the *śūnya* concept of the Mādhyamika, or the *Yahwe* concept of Hebraic heritage, or (although with some reservations) the Supreme Tao of such Taoists as Wei Po-Yang, or perhaps best of all to the *Dharmakāya* or *Tathatā* concept in Mahāyāna in general. The Second God is more comparable to the *saguṇa* Brahman of the *Upaniṣads*, or the *Nirmāṇakāya* of Mahāyāna in general, or the *teh* of the Taoist tradition in the larger framework. Finally, the Third God is more like the *antaryāmi* concept of the *Upaniṣads* or the *Sambhogakāya* of general Mahāyāna, or the *yin-yang* of Taoist tradition since if we omit reference to *teh* (as many commentators do in the late Han) then the Second God would be the other side of the *yin-yang* coin, so to speak. One of the chief differences between Numenius and Plotinus seems to have developed around the nature and function of the Second God.

If the First God is to be considered too exalted for description and all of that, then the question, as always, arises as to how God can be known. Numenius' answer is the classical one for all mystics, east, west, north, south, modern or ancient: detachment from all finite thing until enlightenment is attained spontaneously. Whether for Numenius this means mystical ecstasy, as it obviously does in Plotinus, or *nirvāṇa*, or the *dhyāna* of both Buddhist and Hindu meditational traditions, is difficult to determine.

That Numenius professes the doctrine of reincarnation (metempsychosis) can be interpreted in many ways. Plato himself professed it, although there is little evidence that Aristotle accepted it, and the Stoics generally are silent about it, even though later on Origen, Christian withal, saw no objection to it. We could hypothesize that it was a primordial Indo-European concept which fell into abeyance in some areas and not in others, while with the Cārvākas and the Epicureans it was treated as nonsense. Numenius could just as well have taken it from Plato as from the Buddhists, Hindus or Jainas. China had nothing like it until the entrance of Buddhism there. The Confucianists never did accept it, merely continuing the cult of ancestors, while the Taoists either saw no need for it, having their own conceptions of "continuation", or else merely tried to get longevity in this life. Numenius had a wide variety of views to choose from whatever his sources or influences may have actually been. Thus the possibility of fresh influence from India is open though nothing is conclusive.

The Neo-Pythagoreanism which Numenius included in his syncretistic amalgam was quite esoteric. Its numerology had degenerated into gross superstition, and no doubt Numenius was as much taken in by the Elusinian Mysteries as by the logic of Aristotle. He was curious about exotica from the Orient, but such was the trend of the times. The Sceptics were losing ground even more than the Epicureans and the Stoics, just as the more rationalistic schools in India and China were also continually yielding ground to Mahāyāna idealism and the mysticism of Taoist yoga.

The **Neo-Pythagorean** tradition under which Apollonius of Tyana had had his ascetic training was the chief rival to Neo-Platonism and was often confused with it. Often as not the two were even blended together among both pagans and Christians. Also, Neo-Pythagoreanism was almost a rival to Christianity, many of its beliefs and practices being quite in harmony with Christian doctrines and offering something considerably more rational than what the Gnostics had to offer, even though sometimes no less esoteric.

Of the two major branches of Mahāyāna Buddhism, the Mādhyamika or Śūnyavāda is best represented by Nāgārjuna while the Yogācāra or Vijñānavāda is best represented by Vasubandhu. This second school is known as Yogācāra because it emphasizes the use of yoga for the attainment of enlightenment.

and also as Vijñānavāda because it espouses the idealistic position that reality is cognition (*vijñāna*) only. Yogācāra can be seen as only a modification of Mādhyamika since the two schools do not differ radically in basic tenets, only in emphasis. There are three different aspects or emphases among the various Buddhist schools regarding the attainment of enlightenment : meditation, morality, and wisdom. Nāgārjuna belongs to the wisdom school and Vasubandhu to the meditation school. Morality tended not to become a question of controversy until the arrival of Tantra. The Mādhyamikas engage in a ruthless dialectic by which they arrive at the 'emptiness' of the world of dualities. The Yogācārins engage in the practice of yoga to achieve the same goal. One reason for the development of the Yogācāra school was that there was the danger that some Buddhists would substitute cleverness, dialectical skill, and erudition for enlightenment; thus the Yogācārins countered this danger by urging an exploration of spiritual states via yoga.

It is not easy to locate the beginnings of the Yogācāra school, and the beginnings of other schools for that matter, partly because all the Buddhist schools ultimately trace their teachings back to the Buddha himself, and partly because of the tradition of impersonality, i.e., the sage considers himself to be a small part of a large tradition and he is not interested in fame and copyrights. It would be the irony of ironies if a Buddhist *ācārya* tried in any way to "cling" to his own teachings. Maitreyanātha (270-350) is the founder of the Yogācāra school, to the extent that anyone can be taken as the founder. But even before Maitreyanātha there are several *sūtras* which contain most of the basic ideas characteristic of the school: *Sandhinirmocana*, *Laṅkāvatāra*, *Avataṁśaka*, and *Abhisamayālaṅkāra*. Maitreyanātha was the teacher of Asaṅga, who is taken by a few as the greatest of the Yogācārins. However, most think that Asaṅga's brother, Vasubandhu, who is also known as "the second Buddha", is the greater.

Vasubandhu was first a Theravādin, belonging to the Sautrāntika school. During that time he composed his *Abhidharmakoṣa*, a treatment of the *Abhidharma* which is no less renown than his best known works relating Vijñānavāda, the *Viṁśatikā* and the *Triṁśikā*, which he wrote after espousing Vijñānavāda at the urging of his brother, Asaṅga. The Sautrāntika school holds the doctrine of indirect realism or representationism. This is like the view of John Locke : we do not know "things" directly but only know our ideas of things. Berkeley emerged from this view as an idealist, as did Vasubandhu ". . . Vasubandhu is the only *ācārya* who enjoys equal prestige as an exponent of the two main branches of Buddhist tradition. With one foot planted firmly on the side of the Great, the other on the side of the Little, Vehicle, he bestrides mediaeval Indian Buddhism 'like a Colossus'."[1]

Scheme and Explanation

The guiding intent of our treatment of Plotinus and Vasubandhu is to suggest the many similarities between their respective cosmological schemes. One result of the comparison hopefully will be to show that in principle and spirit Plotinus and Vasubandhu agree on man's nature and destiny, and on the nature of the universe, even though they may disagree on details.

In outline, Plotinus' cosmological scheme is as follows : from the One proceeds Intelligence, from Intelligence proceeds the Soul, from the Soul proceeds the souls, and through the agency of the Soul and souls comes the sensible world. Matter is the final term in this hierarchical procession. In outline, Vasubandhu's cosmological scheme is as follows: *Vijñaptimātra* gives rise to the *Ālayavijñāna* or simply the *Ālaya*, the *Ālaya* gives rise to *Manas*, from *Manas* we proceed to the egos and then to the subject-object duality we call the sensible world. The final term in this hierarchical scheme is, in a negative sense, non-substance, i.e., there is not posited any kind of matter out of which the world is made. These parallel models may be seen more clearly in the following arrangement :

the One	*Vijñaptimātra*
Intelligence	*Ālayavijñāna*
the Soul	Manas
souls	egos, subjects

sensible world	sensible world
matter	no matter

It is not our intent to turn Plotinus into a Yogācārin or Vasubandhu into a Neo-Platonist; but it does seem that it would be difficult to find two thinkers, near contemporaries, in different cultures, who resemble each other more. Though the parallel terms in these schemes are not entirely synonymous, their functions in the schemes as a whole are quite comparable.

Plotinus did not write systematically, that is, begin at the beginning and continue step by step to the logical end, saving the last for last. Each of his *Enneads* treats of his entire scheme, though emphasis may be on one part rather than the others. The reason for this is also the reason why any exposition of Plotinus or Vasubandhu is difficult to begin: each term of the cosmological scheme contains or implies every other term. The one cannot be fully defined until matter and the other hypostases have also been defined. And so with Vasubandhu, the subject-object duality of the sensible world cannot be understood without the *Ālaya* and its function, and vice versa, for each term in the scheme is defined or explained or contained in all the other terms. There is really nothing surprising in this since such a problem in exposition is common to complete metaphysical systems, something we rarely see nowadays, which would mean to Plotinus and Vasubandhu that nothing ever really gets explained in most of contemporary philosophizing.

One way to approach philosophers might be to discern what they intend by an explanation or when they consider something to have been explained. Plotinus and Vasubandhu seem to mean two things by an explanation. First, the term to be explained must be seen in a total scheme, a universal scheme from which nothing is excluded. It is something of the universe in a grain of sand idea. Until a question is seen against the background of the One or the *Vijñaptimātra*, it cannot be truly and fully answered, no matter how many possibilities or probabilities or relative truths are given. Secondly, an answer or explanation, if philosophically important, is of the spiritual order and has a spiritually practical aspect. One understands when one sees not only how something fits into the metaphysical scheme but also what it means in terms of attaining enlightenment. For example, the Intelligence is only partly explained by showing its position and function as the hypostasis between the One and the Soul, and so with the *Ālaya* between the *Vijñapatimātra* and *Manas*. It still must be shown what the Intelligence and the *Ālaya* mean vis-à-vis the attainment of enlightenment. For Plotinus and Vasubandhu the universe isn't just there and functioning in an orderly way, period (the metaphysical scheme of things); but man has a destiny which is to be understood and attained through that universe, and therefore metaphysics and spirituality are two aspects of the same thing.

The One and Vijñaptimātra

The One is unthinkable, ineffable, beyond the reach of thought; it cannot be an object to us as subjects. Our attempts at designating it are at best metaphors. The one is Plotinus' first hypostasis, and from it proceeds or emanates all of the other hypostases; thus, it is the Source of everything. It is itself, however, entirely self-sufficient and has no source. The other hypostases are dependent on the One, but it is Freedom and is without dependency of any kind.

Everything below the One has multiplicity, and multiplicity implies unity; so the One is the ultimate Unity. Multiplicity is imperfection, and imperfection implies the perfection of the One. Only the One is absolutely perfect because only the One is Unity. Still, the One is not to be considered separate from its productions. It exists everywhere and nowhere; it is transcendent and immanent. W. R. Inge suggests that it might have been called the Zero instead of the One if the Greeks had had a word for zero.

The One is without the subject-object duality which characterizes other hypostases. It is the Pure Subject, "Pure" here meaning without an object. It is Thought, and the goal of the philosopher's spiritual quest, the ultimate destiny. The One is equally the True, the Good, and the Beautiful.

The *Vijñaptimātra* is indescribable, ineffable, unthinkable, beyond language and beyond experience (in terms of one particular experience among others). Asaṅga, the brother of Vasubandhu and fellow Yogācārin, said: "It can neither be called existence nor non-existence. It is neither such nor otherwise. It is neither born nor destroyed. It neither increases nor decreases. It is neither purity nor filth. Such is the real *lakṣaṇa* or nature of the transcendental truth."[2] The *Vijñaptimātra* is the Source and Ground of all transformations, or everything real. It is unchangeable and yet is both immanent and transcendent to its transformations, that is, the *Vijñaptimātra* is not to be considered as something existing above and beyond its transformations in an almost deistic sense. All transformations of the *Vijñaptimātra* are dependent on it and unreal apart from it, while it is independent, self-sufficient, and the only Reality.

The *Vijñapatimātra* is variously called Mind-only, Thought-only, Consciousness-only; it is Pure Thought, Pure Consciousness, Pure Subject, the Universal Self. It is not subject to change and is not characterized by subject-object duality or multiplicity found in discursive thought and at all other levels of reality. As pure bliss and omniscience, it is the goal of the yogin, *nirvāṇa*, and is attainable only through spiritual experience. As pure bliss it is not subject to change, for change is suffering (First Noble Truth, *pratityasamutpāda*). The *Vijñaptimātra* is Goodness, Eternity, Liberation. Vasubandu said:

> This is the realm of passionlessness or purity,
> Which is beyond description, is good, and is eternal,
> Where one is in the state of emancipation, peace, and joy.
> This is the law of the Great Buddha.[3]

Just as it was suggested that Plotinus might have called the One the Zero (or something comparable) instead, so indeed the *Vijñaptimātra* is called *śūnya*, the word for zero, but translated as "emptiness".

Vasubandhu's description of the *Vijñaptimātra* could virtually have been Plotinus' description of the One; however, it could also be taken as the description of many of the ineffable absolutes found in various cultures throughout history, Brahman and Tao, for example. Once an ultimate is considered to be ineffable, indescribable, and unthinkable, it is very difficult to see how to distinguish that ultimate from other such ultimates, for any adjectives or qualities attributed to such ultimates have only relative validity. The One and the *Vijñaptimātra* cannot be objects of thought and are beyond discursive thought; but both affirmation and negation are within the realm of discursive thought, so in some senses it makes no difference what we either attribute to or deny of these absolutes, especially if our goal is to make literally and absolutely true assertions about them, for such assertions on the theories of Vasubandhu and Plotinus are always inadequate. Indeed, are not the very concepts of indescribability and ineffability still within the realm of discursive thought ? Calling the ultimate beyond language and then continuing to discuss it is reminiscent of the quip associated with Santayana that there is no God and Mary is His mother.

To say that the One and the *Vijñaptimātra* are quite comparable does not at this point seem to be saying much. However, there are two reasons for saying that they are more comparable than some of the other ineffable ultimates. First, Plotinus and Vasubandhu agree that one can make relatively true and very meaningful assertions about the One and the *Vijñaptimātra* respectively, contrasting somewhat with, for example, the view that the Tao which can be spoken of is not the real Tao. From our position of unenlightenment, such assertions are of the nature of metaphors, not literally true, but enlightening when understood. Such assertions are like a statue or image of a god in a holy place: though none of our attempts at representation may literally apply to the One or to the *Vijñaptimātra*, still it is helpful to have such representations; still the statue or image, though not the god, is not without value in attempting to reach the god. And the assertions, metaphors, 'statues' and 'images' which Plotinus and Vasubandhu choose to give as applicable to their respective ultimates are very similar, as seen above. Secondly, whatever the content of these ultimates, their functions in the cosmological schemes and the spiritual life of the aspirant are very similar, as will be seen more clearly later.

Why did Plotinus choose to call the ultimate "the One" ? Why did Vasubandhu choose to call the ultimate "*Vijñaptimātra*" ? The One is the pure Subject without an object; the *Vijñaptimātra* is Consciousness-only, without an object. In this sense the One could just as well be called *Vijñaptimātra*; the *Vijñaptimātra* could just as well be called the One. "One" is not a numerical designation here; it means Unity. Any hint of a subject-object duality or multiplicity is an indication of imperfection. Here we might make a passing contrast with Sāṃkhya wherein *prakṛti* and *puruṣa* are two eternal, mutually exclusive, co-existing ultimates. But for Plotinus and Vasubandhu, any multiplicity implies a ground for that multiplicity — they could not accept the Sāṃkhyan dualism. Since the major prerequisite for perfection is Unity, Plotinus called the ultimate the One and Vasubandhu called it Consciousness-*only*.

So much for the theme of Unity; but why designate the ultimate as Consciousness, Subject, Thought ? One reason indicated in Conze's following observations about the Yogācārins seems to apply equally well to Plotinus :

> They intended to point to a spot in the world, to a dimension of self-awareness, where we are most likely to find it [the ultimate]. In all our experience, an object stands out against a subject. ... Just as the blade of a knife cannot cut itself, so we cannot experience consciousness directly as an object in front of us. For as soon as we turn to the subject, it becomes an object and ceases to be the subject. ... The final subject — which might be at the end of the infinite regress — is completely beyond our experience, it is not really of this world, it is transcendental. To try to get to it would be to attempt the impossible. This is exactly what the Yogācārins set themselves out to do.[4]

Here again we have the problem of the ineffable and a resort to what we rather loosely have called metaphors. The philosopher cannot through discursive thought lay the ultimate out before you, but he can point to that in the world which may be a doorway to the ultimate. The (seeming) discrepancy or distance between the world and the ultimate is so great that the task may seem impossible indeed. After all, how is one supposed to understand consciousness without that of which it is conscious or a subject without an object in relation to which it is a subject ? As we shall see later, the impossibility of clearly and distinctly conceiving the ultimate will be for Vasubandhu one reason for going on a path other than reason, while for Plotinus this very impossibility will prove to be the essential element in his dialectical method for attaining the ultimate. Some other reasons for the designations of Consciousness, Thought, and Subject should become apparent as we examine the other hypostases.

The Ālaya and the Intelligence

By its inherent power (*śakti*) the *Vijñaptimātra* undergoes the transformation of the *Ālayavijñāna*. However, as eternal and unchangeable, the *Vijñaptimātra* cannot really suffer transformation, so it is better to speak of the *Ālaya* as both the first transformation of the *Vijñaptimātra* and as the *Vijñaptimātra* itself *qua* transformation. The Consciousness-only which suffers transformation is the *Ālaya*, and the *Ālaya* is the first transformation of the Consciousness-only. The *Ālaya* is also considered to be indescribable and incomprehensible without at least near-enlightenment. The *Ālaya* or Great Storehouse of Consciousness or Store-consciousness has been given various and often contradictory interpretations, so much so that Conze makes the judgment that "As worked out by the Yogâcârins, the concept of a Store-consciousness is far from intelligible, and it has led to little more than ardent discussions."[5]

The *Vijñaptimātra* as Unity cannot itself account for multiplicity; thus it is suggested that the Yogâcārins posited the *Ālaya* as a means of accounting for multiplicity. In one sense the *Ālaya* is a positing by the Absolute of an "Otherness" from which shall evolve a multiplicity of egos. Such a process is suggestive of some German Idealists, e.g., Fichte.

The *Ālaya* is variously called the cosmic mind, self-evolving thought, receptacle consciousness. In a micro-macrocosm frame of reference, it is the Stream of the Consciousness shared by each individual stream of consciousness, the Collective Unconscious behind each individual consciousness, the Cosmic Mind expressed in each individual mind. By analogy, it is *saguṇa* Brahman, the *Vijñaptimātra* being *nirguṇa* Brahman.

The *Ālaya* is called the All-Conserving Mind or the Great Storehouse because it contains seeds (*bījas*) and dispositions (*vāsanās*) the fruition of which yields all *dharmas*, both subjective and objective. Everything in the world can eventually be traced back to the seeds and dispositions in the *Ālaya*. But the seeds and dispositions in the *Ālaya* can also be traced back to the world, for they are the results of the past experiences of all individuals. They may be considered as potential karmic forces which are the result of previously actualized potential karmic forces. This depositing of seeds and their fruition is an eternal and beginningless process.

The seeds and dispositions may be either good or bad. In the *Ālaya* they are to be seen as potentiality and definitely as non-material. The seeds are "constructive instincts" or "germs" and the cause of all *dharmas*, which are their effects. *Vāsanā* or dispositions may be seen as an influence left behind after its source is no longer existent, like the fragrance of a flower after the flower is gone; but then as a constructive force the *vāsanā* has the form of a seed. In this view *bijas* and *vāsanās* are virtually the same thing from different perspectives. Another view is that while seeds result from specific events and experiences, the *vāsanās* are the general dispositions or "habit-energies" or tendencies of the *Ālaya* which have obtained at any given point in the process or which reflect the nature of the *Ālaya* as such. In any event, through its seeds and dispositions the *Ālaya* is the cause of all which comes after it (logically and structurally "after"). There is nothing in the world which was not first in the *Ālaya*.

The second hypostasis in Plotinus' scheme is callled *Nous*, which has been translated as the Intelligence, Spirit, Reason, Mind and Intellectual-Principle. It is the realm of the Ideas in the Platonic system; and as in Plato, the sensible world in Plotinus is a copy of the Ideas. There is nothing in the sensible world which is not also in the intelligible world, the Intelligence. It is, so to speak, all possible worlds in the abstract, containing the Pure Forms with which the sensible world is informed. Indeed, the Intelligence is virtually the sensible world minus time, materiality, and exteriority.

It is with the Intelligence that we first encounter Being in Plotinus' scheme. The One is above Being; at the other end of the hierarchy, matter is below Being. The Ideas are the only real or full Being, and that which follows is merely a copy. When the Intelligence proceeds from the One, it "is" not, there is no Being, until it turns back and contemplates the One. The process has been explained thus : "Two stages may. . . be distinguished in the self-creation of Intelligence. . .; in the former, that of Procession (*prohodos*), formless, infinite stream of life flows forth from the One; in the latter, that of Reversion (*epistrophé*), it turns back, contemplates the One, and so receives form and order."[6] There is no Being until there is a subject-object duality, until there is thinking or contemplation, for Being and contemplation are identical.

The Intelligence is thinking thinking about thinking, or thought thinking itself, or thought turned toward itself, as in Aristotle. The Intelligence thus has itself as an object and so in the Intelligence the subject-object duality does obtain whereas it does not in the One, for the One is not thought thinking itself but Thought-only. Still, the subject-object duality in the Intelligence is such only ideally. The Ideas of the Intelligence are not to be considered as a group or series of separate realities. A tendency to think thusly results from thinking spatially and of materiality; but the Ideas are not spatial, temporal or material. "The intelligible world is a world in which 'every being contains all things within itself and sees all things in the other. All is everywhere. All is all'."[7]

Concerning the many similarities between the Intelligence and the *Ālaya*, most obviously they both have the same positions in the cosmological schemes; both are the first evolute, emanation, procession, or transformation from the respective ultimates. Secondly, they have essentially the same functions : they have the ability to account for and to offer the multiplicity needed for a world; they are the ways and means of getting a world out of an ineffable ultimate. In a sense they both mediate between the One and the many. The Intelligence is itself on the verge of non-multiplicity; though multiplicity is to be found therein, it is almost nominal. This is not so true of the *Ālaya*; however, it is said to be "indifferent" to its multiplicity, and its distinction from the *Vijñaptimātra* seems to be almost entirely a functional one. The multiplicity in the *Ālaya* is a multiplicity of potentialities, not of actualities.

The Intelligence's contemplation of the One is synonymous with giving rise to Being. Although the *Ālaya* does not strictly contemplate the *Vijñaptimātra*, it is fair to say that Being is first to be found in the *Ālaya* and not in the *Vijñaptimātra*. Another point of similarity is that both hypostases are presented in an idealistic perspective; having now been presented with two hypostases, we still have only thoughts, ideas, consciousnesses, minds, contemplations and thinkings, and as it turns out that is all we shall ever "really" have. A final point of comparison : though the Ideas of the Intelligence and the seeds-dispositions of the *Ālaya* are certainly not precisely the same, they can be seen to perform similar functions : only in relation to them is there a world, and there is nothing in the world which was not or is not in them. A difference between Plotinus and Vasubandhu is beginning to be present here. With "the Intelligence" and "Ideas" Plotinus definitely has more emphasis on reason and rationality than is found in Vasubandhu, and this difference shall become most apparent when we discuss their respective methods for attaining the ultimate.

Manas and the Soul

The transformation of the *Ālaya* from the *Vijñaptimātra* is called the *vipāka* transformation. The *Ālaya* itself undergoes a twofold transformation : the *manana* transformation is the production of Mind, Self, Soul, or Subject called *Manas*; the *viṣayavijñapti* transformation is the production of the world, of all objects. As a logical sequence rather than a temporal one, the *manana* transformation comes first, and then the *viṣaya-vijñapti*, for *Manas* is the agency by which the world is manifested from the *Ālaya*. The *viṣaya-vijñapti* transformation consists of *vijñānas*, which are cognitions, ideations, consciousnesses, mental facts and events which comprise both terms of any subject-object duality and thus which comprise the world. The *vipāka* transformation is the *Ālaya* as potentiality while the *manana* and the *viṣaya-vijñapti* transformations are the *Ālaya* in its actuality.

Manas is consciousness, but consciousness involved with *avidyā* : false identity and ignorance. Consciousness without *avidyā* is the *Vijñaptimātr*, and indeed beginningless *avidyā* is the force which causes the transformations of the *Ālaya*. The unconsciousness of the *Ālaya* is more to be contrasted with the false consciousness of *Manas*, not with the Consciousness that is the *Vijñaptimātra*. Vasubandhu recognizes eight kinds of *vijñānas*: *Ālayavijñāna*, *pravṛtti-vijñāna* (*Manas*), *mano-vijñāna*, and the five senses. The *mano-vijñāna* is actually considered to be one of the senses, thus raising the number to six. It may be defined as thinking and performs such mental functions as memory and judgment. But it is *Manas* which is responsible for the illusion of an external world and an ego. As the projector of an apparent external world of objects, *Manas* is consciousness, *mano-vijñāna*, and the five senses; but since internal states are just as much objects to a subject as external objects themselves, *Manas* is really consciousness only.

We can view *Manas* from two perspectives : in its association with *avidyā* and without *avidyā* :

> ... it is capable of enlightenment. It is due to its ignorance only that it tenaciously clings to the conception of ego and contaminates the whole mentation with its onerous prejudices. As soon as it realises the full import of the *Ālaya*, it is denuded of its egoistic prejudices and opens the way *to nirvāṇa*. *Manas*, therefore, is the pivot on which turn our spiritual deliverance and subjective ignorance.[8]

Here we confront the problem af *anātman*, "no-soul", one of the most difficult of Buddhist theories. The *Ālaya* is unconscious, and it is only with *Manas* that consciousness and duality in the fullest sense obtain. Without *Manas* there would be no individuality; it is the cause of self-consciousness. So we note that even though Buddhists typically deny the reality of a soul, there is still a something which is a causal agent and which strives for and attains *nirvāṇa* and experiences bliss. So *Manas* can be seen, depending on its association or non-association with *avidyā*, both as the empirical ego involved in illusion and as "the no-soul which attains *nirvāṇa*". One might suspect that *Manas* without *avidyā* is no-soul in the same way that the *Vijñaptimātra* and the One are indescribable and ineffable. One might suspect that the *neti neti*, the *via negativa*, and the *anātman* doctrines are similarily motivated :

whereof one cannot speak without misleading, thereof one should remain silent — or negate. However, we shall leave open for interpretation the question of just how much reality can be attributed to the no-soul and thus to what extent the Buddhist *anātman* can or cannot be turned into the Hindu *ātman*, though we should remark that there is a definite line between Vasubandhu and Śaṅkara.

Manas is said to reflect on the *Ālaya* and to take the *Ālaya* to be its real self. The real *Manas* is consciousness, the false *Manas* is self-consciousness, i.e., anything of which one can be conscious and which therefore one might take as an identity is a modification of the *Ālaya* and cannot possibly be the true self. Identity as an object of one's consciousness is always a false identity. Here it is important to realize that what we call mental states and qualities are also transformations of the *Ālaya*. The true self (anātman ?), the enlightened *Manas*, is not something of which one can be conscious for it is Consciousness itself. *Manas* is very much like *puruṣa* in Sāṃkhya in that *puruṣa* is said to take its reflection in *prakṛti* as its real self rather than realizing that it is entirely free of *prakṛti*.

As the third hypostasis, the Soul proceeds from, and is a copy of, the Intelligence. However, Plotinus' concept of Soul must be seen on three different levels. The third hypostasis is the World Soul; it is below the Intelligence and above the sensible world. It is the Demiurge which fashions the world, informs the world, with the Forms contained in the Intelligence. Above the World Soul as Demiurge there is another Soul or part of the World Soul which remains in the Intelligence : "The primal part of the Soul is above. It remains there always close to the summit in a state of fullness and eternal illumination, and it is the first to participate in the intelligible. The other part of the Soul, which participates in the first, proceeds eternally, a second life issued from the first . ..."[9] Thirdly, Plotinus posits the individual souls which inform individual bodies. Some souls after informing the bodies are drawn to them and thus entrapped. So the Soul spans the spectrum from the fallen souls to the Demiurgic Soul to the eternally undefiled illuminated Soul.

The Soul's production of the world is a reflection of itself. "It is the pride and audacity of the Soul which cause it to plunge into bodies. ... The Soul is not content to radiate. It is attracted by the reflection which it has produced."[10] As the Soul is attracted by the image of itself, it becomes isolated from the whole and becomes more and more attached to individuality. This attraction of the Soul for its image or reflection is likened to the myth of Narcissus and is characterized by self-love, attachment, and false identity. The production of the world is good and a natural result of the law of procession from the One; but the Soul oversteps its bounds when it enters into its production, falls into the sensible world, becomes entagled with false identity.

In noting some similarities between the Soul and *Manas* we may first recall that both are the third hypostasis in the respective schemes. The Soul creates, orders, or informs the world vis-à-vis the Intelligence; *Manas* is the agency responsible for the projection of *vijñānas* vis-à-vis the *Ālaya*. In both schemes the Soul and *Manas* are mediators between the sensible world as potential (the Intelligence, *Ālaya*) and the sensible world as actual. Not only are they responsible for creating the world, but both the Soul and *Manas* then get lost in their creations. Strictly speaking there is actually a slight contrast here between the Soul and *Manas*. *Manas* as the third hypostasis is already associated with *avidyā*, so its very transformation from the *Ālaya* is already a fall. The Soul, however, is not *per se* attached to its reflection in the sensible until after it has performed the act of creation, and apparently not every soul becomes so attached. The Soul as the third hypostasis is less perfect than the Intelligence, but it has not yet fallen to lower possible levels.

There is also a different emphasis in Plotinus and Vasubandhu as to why the Soul and *Manas* become involved with the sensible world. For Vasubandhu, "... the mind [*Manas*] is set in motion by the ignorant references to the mental elements as the self, and from this ignorance about the self is engendered self-love and egoism."[11] Here the emphasis is on ignorance (*avidyā*), with self-love and egoism following as a result. We might also note that "the mind is set in motion" is equivalent to thinking of *Manas* as separate from the *Ālaya*, which was not the case before the "motion", and as the creation of the world of subjects and objects. Again we note that the very activity of *Manas* presupposes the influence of *avidyā*. In Plotinus the Soul can inform the world without reference to imperfection. The Soul does not explicitly become attached to its image because of ignorance but because of self-love and egoism. Since self-love and egoism are certainly states of ignorance from the spiritual perspective, the distinction here between Plotinus and Vasubandhu is not very great. And it is true that both Plotinus and Vasubandhu say that it is because the Soul and *Manas* are ignorant of the nature of their true selves that they become attached to false selves. We might say that Plotinus sees the fall of the Soul as a result of pride while Vasubandhu sees it as a result of ignorance, a difference in emphasis which has had various cultural manifestations through the centuries.

The Soul and *Manas* are found in some sense at each level of the respective cosmological hierarchies. Both are involved with the sensible world, not only as its creator or as the Demiurge, but also in terms of a false identification. *Manas* reflects on the *Ālaya* — the *Ālaya* as not-*Manas* — and takes it as its real self, the result being the self as the object of self-consciousness, a false self. The Soul is attracted by its reflection in the sensible world and likewise becomes isolated and alienated from its true identity. Since *Manas* unassociated with *avidyā* can be found only ideally in the *Ālaya*, there is not a perfect parallel in Vasubandhu's scheme with Plotinus' World Soul; however, as creator *Manas* serves the same function as the World Soul. Since the Soul and *Manas* are due to a procession from or a transformation of the Intelligence and the *Ālaya* respectively, it follows that they are "in" those hypsotases; and Plotinus is quite specific about the Soul remaining in union with the Intelligence even while it also flows out eternally. As we shall see later, we must in some sense admit the Soul and *Manas* (without avidyā; *anātman*) to the respective ultimates also.

Though it is difficult to discern the boundaries of the Soul and Manas, and though it seems that they are found at each level of the hierarchies, there is an important sense in which they are not really found in the sensible world. *Manas* in its function as creator is the unity of consciousness behind the scenes. The self which is the object of self-consciousness is not the real *Manas* but a false self. The self of which I am conscious and which I in my ignorance take to be my real self is not the real self, nor is it *Manas*; yet such reflection is the result of *Manas* activated by *avidyā*, and such false identity is *Manas* taking the *Ālaya* as its self falsely. We could say that *Manas* is in the sensible world as a cause might be in the effect, such as the Unconscious being the cause of the conscious world and yet being found no where in it, which actually is the case with the *Ālaya* interpreted as the Collective Unconscious. The point is that we have to see *Manas* as being both in the sensible world and not in the sensible world. The same is true of the Soul in Plotinus. He refers to the Soul in the sensible world as a piece of gold covered with dirt or as a man covered with mud : wash away the defilement in Jaina-like fashion and there is that which in its essence never was really mixed with the defilement, only the defilement hid the purity. Plotinus used such metaphors "in order to preserve the soul from substantial change and emotional disturbance, in answer both to the Sceptics' charge that a being subject to these cannot be immortal and the Gnostics' admission of sin and ignorance into the spiritual world."[12] But Plotinus kept the Soul even more explicitly separated from the sensible world when he said that the Soul does not herself ever descend into the sensible but it is only an image of the Soul which descends. It is this image of the Soul which commits wrong and transmigrates. It seems to be the general consensus that Plotinus teaches two doctrines concerning the descent of the Soul one doctrine keeping the Soul entirely above the sensible world, the other allowing it to descend through its own vices.

We can then see the Soul and *Manas* not so much in the world but as sort of outside creators of the world. Now looking in the other direction, up toward the Intelligence and the *Ālaya*, we are hard put to make a strict distinction between them and the Soul and *Manas*. The *Ālaya* is the Subject without objects; Manas is the *Ālaya* as subject with objects. In other words, the *Ālaya* under the influence of *avidyā* becomes subject (*Manas*) and object (the sensible world). Again we are reminded of some German Idealisms. Although Plotinus makes a stricter sequential division so that the Soul proceeds before the sensible world, it isn't difficult to see the same separation of the Intelligence into subject and object in his procession.

As we move from the sensible world to the intelligible world in both schemes, we gain in simplicity and unity. Individuality, a multitude of individual subjects and objects, characterizes the sensible world, but the World Soul and *Manas* tend to be spoken of as one unity even though from them comes the multiplicity of the sensible world. However, although mystical union with the ultimate is the destiny of the individual soul, there is some not altogether clear sense in which individuality persists up to this union and thus persists not only in the Soul and *Manas* but also in the Intelligence and the *Ālaya*. One suspects that such individuality is not at all what we ordinarily think of as individuality. At any rate, the Soul and *Manas* are simpler and with less multiplicity than the sensible world. And the multitude of mental faculties, such as memory, understanding, desire, sensibility and emotion, disappear as the Soul and *Manas* return to the Intelligence and the *Ālaya* respectively. Of course there is nothing in the Soul and *Manas* which is not in the Intelligence and the *Ālaya*, but these faculties are there in a different sense, as Forms or potentialities-seeds-dispositions, not as functioning actualities.

The Sensible World

Vasubandhu explains the subject-object duality which is the sensible world (both internal and external) by referring to the dream metaphor. Objects, which are falsely considered to be outside of consciousness, and the ego, which sees itself in relation to objects of consciousness, are both the result of the dreaming subject, *Manas*. The active elements of objects, egos, and *Manas* are the *Ālaya* in a passive state. The subject-object duality which we take to be the real world has no more reality than a dream, though there is reality behind the dream. Just as the dream subject takes the dream objects to be entirely real, so we take our world of objects to be entirely real. As Vasubandhu said : "Before we have awakened we cannot know/ That what is seen in the dream does not exist."[13]

All phenomena, all *dharmas*, both subjective and objective, both internal and external, are *vijñānas* (cognitions). Objects of consciousness only appear to be external to and different from consciousness; ultimately all multiplicity is only a modification of Consciousness; thus every*thing* is really Consciousness-only (*Vijñaptimātra*). The eight *vijñānas* are responsible for the presentation of a world of apparent duality. Behind the *vijñānas*, behind the apparent objects, there is no matter in which forms adhere or on which they are imposed. One of Vasubandhu's major works, *Viṁśatikā*, is almost entirely concerned with refuting atomic theories and indeed any theories which claim that an object is something other than *vijñānas*. For Vasubandhu there is not thought and then that which thought thinks, but thought is both the conception and that which is conceived, both the perception and that which is perceived. There is not mind and that which mind confronts, but there is mind only. Like dream objects, the objects of our daily life have no material foundation; objects do not exist outside of thought, and objectivity is psychological, not ontological. "*Vijñāna*, *avidyā* and *vāsanā* are sufficient to explain everything that is to be met with in the world of experience."[14] Again, *avidyā* is the ignorance which causes subject-object duality via *Manas*; *vijñānas* are the cognitions which are objects or modifications of consciousness; *vāsanās* are the dispositions from past experience which determine which of all possible worlds shall manifest.

The modifications of consciousness which are the world are relatively real modifications. We must say relatively real since the *Vijñaptimātra* being unassociated with *avidyā* is not modified consciousness but Pure Consciousness. Thus Vijñanavāda is objective idealism. At the level of worldly experience, the objects and the ego really are two separate entities. The ego does not project the objects from itself; it encounters objects just as the dream subject does not produce the dream objects but encounters them. To find the source of objects we must go behind both the ego and the objects themselves to *Manas* under the influence of *avidyā*. Still, *Manas* does not project ego and objects from itself, but strictly speaking we must think of *Manas* taking the *Ālaya* as its self (falsely so) and thus projecting. It is not until the *Ālaya* that we find subject and object ideally together, and there they are to be considered as potential.

The transformation of the *Ālaya* results in *Manas* under the influence of *avidyā* and in what we may call the Collective Unconscious, the seeds and dispositions of all past experiences. *Manas* projects these seeds into objectivity in the very process of taking the *Ālaya qua* Collective Unconscious as its real self. *Manas qua* false self is ego or empirical self which really does encounter objects. According to Vasubandhu, in this process there is absolutely no reason to posit matter; all *dharmas* are *vijñānas*.

For Plotinus the sensible world is a copy of the intelligible world. The Soul informs the sensible world by the access it has to the Forms or Ideas in the Intelligence. The sensible world is utterly dependent on the work of the Soul and the souls. Soul, however, is absolutely independent of the sensible world, notwithstanding that through egoism and ignorance souls or images of souls may become bound therein, for such bondage does not in any way alter the essence of the Soul. The Demiurge remains above matter and radiates or emanates an image of the Forms found in the Intelligence. The Soul's attraction to its image is characterized by egoism and separation from a higher unity because matter is the principle of individuation. It is as such that matter for Plotinus is evil, and as such that it is the polar opposite of the unity which is the One. Matter, not Soul, is the source of evil : the weakness of matter is passed on to bodies and thus to embodied souls.

Unlike Vasubandhu, Plotinus does posit what he calls "matter", but it is not the physically hard stuff we usually think of as matter. It is prime matter; it lacks virtually all qualities and is just as ineffable as the One. It is utter deficiency, void, privative, non-Being, and dark. If all forms and order are abstracted from the sensible world, there is virtually nothing left; and this "nothing" is what Plotinus called "matter". Still, Plotinus says that the non-Being which is matter is not nothing. About the most we can say of it is that it has a function in the manifesting of the sensible world, it is evil, and it is the final term in Plotinus' scheme.

The forms which the Soul rediates do not mix with matter but are only reflected in it. Matter is a sort of mirror in which the sensible order is found as a reflection of the intelligible order. Plotinus said of matter, "It is a weak and dim phantom which is incapable of receiving a form."[15] All qualities in the sensible world, such as extension, density and resistence, are existentializations of the forms, not qualities of matter.

In Plotinus the individual soul is given responsibility for the production or informing of its own body; however other bodies and objects are not the creation of the individual subject or soul. Just as in Vasubandhu *Manas* vis-à-vis the *Ālaya* is responsible for the creation of the world of subject-object duality, so in Plotinus it is basically the Soul vis-à-vis the Intelligence which creates the sensible world. Admittedly the individual soul in Plotinus seems to have a role in that creation, but the distinction between the Soul and individual souls is not a strict one. Though the individual soul is responsible for its own body, it is not responsible for the creation of, for example, a tree. Both the individual body and all other objects, as a tree, are combinations of forms or ideas, which forms or ideas are copies of the Forms or Ideas in the Intelligence. Thus both Plotinus and Vasubandhu are idealists, and objective idealists.

It is difficult to see any substantial difference between the *vijñānas* which are the external objects in Vasubandhu and the forms which make up the external objects in Plotinus. The *Ālaya* can be interpreted as pure knowledge, and under the influence of *avidyā* this pure knowledge exhibits forms of knowledge, very much suggestive of the forms in the Intelligence, forms which are also almost indistinguishable from each other while in the Intelligence. It is these forms of knowledge with which *Manas* makes the world. An object then for Vasubandhu is nothing but forms of knowledge, or modifications of consciousness or a combination of *vijñānas*. And so with Plotinus: every quality of an object is a form of knowledge in the sense of a copy of the Forms in the Intelligence.

One of Vasubandhu's chief tasks was to discredit the theory that there is in any sense something called matter which makes up an object. On the contrary, the world is the thought of thinking; it is of the structure and stuff of mind; it is modifications of consciousness; and there is absolutely no matter anywhere to be found. But Plotinus does posit matter, and though he encounters difficulties in doing so, given the rest of his scheme, he insists that matter must be acknowledged. Thus the Soul does not exactly think the forms or ideas, but they are somehow radiated or emanated from the Soul and reflected or mirrored in matter. And that matter is non-Being, real non-Being. Still, if we examine an object from the points of view of both Plotinus and Vasubandhu, we find little difference. In both cases an object is a combination of forms or *vijñānas* which, through the agency of the Soul and *Manas*, can be traced to the second hypostasis. Without the positing of matter we could simply say that the Soul in some sense thinks the world and be done with it, as Vasubandhu does.

Plotinus actually denies matter in the usual sense as much as Vasubandhu does, but trying to discern exactly what it is (rather than what it is not) is rather difficult. Plotinus' cosmological scheme is a spectrum with perfection as one extreme and matter as the other. All the processions or emanations in the spectrum are imperfect since only the One is perfect, and their imperfection has the character of limitation. Just as the One is the Unity which is implied by the multiplicities found at each level of the scheme, so matter represents the complete limitation or imperfection implied by the degrees of limitation or imperfection at each level of the scheme. All of the positives in the scheme imply the One, all of the negatives imply an absolute negative, which is matter. As noted before, Being applies only to the Intelligence, the Soul, and the sensible world, not to the One or matter. The One is non-Being in the sense of being more than Being; matter is non-Being in the sense of being less than Being. The three hypostases which partake of Being do so in degrees; an increase in Being means a decrease in or change of matter (Plotinus also posited a divine matter). To say that Being decreases, to say that non-Being increases, is to say that limitation, imperfection, and "what a thing is not" increase. Matter, in other words, is complete absence, and as non-Being, vis-à-vis beings, it is degrees of absence, degrees which theoretically end in complete absence or privation. Matter is a concept which gives Plotinus' scheme a balance; it is not a thing but a theoretical postulation which his system needed. He lets the concept of matter do a lot of different jobs besides being the mirror for the intelligible world, partly because, whether successful or not, he wanted to keep negativity as much as possible away from the spiritual realms. Vasubandhu does not have that problem *per se* since he admits beginningless *avidyā* into the *Ālaya*.

If we consider matter as the material base for the images we see as objects, both Plotinus and Vasubandhu deny it. Matter as a theoretical absence with no ontological status might even be admitted by Vasubandhu, for such a "thought" what else is it ? — is only a kind of pointing, and any pointing is itself admissible. When Vasubandhu says there is no matter behind the *vijñānas*, he is himself pointing, making a reference to an absence; and how much reality does a referent *qua* referent have ? Matter as a base for images is a referent for both Plotinus and Vasubandhu, and they both say it is absent; like *anupalabdhi*, they both recognize the reality of the cow which is not sitting on your desk, but they do not give it ontological status. In short, they both deny that there is any matter in which the forms inhere or to which they relate existentially; such matter is posited only in order to deny it. When Plotinus does then go on to discuss matter, it is for theoretical reasons relating to the rest of his cosmological hierarchy in general.

The Schemes as Systems

We may look at Plotinus' and Vasubandhu's schemes as dynamic systems which are self-perpetuating. What are the sources of the dynamism ? The One is super-abundance and naturally overflows or proceeds or emanates, as light proceeds from the sun or cold from snow or heat from fire. But emanation is not an act of will on the part of the One, nor is the One in any way diminished or bettered by it. The *Vijñaptimātra* is transformed by its inherent power; again, the transformations are not a result of will and the *Vijñaptimātra* is not affected by them. Just as the One necessarily produces because, according to Plotinus, it is the nature of the Good to produce an image of itself, so each of the spiritual hypostases in his scheme also overflows and thus produces the hypostasis below. Superabundance and overflowing are not the causes of transformation in Vasubandhu; rather, *avidyā* working through the *vāsanās* in the *Ālaya* causes the production of subject-object duality which characterizes everything below the *Ālaya*. Without the influence of *avidyā* there would be no subject-object duality, no world, only the *Vijñaptimātra* and theoretically the *Ālaya*, though there is some doubt that the *Ālaya qua Ālaya*, without activity, has any ontological status. Both Plotinus and Vasubandhu are presenting a beginningless process, and in order to understand we tend to stop it and separate out each part and ask where it came from. *Avidyā* is not to be considered as a product of the *Vijñaptimātra*; rather, it is simply an inherent part of the system as such and cannot otherwise be accounted for. On a lower level, the system operates via the law of karma. In a sense we may see the *Ālaya* as the machine which makes the system go after it is started by the *Vijñaptimātra*, for *avidyā*, karma seeds, and the creating Subject *Manas* are all (theoretically) located there. Though each of Plotinus' spiritual hypostases is equally productive, we might see the Soul as the major perpetuator since it takes the Forms in the Intelligence and creates the sensible world and then becomes attached to its creation.

Each of the hypostases is dependent on the one above and contains everything in the ones below, only in a more unified way. Dependency and unity are major themes in both Plotinus and Vasubandhu. In both the processions and transformations are ultimately dependent on the One and the *Vijñaptimātra* respectively. The *pratītyasamutpāda*, the law of dependent origination, means that anything which has dependent origination is neither ultimately real nor free; thus the *Vijñaptimātra* is the only Reality and the only Freedom. Essentially the same can be said of Plotinus; he especially emphasizes the temporality and changefulness of the sensible world, saying that it is full of suffering, which is suggestive of (though technically different from) the principle of *kṣaṇavāda*, all is momentary, and of the First Noble Truth, all is suffering. It has already been noted that Plotinus' scheme is a hierarchy of Unity-multiplicity, with all subject-object duality disappearing in the One even as in the *Vijñaptimātra*. For Plotinus, the degree of unity of an hypostasis is proportionate to its degree of reality.

For both Plotinus and Vasubandhu, a higher hypostasis contains a lower hypostasis, and all are contained in the ultimate. It may be said of both ultimates that "It is not necessary to go in search of the universal being as if it were in some remote place, but merely to feel its presence,"[16] It is difficult but essential that we avoid spatial thinking when considering the hypostases. In Plotinus, for example, the body is contained in the Soul, the Soul is contained in the Intelligence, the Intelligence is contained in the One; and a parallel to this can be found in Vasubandhu. Their respective ultimates contain the emanations or transformations in much the same way as a theorem is contained in a science: one theorem implies all others, and the science and its theorems are not two things but one, even as Plotinus said of the One : "It and its production of itself are not two things but only one."[17] The same analogy of a science and its theorems can be applied to the Intelligence and its Ideas. The sensible world being the last and least real of the hypostases cannot express the intelligible all at once, so to speak, as the Ideas themselves are expressed, but must rely on temporal succession.

Methods

Thus far we have been concerned to show Plotinus' and Vasubandhu's respective schemes of things; but as we said in the beginning, an explanatio1 also requires, in order to be complete, that there be some relevance to the attainment of enlightenment. So it remains for us to show their respective methods for enlightenment and the nature of the highest state, relating these as much as possible to their cosmological schemes.

We might say that Vasubandhu always has two primary concerns : to disprove the existence of a lump of matter in regard to external objects, and to show, or encourage one to discover, that the subject-object duality is not ultimately real. Vasubandhu said:

> To hold something before oneself,
> And to say that it is the reality of mind-only
> Is not the state of mind-only,
> Because it is the result of grasping.[18]

Thought alone can never attain the *Vijñaptimātra* for thought by its very nature "grasps", must have an object. Thought and reasoning can, however, be effective in disproving the existence of matter, and Vasubandhu did not hesitate to engage in refutations of the views of his contemporaries who did posit matter behind the images. There is an interesting parallel between Vasubandhu and Berkeley concerning their attitudes towards materialism :

> In endeavouring to establish the truth of their respective propositions, both the Irish bishop and the Indian *ācārya* were influenced by practical and religious, rather than by theoretical and academic, considerations. Berkeley, to whom materialism was synonymous with atheism, atheism synonymous with irreligion, and all synonymous with vice, believed that by disproving the existence of matter he rendered materialism impossible, vindicated religion, and promoted the cause of virtue. According to Vasubandhu, when ... we realize that the so-called objective universe exists nowhere save in our own mind, all attachment to it will be destroyed, and with the destruction of that attachment liberation will be attained. In the *ācārya*'s own words, "Where there is nothing to grasp there is no more grasping."[19]

Part of Vasubandhu's method for attaining enlightenment is to gain an understanding via rational arguments that matter does not exist, but an understanding promoted by right motives. Academic cleverness is not only beside the point but detrimental to spiritual advancement, but philosophical ignorance is also not an auspicious base from which to seek wisdom.

First and foremost, however, Vasubandhu's method for attaining enlightenment is yoga; thus the school is called Yogācāra. As Vasubandhu said : "Before we have awakened from a dream we cannot know that what is seen in the dream does not exist." No one can "awake" for you; you must do it yourself. To pursue his most informative metaphor, the dream subject is still in the dream until there is an awakening, no matter how erudite or clever or sensitive the dream subject may be. Yoga, while not without its intellectual aspects, is basically a path leading toward spiritual experience, and it is only through this experience that we can fully understand the

Yogâcāra philosophy. Indeed, as Conze notes, some of the insights of that philosophy result from the Yogâcārins familiarity with trance (*samādhi*):

> The highest insight is reached when everything appears as sheer hallucination. The Yogâcārins based this conviction not merely on a number of logical arguments which proved the impossibility of an external object, but on the living experience of ecstatic meditation. In the higher stages of trance the yogin was accustomed to meet with vivid visual images without a corresponding external stimulus.[20]

We cannot here explore the details of the yogic method which lead to the Subject behind the subject-object dualities, to the *Vijñaptimātra*. We can mention that "for the regulation of moral life, the Yogâcāra with the other Mahâyāna schools, proposes the practising of the six Pāramitās (virtues of perfection), which are: 1. Dāna (giving), 2. Çīla (moral precept), 3. Kṣânti (meekness), 4. Vīrya (energy), 5. Dhyâna (meditation), 6. Prajñâ (knowledge or wisdom)."[21] With Vasubandhu as with so many other great thinkers, though apparently not so much so nowadays, ethics and knowledge are inseparable complements, at least until the attainment of enlightenment at which stage such distinctions tend to disappear along with all others.

According to Plotinus we must leave the sensible world behind and enter into the realm of thought, the intelligible world, in our pursuit of enlightenment. There are four epistemological (and spiritual-ontological) steps in this progress toward the One: perception, understanding, reason, and ecstasy. Perception is merely sense perception and applies to the sensible world; understanding is discursive thought, logical proofs, reflection on an object; reason is immediate apperception or intuition, but still implies a subject-object duality; ecstasy is reason-in-love or reason-in-drunkenness and transcends reason itself. Philosophy is the way to enlightenment, but it must be discarded or rather surpassed on the way, a view suggestive of Nāgârjuna with whom several parallels can be found with Plotinus in terms of method. Reason goes only so far; ultimately an experience is required. The One is, after all, ineffable and beyond thought, so thought cannot take us all the way, "Anything we can think belongs to the intellectual world we are trying to transcend."[22]

In the process of becoming receptive to the One via thought we first use the categories of thought to abstract from the sensible world and to enter the more unified and thus more real intelligible world. Building on perception and understanding, we then engage in dialectical speculation, which results in categorical transcending or the surpassing of reason.[23] Thought surpasses itself by attempting to think the unthinkable, the ineffable, by employing the categories of thought which do not apply to the unthinkable, both the One and matter. For example, we think in terms of form and matter, but "by way of form Plotinus arrives at what is no longer form because it is without matter, the Supreme One. By way of matter he arrives at what is no longer matter, because it is without form, the non-Being of matter."[24] Similarly, Being and the ground of Being are the same in the One; potentiality and actuality are one in the One; the One is absolute Unity and yet is the source of unity; the One is the Only and yet the source of "the others". Speculative dialectic, attempting to think the unthinkable with such categories as form and matter, or identity and difference, categories which do not apply to the One since no categories apply to it, results in categorical transcending, i.e., the thinkable shatters against the unthinkable.

> This speculative dialectic achieves a meaningful failure in the failure of discourse. Meaningful, first because it makes us receptive to that which cannot be apprehended as thinkable, and second, because it enables us to think the thinkables in such a way as to free ourselves from them and overcome our tendency to find an ultimate and absolute in any object of thought.[25]

In short, thought is not discarded even though thought itself cannot take us to our highest destiny; rather, thought is exhausted, pushed to its limits, shattered, which is somewhat suggestive of some Zen methods of preparing the aspirant for *satori*.

The processions or transformations were seen in terms of the descent of the soul into illusion; and now we are dealing with the ascent of the soul from its fallen state in the sensible world to the One or the *Vijñaptimātra*. Neither Plotinus nor Vasubandhu considered it spiritually profitable for the soul to contend with the sensible world; rather, one must simply extract oneself from it and its bondage. Thus they were not concerned with politics or political theory, and neither made any effort to employ or advance the physical or biological sciences; however, both were certainly concerned with psychology (study of the *psyche*, soul), though it was not yet separated from philosophy.

Of course the aspirant is not suddenly relieved of all dealings with the world simply because he senses a higher reality; so both the Neo-Platonist and the Buddhist considered the ethical life of the aspirant as a member of a community. The community for a Buddhist was mostly the *saṁgha* with its rules and regulations; and the *saṁgha* as such could well be considered an integral part of the method for attaining *prajñā* or enlightenment. Plotinus, however, tended to see the sage as alone with the One, engaging in dialectics Platonic style, but essentially responsible for his own spiritual advancement. We might see here the contrast between the *Arhat*, who has the aid of a teacher and the *saṁgha*, and the *Pratyekabuddha*, who makes his spiritual quests alone. Plotinus acknowledged that the sage must live in the world and should do his duties as they come, but always he must keep the intelligible world uppermost, and, if necessary, family, friends, and country, even this life, may be abandoned for its sake.

Plotinus and Vasubandhu agree that one advances from "here" to "there" only by a series of experiences. One must find truth for oneself by following yoga or (as Plotinus means it) philosophy to its conclusion. Plotinus said: "We speak and write only in order to lead to it, to *awaken*, to indicate. For instruction serves only to show the way; if you wish to see, you yourself must do the seeing."[26] And this "seeing" is always more than mere knowledgeability for Plotinus even as for Vasubandhu. Indeed, it is difficult to see that Plotinus' philosophy *per se* gives us any knowledge whatsoever when we only study it as an academic exercise. His philosophy is a *mārga*, a way, no less so than Vasubandhu's philosophy. "The prevailing motive in such a philosophy could not be the purely intellectual, Aristotelian 'desire to know', nor even the practical 'way to life' of the Stoic. It was a way of salvation, man's way to God."[27] Examining Plotinus is not much different from examining yoga when one has never practiced yoga; such examination, unless followed by practice, is mostly useless and beside the point. One must follow thought "beyond the utmost bounds of human thought" and thus discard that self-love and egoism which keeps most of our thinking bound to the sensible realm. In short, for Plotinus thinking is an experience no less than yoga is an experience for Vasubandhu.

Still, we must not turn Plotinus into a yogin. Using the traditional Hindu scheme of *mārgas*, we would associate Plotinus with the *jñānamārga* (the way of knowledge) and Vasubandhu with the *yogamārga* (the way of yoga), remarking, however, that the final difference is one of method, not ends. Both Plotinus and Vasubandhu seem to disparage the *karmamārga* (the way of action). We might be tempted to see a major contrast between Plotinus and Vasubandhu regarding the role of reason in their respective methods, and there is a difference which should not be neglected. However, Plotinus also must not be seen as pure rationalist, for reason has its limitations.

> In asserting that Intelligence is not the ultimate principle, that the source of beings escapes every intellectual determination, does not Plotinus become the first author in the West of an irrationalistic metaphysics? . . . Is it not likewise true that he considers the problem of the rational structure of reality as insoluble? Indeed, to acknowledge an experience which is absolute, an experience which through its nature is susceptible to no analysis whatever, is to acknowledge a datum impervious to intelligence.[28]

And as for presentation of their philosophies, as for strict philosophical argumentation, Vasubandhu is really less metaphorical and less poetic than Plotinus, who is replete with metaphors and contradictions. Vasubandhu does not engage in spiritual testimony or philosophical rhapsodies, but, in his refutation of materialism, for example, appeals to rational argument; and it might be noted here that Vasubandhu is one of the major sources for the development of Buddhist logic which grew from the art of philosophical debates such as Vasubandhu engaged in. Still, it might be best to see the schemes of Plotinus and Vasubandhu as metaphors for the spiritual life, for one must suspect that they have not so much literal validity as metaphorical efficacy: they provide an orientation, a perspective, a pointing of the way, and as such we may query whether speculative philosophy in general is as far removed from art as it is generally considered to be.

Plotinus' and Vasubandhu's cosmological schemes may also be seen as psychological schemes and as outlines of the spiritual path. To trace the descent of the soul is to virtually define the soul itself and observe its alienation from itself. The ascent of the soul therefore simply becomes a matter of retracing the steps of the descent in reverse. The soul extracts itself from the sensible world and again becomes one with the World Soul and enters the Intelligence where it contemplates the One, eventually even rejoining the One. Such an ascension is explicitly given in Plotinus, and we can easily see the same process in Vasubandhu : the dream subject or ego finds the dreaming Subject or *Manas* and returns to the *Ālaya*, eventually to rejoin the *Vijñaptimātra*.

Goals

The Yogācārin's goal is to find the Pure Subject which does not stand against an object, to ascend to the *Vijñaptimātra*, to attain *nirvāṇa*, *Tathatā*, Buddhahood. *Nirvāṇa* is characterized by bliss, omniscience, and pure consciousness; however, *nirvāṇa* is indescribable. When *avidyā* is no longer operative, when there is nothing else to grasp, then liberation is attained, for bondage is essentially ignorance and clinging to false identities. We have already mentioned the difficulties of the *anātman* doctrine and the tendency to interpret an *ātman* principle into Vasubandhu.

The Neo-Platonist's goal is to return to the One, to attain "the state of ecstasy and communion with the One, in which 'the Soul is no longer even a Soul'. . . ."[29] The One and self-knowledge are the same goal, for absolute knowledge of the Self is the Absolute. "The Soul discovers the One within its inmost depths as the pure subject which makes the Soul a substance, an autonomous and independent being."[30] Individuality is discarded, and that the Soul is no longer even a Soul is suggestive of the *anātman* doctrine; however, both of these points are moot. It is thought which brings the Soul back to the Intelligence, but it is love which takes the Soul from the Intelligence to the One. When the Soul in the Intelligence — really two aspects of the same thing — has this love for the One, it "casts off every form it has, even the intelligible form,"[31] and experiences ecstasy. When the Soul casts off every form, it is mystically unified with the One and experiences "the absolute consciousness which imprints finite consciousness."[32]

For both Plotinus and Vasubandhu the ultimate goal of the sage or yogin is self-knowledge, the identity of knower-knowledge-known, which is equivalent to a return to the Source. This is accomplished primarily by sloughing off all that is alien or detrimental to the soul. For Plotinus this means first the sensible world and then even the intelligible world. Vasubandhu thinks more specifically in terms of casting off the bondage of ignorance and illusion. But in both cases the soul does not become through the processes of purification any more than it already was in the beginning; it does not so much gain anything as lose that which has been added to it. To gain freedom, one must not grasp, but ungrasp, not add, but throw away the shackles.

Perspectives

In both Plotinus and Vasubandhu we find a presentation of perspectives. Vasubandhu presents the doctrine of *svabhāvas* (own-being) which consists of three perspectives and refers to three levels of being: (1) *parinispanna* : absolute reality, Consciousness-only, transcendental perspective; (2) *paratantra*: relative reality, *Manas*, the perspective of the dependency of beings; (3) *parikalpita*: illusion, the false subject-object duality in which objects are imagined to exist independently of mind, the naive perspective. *Parinișpanna* is equivalent to the *pāramārtha* perspective, and *paratanatra* and *parikalpita* together are equivalent to the *vyavahāra* perspective. From these perspectives we have the doctrine that *saṃsāra* is *nirvāṇa*, which means :

> . . . the *Bodhisattva* perceives the working of birth and death in *nirvāṇa*, and *nirvāṇa* in the transmigration of birth and death. He sees the "ever-changing many" in the "never-changing one", and the "never-changing one" in the "ever-changing many". His inward life is in accord at once with the laws of transitory phenomena and with those of transcendental Suchness.[33]

Plotinus also often presents his theories from two different perspectives; and although he does not call them *pāramārtha* and *vyavahāra*, we might see them as such and thus also find implicitly in Plotinus the doctrine that *saṃsāra* is *nirvāṇa*. Plotinus sometimes seems obsessed with getting out of the sensible world, but then Vasubandhu is no less so. *Saṃsāra* and *nirvāṇa* are more perspectives than places; there is no "place" to get to or to get out of, but there are perspectives. The attainment of the *pāramārtha* perspective is virtually the same as enlightenment, though in its supposed mainfestations it may to us, from the *vyavahāra* perspective, seem more like resignation or romantic euphoria. For Plotinus, "the difference between 'here' and 'there', between upper and lower, no longer signifies anything but the difference between the dispersion of sensuousness and inner concentration."[34] And as we noted earlier, according to Plotinus, "it is not necessary to go in search of the universal being as if it were in some remote place, but merely to feel its presence. And we feel it through a simple change of perspective."[35] Some of the different perspectives in Plotinus and Vasubandhu representative of the *pāramārtha* and *vyavahāra* perspectives are presented in the following outline :

Perspectives

Vyavahāra	*Pāramārtha*
1. the goal is to leave *saṃsāra* and attain *nirvaṇa*	1. *saṃsāra* is *nirvāṇa*

2. matter is evil	2. matter is ineffectual
3. the Soul has fallen, is entrapped in the sensible world (*jiva*); the greatest good is to get out	3. the Soul is a creator, overflowing even as the One; its illumination of body is a blessing; it is entirely uneffected by the sensible world (*puruṣa*)
4. we are separated from God, the Good, the One	4. the Soul never left the One; we are still there but don't realize it
5. matter has always existed, is set against the other cosmic terms, and may vie with them	5. regarding the procession, matter is a sterility, an absence
6. procession : perspective of separation	6. reversion : perspective of unification
7. better if the Soul had not proceeded from the One	7. necessity of procession; the Good produces an image of itself; beginningless working of karma/*avidyā*
8. enlightenment is the absence of *avidyā*	8. enlightenment and *avidyā* are one
9. transformations are a superimposition on the ultimate	9. transformations and the ultimate are one
10. enlightenment is a goal to be pursued	10. enlightenment and non-enlightenment are one

Conclusion

In conclusion we shall simply present some of the many themes which could be developed in comparing and contrasting Plotinus and Vasubandhu. (1) The One and the *Vijñaptimātra* are quite similar theologically. God does not exercise divine will but creates, we might say, spontaneously. God is the goal of spiritual endeavors, but there is no doctrine of grace, and the *bhaktimārga*, the way of devotion, is not (alone) efficacious. For Plotinus, man's love for God is his motive force for questing, but God is impersonal and does not love man in return. The motive force in Vasubandhu may best be taken to be the First Noble Truth that all is suffering. Though the *Vijñaptimātra* may also be seen as impersonal, still Vasubandhu must also be seen against the background of Mahāyānism wherein we find the Compassionate Buddha, love, a role for piety, and various religious trappings which are of dubious strict philosophical significance. (2) In characterizing their respective ultimates, at one point Vasubandhu and Plotinus seem to be at polar opposites : the One is super-abundance, the *Vijñaptimātra* is *śūnya* ('empty'). On the principle that extremes meet, these would be the same. But then what about matter in Plotinus, which is the polar opposite of the One and which might also be called 'empty' ? (3) In Vasubandhu we find the *Bodhisattva* ideal, but there seems to be nothing comparable in Plotinus. The *Bodhisattva* works for the liberation of all beings, but the sage, again like the *Pratyekabuddha*, seems to be concerned almost entirely with his own liberation, which he attains alone. We might find some similarities between the *Bodhisattva*'s *karuṇā* (compassion) and the role of love in Plotinus. The saint, mystic, sage or *Bodhisattva* may effect the physical-social realm by working on the transcendental realm; for example, in several traditions we find the equivalent of the *parivarta* doctrine, the turning over of merits by the *Bodhisattva* for the benefit of others. Also, (4) Plotinus adopted the Stoic doctrine of universal sympathy, which means that instead of the apparent disconnection of parts in the world all things are intimately connected, "all is all; each being is all". This sympathy is the basis of magic, in which Plotinus had some belief. It is some theory like that of sympathy which would explain the operations of *parivarta* and karma, especially community karma. This sympathy which operates in the lower realms is only an extension of the unity-in-difference which characterizes the Intelligence. If as Plotinus says, "each being is all", then the love which the sage has for the One must, when followed, work for the advantage of all. (5) Plotinus did believe in transmigration, and the working out of transmigration is not dissimilar from the law of karma and is related to the doctrine of sympathy. (6) Given that their ultimates and processions/transformations are so similar, and that the ends of the spiritual quests are at least often descriptively similar (while ineffable), it is interesting that Plotinus adopted the Stoic doctrine of eternal recurrence and that Vasubandhu did not have such a doctrine. This would seem to indicate some basic difference in their conceptions of the ultimate. Because the One emanates out of necessity, after all souls have returned to the One it must necessarily emanate again, and so on eternally. Since the process outlined in Vasubandhu is beginningless, we might wonder whether it is also endless; but if so, what about the *Bodhisattva,* who puts off *nirvāṇa* until all suffering beings are liberated ? But then, *saṃsāra* is *nirvāṇa.*

Finally, we should mention two other themes : (7) Plotinus does not find the sensible world entirely negative and detrimental to the spiritual life. Beauty in the sensible world is a reflection of the intelligible world, and as such it is a means of communing with the higher reality. Vasubandhu does not seem to have so much use for the sensible world or such an aesthetic emphasis as may be found in Plotinus. However, the conflict between externality and the subject, the conflict between the self and the not-self, suffering in the sensible world, in short, leads to a quest for the real self. (8) One way or another, ineffability can be found at virtually all points in Plotinus and Vasubandhu; and one could fruitfully compare-contrast their uses of *via negativa* and metaphors.

Perhaps the greatest comparison between Plotinus and Vasubandhu is not between any of the doctrine we have presented but in the spirit of philosophy as found in them. To follow one rather than the other may mean a difference in method, but their views of the nature, destiny, and dignity of man are virtually the same.

B. Neo-Taoism

Introduction

Taoism after the Axial Age developed in virtually every direction; during the Wei-Chin Period (220-420) there is Taoism which is nihilistic, hedonistic, religious, alchemical, fatalistic, mystical, metaphysical, and even Confucianist. Not only did there develop so many different characteristics, but nearly every school during the Wei-Chin exemplifies several of the characteristics so that it is difficult to make a strict division between the different schools.

> The Taoist movement was always a mixture. Every element in that mixture had something in common with every other element, but nothing in common with all the other elements. Alchemy, hygiene, philosophical Taoism, and the Taoist church — these were now the elements. The pursuit of immortality, the use of the *Tao Te Ching* as a fundamental text, the Taoist pantheon, and in individualistic revolt against the demands of society — these were the features they most often had in common. But the Taoist movement was never unified.[1]

We shall be primarily concerned with Neo-Taoism, which developed at the beginning of the Wei-Chin Period with Wang Pi (226-249), Hsiang Hsiu (221-300), and Kuo Hsiang (d. 312).

Before discussing Neo-Taoism, we might note some of the other philosophical Taoists and schools after Lao Tzu and Chuang Tzu. Yang Hsiung (53 B.C.-18 A.D.) in his doctrine of the Great Mystery does not differ significantly from earlier Taoism, but as so many Han thinkers he was syncretistic in combining Taoist metaphysics with Confucian ethics, and he is noted for his doctrine that human nature is a mixture of good and evil. Huai-nan Tzu (d. 122 B.C.) is important because he helped preserve Taoism through a period of strong Confucian dominance and is sometimes seen as a precursor to Wang Ch'ung; but the *Huai-nan Tzu*, actually the work of many hands, does not deviate appreciably from Lao-Chuang. The Taoists Wei Po-yang (fl. 147-167) and Ko Hung (253-333) are usually considered to belong to alchemical-religious Taoism rather than philosophical Taoism. Wei Po-yang is primarily known for compiling what is now the oldest extant alchemical treatise; Ko Hung has been treated elsewhere.

The *Lieh Tzu* claims to present the views of Lieh Tzu (c. 450-375 B.C.), and the seventh chapter of the *Lieh Tzu* claims to present the views of Yang Chu (440-360); however, it is now recognized that the views of these two Taoists are not fairly represented therein. The *Lieh Tzu* is most probably a work of the third century A.D. by some writers who wanted to use Lieh Tzu and Yang Chu as a traditional base and authority for their own views. The philosophy presented in the *Lieh Tzu* and especially in the Yang Chu Chapter is, like that of the Cārvākas, hedonistic, fatalistic, and entirely negative. It holds that there is nothing after death and no high spiritual goal which one can attain in this life; thus pleasure is the only value and the degree of pleasure is the criterion for the good life. Unlike the Epicureans, the *Lieh Tzu* does not value intellectual pleasure and does not teach delayed gratification in order to attain a higher pleasure. One should take immediate bodily pleasures and forget about the future, for ultimately we have no future. These views and the reasoning behind them are both Taoist and un-Taoist :

> The ideas of the equality of all things, indifference to life and death, following one's nature, and accepting one's fate are all original ingredients of Taoism. But the hedonistic philosophy in the "Yang Chu Chapter" is directly opposed to the Taoist philosophy of having no desire. In the *Lieh Tzu*, the Taoist doctrine of inaction, i.e., taking no artificial action, has degenerated into a complete abandonment of effort. Spontaneity is confused with resignation. And the Taoist doctrine of nourishing one's nature is forgotten.[2]

Much in the *Lieh Tzu* is suggestive of the Cyrenaics. For example both have the view that laws and restrictions are entirely social and founded solely on consensus and power. Since they have no intrinsic value or metaphysical basis, and since they are designed for the future, which is only death, such laws can be seen as hindrances to pleasure and should be ignored when possible. We also find the teaching that death is not to be feared since it is complete and literal extinction, and since fear of death can interfere with pleasure and thus reduce the only value of life.

The *Lieh Tzu* is sometimes treated within the movement called Neo-Taoism; but because of its purely negative views, because it does not follow Lieh Tzu and Yang Chu very closely even while utilizing them, and because its teachings do not share many of those tenets and characteristics common to the other Neo-Taoists, we prefer to see it as one of those philosophical positions outside of Neo-Taoism.

Neo-Taoism is not one teaching but many teachings; however, we may note these general similarities: (1) the search for a reality behind the endless phenomenal changes (*hsüan hsüeh*); (2) mystical identification with that reality; (3) the sage as one who has identified with reality mystically; (4) often the incorporation of Confucian social and political philosophy with Taoist metaphysics; (5) often Confucius is seen as a greater sage than either Lao Tzu or Chuang Tzu: (6) a turning away from the scholasticism which had grown up around the Confucian classics; (7) a reconciliation of the conflict between living in the mundane world and attaining enlightenment; (8) the use of logic (*ming li*) and dialogue or conversation (*ch'ing t'an*); (9) criticism of and giving new meaning to the *Chuang Tzu*, *Lao Tzu*, and *I Ching* or, in other words, giving new meaning to such traditional Taoist principles as *wu wei*, constant change, Tao, and the equality of all things.

Neo-Taoism was known as *Hsüan Hsüeh*, which is variously translated as Mysterious Learning, Metaphysical School, Mystical Studies, or Cosmological School. Their concern for Hsüan, the "mystery of all mysteries" or the "beyond behind the beyond",[3] has led to the conclusion that the Neo-Taoists "may rightly be said to have been wholly mystics, nothing but mystics"[4]; however, it is doubtful that most of them were any more (or less) mystical than Plotinus or Vasubandhu, and many of them did philosophize as well as rhapsodize.

A common method among the Neo-Taoists is *ch'ing t'an*, which is variously translated as light conversation, pure conversation, pure talk, philosophical wit, or the art of philosophical conversation. "*Ch'ing t'an* at its best was a form of philosophic dialogue in which two or more participants clarified their ideas and quickened their perceptions in vigorous and spirited interchange of argument and rebuttal."[5] Neo-Taoism as a whole is sometimes designated as the Pure Conversation School since *ch'ing t'an* in some form was common to all of them. *Ch'ing t'an* and that aspect of it known as *ming li* ("name-principles") may be traced back to the School of Names or Dialecticians of the Axial Age, who were very influential among the Neo-Taoists. *Ming li* is dialectical skill, the exploration of paradoxes, a dealing with abstractions and the logical implications of terms and definitions. It is basically an involvement in pure speculation without concern for actualities or practical results. As such it may be seen as rather un-Confucian and as that which the pragmatist or common man may refer to as "so much talk". Because of the political corruption, intrigues, wars, natural disasters and general chaos of the times, many intellectuals became dissatisfied and withdrew from society to discourse among themselves on non-mundane issues. Such discourses or dialogues, *ch'ing t'an*, could span the spectrum from sex and poetry to the nature of Being and non-Being; and though the purpose of these dialogues may have often been only escapism at first, eventually *ch'ing t'an* always had as its goal an awareness of, insight into, or identification with, the Tao.

Although the terms *Hsüan Hsüeh* and *ch'ing t'an* apply to Neo-Taoism as a whole, these terms are also used to distinguish two different segments within Neo-Taoism. Thus *Hsüan Hsüeh* or the Metaphysical School designates those Neo-Taoists who tend to be more strictly philosophical, that is, present a written, coherent, and consistent perspective, such as Wang Pi and Kuo Hsiang do. *Ch'ing t'an* or Light Conversation School designates those Neo-Taoists who tend toward the mystical without presenting their philosophical foundation in a complete or detailed form, but who rely more on poetry, wine, and conversation. The best known of the Light

Conversationalists were the Seven Sages of the Bamboo Grove. These two schools are not completely separable but more represent two ends of a spectrum. Hsiang Hsiu, for example, is one of the Seven Sages but also belongs to the Metaphysical School. Also, these two schools are not homogeneous but contain a variety of views.

Wang Pi

Wang Pi is probably the best known and the greatest of the Neo-Taoists. He wrote commentaries on the *Lao-Tzu* and the *I Ching*, bringing these two different works closely together for the first time. Though he lived only twenty-four years, it has been said of him that he "had no successor of equal rank."[6] In interpreting the *I Ching*, Wang Pi broke with the burdensome Han method of nice distinctions and inexhaustible commentaries on unexhausted commentaries on a few words of text. Also, most of the Han scholars kept closely to particulars of the concrete world, reflecting in part the continuing influence of Tung Chung-shu; but Wang Pi entered the realm of metaphysics, being able to suspend the world of existential actualities. He is sometimes considered to be the first truly important Chinese metaphysician, as opposed to cosmologist, and to have very much influenced the direction of Chinese philosophy generally in the direction of metaphysics. His rationalist tendencies and his theories of substance-function and principle especially influenced the Neo-Confucianists; Chu Hsi (1130-1200), the major Neo-Confucianist, explicitly acknowledges his respect for Wang Pi. Wang Pi provided material for future thinkers in part because he is often rather unclear as to his precise intent and does not develop his theses to their logical conclusions. Still, he was one of the first major Chinese thinkers to attempt to handle metaphysical problems on a metaphysical basis.

Perhaps more emphatically than with the other Neo-Taoists, Wang Pi's problem is that of the One and the many, the unity behind multiplicity, the permanence behind the ceaseless changes of the phenomenal world. He is in search of a principle which will account for there being order rather than chaos in the world, a principle which will concomitantly throw light on the problem of the nature of human destiny and enlightenment. Wang Pi discovers the solution to the problem of multiplicity and change in the *I Ching* wherein he notes that just as in government one ruler controls the masses, so one of the six lines of any given hexagram controls the other lines. Also, only forty-nine of the fifty sticks are used in throwing the *I Ching*; the forty-nine sticks used represent multiplicity while the one not used allows the others to be used and in a sense governs them. Though Wang Pi's philosophy begins with the problem of multiplicity and change, it also begins with its necessary solution; "all multiplicity must be ruled by oneness, and all activity controlled by quiescence. This is the first of his metaphysical principles."[7]

In the *Lao Tzu* and the *I Ching* Wang Pi found ample material for his view of a metaphysical Unity or Oneness behind multiplicity; his Oneness is very closely related to the Tao of Lao Tzu and the *T'ai Chi* of the *I Ching*. Wang Pi calls the highest metaphysical reality *wu* (non-Being) or *pen-wu* (original non-Being). In relation to the problem of order vs. chaos, it may be translated as Dynamic Order, Principle, or Original Substance; and in relation to the problem of unity vs. multiplicity, it may be translated as the One. Since *wu* is formless, immaterial, unlimited and undifferentiated, it may be translated as No-thing; as such, *wu* is to be contrasted with all objects and indeed with the very concept of "object". As nameless and ineffable, *wu* is to be contrasted with all that we know and with the very concept (or our usual concept) of "knowing", i.e., it is not simply another object among objects or another knowable among knowables. As the source and ruler of change or activity, *wu* may be translated as Quiescence. In short, the translations of, or adjectives applied to, *wu* (literally non-Being) seem to depend on which aspect of Wang Pi's metaphysical problem one wants to emphasize.

All things are produced from the One; it is the source of Being and multiplicity. Being (*yu*) is necessary for non-Being (*wu*) to manifest; without Being the One could not manifest. So the One produces Being, and from Being come the ten thousand things. But non-Being is not opposed to Being; it is something else altogether. Quiescence as the source of change and activity is not opposed to change and activity; it is something else altogether. As Wang Pi says in a metaphor, "The cessation of speech means silence, but this silence is not something opposed to speech."[8] Because all things come from, and are governed by, the One, change is not chaotic but orderly: "The Original Substance is above appearances, but it gives birth to and nourishes the whole world. All changes are given their laws by Order, which is ultimate, and everything has its definite task and place in it, because it represents an application of the Original Substance."[9] In his desire to establish a metaphysical source for order, Wang Pi is often considered to have gone to the extreme of determinism.

Needham presents an interesting interpretation along scientific-naturalistic lines of the relation of the One or Tao vis-à-vis the problem of change and order:

> At first sight we are surprised to find the Aristotelian conception of an unmoved mover emerging from the phraseology of Wang Pi. If this was really his thought we might be tempted to attribute to him a visualisation of laws of Nature enacted by a transcendent lawgiver. But we may be sure that in speaking of the One he had in mind the immanent Tao. What he was trying to describe was perhaps a series of fields of force (as we might call them), contained in, but subsidiary to, the main field of force of the Tao, and each manifesting itself at different points in space and time. He believed that to each of these there corresponded one of the hexagrams of the *I Ching*, its sufficient characterisation being given in the *thuan* or 'explanation' attached to it in the Book of Changes. In this way man could know the most important 'dominant factors' or 'root causes' of things, and feel able to affirm with unshakable faith that though there was manifold complexity in the universe, there was no confusion.[10]

Whatever the precise interpretation (and Wang Pi is often unclear), philosophically the One as Unity and Order is the Law behind and governing change and multiplicity, as well as being the Source of all things.

The One or Tao as manifested through Being is *teh*. The One and *teh* are not different except that *teh* is the One with an ontological status while the One *qua* the One is not ontologically limited. The One is both *wu* and *yu* at the same time; and though non-Being is the source of Being, they are not to be considered dualistically. The One is all-inclusive, so there cannot be that which is outside of the One. This is monism.

Wang Pi writes : "The ten thousand things have ten thousand different forms but in the final analysis they are one." The only reality is the One, but the manifestations of the One through Being are equally real; in other words, Wang Pi does not posit a *māyā* doctrine. Multiplicity is not illusory in essence but is itself the One-in-manifestation. It is doubtful that some of the suggested contradictions in this view are completely reconciled. At any rate, the One manifests, and the manifestations return to the One. "Tao is concurrently Being and non-Being. All that is formed by Tao returns to it. This latter concept is the usual unbroken cycle of objective idealism and Wang Pi's thought falls within that general category."[11] Since the manifestations return to the One, Wang Pi understands destiny as this return. Since all things return, all things have this destiny.

Wang Pi "seems to imply that there are numerous different categories of things and events in the universe, and that each of the hexagrams in the Book of Changes represents one or several of these categories."[12] These categories have a higher epistemological and/or ontological status than the concrete particulars within the categories. Once we understand the categories by observing the particulars, we may discard the particulars and keep only the categories within our minds, or in Wang Pi's words, "once the ideas have been grasped, the symbols may be forgotten."[13] To arrive at categories through abstraction from the multiplicity of the world is to "unify", to come closer to the One, closer to truth. "The greater the number, the further we go astray. We are nearer to [truth] if the number is reduced. When it is reduced to the least (one), we shall arrive at the ultimate."[14]

Although Wang Pi does not develop a clear and distinct rationalist view, he has very strong tendencies in that direction. Wang Pi said : "If we know the general principle of things, we can know through thinking even if we do not travel."[15] By "even if we do not travel" he means even if we do not explore or deal with the ten thousand things, the concrete particulars. Here he is indicating that it is the mind, the reason, which can penetrate reality by abstracting from existentials and arriving at categories. The implication is that these categories behind the infinite variety of particulars can themselves be unified by the final category of the One, but Wang Pi seems to stop short of the rationalist position that reason can comprehend this final category also. In the end, he remains the mystic, though we might call him a rational mystic. In the end, it is *wu wei*, natural action, and tranquillity which reveal and make us one with the One. We might say that Wang Pi employs equally the *karmamārga*, *yogamārga* and *jñānamārga* (karma, his Confucianism; yoga, tranquillity/*wu wei*; *jñāna*, his rationalist tendencies and emphasis on thinking).

Concerning Wang Pi's relation to the Neo-Confucianists, Chan notes that "where Lao Tzu had destiny (*ming*, fate), Wang Pi would substitute principle, thus anticipating the Neo-Confucianists, who preferred to speak of the Principle of Nature (*T'ien-li*) instead of destiny decreed by Heaven (*T'ien-ming*)."[16] Destiny as principle is more "natural" than having a destiny/fate decreed by Heaven, and less likely to acquire anthropomorphic connotations. A decreed destiny almost suggests an after-thought while principle suggests an integral and unchangeable part of the scheme of things. Principle and category are apparently closely related, much as metaphysics and ethics are related. On the metaphysical level, category and principle are virtually synonymous with Nature. To follow one's destiny (principle) is now quite literally to follow Nature.

It is a typical Neo-Taoist view to consider Confucius to have been a greater sage than either Lao Tzu or Chuang Tzu. The reason Confucius is considered the greater is because he found no antithesis between Being and non-Being since they are simply two different aspects of the Tao or the One. Lao-Chuang, however, tended to consider the world and the transcendental to be in opposition so that one wanted, or should want, to get out of the mundane into the beyond. Bringing in terms from another culture, we might say that Confucius had the *pāramārtha* perspective through which all oppositions were synthesized, whereas Lao-Chuang had only an elevated *vyavahāra* perspective through which they were directed away from one part of the universe toward a (supposedly) higher part. Thus we find Lao-Chuang advocating such positions as the best government is no government and the ideal life is manifested as that of a free-spirited wanderer.

"Those who know do not speak; those who speak do not know." This basic dictum of the early Taoists can be used to show that they themselves did not know since they talked about the Tao. Confucius, on the other hand, does not talk about *wu* since he is truly identified with *wu*. Lao-Chuang talk about that which they lack, and their discussion itself indicates the deficiency. But Confucius, being identified with *wu* and recognizing its ineffability, does not talk about non-Being but about Being (*yu*). Thus somewhat ironically Confucius is seen by Wang Pi and others to have been the greatest sage because he did not claim to be a sage and concerned himself with what would appear to be many non-sagely things.

To return to the Source, to the One, and to become a sage, does not entail going outside of oneself to some transcendental separate from oneself, nor does it entail going out of society onto the mountain tops or into the forests. As Wang Pi says: "If we know it, we do not need to go out of doors. If we do not know it, the further we go, the more beclouded we become."[17] We become more beclouded because the whole idea of "going out to find it" is a misconception, a path going the wrong way. Enlightenment is not a change of place or situation but the attainment of the absolute perspective. The One has the two aspects of Being and non-Being. Having identified with non-Being, the sage has also identified with Being, not escaped from it. Having become one with the One, the sage will exhibit both aspects of the One: immanence and transcendence. "To one who acquiesces in the world of forms and individual things but is ignorant of their origin, the *I* and the *other* become distinct, and disputations arise."[18] But for the sage, though he is still in the world of dualities, there is no duality. This paradox is analogous to the *wu wei* principle by which no action is taken even though there is activity. In the complete naturalness and nonassertiveness which characterize the sage, there is no action, no dualities, no transcendence, no immanence; there is only the synthesis of oneness and manyness. Being a paragon of the ideal of sageliness within and kingliness without, the sage is identified with *wu* but also functions in *yu*, and these are really not two different things for the sage. Another way of stating Wang Pi's criticism of Lao-Chuang is that they attempt sageliness but repudiate kingliness, and thus they are in the peculiar position of seeking Tao and rejecting Tao both in the same step.

Though the sage is in the world, and though, like Confucius, he may appear to be just like many other men, internally the sage is much different. He is in such sympathetic harmony with the universe that he immediately intuits all changes and tendencies and responds accordingly, and thus he remains in perpetual harmony. Unlike other men, he is not forced to rely on an analysis of data, discursive thought, or authority in order to make a decision; rather, his spontaneous responses and truth coincide at all times. According to Wang Pi the sage is like other men in that he does have emotions, for emotions are natural and nothing natural can be avoided. Earlier Taoism had considered the sage to be without emotions, for to them emotions automatically meant bondage. Herein Wang Pi differs and offers a new alternative: the sage has emotions but is not bound by them. Because the sage is identified with *wu*, he has the superior "spirit-like intelligence"; but because he is in Being also, he has the emotions.

When we consider that Confucius is the ideal sage, then the influence of Confucianism on Wang Pi is clear. But it is only the social and political aspects of Confucian philosophy which remain in Wang Pi and other Neo-Taoists; the rest is replaced by, or the social and political Confucian philosophy is supported by, reinterpretations of earlier Taoist thought. It seems to be the general consensus that the Confucian way was becoming an empty shell of externalia that had little meaning, like much that was going on in the Roman Empire about the same time. Stoicism had virtually dried up and Scepticism was or had long since become sterile, while the Peripatetics had done nothing new but had rather lapsed into a scholasticism of Aristotle's scientific investigations. Even Plotinus' attempts at re-infusing some life into the skeleton of Roman religion failed, while the Neo-Pythagoreans never had much to do with the external order of things, having, as it were, their own religion and aesthetics as a community of a monastic sort not completely unlike the Taoist monasteries. Christianity and Buddhism were not yet major forces.

Wang Pi is in many ways so similar to Vasubandhu and especially to Plotinus that extensive comparisons could be made. We shall here only suggest some of these comparisons and some contrasts. In making comparisons with Wang Pi one must be a little hesitant for two reasons : first, Wang Pi is himself often very suggestive but imprecise so that some comparisons which seem valid really need much qualification; and secondly, many of the scholars of Wang Pi are themselves not in agreement in their interpretations, and those interpretations often are not conclusive.

Looking at Wang Pi and Plotinus, we note that they had conceived of the primary philosophical problem in almost exactly the same terms : multiplicity *per se* means imperfection and implies an ultimate Unity behind that multiplicity; and they offered almost exactly the same solution : the One. There are some differences, however; for example, Plotinus makes the One the source as well as the 'container' of multiplicity, whereas Wang Pi makes non-Being (*wu*) the source of multiplicity and considers the One as the all-in-one/one-in-all Unity resulting from considering *wu* and *yu* as the same thing in two different aspects. In other words, the source of multiplicity for Plotinus is not non-Being, though his source, the One, is "above" Being. Considering that both Wang Pi and Plotinus consider the ultimate to be ineffable, above discursive thought, and that while they both have strong rationalist tendencies, still reason cannot penetrate all levels of reality, it must for now remain an open question as to whether there is any substantial difference between their conceptions of the One. It seems to us that they both provide for Unity, but Plotinus gives the One a cosmological function while Wang Pi leaves the One as a concept of unity and attributes cosmological functions to non-Being (*wu*).

Wang Pi usually presents non-Being as the uncreated, eternal source of multiplicity; however, noting again his lack of complete consistency and clarity, we do find the following also which makes his One resemble Plotinus' One even more :

> All things are produced by the One and this is why it is the master of all. And all things achieve their completion because of the One. All things in the world came from Being, and the origin of Being is based on non-Being. In order to have Being in total, it is necessary to return to non-Being.[19]

In Wang Pi we find a series of manifestations, emanations, or transformations much as we found in Plotinus and Vasubandhu : the One, non-Being, Being, categories, the ten thousand things. In all three the problems of unity, order, and change are solved by presenting a hierarchical (or apparently so) universe in which the higher levels are nearer to truth (because more nearly unified) and, especially with Plotinus and Wang Pi, the lower models itself after the higher.

Soul, *teh*, *Manas* : these are the indissolvable connections between the individual and the ultimate. All three thinkers urge a return to the origin through these, and for all three the quest for the ultimate is not seen in traditional religious terms but in what might be called a spiritual naturalism : there is no grace, virtually no theology, no efficacy of prayer, no "sin", no personal God, and (apparently) no *personal* immortality. It is with the question of human destiny that we find both the greatest similarity among Plotinus, Vasubandhu, and Wang Pi and the greatest contrast. All three are concerned with what is essentially a mystical enlightenment, a return to and identification with the source of all, becoming one with the One and transcending personality; but while Plotinus and Vasubandhu want to get away from the sensible world of dualities, Wang Pi does not, which reflects his Confucianism. Vasubandhu turns away from the world via yoga; Plotinus turns away via abstractions; but Wang Pi stays firmly in the world and finds non-Being by observing its operations in the world. It is doubtful that Plotinus could ever have seen Confucius as the greatest sage, for to Plotinus the spiritually inclined man keeps his relation to the world at a minimum whereas Confucius was constantly concerned with the kinds of questions, like government and social institutions, which Plotinus virtually ignored. We can, however, raise the question as to whether Vasubandhu might not be able to see Confucius as a *Bodhisattva*. We also shall not explore the question here but suggest that the theme of *saṃsāra* is *nirvāṇa*, or the theme of the *pāramārtha* vs. the *vyavahāra* perspective, can be found in Wang Pi even more so than in Plotinus.

To mention a few other themes: all three thinkers are concerned with dualities and consider dualities to be transcended in enlightenment. All three rely on past authorities and are syncretistic as well as original: Plotinus had Plato, Vasubandhu had the Buddha and indeed the Mahāyāna and Theravāda traditions, Wang Pi had Lao Tzu. Although Wang Pi implies the role of egoism and ignorance in the human condition, he does not seem to do justice to the question of a "fall" and the causes for imperfection, evil, and disharmony in the universe. Though he is very similar to Plotinus and Vasubandhu, yet he does not utilize fully such concepts as rebirth, *māyā*, and ignorance; nor is his method for attaining enlightenment very clear, though it seems to be much like Plotinus' method.

Any thesis which could be supported by showing three global contemporaries who are essentially similar would be supported by comparing Plotinus, Vasubandhu, and Wang Pi. We strongly suggest that instead of examining Plotinus, Vasubandhu or Wang Pi in isolation, it would be pedagogically more effective to examine all three together; and we especially suggest, with the case of these three thinkers providing an example, that it would almost always be more profitable to explore a thinker in relation to his global contemporaries than to see him only against the background of his cultural contemporaries and predecessors. Neo-Platonism, Yogācāra Mahāyāna, Neo-Taoism : are not these the results of an intrinsic logic from the Axial beginnings ?

Kuo Hsiang

After Wang Pi, the next major Neo-Taoists are Kuo Hsiang

and Hsiang Hsiu. Just as Wang Pi wrote a commentary on the *Lao Tzu*, so Kuo Hsiang and Hsiang Hsiu both wrote commentaries on the *Chuang Tzu*. Kuo Hsiang's commentary is considered *the* commentary; however, he relied on, and apparently plagiarized from, Hsiang Hsiu's commentary. Thus we may consider this aspect of Neo-Taoism to be the result of the efforts of both, though Kuo Hsiang is generally given more credit.

The biggest difference between Wang Pi and Kuo Hsiang is in their conceptions of Tao or the reality behind multiplicity, and thus in their differing views of the nature of multiplicity. Where Wang Pi found non-Being, and by extension the One, Kuo Hsiang found literally nothingness. For Kuo, non-Being (*wu*) means nothingness, whereas for Wang Pi it almost has connotation of super-abundance such as we found in Plotinus. We may say of Kuo Hsiang that for him Tao is replaced by a completely naturalistic concept of Nature, or we may say that for him Tao is nothingness and that there is thus nothing behind the multiplicity of nature which unifies or governs it. In either case, each individual thing in Nature is self-sufficient. There is still order rather than chaos in nature because, as Kuo writes, "Everything has its own nature and each nature has its own ultimate."[20] That is, everything has its own principle (as opposed to there being only one Principle in which each individual participates), and everything changes spontaneously according to its own principle. This theory of self-transformation also means that each individual thing causes itself to exist; there is no super-Creator, Governor, or God beyond the self-transforming multiplicity. According to Kuo, questions of ultimate origin or First Cause must continue *ad infinitum* or until we stop at a self-produced something which we usually call God or Tao and which is essentially a mystery; thus Kuo simply stops with things themselves right at the beginning. So while Wang Pi thought it necessary to go beyond the multiplicity of Being to the unity of non-Being in order to establish order, Kuo Hsiang, through his theory of self-production and self-transformation vis-à-vis individual principles, is able to remain completely within the eternal realm of Being, which is nothing more than the multiplicity of individual things.

That everything necessarily and rightly follows its own principle and always follows its own principle leads Kuo Hsiang to the position of fatalism and determinism. The response of the individual can only be to find contentment with whatever is and to follow his own principle, a position suggestive of the *Gītā*'s *sva-dharma* and the Stoic *apatheia*. Kuo ardently advises that the individual be true to his own self and not follow others, for only thus can one be truly genuine. This is true even to the extent of not trying to imitate the sage, for if it is not naturally part of one's nature to become a sage, then to imitate a sage can only result in artificiality. After all, the sage himself in being a sage is only following his nature and is not taking any unnatural action. If one who is not naturally a sage attempts to become one, he will in the end lose his true self in the effort and accomplish nothing. It may be that Kuo would see Vasubandhu's yogic method as unnatural.

As with Lao Tzu and Chuang Tzu, the principle of *wu wei* (non-activity) plays a central role in following one's own nature. "Hence let everyone perform his own proper function, so that high and low both have their proper places. This is the perfection of the principle of non-activity."[21] While this theme that not all men can become sages is recognized by Plotinus and Vasubandhu, it does not receive so much emphasis as here in Kuo Hsiang or in the *Gītā*. Non-activity is really nothing more than following one's own nature, whether one be low or high, a common man or a sage. "Lift what is within one's nature, and though it be the burden of a myriad stone, its weight will not be felt. But assume anything additional, and though its weight be less than a hair, you will be unable to endure it."[22] Any man, be he a sage or only sage-like, can be happy if he follows his nature, stays in his proper place, and takes no unnatural action.

The hardest lesson to learn is that everything is as it should be. Because we think that there are states higher than our natural ones to be attained, we have desires, as for fame or sagehood, and fears, as of death. But our human condition and our social position must be seen from the perspective of "the equality of things". It is this principle of the equality of all things which is at the basis of Kuo's mysticism. "Therefore he who makes excursion into the realm of non-distinction between small and great, is himself without limitation. He who ignores the distinction between life and death, himself has no terminal."[23] The sage not only understands but identifies himself with the principle of the equality of all things and thus becomes one with the process of Nature; and in becoming one with multiplicity and transformation, he actually transcends them. Kuo Hsiang's mysticism is not greatly different from that of Wang Pi, and we might make some similar comments about it vis-à-vis Plotinus and Vasubandhu; but with Kuo's mysticism there seem to remain more unanswered questions about the relation between psychology and ontology, and the very possibility of transcendence within a naturalistic framework.

Even more than with Wang Pi, for Kuo Hsiang the sage must be sagely within and kingly without; and for this reason he, as Wang Pi, found Confucius to be the greatest sage. Kuo also criticizes Chuang Tzu for confusing knowledgeability with identification : to know sagely things is not to be a sage.

Kuo's determinism extends quite logically to history. Although we cannot point to any specific events in the past as the causes for any specific events in the present, still the past taken as a whole is the cause for the present taken as a whole. And though men often think they control events, and think it is their actions or lack of actions which are responsible for the various conditions of order and disorder, Kuo says: "The human sphere, too, is equally a part of the natural process. Thus, order and disorder, success and failure, what happens and what does not happen: none of these is caused by man; they are all natural."[24] Because change is continuous and eternal, and because it is the natural way of all things, even societies, the natural response for man should be to continually adjust to the present conditions and not cling to the past. If we let the past go, then the present will take care of itself; but if we attempt to carry the past into the present as a way of dealing with the present, then the past will only prove to be an obstacle. Institutions, which by their very nature are temporally extensive, are not bad *per se*; they are bad only when they become unnatural, that is, when they are extended artificially beyond their time in an effort to make the present like the past.

Kuo Hsiang and Hsiang Hsiu were not merely explicators of the *Chuang Tzu*; they were critics of Chuang Tzu as well as admirers, and in their commentaries did not hesitate to correct him, just as Wang Pi corrected Lao Tzu. Plotinus and Vasubandhu, on the other hand, never claimed to go beyond the teachings of Plato and the Buddha respectively, but only claimed to present their real teachings in another and clearer form. "The Hsiang-Kuo correction of the early Taoists consists in its most important aspect in resolving the antithesis between Being and non-Being, between Heaven and man, and making a synthesis of the antithetical states of being in the world and being outside of it."[25] Their resolution of the antithesis between Being and non-Being consisted simply in discarding non-Being and introducing the principle of the self-production of all things: if the multiplicity of Being has no cause outside itself, then there is no need to posit such a cause, i.e., non-Being. The antithesis between Heaven and man is resolved by their naturalistic emphasis and determinism : nothing man does is unnatural or separated from the rest of the universe. Even though there are the distinctions of the sage, the common man who follows his individual principle, and the common man who does not follow his principle and is thus in bondage, still all three are located in this world, in the realm of Being, for that is the only world there is. Unlike Plotinus and Vasubandhu, who tend to posit two worlds, one real, the other more or less unreal, so that the final end of all activity is to "get out of here" (although this must be qualified by the *saṃsāra-nirvāṇa* principle) — unlike this, Hsing-Kuo recognize only a real world, not any unreal ones, though within that world there are variations among men as to their degrees of harmony and identification with Nature. Also, since each individual has his own principle, there is no need to appeal to something like a Will of Heaven considered as being outside of oneself. The ideal of being sagely within and kingly without, and the principle of identification with Nature — "There are ten thousand things being transformed in ten thousand ways, and the sage is in process of transformation with them."[26] — means that ultimately there is no difference between being in the world and being outside of the world; again, with qualifications, as Vasubandhu would say, ultimately there is no difference between *saṃsāra* and *nirvāṇa*.

Seven Sages

Concerning the Seven Sages of the Bamboo Grove, one can never learn quite enough to get a complete picture of just what their role was or of what they actually talked about in their *ch'ing t'an*, their pure conversations or enlightened discourses, for often they did get drunk and, according to some accounts, not always completely retained their dignity. For example, Welch says of the Pure Conversation School:

> Their lyricism is often termed *feng liu* ("wandering from convention"). *Feng liu* is best exemplified in the activities of a group known as the Seven Sages of the Bamboo Grove. Not far from Chi K'ang's luxurious estate in Honan was a grove of bamboo where he and certain Taoist friends used to walk in the heat of the afternoon, making up poetry, drinking a little wine, and playing the lute. Here, too, they indulged themselves in "pure conversation" which would end, as Fung Yu-lan puts it, when they reached the Unnameable and then "stopped talking and silently understood each other with a smile." Their strolls invariably wound up at the local tavern. There they would turn to serious drinking. By the end of the evening they would be in a stupor of glorious indifference to the world and intimacy with Tao."[27]

Even though subject to such characterizations as the above (which is no doubt not false), it may also be gathered that these Seven Sages really had important issues to discuss. Possibly their assembly was like modern philosophical societies' conferences (at which, indeed, not everyone stays entirely sober all the time either) except that they met in places more aesthetically compatible than our modern hotels and university compounds. They discussed more than politics (though that philosophers in all places and at all times are prone to discuss), reviewing, among other things, the "informed opinions" (*ts'ing yi*) of previous generations of thinkers, and generally discussing as comprehensively as any similar Roman assembly the whole situation of Chinese civilization.

Continuing with Welch's characterization we may note the following which, if nothing else, can illustrate the view that philosophy is something to be "lived"; and it also provides an interesting and radical contrast with a Plotinus or Vasubandhu, illustrating the wide variety of responses found, not only in China, but globally during this period:

> The most celebrated drinker among the Seven Sages was Liu Ling (221-300). His eulogy of wine is still preserved. He used to have a servant follow him about with a flask in one hand and a shovel in the other — the first in case he wanted a drink, the second for digging his grave wherever he fell. Liu Ling is also the person who liked to go about his house naked. Once he was interrupted by some stuffy Confucian visitors. They expressed surprise at the absence of trousers. Liu replied : "The whole universe is my house and this room is my trousers. What are you doing here inside my trousers?"[28]

Although it appears to be historically true that the striving towards selflessness through mystical disciplines became much more universal in all of Eurasia by the end of our present epoch, about 325 A.D., the nature of that "selflessness", discipline, and mysticism was not constant, especially in form.

As to their anti-ritualism, Holzman[29] claims that these gentlemen formed a sort of avant-guarde who deliberately set about to expose the emptiness of the older Confucian ceremonial and to replace it by meaningful, more humane, ways which allowed more freedom for individuals. Indeed, it is this antiritualism that made them famous as the archetype, the living historical symbol, of nonconformity. Their role as nonconformists, as establishers of a counter-culture in the China of that period, was only another crack in the old Confucian mask which later was to be removed almost forever by the advent of Buddhism. China was ready for something different, and that is what Buddhism supplied.

The Seven Sages were Hsi K'ang, Jüan Chi, Liu Ling, Wang Jung, Jüan Hsien, Chan T'ao, and Hsiang Hsiu, all of whom lived during the last half of the third century. In general,

Taoism had always been opposed to the ritualism of Confucianism, and so these Seven Sages were really, in a sense, conforming to the nonconformity which had a long history. Thus we may see the metaphysical Taoists, like Wang Pi, as being really more radical and effective since it is often easier to cause change by embracing the opposition and altering from within than simply openly opposing.

We may see the spontaneity of the Taoist Way as the dynamism which kept the Confucian structure of society alive and moving. That other societies manifest this same polarization in essence we shall often note down through the centuries. As Christianity replaced the official Roman religion (which had had its counterpart in the Oriental mystery cults) and the official Greek philosophies of Stoicism and Epicureanism, it also experienced the same polarization. The emergence of the papacy was countered by the rigors of the Desert Fathers; and it was not too long before theologians were beginning to think, talk, and write in terms of both priestly and prophetic vocations. In India, likewise, Vaiṣṇavism with its spirit of spontaneous enjoyment evolved as a polar opposite of the sterner Śaivism; and it was not long before Tantrism burst forth from the formalism into which Mahāyāna Buddhism had developed.

According to Holzman, the one word which typifies the social and political milieu of the Seven Sages is *transformation*. There was a transition from the older centralized monarchy to a decentralized order which was feudal in form and dominated by a relatively few major families. Theoretically, of course, the emperor was supposed to treat the whole empire as though it were his own family and, in return, according to Confucian filial piety, he was to receive absolute obedience. But often enough we have had occasion to notice how the discrepancy between theory and practice in this regard, especially at the end of later Han Dynasty, became at least as wide as it was in Rome, if not more so. Not only that, but the remedy — or what theoretically should have become the remedy according to Confucian theory whereby the Son of Heaven received the Mandate to rule only if he had the welfare of the people at heart — became a part of the disease. Everyone with any property, wealth, or pretense would wage battle with fellow rivals for the Mandate. The net result: chaos not completely dissimilar from the period of the warlords before Chairman Mao finally succeeded in reuniting the whole of China in our own time. Parenthetically, there was a high degree of disunity all over Eurasia during this century, the only possible exception being the rise of the Sassanian Dynasty in Iran. India was only partially reunited under the Guptas in the north, while in the south, rivalry had begun between the Pallavas, the Pandyas and the Chalukyas.

Thus the Wei-Chin Period became more favorable to Taoism, although it was a Confucianized Taoism. But even that would not be enough. So in retrospect we notice, as many contemporaries did not, Buddhism literally walking in on foot without any political or economic much less military backing, but with only popular appeal, infiltrating the masses first and gradually gaining converts among the literati. Soon it would get official patronage of a sort and, much later, full patronage under the T'ang Dynasty. As is often said, Buddhism walked into a vacuum and filled it. The antiquities had failed to meet the demands of the age. Just as Confucianism and Taoism will continue either in the background or in exile almost until the revival with Li Ao and Chou Tun-yi and others, so even after Christianity in Europe comes in with fresh hope to a world whose intellectual and spiritual resources had become exhausted, nevertheless, Platonism and Aristotelianism will survive, especially in the Greek East.

It is against this background of Confucian corruption and increasing Buddhist influence that we can see metaphysical Neo-Taoism generally as a final attempt to put together a working order based on tradition. The Seven Sages tend to represent an abandonment of the world as lost, at which time one should naturally turn to the Tao. Perhaps there are times historically when circumstances indicate responses like those of the Seven Sages.

In general, the Seven Sages or Worthies of the Bamboo Grove were a strange lot from our present perspective (and no doubt from the perspective of most of their contemporaries), and we certainly cannot call them heavy philosophers based on any written philosophizing they did. Still, in many ways they exemplify, with qualifications, the teachings of the metaphysical Neo-Taoists; they exemplify through their nonconformity many of the conditions of the times; though their way was certainly unorthodox, it was nevertheless one of the possible paths to enlightenment, and as such they can be seen as a parallel to some future Tantric schools; and finally, at least one of their number, Hsiang Hsiu, is recognized as a substantial thinker in the naturalistic branch of Neo-Taoism. In the Neo-Taoism of these Seven Worthies, the romanticism of Chuang Tzu continued.

Hsi K'ang (223-262)

Hsi K'ang was offered a rather advantageous position but refused it because he thought his honor was at stake. The emperor however took it as an insult or an unwanted criticism of himself and put Hsi K'ang in prison and had him executed. Balazs calls Hsi K'ang one of the world's great conscientious objectors. Consistently independent, he enjoyed wandering in the woods and mountains, cultivating the books of Lao Tzu and Chuang Tzu. Whether it was thought that music had therapeutic value or not, it was cultivated, as we have seen in many contexts, by both Taoists and Confucianists as a means of getting into harmony with the universe, or at least of inducing a feeling to that effect. Both Balazs and Howard stress Hsi K'ang's love of his lute.

Hsi K'ang gained a reputation for being obstinate. He was contemptuous of the Confucian observance of external forms of ceremonial etiquette and ritual since he considered those to be hypocritical and ineffectual. Nevertheless, he was probably not unaffected by circumstances, for during his lifetime Loyang became a major center, if not the major center, of intellectual and cultural activities. We might add that it was at Loyang, and probably during Hsi K'ang's own lifetime, that Buddhism began to make its first impact on China.

According to Howard,[30] Hsi K'ang's renunciation of officialdom did not mean that he had no concern for the welfare of the country or of the people. Rather it was the Taoist philosophy that that government is best which governs least. This sort of non-action (*wu wei*) and the *yin-yang* dialectic are basic to his philosophy. Enough to note that he incorporated in varying degrees virtually all that had preceded him, whether by affirmation or by denial.

It should be noted that Hsi K'ang was certainly no exception to the trends of the times, though he did not go to the extremes that some of his fellow aristocrats did. As one of the Seven Sages of the Bamboo Grove, he included quite a bit of esoteric lore in his syncretistic amalgam right along with the best of the classical heritage, which included not only Lao Tzu and Chuang Tzu but also the *Huai-nan Tzu* and the works of various Taoist magicians. In addition he had some knowledge of the Buddhist apologist Mou Tzu's works and ideas. However, we should not especially emphasize Hsi K'ang for these influences for, typical of his era, he was a sort of omnivid who had studied almost everything that had preceded his own work, which included Wang Ch'ung right along side the Taoist magicians. Thus within his syncretism we infer, much as we find today among the counter-culture and such as was popular in Rome also, a rather striking blend of scepticism and esoterics.

In Hsi K'ang and the other Seven Sages we encounter something strangely familiar: civilization and its discontents. The romanticism of Rousseau and Freud is really very old. The "return to nature" is never advocated by the struggling masses but becomes a dream of elites who are caught in their corsets, so to speak. Even excessive intellectual activity is to be avoided since that also can upset the balance of nature in the organism by inducing too much stress and strain. The objections which would be raised today are already there in the objections of Hsi K'ang's record. He is not escaping; rather, he can contribute more to society by "minding his own business." If he can make his own life longer and happier, then others may follow his example.

Hsi K'ang shows a healthy realism which is refreshing; and indeed in this may demand a slight revision of some of our own more extreme remarks about those Neo-Taoists who appear to be either dreamy idealists or refugees from public responsibility. Rather, Hsi K'ang himself complains about such men. Somewhat of the same spirit is manifest in regard to yogic practices. Now as then, and likewise among many Gnostics in the Roman

Empire, all sorts of people were resorting to such practices hoping for magical and quick (if not instant) results. But they were failing miserably and even falling into greater calamity for the simple reason that their motives were wrong and therefore they had become inconsistent. For the acceptance of any yoga, whether Taoist, Hindu, Buddhist or Christian — and we should not forget that the Desert Fathers were no less yogis than their contemporaries elsewhere — entails the acceptance of a total discipline and not merely the dilettantish experimenting with something sensational or faddish or a technique for sale on the get-rich-quick market.. Yoga, even Zen yoga, is not magic; it is not for merely personal advantage; and above all it is a matter of complete dedication of one's whole being to the pursuit of nothing less than virtue (not power) and wisdom (not miracles).

In Hsi K'ang we find the typical appeal to the natural as the good; and undue stresses as well as inordinate appetites, and all the interruptions from the hurly-burly world, are regarded as unnatural. He is thinking not only of the sins of the flesh but also of pride and position. There is nothing wrong with the possession of wealth as such, or with holding a position of great public responsibility, but to become obsessed with the acquisition of these or to use them merely for one's own enjoyment or advantage is wrong. As with almost all philosophers of Confucian heritage, it is not just that altruism is a virtue but that one's own integrity must be conserved and cultivated lest compromise of principles demean one's own human dignity. One must be especially cautious of enticements which are very subtle or appear to be only a case of accepting a little recognition or consideration for extra effort, for corruption does not arise from deliberate evil so much as from such rewards and tokens of appreciation, as well as from anxiety about one's public image.

For Hsi K'ang it is not that things are inherently good or bad, but rather that appropriateness of conduct according to the proper occasion should be the basis of good judgment. It seems that typically he is merely combining Confucian and Taoist virtues, the former giving integrity, the latter, simplicity. What is involved is not only the need of non-bestial, truly human or humanistic perspectives, but a realization of the hierarchy of values. Utilitarianism and pragmatism also have not withstood his scrutiny, for he is always appealing to principle, not just to *ad hoc* situations; and, whether we like it or not, he still thinks in elitist terms, showing occasionally almost a contempt for the passion-swayed masses.

Hsi K'ang brings to mind Plutarch's *Moralia.* Compared with Sextus Empiricus's work on ethics, on the other hand, we find some rather sharp contrasts since Sextus argues that there are no natural virtues and remains much more uncommitted than Hsi K'ang. The scepticism one senses in Hsi K'ang is no doubt an echo of the scepticism in Wang Ch'ung, though it is never as sharp. Actually neither of them totally rejected the notion of spirits nor the practice of placating them. In Hsi K'ang's case at least this is in part due to his inclusiveness. In Hsi K'ang and Wang Ch'ung, as to some extent in Galen and Sextus Empiricus also, we find fascinating mixtures of superstitious practices not only with what might be considered as alchemy but a canon of very scientific information about the medicinal properties of many plants and herbs. However, what is more significant than the cataloging of these things is the fact that everything concerning them is considered as natural phenomena. From the results of transplanting orange trees to fabled reports of ancient sages like Ch'ih Sung's supposed ability to ride on the clouds because he ate crystal, all phenomena are taken, not as miracles, but only as examples of a cause and effect pattern of nature, inadequately tested, no doubt, but nevertheless interpreted in a nonsupernatural frame of reference. Though an action may be unnatural in an ethical sense, there is no real separation between the natural and the supernatural.

FOUR

PATHS AND PRINCIPLES

A. Global Apologetics

Justin Martyr

The controversy may continue for a long time as to whether one can truly speak of a Christian philosophy as such since, in contrast with Buddhism and Jainism which were really philosophies that became religions, Christianity was really a faith that had to adjust to the philosophies it encountered — chiefly Stoicism but also the full range of Hellenistic philosophies from rank hedonistic materialism to extremely ascetic and very esoteric Neo-Pythagoreanism. The traditional claim was (and in some circles still is) that with all its richness and variety the whole history of Greek philosophy for more than five centuries had left the basic problems of human existence unsolved, and that Christianity solved them. According to Gwatkin[1] Christian faith came in as a middle way between Greek philosophy and the gross superstitions of the time. It was able to do this by virtue of the doctrine of the Incarnation which stressed, so to speak, the "down-going" compassionately of God more than the "up-going" of man which characterized the Neo-Platonic and Neo-Pythagorean schools. Essentially the same de-emphasis on the "up-going" of man could be asserted of both Mahāyāna Buddhism in China and Vaiṣṇava Hinduism. In practice, however, it was not long before the association of Neo-Platonism with the Christian faith became so strong that they were scarcely distinguishable, and it was this trend which brought about the victory of Athanasianism in the Mediterranean whereas to the "barbarians", including even the Goths under Theodosius, Arianism, being more realistic and less fanciful, made more sense.

The language may be different but the basic problems dealt with by Justin Martyr (100 ?-165 ?) and the other Christian apologists are not in the least dissimilar from the basic problems of the Taoists and Buddhists : the great meta-cosmic movement out of the undifferentiated 'Father'; the establishment of the Divine Order undergirding the structure of nature and the relation of this to the great possibilities of human destiny; the right discernment of the inherently divine in all things; the establishment of the spiritual community with the church-at-large as the instrument for lifting humanity; and the eventual, if not the constantly occurring, return to the Source, *regressus-in-Deum*, *pralaya*.

Justin Martyr had been brought up in completely pagan circles, not hearing of Moses and the rest of the Biblical lore until rather late in life. He seems to have had a mixture of Greek and Latin traditions in his upbringing. It is a bit odd that it was under Marcus Aurelius that he was martyred, this event having been the result of a conflict between himself and a certain Crescens the Cynic. From autobiographical notes in his writings we learn that from early youth he had been a very earnest if not an almost desperate searcher after truth and personal peace of mind. Barnard quotes the famous passage from his *Dialogue* in which he expresses his reverence for all philosophers : "For all philosophy is, in fact, the greatest possession and most honorable before God, to whom it leads us and alone commends us; and these are truly holy men who have bestowed attention on philosophy."[2] This attitude led him, typically for his age, through a rather eclectic career, sampling the Stoics, Peripatetics (who, it may be inferred, had become rather commercialized, more bent on collecting their fees than research into scientific matters), Pythagoreans (who insisted that a long course in music, astronomy, and geometry is needed as a propaedeutic to the higher reaches of the spirit; Justin, being ignorant of these things, was not qualified to enter into their mysteries), and finally finding a Platonist philosopher with a better disposition, he records that : "The perception of immaterial things quite over-powered me, and the contemplation of ideas furnished my mind with wings."[3] But, of course, not long after that he was introduced to the *Old Testament* Prophets and the teachings of Jesus and the Faith that had already been built around him.

Barnard stresses the fact that Justin's conversion was in a sense hardly a conversion at all, or at least it certainly did not entail a crisis such as those recorded by and about Saint Paul and Saint Augustine. For Justin it was a matter of calm, rational conviction that at last he had found the true *gnosis*, the true Wisdom beyond the mere search for wisdom or "love of wisdom", which remains the literal meaning of "philosophy". In this respect as well as in his role of apologist, Justin and Mou Tzu (b. 165) are remarkably alike. Mou Tzu, a veritable contemporary of Justin Martyr, was writing what amounts essentially to apologetics for the new Faith of Mahâyâna Buddhism for the sake of the 'Gentile' Confucianists. These two religions, as Toynbee and others have reminded, were so remarkably similar that it is difficult to avoid the hypothesis that they issue out of the same Eurasian cultural nexus (*zeitgeist*).

The Platonism which had occupied Justin was what is now called Middle Platonism represented by Albinus (d. cir. 200) who had inherited a certain Aristotelianism and infused it into the Platonic tradition, at least in regard to the transcendence of God or the Supreme Good as *To hen*, the One, as well as the Unmoved Mover concept of God. However, it seems that Albinus had also left large room for gradualism of stages of approach to the ultimate. Barnard claims that Albinus did not measure up to the standard later set by Plotinus as far as mysticism goes, and that he was typically eclectic even to the point of inconsistency. We may or may not regret that Justin had not inherited a better, less diluted interpretation of Plato, but such historically is the case.

Justin seems to favor the *Timaeus* most of all, perhaps to the neglect of the more dialectical dialogues. The *Timaeus* gives a hint at an imaginative doctrine which already seemed to bridge Greek paganism with Judeo-Christian cosmology, psychology and ontology. It is not surprising to learn that Justin was among those who adopted the notion (whatever its origin) that Moses and Plato had had some connection, or even that Plato received something of 'revelation' from Moses.

Justin's doctrine of the sacraments and the Church are of theological but not necessarily of philosophical interest. However, his teaching on the concept of God is worth noting. Barnard remarks:

> Justin retained the Middle Platonist emphasis on God as the unknowable and transcendent Cause far removed from the world and disconnected with it. ... Justin, as a Christian, knew the living God, yet it would seem that he could not formulate the divine indwelling in intellectual terms. In the *Dialogue* he defines God as "that which always maintains the same nature, and in the same manner, and is the cause of all other things". He also appeals to Plato's description of that "Being who is the cause of all discerned by the mind, ... beyond all essence, unutterable, and inexplicable, but alone beautiful and good, coming suddenly to souls that are naturally well-dispositioned on account of their affinity with, and desire to see, him". Justin had no real theory of divine immanence to complement his emphasis on divine transcendence. His doctrine of the logos ... in fact kept the supreme Deity at a safe distance from intercourse with men and left the Platonic transcendence in all its bareness. ... It was not given to him, as a pioneer second-century Apologist, to unite transcendence and immanence in a system at once rational and biblical.

Every topic, every field, has its levels of penetration, its plateaus of understanding, its orbits of comprehension, and of virtually no other field is this more true than of this field of Christian apologetics and patristic studies of the first four centuries. Thus, it is one thing to read Justin Martyr merely from the standpoint of personal piety; another to study him as an authority as close to the original Christian gospel as anyone acquainted with the full range of Greek philosophy; and yet another to understand him as a philosopher contemporary with Epictetus and Marcus Aurelius; and it is still another to see him in his position in world history as roughly contemporary with Nāgārjuna, the *Laṅkāvatāra Sūtra*, and Mou Tzu (the first Buddhist apologist in China), and as living shortly after the Chinese sceptic Wang Ch'ung and during the lifetime of the Taoist Wei Po-yang.

Milinda Pañha

The *Milinda Pañha* or *Questions of Milinda* may be seen as an apologetic work written for Greeks or bi-lingual semi-Greeks. Milinda or Menander was one of the Indo-Greeks in Bactria. It is during his reign, as well as just before and for some time after, that Buddhist art assimilated a considerable measure of Greek influence; and for this reason it is commonly suspected that the dialogue form of these *Questions* was the result of influence from Plato. However, this is by no means necessarily true since many of the earliest *Upaniṣads* are also in dialogue form as are most of the earliest Theravâda scriptures in Pāli. Some scholars doubt that the Buddhist claim that Menander became a convert can be authenticated; but even the most conservative opinions must at least concede that he did give considerable patronage to the Buddhist monks, represented in the *Questions* by Nāgasena.

In the *Milinda Pañha* we find some of the best arguments for many Buddhist doctrines. There is, for example, the famous simile of the chariot, which Nāgasena uses to convince Menander that personality is not a substantial unity but a composite, just as a chariot is a composite of the different parts. There is also the metaphor of the passing of a flame from one lamp to another to indicate the doctrine of transmigration. In itself the work contains no especially radical doctrine or interpretations; rather, it presents many of the Buddhist doctrines with a clarity and literary excellence seldom equalled. Indeed, Rhys Davids says that "the work, as it stands in the Pāli, is of its kind (that is, as a book of apologetic controversy) the best in point of style that had then been written in any country ... it is the masterpiece of Indian prose."[5]

It is characteristic that in some measure both Theravâda and Mahāyāna Buddhists claim these *Questions* as authoritative literature; and for this reason it may be representative of a transitional period between them, although this is not necessarily true. The *Questions* seem to be closer to the Theravâda tradition; they have very little if anything at all that could be compared to Nāgārjuna's dialectics or Vasubandhu's trend towards idealism.

Mou Tzu

We have noted from time to time how parallel developments both in external affairs and in trends in philosophy obtained in China and in Rome, with Mahāyāna Buddhism slowly filling the vacuum between the empty Confucian orthodoxy, hypocritical and irrelevant as it had become, and the Taoist fascination with esoterics to the detriment of the maintenance of public order and stability, in a way remarkably parallel with the way Christianity seems to have filled the vacuum between the empty formalism of Stoicism and the hedonist disdain for world. Thus, it should be possible to see Justin Martyr and Mou Tzu in positions fairly parallel vis-á-vis their cultural milieu and their newfound Truth.

Concerning Mou Tzu (b. 165), ever since Pelliot made his translation of the work bearing his name there has been considerable controversy. It seems that a goodly part of the controversy stems from the use of dialogue form, which had not been the practicę in China before Mou Tzu introduced it. It would be difficult to claim that the dialogue form indicated Greek and only Greek influence since, as noted, the Pāli Canon reveals such an extensive use of it. So, since Mou Tzu was a Buddhist himself, it should not be the least surprising for him to use the same form.

Like Pyrrho, Apollonius of Tyana, Philo, Mani, Plotinus and many others, this pivotal figure of Mou Tzu manifests testimony to intercultural contact or interest that would be parallel to a global interest in our own time, attempting to bridge if not to completely unify different traditions. He was a convert to Buddhism, but he carries into his apology a lot of Confucian and Taoist lore even though he ridicules superstition almost as much as Wang Ch'ung. Moreover, he warns — with little effect, however, judging from subsequent history — against mixing too much Taoism with the newly arriving doctrine. Hence it is only with some caution that we can accuse him of outright syncretism.

It is difficult to get an adequate impression of what Mou Tzu's role really was. Certainly he was a scholar, exhaustively so, having encompassed all of the Chinese classics and evidently most of the commentaries up to his time. He had also acquired knowledge of the vast range of Buddhist literature, which was a great discovery to him. He bases much of his apology on his belief that the Buddhist classics are more ample than the Confucian and Taoist scriptures, and more meaningful as a personal guide to life as well as manifesting genuine philosophical and historical understanding of the world. Whereas Wang

Ch'ung had ridiculed the current superstitions about ghosts and spirits from a sceptical humanist Confucianist point of view, Mou Tzu bases his ridicule of these superstitions on Buddhist enlightenment — a rather ironical point since later popular Chinese Buddhism was to lose this humanist spirit and get very much mixed with Taoism both in vocabulary and in practice.

Mou Tzu says that by understanding the Buddhist Sūtras he also gained fruitful understanding of the Confucian and Taoist classics, and especially an understanding of such concepts as the Taoist "non-action" (*wu wei*). He says that before attaining Buddhist enlightenment he was engrossed with the multifarious things of the world; but after enlightenment he gained such a perspective as enabled him to see all of his "vital and urgent concerns" as no more than an ant hill. Before Buddhism he was fumbling around in the dark, but when he saw the light (his own metaphor) all other things became perfectly clear.

However, the differences between the Buddhist and Confucianist world-views were not easy to reconcile. After all, Yao and Shun and Confucius himself did not know about the Buddha and all of this Buddha lore; and since they were the very image and embodiment of perfection, how could the Buddha and his teachings have any value ? The attitude was no doubt not far from that expressed by Plotinus (or rather by Porphyry, with Plotinus depending on his report) concerning the Christians: if they did not have Socrates, Plato and Aristotle, then they could not be worth very much. In short, ethnocentricity is very difficult to overcome or even to penetrate, and this was Mou Tzu's problem. Not only was there ridicule of the tonsure and the "queer clothes" that the Buddhist monks wear, but more seriously there was great concern over the horrifying and really ominous notion of taking vows of celibacy, thereby leaving no progeny to honor one as an ancestor and even insulting ancestors by not honoring them above loyalty to the *saṁgha*. Filial piety as one of the key Confucian virtues could easily cause conflict for a Chinese youth who wanted to join the Buddhist *saṁgha* and renounce the world against his father's wishes. Also, the question of metempsychosis must have bothered orthodox Confucianists and others as much as it bothers modern Americans. There are many parallels in the encounters between Chinese Confucianists and Taoists and the development of Buddhism in China on the one hand and, on the other, between Hebraic and Greek traditions. Many of the resulting problems still have not been resolved.

Since the Taoists insist that the Absolute, the Tao, cannot be expressed, even as the Buddhists talk about the ineffable *śūnyatā*, how is it that they talk so much about it? Mou Tzu replies that there is a difference between the Tao of Heaven and the *tao* of man. When Lao Tzu was speaking about these things, he meant that although the Tao of Heaven as all-comprehensive was too much for finite man to express, nevertheless the *tao* of man has to do with everything that man does and thus evokes verbal attempts at linking personal, familial and political affairs together as harmoniously as possible so that the proper proportions are maintained between Heaven, earth, and man.

Forke[6] concludes his treatment of Mou Tzu by saying that he is the first to incorporate all three Chinese traditions in his perspective, namely, Buddhism, Taoism and Confucianism. We shall be seeing through the centuries to come how these continue to stimulate each other and in turn to respond variously to the impact of the Hebraic-Greek synthesis (if it is that) culminating in the present cycle of ascendency of Maoism.

B. Upatissa Thera

It is difficult to single out any particular individual for Theravâda Buddhism during the Han-Hellenistic-Bactrian Period except Upatissa Thera (fl.66-129). But it is perhaps foolish to demand recognition of individuals in this connection since the basic teaching of Theravâda induced selflessness and anonymity. There is considerable dispute as to the real identity of Upatissa Thera; but as important as it is to historians and philologists, it is not our concern to go into details of that controversy for we are much more concerned with the contents of the teachings as at least representative of Theravâda teachings during the general period when the Mahāyāna canon of sūtras was taking shape, notably the *Lotus* and the *Smaller Prajñāpāramitā* and possibly even the *Laṅkāvatāra*. It was the period of the earliest Christian martyrs and attempts at adjusting the Christian religion to Greek philosophy after the pattern set by Philo of Alexandria; it was the period of the Neo-Platonists, of the development of Han Confucianism and Neo-Taoism in China, and possibly (dates still being highly controversial) the period of Nāgārjuna.

The *Vimuttimagga* of Upatissa Thera should not be confused with the *Visuddhimagga* of Buddhaghoṣa. The similarities of the *Vimuttimagga* and the *Visuddhimagga* are not merely accidental, for Buddhaghoṣa relied very heavily on the former. The fact that they are so much alike is ample testimony to the stability of Theravâda tradition whereas the various splinterings and syncretisms of the broad range of Mahāyāna Buddhism leaves virtually anything and everything open to be included under the name of Buddhism. Parenthetically, Christianity was no less syncretistic in its origin than Mahâyâna Buddhism was in its development.

The *Vimuttimagga* is very sane and sound counsel based on several centuries of accumulated experience as well as being, no doubt, closer than much Mahâyāna literature to the clear-headed humanism of the Buddha himself, unburdened by esoterics of mantras and magical formulas for achieving supernatural powers and even unentangled from the subtleties of devastating dialectical logic aud vituperative diatribes against heretics. Indeed, one senses almost a spirit of healthy scepticism all through the discipline. But most of all one cannot but be impressed by the 'scientific' thoroughness with which every topic is treated. It is difficult to understand why modern psychologists are so adverse to the reinvestigation of such texts since therein they might find some guidelines for fresh research to see whether some of the level-headedness of this sort of Buddhism might not be of considerable value in our own muddle-headed and crisis-ridden world. Actually, the *Vimuttimagga* is intended as a *vade mecum*, a guide to right living for daily cultivation, and not as a dogmatic treatise to be argued about. Quite apart from its historical value, it might again prove to be such for many.

Almost uniquely, the *Vimuttımagga* is not very eclectic or syncretistic. Where elsewhere we have freely used generalizations about Eurasia as the unit of study with far more parallel developments than geographically distributed differences, in almost every case Sinhalese or Theravāda Buddhism may indeed provide the great exception. The typical classical reserve, the purity of exposition without undue elaboration or ornamentation, the humanist good sense that typified the Buddha's own teaching — these seem to have prevailed in this tradition. Above all, one does not find any of the intellectual gymnastics with which one is confronted in Nāgārjuna's flaunting of negations in the face of all possible assertions. Yet neither internality nor externality, neither subjectivity nor objectivity, is neglected. Theravāda stands, therefore, encompassingly in the middle of all the other extremes that characterize the period, from contempt of esoterics on the part of Wang Ch'ung to the aspirations of complete transcendence on the part of Philo and the completely interior way of Epictetus and Apollonius of Tyana.

From all the richness of Upatissa Thera's charismatic text it is difficult to choose what is most historically representative of this first century A.D. The texts of early Christian thought do not contain any systematic approach to the problem of expansion of fields of awareness. The texts from Wang Ch'ung as well as from others of sceptical tendencies, including those in the Mediterranean region, although filled with a real social concern, are, by comparison, rather negative, offering little remedy for the misplacements of judgment committed by the masses as well as by degenerate aristocracies except ridicule of superstitions. And at the other extreme, the Mahāyāna Sūtras seem to be too radically into the esoteric realm to be very applicable universally, while the eccentric antics of many Neo-Taoists, as well as the risk of fresh superstitions coming in at the expense of scientific (proto-scientific) experiments with alchemy and other means of transforming human nature, impress us more as historical curiosities than as having universal and permanent value, valiant though their motives may have been. The *Vimuttimagga*, then, remains in a definite sense unique in its period as a rational, stable, universally applicable, sane method, not of argumentation, but simply of what all human beings normally need, namely, an expanded cultivation of wider awareness accomplished by natural means, without drugs or magical formulae or short-cut but dangerous leaps of faith.

That the *Vimuttimagga* may be more psychological than philosophical in the modern sense must be admitted. But there is a definite philosophy which undergirds this 'psychologism', a definite awareness that knowledge is not easily gained by the usual naive methods. It is a philosophy that is also aware that without such cultivation of awareness ethical do's and don'ts will only lead to tension, conflict and guilt. Still, it may be true that it has not enough social or political wisdom; and it may be argued that, lacking the *Bodhisattva* ideal of renunciation of *nirvāṇa* for altruistic reasons, it is not sufficiently altruistic in its outlook — though it is relatively difficult to see anything wrong with the less exaggeratedly ambitious goal of the *Arhat*. And to still others of a more metaphysical turn of mind, such as the early Neo-Platonists, it may be lacking in ultimate values and/or be insufficiently theistic, for although the Person of the Buddha is one of the many objects to meditate upon, there is certainly no worship even of any Hyperion Zeus, much less of a *Yahwe*, Viṣṇu, Śiva, or any such Deity.

Finally, those who object that meditation has nothing to do

with philosophy, especially in the modern Western sense, might do well to re-examine their own heritage, such as the *Imitatio Christi* or even the writings of Meister Eckhardt and Epictetus. Even those who are attracted to the currently popular transcendental meditation cult — which is a healthy corrective to its opposite which prevails in most modern super-secular universities — might well profit from an examination of the methods taught in this tradition, which is not dead in Thailand, Burma, and Ceylon, and which is undergoing a revival at the hands of such organizations as the Mahabodhi Society.

It is not easy to choose the most apposite portions of text to comment upon, for often the most fascinating existentially will not necessarily be the most important historically. Nevertheless since there is always an interest in supernormal powers among all peoples, whether they are achieved by artificial means or by "yoga" tricks, we should not ignore the chapter which deals with these. All charismatic figures were accredited with miracles during this first century and subsequent centuries. Although such stories are easily exaggerations and must be reduced to the minimum of credibility, nevertheless, they cannot be dismissed altogether. If miracles are evidence of prophethood (as in the Muslim world) or incarnation of the Deity, one gets into trouble if one insists that his prophet or avatār is unique. It will be remembered that the Patañjali *Yoga Sūtras* contain a rather substantial chapter dealing with these matters, and there they are not treated as supernatural but only as supernormal. That spirit seems to follow through into the Buddhist world of both theory and practice, at least in the Theravāda tradition even though in some later versions of Mahāyāna traditions the cult of miracles comes into play scarcely less than in any other Eurasian Medieval culture, along with the worship of the Divine Mother, speculations about trinities, expectations of Messiahs, Mahdis, *Bodhisattvas* and Avatārs.

From reading other minds and elementary ESP phenomena, the *Vimuttimagga* goes on to discuss many (not all) of the traditional "tricks". In India those who do these are called Jādūwāllāhs, tricksters, and are not very highly regarded for these things have nothing to do with sainthood nor have they any ethical foundation. In fact, they can be used for evil as well as good purposes. As one progresses evidently one learns to ignore these tricks as temptations, for they may even be hindrances to higher spiritual achievements. Indeed, there are many stories about the Buddha himself in this regard.

Past the more tempting and more nearly sensational matters, however, as in all mature texts dealing with spiritual themes, beyond the supernormal powers, lies wisdom. And this is the end to be striven for, preferably under a competent guru or guide who has received similar training and has arrived at sufficient proficiency to guide others safely through the trials and tribulations as well as the temptations involved. Many texts, however, do allow the following of adequate texts as guides since the human guides themselves may be tested by these more permanent records.

In the more substantial than exotic matters, there is perhap less difference between the Mahāyāna and the Theravāda ways. The same word for wisdom is used, Pāli *panna* and Sanskrit *prajñā*. Whether a parallel can be drawn between this concept of wisdom and, for example, the sort of esoteric *gnosis* sought by the Gnostics and the *sophia* sought by the more sedate and less sensational but more thorough Neo-Platonists and Neo-Aristotelians during our present period, and likewise between the Neo-Taoist practices and the more thorough Han Confucianists, remains another of those challenging studies yet to be done by experts.

The title *Vimuttimagga* means "path of liberation" or "path of freedom". Its highest teaching is nothing more or less than the Four fold Noble Truths taught by the Buddha himself. All the supernormal powers are far less important than this profoundly simple formula which means, essentially, that although we and the world are indeed in a sea of suffering, there is a way out. That mediation is essential for deliverance, and not mere calculations or intrigues or even revolutions and counter-revolutions, should be clear. Freedom, in short, is a matter of wisdom and not merely something to "fight" for in a way that will cause others to suffer. For suffering comes from the endless chain of causation, and deliverance from that comes from the

Middle Path, not the extremes, attractive though they may appear at times.

As noted, Pāli *panna* and Sanskrit *prajñā* are virtually the same word. However, in the Mahāyāna context it becomes highly esoteric whereas in the Theravāda it is the fruit of habitual discipline and is a human virtue, not a metaphysical, not to say a theological, 'gift' of supernatural grace or a matter of magic or alchemy. *Panna* is often translated, not as wisdom, but simply as "understanding". True, it is more associated with faith — *śraddhā*, not blind acceptance of mythical truths nor demand for literal facts, but rational confidence and commitment to a way of life — than with knowledge of particulars of the myriads of things, of the facts and figures.

There is a popular notion abroad in many circles still, a notion which can do much damage unless corrected by proper historical perspectives, that there is little difference between Hindu and Buddhist 'mysticism' and Gnosticism. In the case of some extremes of Vijñānavāda and some sub-varieties of Advaita, this is partially true, and historically they are very closely related. According to the Theravāda teaching not only are there experiential aspects of spiritual, intellectual and/or aesthetic deliverance from animality and the ignorance of the *natur-mensch*, but an ethical basis is a *sine qua non* for enlightenment. In contrast, the discipline of some Neo-Taoists, as with their use of alchemy, was not necessarily ethical; it was, or had become, far too esoteric. Generally during our period there was not the same emphasis on ethics in other paths of enlightenment as one finds in the Theravāda tradition.

As concerns wisdom and/or knowledge, the Theravāda as exemplified by Upatissa Thera remains the "middle" path, not in the sense proposed by Nāgārjuna, but in the sense of moderation or the "sweet reasonableness" of humanist concern for the welfare of mankind rather than any extreme devices for escape from responsibility for one's own destiny or the shape of the future of human destiny. In this sense, Upatissa Thera might be better compared with some of his Confucianist contemporaries, although they would be very much taken aback by his monastic vows, as we may see from the objections recorded by Mou Tzu. Also, the end of the Theravāda disciplines, the signless concentration of mind, is not too far removed from the imagelessness at the end of the Neo-Platonic *via negativa,* or the purging of the phantasms in later Averroist discipline.

Theravāda is realistic in its metaphysics, in sharp contrast with the Śūnyavāda of Upatissa's contemporaries. And it scarcely needs to be punctuated that in the Theravāda tradition there is very little, if any, separation between ethics and epistemology. What is termed as the highest knowledge is the fruition of the realization that all the experienceable world around us is pervaded with ill, something that is very close to the present day existentialist *Angst.* But even this "realization" — that is really a better term than "knowledge" for it is a matter of spiritual, psychic states of awareness rather than definite things that are "known" — does not normally come all of a sudden.

Most of the contemporaries of Upatissa Thera were much more speculative and often openly esoteric, mixing magic with mysticism. But Upatissa Thera, by comparison, is extremely restrained. One finds no references to demons, angels, archangels, *Bodhisattvas-Mahāsattvas,* chants or magic spells, but rather what might even be called a scientific humanism. Not that he is colorless and impersonal. On the contrary, the whole Pāli Canon is replete with vivid metaphors designed to assist understanding, and Upatissa even lists many of these and labels them as metaphors evidently lest they be taken as dogmas in themselves rather than as merely illustrative figures of speech. Not only avoidance of dogmatism is a part of the teaching in Theravāda Buddhism, but — differing herein very radically with most other traditions in that century — one must positively avoid addiction to all ritual forms.

C. The Rise of Mahāyāna

Mahāyāna Literature

If we may accept Conze's datings as reliable, the early *Prajñāpāramitā* literature, which later mushroomed into a huge corpus, took form during the century from 200 to 100 B.C. Right from the first it took on a speculative and metaphysical spirit that is quite different from the realism and anti-speculative manner of the Theravāda tradition. The *Larger Prajñāpāramitā Sūtra* (first century A.D.) is a seminal work in the Mahāyāna tradition, especially as concerns later influence in China, Korea and Japan. It would appear that the *Prajñāpāramitā* literature is more closely associated with the Mādhyamika tradition and the *Laṅkāvatāra Sūtra* with the Vijñānavāda, while the *Lotus Sūtra* (*Saddharmapuṇḍarika*) becomes more closely associated with the Amida tradition. However, this should not be exaggerated since the syncretistic trend of the period is such that one would be surprised if devotees did not study all of them. Only after several centuries, and then much more in China and Japan than in India, does sectarianism become critical. Indeed, from the standpoint of the history of religions rather than the history of philosophy, it is interesting to note that no variety of Buddhism ever developed a "Bible" as a revealed scripture comparable to the Judaic or the Christian canon, the *Qur'an*, the *Vedas*, or, for that matter, even the Pre-Confucian Classics. It is certainly true that in later centuries as sectarian differences developed each sect or tradition did adopt its favorite texts; but the others, with the possible exception of Nichiren, were never anathematized as heretical. In the development of the Mahāyāna canon, the opposite is true : syncretism runs riot, and before long there is scarcely any notion or myth or product of the imagination, no matter how terrifying or serene, which does not come under the designation "Buddhist".

Above all, it is in the *Larger Prajñāpāramitā Sūtra* that the concepts of the *Tathatā*, the *Tathāgata*, and the *Bodhisattva* take on full development. And within this context we seem to find the beginning of what later in Christian and Sufi traditions comes to be termed mystical theology in the technical sense, i.e., an attempt at systematically — and therefore we shall say 'scientifically' — treating the various possible schemes of achievement of spiritual perfection. The basic theme of the Sūtra promises that certainty is not impossible even though it evidently is not the ultimate achievement — a rather humbling thought !

Buddhist texts frequently emphasize the necessity of a good spiritual friend (*kalyāṇamitra*) and it is mentioned in this Sūtra as well. The true friend is one who helps us to win a better destiny or the ultimate goal of Buddhahood. Where a guru is not available, the fellow traveller is a good second best; and even where there is a guru, fellow disciples are supposed to assist each other, like young saplings in a forest which will withstand a storm together where singly they would be blown down or uprooted. The Buddhists have always insisted upon the necessity of the *saṁgha*, the community of monks, whereas the Hindu tendency is toward isolated individual, solitary effort.

We are warned that it is utterly vain and a waste of time to argue about the ultimate goal. We should rather apply ourselves to the means at our disposal for actual practice at the beginner's level until we are invited, as it were, if not literally by a guru, into the next higher stage. In these matters as well as in matters of engineering and technology, considerable intelligence and technique are needed and these require much training. Eventually, at least by some, the goal is finally reached; however, the *Prajñā* is not quite so optimistic as the *Lotus* about everyone "making it".

Revived interest in the increasingly famous *Lotus Sūtra* is now being spread under the umbrella of the Soka Gakkai. Conze gives 100 B.C. for the approximate time when it came into circulation. This is the Mahāyāna Sūtra *par excellence* in that it departs from the older Theravāda *Arhat* ideal according to which those who undergo the proper training and discipline may achieve *nirvāṇa*, not to say Buddhahood since in Theravāda tradition there was no theology of Buddhahood as such. The *Lotus Sūtra* replaces the *Arhat* ideal with that of the *Bodhisattva* and teaches that everyone, without qualification, can achieve not only *nirvāṇa* but Buddhahood, a sort of comparticipation in the eternal Buddha nature.

An objection might be raised to the effect that the *Lotus Sūtra* contains little that is genuinely philosophical and belongs more to the history of religions than to the history of philosophy. To this we must indeed concede quite a bit, but we must quickly and emphatically add that even in the case of Stoicism and Epicureanism the trend is increasingly religious. The importance of the *Lotus Sūtra* really lies in its influence and popularity in the historical developments of Buddhism in China, Japan and Korea. Nichiren claimed that it was the *only* authoritative Buddhist scripture, while the other Japanese Buddhists of the medieval period also acknowledged its primary importance even when they would not discard other texts in its favor.

As for its basic characteristics, we cannot avoid the description syncretistic, no less so, but perhaps scarcely any more so, than any text of the same period anywhere in Eurasia. The form, as in the *Milindapañha* and many Pāli texts, is a dialogue. In contrast to the Pāli Canon, in the *Lotus Sūtra* we find the historical Buddha (*Nirmāṇakāya*) deified and speaking as the manifestation of the Eternal Buddha (*Dharmakāya*). Already we find the *Bodhisattva* vow not to enter final *nirvāṇa* until all suffering creatures have been "saved" from *saṃsāra*, and we find the prophecies of the Buddha Śākyamuni concerning the innumerable *Bodhisattvas* to come.

In the famous parable of the burning house it is told how the children do not understand the father's warning since they do not even know what fire is. Fire here symbolizes *saṃsāra*, the First Noble Truth that all is suffering. Herein may be an answer to those who object to other-worldliness as escapism. Escape indeed ! Consider the alternative ! Consider the fire !

Chapter VII of the *Lotus Sūtra* contains a horrendously supernatural account of the Buddha's enlightenment which historically consisted in the realization that the supernatural may and should be neglected in favor of activities positively leading to relief of suffering and that metaphysical disputes are indeed a cause of suffering. This mythologization of a supremely anti-mythological perspective exemplifies the basic cultural phenomenon of re-mythologization following a period of scepticism such as we may well yet see again in our own time. An elaborate heavenly hierarchy figures prominently, reminiscent of the Byzantio-Russian Liturgy. Splendor, luxury, magnificence, awesome majesty and all the superlatives have replaced the quiet simplicity of the Theravāda tradition. We even find a sort of Heavenly Jerusalem the description of which is scarcely rivaled by the Book of Revelation.

The *Sūtra* continues for nineteen more chapters — although there is considerable doubt about the authenticity of some of the last sections — of extremely elaborate language, almost sensuous at times, certainly ornate in the extreme. Towards the end of the text as it now stands is an account of the *Bodhisattva* Avalokiteśvara the mere remembrance of whom is still considered by many to be sufficient for salvation and who is later transformed, as it were, into the Chinese Protectoress and Mediatrix Kuan-yin (or Kuanon in Japan).

Now out of all of this elaborate and ornate mythologizing, what can be derived that is philosophical? The answer must frankly be, not much. However, if all of this is taken as a manifestation of a radical change in the concept of man, or rather of what any man can become, then we do have a challenge. Once again, as in Byzantino-Alexandrian Christianity, the issue is no longer human nature as a natural given whether good, bad, neither, or both in mixture; but the issue is human nature *sub specie transformationis*. And that in world history is truly revolutionary. It is for this reason that we would emphasize the *Lotus Sūtra* over most of the other Mahāyāna sūtra literature, most of which carries the same themes.

The Bodhisattva Ideal

The *Bodhisattva* ideal is one of the major developments of the Mahāyāna. Aside from the *Gitā* and Śabara Mīmāṁsā, there is little that is datable that is distinctly Hindu from this period, the whole of India evidently having been dominated by Buddhism and Jainism. Generally, Jainism developed nothing comparable to the *Bodhisattva* vow but remained (and remains today) more akin to the Theravāda than to the Mahāyāna pattern. It may be that it was from the *Larger Prajñāpāramitā Sūtra* and the *Smaller Prajñā* that the concept of stages in the mystical way spread throughout Asia.

Perhaps one of the obstacles to understanding the *Bodhisattva* and his *mahākaruṇā* (great compassion) is the structuring of Good at the transcendental (*pāramārthika*) level, a Good beyond the opposites, beyond the chain of endless causation, in complete freedom in the metaphysical as well as moral sense. The trouble is, evidently, that this cannot be understood in a merely lexicographical sense but must be *lived*, and that perhaps in an entirely different environment, in a Buddhist monastery rather than in a secular university. The transcendental or absolute level (inevitably theologized, of course) is conceived of as a super-abundance of everything, saving the world even when it does not deserve it; and hence everything is exaggerated to the extreme, to the highest imaginable degree. The *meden agan*, the middle way, has given way to the *ouden agan*, "nothing is too much". We cannot stretch upward far enough, for the Ultimate is ever beyond our wildest imagination; and the extremes are where the encounter with the Divine occurs, so that fantasy replaces fact and miracles replace rationally planned human enterprise. Science goes into cold storage, as it were — with a slight exception among the mathematicians in India — and in the *Lotus* and the *Prajñāpāramitā Sūtras* one is definitely instructed *not* to study 'philosophy' because it will contaminate faith.

It is more than mere altruism which motivates the *Bodhisattva*; he is more or less an integral power in the turning of the Wheel of the *Dharma* in history, and his vow to refrain from final *nirvāṇa* is as essentially a part of his own salvation as it is necessary for the salvation of others. This stage of the development of his charisma is only the next to last, for after leaving this world he becomes a mediating demigod, or saint-with-a-cult, remarkably resembling that of the Catholic system of canonized saints, but perhaps exalted more as saviours or archangels, almost as avatārs of a whole era. Yamaguchi lists some chief *Bodhisattvas* :

> Manjusri Bodhisattva is the Bodhisattva of Wisdom, the prajna of the Madhyamika theory which was set forth in

> history by Nagarjuna. Manjusri is said to represent the wisdom of the Buddha. The sharp sword which he holds in his hand symbolizes wisdom which cuts through the cloud of ignorance, which cuts away human attachment to the illusion of subject and object.
>
> Samantabhadra Bodhisattva stands for the mercy (*karuna*) of the Buddha. He has vowed to serve all sentient beings by guiding them to a happy life which is attained by the profound intention to be free from all attachment and resistance to things. In him, action is identical with his vow. Mahasthama-Prapta represents the wisdom and mercy of the Buddha. *Maha* means great, *sthama* means power, and *prapta* means to reach. The power of wisdom is supposed to run through the dharma world in ten directions and to cut off the attachment of the ignorant. He especially represents the wisdom of Amida Buddha.
>
> Avalokitesvara is one who observes (*avalokita*) the world and saves all sufferers freely (*isvara*). Avalokitesvara represents the mercy, the compassion, of Amida Buddha.
>
> Maitreya Bodhisattva has not yet arrived at this earth. His abode is in the Tushita heaven. He is supposed to be a future Buddha who is to come to this world to preach the dharma when the teaching delivered by Sakyamuni Buddha decays. *Maitreya* literally means benevolent, and he will come to the world as an incarnation of great benevolence, just as Sakyamuni Buddha did.[1]

This includes developments later than we shall be immediately concerned with, for although evidently the *Bodhisattva* ideal had rather early origins, the emergence of these particular *Bodhisattvas* in this full role of plenipotentiary mediators, and as not only founders of new sects but as virtual world saviours, is of later development. What concerns us most is that the Mahāyāna Bodhisattva ideal replaces the Theravāda *Pratyekabuddha* and *Arhat* ideals — the *Pratyekabuddha* is one who attains enlightenment without the help of a teacher whereas the *Arhat* is helped by a teacher; neither is especially concerned with helping others.

Sangharakshita lists the ten vows (*praṇidhānas*) of the *Bodhisattva* according to the *Daśabhūmika Sūtra*:

> (1) To provide for the worship of all the Buddhas without exception. (2) To maintain the religious Discipline that has been taught by the Buddhas and to preserve the

> teaching of the Buddhas. (3) To see all the incidents in the earthly career of a Buddha. (4) To realize the Thought of Enlightenment, to practise the duties of a *bodhisattva*, to acquire all the *pāramitās* and purify all the stages of his career, (5) To mature all beings and establish them in the knowledge of the Buddha, *viz.*, all the four classes of beings who are in the six states of existence. (6) To perceive the whole Universe. (7) To purify and cleanse all the Buddha-fields. (8) To enter on the Great Way and to produce a common thought and purpose in all *bodhisattvas*. (9) To make all actions of the body, speech and mind fruitful and successful. (10) To attain the supreme and perfect Enlightenment and to preach the Doctrine.[2]

Along with these vows, the path of the *Bodhisattva* consists of the *pāramitās* (perfections) and the ten *bhūmis* (stages).

> The Six Perfections are (1) the Perfection of Giving (*dāna-pāramitā*), (2) the Perfection of Morality (*sila-pāramitā*), (3) the Perfection of Patience (*kṣānti-pāramitā*), (4) the Perfection of Vigour (*virya-pāramitā*), (5) the Perfection of Meditation (*dhyāna-pāramitā*), and (6) the Perfection of Wisdom (*prajñā-pāramitā*).[3]

Though these are the traditional Six *Pāramitās*, the *Daśabhūmika Sūtra* adds four more — *upāya-kauśalya-pāramitā* or the Perfection of Skilful Means, the *praṇidhānas* as a *pāramitā*, *bala-pāramitā* or the Perfection of Strength or Power, and *jñāna-pāramitā* or the Perfection of Knowledge[4] — and then correlates these ten *pāramitās* with the ten *bhūmis* or stages in the *Bodhisattva*'s career.

Concerning the *bhūmis*, one may wince at the great psychic expanse involved and the tendency to compound superlatives in the elaboration of each. It is rather to our shame that we have evidently lost the spiritual discipline necessary to experience these planes of existence by being entirely too much engrossed in exterior affairs. The 'interior' world is much more vast than the 'exterior', and although few are capable nowadays of even penetrating the first barrier, the challenge is vividly before us to re-explore these regions. Sinha gives us a relatively concise presentation of the *bhūmis* :

> The first is the stage of joy (pramuditā); in it he feels joy because he devotes himself to the work of a saviour; he

> realizes the selflessness (nairatmya) of the self, and of other things; he realizes the Norm (dharmatā) as the common nature of them all. The second is the stage of purity (vimalā) free from egoism and sin; in it he practices moral precepts, meditation (dhyāna) and trance (samādhi). The third is the stage of illumination (prabhākarī); in it he practises bhāvanās or sublime meditations and patience and forbearance; he shines with tolerance with people; he sheds anger, hatred, and delusion. The fourth is the radiant (arciṣmatī) stage; in it he practises the greatest energy in good actions and meditation. The fifth is the invincible (sudurjayā) stage; in it he practises meditation on the four noble truths, which leads to transcendental knowledge (prajñā). The sixth stage is called turned towards (abhimukhī); in it he turns to the chain of causation (pratītyasamutpāda) and unsubstantiality; he is right in face of Nirvāṇa; he transcends good and evil, and achieves transcendent purity; he is now Arhat or Bodhisattva. The seventh stage is called far going (dūraṅgamā); he becomes an adept in all means of leading others to salvation; he feels great compassion for them, and helps them in their troubles; he seeks enlightenment which will enable him to effect universal salvation. The eighth stage is called immovable (acalā); in it he attains supreme knowledge, transcends duality of selfishness, knows all things as rooted in Suchness (Tathatā), and teaches the Dharma to others. The ninth stage is called the good (sādhumatī); endowed with the highest knowledge, he becomes a preacher of the Law, and prepares the creatures for Nirvāṇa. The tenth stage is called cloud of the Law (dharmamegha); in it he is enshrined in the heart of the Dharmakāya, acquires the powers of Buddha, and reaches the end of his career.[5]

Conze reports that the schematization of the stages of spiritual progress or ascesis did not receive much attention among the Mādhyamikas or the Sarvāstivādins, but did get full elaboration among the Yogācārins. It might be noted that although there are hints of such things already in Philo and certainly in Plotinus, they are not developed until we get to such persons as Clement of Alexandria, and not fully until Dionysius the Pseuda-Areopagite. Among the Arian and Coptic traditions and in Tertullian there is scarcely anything comparable. It is possible that Neo-Platonism is the prime source of the elaborate schematization of the stages of spiritual progress and that its influence was very widespread.

However, it is just as possible that Yogâcâra, as expressing the *Weltgeist* of the time, was the source and it spread from there. Still, the safer hypothesis may be that chronologically the idea of mystagogy, whatever its source, develops everywhere after about 325. Again, this is one more of the very many questions which it is our job to open whether we have an answer or not.

Mystagogy enters as a 'science' much as psychoanalysis has in our own time. Of course there is not complete consistency in the reportings of these schematizations anymore than there is complete consistency among psychoanalysts or even sociologists today. These matters being subjective by nature, it is commendable that an attempt is made nevertheless to treat them 'scientifically' by ordering them as rationally as possible, Likewise, it may be naive to presuppose that the experience reported is always the same, just as it is not always that we get the same report from different witnesses about the same event. Conze explains that in these stages of spiritual progress we are dealing not with merely rational processes but with a different dimension of reality and experience, that of various degrees of concentration, levels of awareness, and that indeed the last stages must be realized only in a sort of trance experience. Thus, once again, the praiseworthy thing is that a sense of system is finally emerging historically just where one might least expect it after a long twilight of eclecticism and unsystematic syncretism. Comparative mysticism with its sense of system and sensitivity in observation of interior phenomena (which are not necessarily 'subjective' altogether in so far as they are universal or universalizable) might be helpful to some modern psychologies which, however, are concerned as pathology with the sub-normal rather than with the supra-normal.

The last term in the ten stages is supremely important. The aspirant who reaches this level affects all aspects of life from art and ritual to politics and economics. The method for this is not in the planning and execution of social programs but in gaining control of those unseen factors and forces that control human destiny, the 'principalities and powers' in the region well past the hurdle of the Cosmic Ego.

The relative success of Buddhist tradition in all aspects of the subsequent cultural developments in Asia is best judged by its own criterion and not by any imposed from without by Aristotelian canons. It is generally asserted that the Buddhist systems as world-negating have been a deterrent to the development of a sound social order and of culture in general. The opposite is quite the case. To see this one need only trace out the influence of Buddhist rulers, not only in India and Bactria, but also in Cambodia, Burma, Ceylon, Laos, etc., as well as in China and Japan. Not that Buddhism has necessarily a better record than Christianity or Islam or Confucianism; by its own standard it too has failed miserably in bringing about the Kingdom of God on earth, which is, perhaps, the nearest equivalent to the *Dharma-megha*.

The Trikāya Doctrine

One of the chief features of the Mahāyāna is the development of a Buddhology not unlike the development of the Christology by the Church Fathers of a slightly later period. This may not be of interest to those whose concern is philosophy in the narrower sense, but it does represent in the history of the world's motivating ideas an opening of the realm of personalism: a metaphysics of the Person almost replaces a metaphysics of the Self.

The most controversial point in the development of a Buddhology was whether more than one Buddha could exist, and next to this, whether the real Buddha is simply the historical person or a Cosmic Being incarnated in the person of Śākyamuni. While the *Questions of Milinda* insists that there can be only one great Buddha, the fully developed Mahāyāna position qualifies this. On the analogy of many rulers existing in one world, because of the necessity of saving all beings scattered throughout the world, because of the danger of the *Dharma* lapsing in different periods of the world's history, because of the imperfection of the great mass of mankind, and for similar reasons, the principle of hierarchy begins to replace that of dialectic, and there begins to appear a hierarchy of *Bodhisattvas* and Buddhas. This quasi-polytheistic element is made possible not in spite of, but because of, the idealistic metaphysics, since the idealistic comprehension of unity (or so it is argued) is more vast and therefore can more readily include the many in proper perspective.

The concept of Unity that is 'big' with relations is new and becomes fairly common in Eurasia from 100 A.D. or so down to the present. The various trinities may be considered as fresh projections of the idea of perfection or interpreted in terms of the contemporary trend towards model construction. Why a triadical Ultimate ? Because it must be inclusive of relationalities. What, then, are the possible relative emphases within any possible triad ? Domination by one, subordination of the other two; domination of one by any other two; or, if complete equality, is this an equality of reciprocity or one-way relations ? Does the nexus of interrelations in such an ultimate triad generate or already contain all possible relationalities, or is the triad only a bad compromise between extreme monism and pluralism ? And if there is a distinguishable third between these, is that going to satisfy the dualist, especially in the matter of transcendence and manifestation on the one hand in the 'descending' ontogenetic scale, and the dualism of empirical vs. *a priori* conceptions on the other in the 'ascending' epistemological scale ? Does triadizing simplify, then, or make even more complex the problem of knowledge of transcendentals ? And yet, how else to deal with indefinables ?

The trinities should be seen as sincere attempts to deal with metaphysical problems. They represent a new cycle of the old problem inherited from the *Upaniṣads*, *Tao Teh Ching*, and the Pre-Socratics, i.e., the problem of the One and the many. If the ultimate is the One, then there can be no "other"; but since there at least seems to be some other in some sense, the One must be inclusive, that is, inclusive of the characteristics of Deity or of whatever structurally replaces Deity if atheism is asserted. But if the One is inclusive, then it is no longer the One pure and undefiled. Such is the problem. As for solutions, they were exhaustively discussed in India, China, and the Levant, if not also in Rome, North Africa and Spain, during our period to the modern period (circa 1500).

The *Trikāya* Doctrine, the levels of embodiment of the Buddha and evidently to some extent of *Bodhisattvas* also, includes the Earthly Body (*Nirmāṇakāya*), the Subtle Body (*Sambhogakāya*), and the Unmanifest Body (*Dharmakāya*). The arguments concerning the interrelations of these three levels in the different Mahāyāna schools became as desperate and intense, as abstract and abstruse, as those arguments concerning the nature of the three Persons of the Christian Trinity: Father unmanifested, Son manifesting, Holy Ghost manifested and emanately operative. It remains to be determined whether there may have been any mutual influence. However, our thesis is that the tracing of influences is not so important as the discovery of the deeper common ground out of which these developments grow. Again, if it be objected that this is theology and not philosophy, the answer should be plain enough: there was no division between the two in East or West (or North or South) until a much later date. No one ever thought of proposing a two-truth theory, such as one finds in Averroes and Aquinas, during this Han-Hellenistic-Bactrian Period.

The Buddha, the *Dharma*, the *saṁgha*, as all Buddhists of all denominations still affirm, correspond to the Christian affirmation of the Christ, the moral code in the Ten Commandments and Jesus' summary of the law, and the faith in the Holy Catholic Church. In Islam one may find essentially the same thing. There is no fancy metaphysics or supernaturalism here necessarily since it is simple common sense to realize that these are the irreducible components of any tradition whatsoever: the charismatic figure, the teachings (usually moral, though not necessarily or exclusively so), and the society for the promotion thereof.

The Tathatā Doctrine

The *Tathatā* usually simply translated as "Suchness", is perhaps the most fundamental concept developed by the Mahāyāna schools comparable to the Vedāntic *nirguṇa* Brahman or the Neo-Platonic "the One". To anyone familiar with the literature of the *Upaniṣads* or with the later Advaitic tradition of Śaṅkara and his school, that this concept of "Suchness" or "Thusness" sounds very much like the *nirguṇa* Brahman of Śaṅkara should not be surprising since he is in direct line of influence from Aśvaghoṣa and was strongly influenced by Vijñānavāda. In Nāgārjuna *Tathatā* is virtually equated with *śūnya*, "Emptiness" — we prefer this translation to "the Void" because the latter in Greek has a quite different connotation — which also takes a much more metaphysical range of meaning in Mahâyâna than we found in Theravâda. Much of the Mahâyâna literature uses the terms *Tathatā* and *śūnya* interchangeably as though there were no difference.

The *Tathatā* is 'realized' at the end of a long process of 'emptying' in meditation. Having come to an awareness of the 'emptiness' of all things, one can then see things for just what they are and are not, from the great expanse of the cosmos to one's own or others' slightest psychological quirks. Thus it is that the Buddha himself becomes the *Tathāgata*, the one who has realized Suchness. In addition to *karuṇā* (mercy), *prajñā* (wisdom) must also proceed out of this *Tathatā*. As Yamaguchi puts it :

> In other words, Suchness in its entirety is to be realized through the inseparable connection of coming and going, that is, of entering into and emerging from, the Suchness. This is what is called the altruistic Nirvana (literally "nonresident Nirvana"), the Nirvana of one who does not reside in the world of transmigration because he is wise, and does not reside in Nirvana either, because he is merciful. Such an inseparable connection between wisdom and mercy is a belief running through all Mahāyāna Sutras.[6]

Since the concept of the eternal is still subject to dialectical opposition to the temporal just as process is opposable to Being or subject to object, perhaps the best indication is that *Tathatā* is that which is left over after all dialectic has exhausted all possibly conceivable principles. "Beyond all possible dialectic" is to be taken seriously even if it seems impossible, for the intention is the 'just thereness' which is beyond all our bickerings in terms of affirmations and negations and beyond all of our terminologies and definitions. To say that it is a principle of no-principle is to come close to it, although still this does not adequately distinguish it from the *anirvacanīya*, the indescribability of Brahman. Such locutions as "principle of no-principle" are common in the literature of this period, not only in Taoism but also in Mahāyāna and Neo-Platonism.

With the Mahāyāna in general and with Śūnyavāda in particular, the problem of the indefinables is the problem *par excellence*. This is also the problem of the Greek Fathers following after Philo, especially Gregory of Nyssa and also Plotinus to some extent, in the form classically known as the *via negativa*, which is very much like the usual interpretations of the *neti neti* of the *Upaniṣads* or the indescribability of the Tao. The *via negativa* completely — or almost completely, for there were others like Wang Ch'ung later — dominated Eurasia from about 200 A.D. at least until Abelard, Rāmānuja, Chou Tun-yi, and al-Fārābī, and really even somewhat after them.

Neither positive nor negative, yet including both positive and negative, the *Tathatā* is that without which even positive and negative cannot be defined. More a perspective than a concept, it at once sublates and transcends the difficulty encountered by all logic in properly relating the both/and and the neither/nor. Even logically such a position is seen as necessary, and yet few systems have been bold enough to back into it for fear that all else will 'disappear' once one has gotten into it. But the meditative discipline is designed to deliver the philosopher from this fear.

How can we know the unknown? The answer comes that the *Tathatā* is neither known nor unknown but is that absence by which the known and the unknown are distinguished from each other. Mookerjee points out that the argument between the Mīmāṁsā philosophers Prabhākara and Kumārila and the Buddhists hinged largely on the issue of the objectivity of negation as such. The Mahāyānists argued that negation is itself illusory, at least as illusory as a notion founded on uncertain, momentary perception must be. Therefore, negation is also only a fiction, eventually to be eliminated by its processes as unsubstantial as the things about which the thoughts occur. As such, therefore, even the subject-object relation breaks down, for it is also a sort of infinite series of degrees of connection always likewise capable of disjunction. What remains? Only an empty locus whereby one observes these mental 'tricks' going on. That locus is the *Tathatā*. And yet even to call it a locus is being too definite, for the *Tathatā*, perhaps even more than the most astute theorizings about the Tao, is also beyond-and-inclusive of both the definite and the indefinite. Perhaps at best the Neo-Kantian may read into it something like a limiting concept; but his also is inadequate because the limiting concept involves the concept of limitation, and although in a sense the *Tathatā* is itself beyond limitation and non-limitation, in a more radical sense it is that by which both limitation and the concept of limitation are discerned as coming into being and passing away. The infinite series, valid or invalid, only gives way to the suspicion that there is a 'nothingness' and only a 'nothingness' behind the series. Therefore, one has no choice but to seek for *nirvāṇa* wherein one is finally delivered from these quandaries. But even the assertion of liberation, either in the moral or in the intellectual sense, is also non-liberation. *Nirvāṇa*, it is said, is *saṃsāra*, and *saṃsāra* is *nirvāṇa*; otherwise, one is still condemned to a quasi-dualism.

The Buddhist genius is largely based in the way of non-clinging; to "let go" even one's most cherished preconceptions, this is the approach. According to Yamaguchi, if one does not come into this realization, this awakening to the truth that even the best absolute is not so absolute after all, one does not easily become open to the exercise of compassion (*karuṇā*), for the essence of suffering is bondage to the false notion that there is anything one *can* cling to. One may not become established, enlightened, if one does not become, in a profound sense, self-reliant. The Buddhist self-raliance is not a valiant self-centeredness flaunting conventions uselessly or committing *hybris* in any other way; rather, it is the quiet confidence attained by total detachment in the field of ideas as well as in morals. Such is the Buddha's secret of peace and the capacity of the *Bodhisattva* to reject *nirvāṇa* for the sake of those still bound to the fetters of belief and disbelief. But scepticism is also avoided because of the profound contemplative reservoir of spiritual energy fully under control.

If one takes scepticism in the classical sense, such as that espoused by Carneades or even by Sextus Empiricus himself, then that is closer to the Mādhyamika than many would like to assert since censorship of that school ever since the time of Saint Augustine has conditioned a wrong attitude. The "suspended judgment" idea is not far, perhaps, from the Buddhist detachment, the Middle Way, free of dogmatism. In both cases, wisdom (*prajñā*) is cultivated as a general guide to right action and philosophy is a way of life, not merely a set of definitions and deductions. This does not indicate an either/or situation, however. One should be as expert at logic and debate as anyone; but one should realize that logic, like a computer, is only an instrument and that something more is needed in order to know how to use it wisely. By accepting metaphysics and thereby running the risk of ontologizing processes or absolutizing some ultimate or other and thus unintentionally providing something to cling to, some God or Buddha to worship, some means of security in a crumbling world other than mere human self-reliance, these Mahāyāna schools, especially Vijñānavāda, may have rejected scepticism only to fall into fresh dogmatizing and to allow gross magic and superstition to re-enter what had been a rational humanist movement but which becomes a religion in the full medieval sense as exemplified in the pure fideism of the Amida cult with its theology of grace.

Once you try to define the undefinable or try to locate the transcendent, then even in the attempt to do so, dialectically you will soon find yourself talking about everything else in relation to it. Since it can be defined only in terms of what it is not, then it is whatever it is by virtue of its not being everything else. Then, and not unrelated to this process, it gets combined in moderated form with everything else since the human mind just cannot conceive of a that-beyond-all-relationalities since that-beyond-all-relationalities is itself a relation. Hence, in addition to being posited at first as relationless and completely transcendent, it becomes or comes to be considered as inclusive of all relationalities actual and potential. And that, evidently, is what the *Tathāgatagarbha* is. It is probably wrong to try to comprehend the *Tathāgatagarbha*, the Great Matrix of Becoming, since it is by definition, as it were, the incomprehensible. Better perhaps just to acknowledge that there may be that which we do not and cannot understand — a very good exercise in mental health, that, to give us a little humility. Perhaps we might try taking the Buddha or Jesus as our model instead of Prometheus.

Further comparison of *Tathatā* could and should be made

with the Neo-Platonist concept of "the One" and the corresponding discipline of the *via negativa*, especially as developed by Origen and Gregory of Nyssa, the brother of Saint Basil. As for a comparison with the Tao in China, an affirmative answer is inevitable, the only qualification being that most Taoists between Chuang Tzu and Ko Hung were less enfatuated with the inexpressible Tao than with alchemy, magic and minimal speculations about the practical application of the *yin* and *yang* — a note not easily found in Aśvaghoṣa or others immediately after him. Nevertheless, it was not long before the amalgamation of these Mahāyāna concepts of transcendence with Taoism began (designated *Ko-i*). Taoist terminology was the only language available for translation of these Sanskrit technical terms, and thus it at first appeared to the Chinese that Buddhism was simply Taoism in another dress. In spite of the fact that evidently *Tathatā* did get translated as Tao in the *Ko-i* sequence and syncretism, there might be the distinction that the Tao has echoes of the harmony of all things and is more like the *Tathāgatagarbha* than *Tathatā* itself.

The atmosphere of syncretism became so heavy by the end of our present cycle from about 100 A.D. down through 325 and on into the seventh and eighth centuries that both *Tathatā* and *nirvāṇa* got mixed up with everything. If the Undifferentiated (*Tathatā*, Tao, *nirguṇa* Brahman, *Yahwe*) becomes the primary focus for thought, then all finite distinctions get blurred. And so it happens that in many texts by the time Buddhism has penetrated China and entered Korea and Japan there are assertions that there is no difference between *saṃsāra* and *nirvāṇa*, between good and bad, ugly and beautiful, *māyā* and reality.

Aśvaghoṣa

As usual, dates are not certain, but it is known that Aśvaghoṣa had patronage from Kanishka whose reign was from 78 to 102 A.D. Aśvaghoṣa was a poet and dramatist and so belongs as much to the history of literature as to the history of philosophy or religion. It is only relatively recently that manuscripts of three of his dramas have been discovered. Such is a basic problem in dealing with many thinkers of our Han-Hellenistic-

Bactrian Period : who knows where or when there will be further finds that will revolutionize interpretations ? Therefore, much must be taken as tentative. We might mention that these dramas concern the conversions of Maudgalyāyana and Sāriputta, famous disciples of the Buddha, and include some heavily philosophical dialogues. Indeed, it should not be surprising to us to find Aśvaghoṣa using allegory just as freely as Philo and many other writers of this period.

Virtually all of the themes in Mahāyāna which we have discussed can be found in Aśvaghoṣa's work *The Awakening of Faith*, and it is here that they are all first to be found together. Thus Aśvaghoṣa is generally taken to be the first systematizer of the various Mahāyāna doctrines, and the subsequent Mahāyāna schools can be traced back to him. For example, Aśvaghoṣa's "point that Reality is Indescribable and beyond all the categories of intellect and that therefore it can be called neither *śūnya* nor *aśūnya* nor both nor neither, was developed by Śūnyavāda, and the point that Reality is Consciousness was developed by Vijñānavāda."[7] Also, in *The Awakening of Faith* we find the *Bodhisattva* ideal with the delay of *nirvāṇa* out of compassion (*karuṇā*) for suffering beings, the doctrine of levels of understanding so that Aśvaghoṣa claims to be presenting the real teachings of the Buddha which had been only partially understood heretofore, an emphasis on the role of ignorance (*avidyā*) and wisdom (*prajñā*), the view that while the intellect should be developed still it cannot of itself lead to enlightenment, and so on with most of the other traditional Mahāyāna doctrines, especially as found in Vasubandhu and Nāgārjuna.

The traditional interpretations of Aśvaghoṣa stress his position as the first comprehensive expounder of Mahāyāna and his doctrine of *Tathatā*. As with so many other ultimates, *Tathatā* seems to be both multi-faceted and yet nothing that we can very easily or conclusively categorize.

> Reality is Tathatā. As the ultimate Existence, it is called Bhūtatathatā; as Pure Spirit it is called Bodhi or Prajñā or Ālayavijñāna; as a Harmonious Whole, it is called Dharmakāya or Dharmadhātu; and as Bliss having infinite merits, it is called Tathāgatagarbha. Viewed from the empirical standpoint, it is saṁsāra, the cycle of birth

> and death; viewed from the ultimate standpoint, it is Nirvāṇa or the realization of positive bliss. It is essentially Indescribable because intellect cannot compass it. It is beyond the four categories of the understanding. It is neither existence nor non-existence nor both nor neither; it is neither unity nor plurality nor both nor neither; it is neither affirmation nor negation nor both nor neither.[8]

As we have noted, though there has been endless controversy over the precise meaning of *Tathatā*, it might best be expressed by Suzuki's term "Suchness", or by the simple phrase "that which has become such", or even by the term "quiddity", for later Mahāyāna began (as did Duns Scotus) to distinguish "thatness" from "whatness".

The concept of the *Ālayavijñāna*, the Great Storehouse of Consciousness wherein all psychological possibilities are present and appear to belong to an objective world, is also found in Aśvaghoṣa. The *Ālaya* is spoken of as moving towards the Absolute or at least knowledge of it, which is the realization that everything possible has actual existence only by virtue of its being a part of the Absolute. What is involved here is a double reflexivity wherein notions move within the totality of the *Ālaya* until it is realized that they are contained, as it were, in something. Then that 'container' concept is absolutized in the realization that it can have neither outside nor inside; and from that its uniqueness is inferred along with its absoluteness, its *Tathatā*, its "being-thereness".

We must, however, be wary of the word "Absolute", towards which one may acquire a strong negative bias when it comes to the Buddhist systems. The spirit of Buddhism in all its manifold branches has been to insist on change as primary over permanency, and "no soul" as opposed to a substantial, eternal entity. Therefore, it is not clear how any Buddhist could have any Absolute without becoming a Hindu. Some claim that this is just what happened and that Aśvaghoṣa, a convert from Hinduism to Buddhism, is one of the chief thinkers who is to blame for this re-Absolutizing of Buddhism.

Bimala Churn Law, on the other hand, concludes that Aśvaghoṣa was closer to the Theravāda tradition.[9] According to Law, Aśvaghoṣa emphdasize the Four Noble Truths, *nirvāṇa* being no more or less than the cessation of suffering. He stressed avoidance of the extremes rather than (as one might infer from other interpretations) idealist metaphysics, which of course is one of the extremes to be avoided if one is to stay close to the original teachings of the Buddha himself. According to Law, Aśvaghoṣa's teaching is primarily ethical, and he puts rather strong emphasis on faith as almost a means of knowledge, or rather a precondition for knowledge, since if one does not believe that the fruits of ones efforts will be useful or valid then the effort involved will not be worth the trouble. He also points to the very likely influence of the *Gītā* on Aśvaghoṣa.

In Aśvaghoṣa, according to Law, the terms *śūnyatā* and *Tathāgata* are used more in the context in which they are used in the Theravāda tradition than in the later Mahāyāna. The emphasis is always on the simple, basic, universal Buddhist teachings of the Fourfold Noble Truths, the Eightfold Noble Path, and the doctrine of no-soul. Evidently, Aśvaghoṣa simply embellished these things so that they would be attractive to all and sundry for centuries to come, and that itself he did so well that the whole world will forever be indebted to him. Traditionally Aśvaghoṣa was one of the greatest preachers/lecturers of all time. Holding debates with everyone (he travelled widely), he was scarcely rivalled by anyone. On occasion he could move even the sternest of audiences to tears of penitence and — a rare thing these days — tears of compassion for the suffering of humanity and all living beings. We cannot pretend to be in a position to arbitrate the different interpretations, but there can be no question of Aśvaghoṣa's pivotal position in the history of Buddhism.

D. The Rise of Christianity

Clement of Alexandria

Clement of Alexandria (150-216) really needs no introduction that would not, in essentials at least, apply also to Origen (185-254). They go together for the most part since Origen follows him implicitly except in details which are significant only to specialists. Nevertheless, to omit Clement would be historically inaccurate since his position is rather unique within the history of Christianity. He is transitional between the earlier apologists such as Justin Martyr and the later fullfledged philosopher-theologians who no longer were under constraint to refute living pagan philosophers for the simple reason that there were very few of them left. The Church was growing strong enough to stand on its own feet, so to speak, even if there were many heathens outside and many heretics inside; and Clement was one of those who, at least in the intellectual realm, helped in its strengthening. He begins in earnest to build a complete world-view from both the Greek and the Hebraic sources, to develop a synthesis, indeed. So Clement cannot be neglected even though he may be said to be a lesser figure than many of those who follow after him.

Since the century when Philo, Seneca, Aenesidemus, Apollonius, Jesus and Paul and others had lived and struggled for reform, things had gotten worse, not better. It was a time of decay and degeneracy, and the Christian Church as a proletarian institution which was feared as subversive by the officialdom was gaining strength, although by no means had it yet assumed the responsibility, as later within even a generation or two it had to do, of pulling things back together after the virtually total collapse of the Empire and the re-separation of Greek and Roman worlds into the Greek East and the Latin West.

Quite in keeping with the spirit of the times, in which not only the Sceptics but even Seneca had already some familiarity with India, and in which virtually every educated man would have read *Tá Indika,* we know that Pantaenus, Clement's teacher, had been to India — although that was not so uncommon as many have hitherto supposed — and had studied something of Indian philosophy, although we must quickly ask what kind of Indian philosophy, whether such as converted Pyrrho and Carneades to Scepticism or some brand of Mahâyâna Buddhism or perhaps even Jainism. This shows the other side of Jayrazbhoy's theme of the influence of Greece and Rome on India, i.e., it shows mutual communication. Therefore, we should not be surprised if there are parallel trends of development with increasing interiorization of focus for philosophizing with only a minority such as Wang Ch'ung and Sextus Empiricus going to the opposite extreme of scepticism and with neither trend giving much hope for development of the empirical sciences.

Before his conversion to Christianity, Pantaenus had been a Stoic. The date of their first meeting is given as 180 A.D., a date marked by Marcus Aurelius' futile attempts on the Danube and other shrinkings of the Empire on the eastern frontier as Central Asia gains strength; Kanishka is at his zenith, and in China court intrigue among the eunuchs and general decadence and neglect had provoked the famous Revolt of the (Taoist) Yellow Turbans.

It was at Alexandria where Philo had lived and worked most of his life; it was at Alexandria that the vast library — perhaps not so vast as those at Nalanda in India and at Loyang in China, who can say ? —was accumulating; it was at Alexandria that science and engineering during this Han-Hellenistic-Bactrian Period made any advance at all; but most of all, it was at Alexandria that one found one of the most cosmopolitan collections of people from almost every country in the world.

Even more than Justin Martyr before him, and almost as much as Origen who soon followed after him, Clement appears to have virtually exhausted all the major works in Greek philosophy up to his time. Even Saint Jerome praised Clement as being the most learned of all Christians to his time, although it is quite likely that his way was a sort of eclectic use of the compendia of philosophy or other digests such as Plutarch, for example, had produced scarcely a generation earlier, for such were rather popular then as now. Because of his profuse use of the Greek classics, Clement was accused by some of his fellow believers of actually "doing the devil's work to pretend that anything more than simple faith was required."[1] It seems that after almost two thousand years this problem would have been solved; but we seem to have still the same spectrum from the Bible-pounding hot-gospellers to those who would rather not draw any line at all between being a Christian and being a Hindu, Muslim, Zen disciple, Theosophist, or what have you.

The stereotype characterization or memory-peg identification for Clement is that he is the first seriously to propose philosophy as the "handmaiden of theology", the formula which Thomism still affirms. Clement says in the *Stromateis* (*Miscellanies*): "Greek philosophy as it were provides for the soul the preliminary cleansing and training required for the reception of the faith on which foundation the truth builds up the edifice of knowledge."[2] But while, like Saint Basil later on, Clement does not discourage but rather sanctions a discrete study of the Greek classics — not philosophy only but even Homer and the poets and dramatists — he does not allow a careless syncretism. Just because it is written in Greek does not necessarily mean that it is really 'civilized' literature. Actually Clement was scarcely doing more to Greek mythology and popular religion than Plato had attempted, but without. effect. Indeed, whether it can be claimed that Christianity in general and Clement in particular were historically any more successful than Plato might be debated, for no matter what name the religion bears the masses will probably still manifest a semi-superstitious and emotional approach to religion while it is in every culture thus far known only the elite who filter out logically consistent theology from the traditional practices.

Clement resembles Origen very closely in that he does not allow anything and everything into the Church. Evidently he wants to avoid both fanaticism and that sort of toleration which even ignores logic and ethics. For within the Church, as well as among those who were definitely on the periphery, there was not agreement between the extreme ascetics, such as Marcion and Tatian (fl. 172), and those whose faith taught that Christian redemption had restored the innocence of the Garden of Eden — though scarcely any one then took these things literally, and Alexandria was the chief seat of allegorizing — and that under such a Dispensation all things were legal, including communal marriage or free love within the holy community. The archetypes of both extremes of rigorous, even self-torturing asceticism and orgiastic exhaustive indulgence were Basilides and Valentine, at least by reputation. Both were respected by Clement who realized that there was a profound human problem here which would not be solved by any number of anathemas and excommunications. This sect and that one, now as then, from the Soka Gakkai to the Jehovah's Witnesses and perhaps even the Trotskyites, each has the *only* way.

In the *Stromateis* Clement makes his review of the history of Greek philosophy up to his time. His history makes a fascinating comparison and contrast with the similar works of Sextus Empiricus who was working only a generation or so after Clement. What they have in common is a typical — typical for the age, we reiterate — eclectic base, although of course Clement relies almost without question on Philo for his interpretation of the *Septuagint*. Clement says: "And philosophy — I do not mean the Stoic, or the Platonic, or the Epicurean, or the Aristotelian, but whatever has been well said by each of those sects, which teach righteousness along with a science pervaded by piety,— this eclectic whole I call philosophy."[3] Even if this were a unique passage it would in itself be quite enough to show that right from the outset among the Greek Fathers there was not the same sense of conflict between philosophy and the Christian religion or between reason and faith that has plagued the Latin West ever since Tertullian.

Clement's dependence on, and critical reappraisal of, the history of Greek philosophy can be exaggerated if one omits his equal or frequently even greater use of the *Septuagint* and his own originality in pruning these towards the development of specifically Christian philosophy. He attempts a synthesis of two very divergent traditions just as to some extent Philo had already done. Or should we say that Philo really had not done that but had simply attempted apologetics, trying to make Jewish doctrine at its best comprehensible in terms of the Greek philosophies of his time; whereas Clement, unlike even Justin Martyr in this respect, was no longer writing apologetics but was trying to get beyond that and to move from eclecticism towards synthesis, even though the actual result is really syncretism, not yet synthesis, which may not be said to reach full maturity until the time of Maximus Confessor or may be not even until Photius ?

Clement teaches that faith leads to truth, but faith to Clement is not just blind credulity or even the systematic opposite (but not contradictory) pole to reason that it is in the Thomist tradition and in al-*Gh*azāli or Madhva many centuries later. Rather, in his own words :

> Faith is then, so to speak, a comprehensive knowledge of the essentials; and knowledge is the strong and sure demonstration of what is received by faith, built upon faith by the Lord's teaching, conveying (the soul) on to infallibility, science, and comprehension. And, in my view, the first saving change is that from heathenism to faith, as I said before; and the second, that from faith to knowledge. And the latter terminating in love, thereafter gives the loving to the loved, that which knows to that which is known.[4]

Clement expresses his thankful reverence for Plato, a reverence which is almost as great as that of Ficino many centuries later. But one who has been brought up on twentieth century scholarship in Plato with heavy emphasis on the so-called Socratic dialogues rather than on the *Timaeus* may wonder. For it is really a concept of God perhaps even superimposed on Plato's own devastating dialectic that attracts Clement. Platonist though indeed Clement was, he is not content with panpsychism, as to a great extent both Plotinus and Proclus and others after him were. The dissatisfaction with panpsychism, however, was already somewhat present in Philo, who also wants to avoid pantheism. This constitutes a major problem which keeps bothering Jewish, Muslim, and Christian philosophers all through the centuries since Clement's punctuation of it.

Origen and Tertullian

It might be well to look at one of the primary Christian philosophers, namely Origen (185-254), to see not only how he looks in traditional interpretations (too many of which are biased from the standpoint of the Latin West as distinct from and often in conflict with the Graeco-Byzantine-Russian East) but also to seek new perspectives whereby reinterpretation in the light of his contemporaries in Eurasia becomes not only illuminative but perhaps even essential.

What we are concerned with is not the particularities of who then or now has the greater, better, or truer synthesis, but with the dynamics whereby the interfusion of philosophical themes brings forth a full spectrum of varieties in any intercultural encounter such as we know was going on during Origen's life-time. What, then, are the metaphysical principles here involved? (1) Degrees of reality of "the world"; (2) personification, growing into avatarhood and Buddhahood and Christhood, of ideals of human (now equals divine) perfection such that metaphysics and ethics fused inseparably in concept-goal of transformation; (3) infatuation with logic of negation and the problem of indefinables side by side with remythologizings of revelation as the basis of theology; (4) emergence of trinitarian principle, triadic patterning of problems gradually replacing older dichotomic dialectics, thus attempting bridge between mysticism and practical experience; (5) democratization of the science of spiritual progress, along with hierarchization of world view into multiple levels from Undifferentiated Absolute through angels and archangels and *Bodhisattvas*, Buddhas, Mediatrixes, and Christs, and ordinary saints and ordinary sinners to damned sinners, ghosts, demons, devils, etc., corresponding with the appearance of a whole gamut of heavens, purgatories, and hells; (6) finally and almost universally, neglect of natural sciences and public administration except under necessity or duress as responsibility rather than as ambition or inherited privilege.

Who were Origen's contemporaries and what was his historical milieu? In the Mediterranean, Alexandria had become the melting pot where every sort of ideas, cults, and virtues and vices could be found. It was a multi-national crossroads containing people from literally everywhere, including merchants from India and Iran and probably from what is now Southeast Asia as well. The Gupta Dynasty in North India was just beginning its efforts at reviving the Mauryan unification of all of India. The silk routes for trade with China had opened, but ideas also travelled along the same routes on two feet, as it were, in the heads of Buddhist monks and not long after Origen's time also in the heads of Nestorian Christians and Manichaeans, giving justification for speculation about the relation between Chinese Mahāyāna of the T'ien-t'ai and Pure Land Schools and these Eurasian 'faiths'. There is scarcely any period in world history as comparable to our own as that in which Origen and his contemporaries lived and tried to think and tried to pray; and yet it is also a period now woefully neglected.

Although Origen has been accused of being too syncretistic, the marvel is rather that he was not more so. Mani (215-276) was, needless to say, the super-syncretist of all time. As soon as Buddhism came into China, syncretistic combinations of it with the various Chinese schools began, not only by virtue of language adaptation but also because syncretism was already in the atmosphere, having virtually exhausted all the possible combinations of Confucianism and Taoism and, though not recognized as such openly, Legalism and Mohism. Thus in the world-wide scene it might be said that Origen represents a middle position between syncretism and rigorous orthodoxy. Even from his teens he was zealous in practice as well as in arduous study of the Scriptures to the point of desiring to follow his father into martyrdom. But this did not prevent him from adopting through Clement of Alexandria almost all of Philo's allegorizings about the *Old Testament* virtually without qualification and almost everything from Plato that did not lead to scepticism. Again, in contrast to Plotinus his contemporary, Origen's learning and affirmations in these and related fields did not lead him to a mania for cleansing and purifying as well as reviving the "pagan" past which had been admittedly glorious but which had become exhausted and even degenerate, no longer eliciting any true allegiance much less devotion.

To a Tertullian, indeed, such compromising syncretism as the Alexandrians like Origen, Cyril, Gregory of Nyssa and Gregory Nazianzen were risking was giving too much ground to the enemy, to paganism. If the true Christian was to fulfill his mission, even at the risk of fanaticism and dogmatism the new vitality should not be diluted with apologetics but presented as a challenge, a challenge uncompromising even to the point of martyrdom. But with the Greek Fathers we do have something much more civilized, urbane, and even rational. Origen wanted to present the new-found Faith (and even to interpret it to himself, perhaps) in a way that would be acceptable both to Alexandrian Jews who were already so Hellenized that they could not understand their own *Septuagint* except in Philonian allegorizings in the language of Plato and the Stoics, and also to the unconverted pagan intellectuals, whose sincerity Origen no doubt respected as highly as he did the classics of Greek philosophy and literature even though they also, like the *Old Testament*, had to be screened and reinterpreted lest the scandals of Homer and the cruelty of some biblical characters mislead the immature.

In Origen's philosophy of natural and divine law the emphasis on the biblical source is not so strong as in Tertullian, but the law of nature and the moral law are considered as equally grounded in the divine law. Origen's concept of law is comparable to the Stoic concept of Providence, but Providence to the Stoics was impersonal, indeed, impersonally rational, and not under the merciful judgment of a single, transcendent, benevolent, compassionate Deity. For Origen Christian Providence is the positive Providence that dispenses freely given grace, not just the impersonal justice that evens everything out in the long run so that Stoic fortitude and resignation to fate are necessary, but rather faith, hope, and *agapé*. This is often exaggerated even in Fundamentalist sermons, and is certainly worn threadbare by Anglican divines and a few Roman Catholic Neo-Augustinians, although it is not enlarged on enough by Thomists or Neo-Thomists. The French Personalists today seem to have recaptured something of this, and Marcel has, in opposition to (Tertullianish) Sartre, caught something of it from them in turn. This New Dispensation under Freedom which is yet in accordance with a personalized conception of Law more Greek than Roman becomes a sort of dogma for later on the latter was and still is rather inexorable. Even though Origen might be said to be one of the prime sources for its development, he is not to blame for its later crystalization.

Right from the beginning, even in the teachings of Jesus, not to mention Paul and the other *New Testament* documents, including some of the *Apocryphal New Testament*, the concept of a New Dispensation or a New *Dharma* which was inclusive of the best of both the Jewish and pagan pasts was very basic. One may risk the assertion that with the Alexandrians this New Dispensation or *Dharma* was inclusive of the past of the two known civilizations — if not others also, if one reads correctly the Epistle to the Hellenized Alexandrian, even Philonian, Jews in the *New Testament* — whereas Tertullian as a rigorist thinks that the old must be annihilated in order to make way for the new.

For Origen and others, the rational is not replaced by the divine, nor does it complete itself, so to speak, by becoming divine, but mirrors the divine in a way that could not be understood without the fact of Christian revelation. Whereas Plotinus and the Stoics and Sceptics had struggled upwards and outwards towards transcendence and universalization, Origen sees the operation of the *Logos* not only as the existentialization of the Platonic Ideas, but also as affording man a participation (*gnosis*) in the knowledge that God has of his creation, thus completely inverting the classical problem of epistemology. Knowledge in its various levels is now posited as a gift from God, a trust, not as a merely human accomplishment or acquisition. Therefore, God is posited as the perfect knower.

In terms of toleration, dignity, generosity of spirit, sense of public responsibility, and even critical (but not careless) syncretism or attempt at systematic synthesis, Origen is very much like his Han Confucian contemporaries. He is also closer to the Han Confucianists than to his fellow Christian Tertullian whose castigations of the pagan world are more dependent on the revealed law. According to Tertullian, the whole of society through the Church is supposed to be lifted to the supra-rational standards of complete redemption and transformation into spontaneous righteousness and goodness — a spontaneity, nevertheless, which does not preclude predestination. Origen could more specifically be compared to Hsün Yüeh

(148-209) or perhaps to Hsu Kan (171-218) since they were the prime sources for the later Neo-Confucian (post-Buddhist) revival of the seventh and eighth centuries in the same way that Origen, Basil, and the Gregories are the basis through Photius for the continuation of the pagan Greek heritage in Byzantium which was lost to the Latin West. Or Origen could be compared to one of the early Chinese Buddhist apologists, especially of the Southern School of Gentry Buddhism, such as Chih Tao-lin (alias Chih Tun, 314-366) even though he comes a century or so later.

Origen is, howsoever Christian, still Greek, and his ethical philosophy is thus more in accord with his ontology and cosmology, whereas in Tertullian there is a strange hiatus between his ontology and what Hegel calls the contrite consciousness : he is so obsessed with the conviction of sin that he cannot see much hope for reason aside from revelation. Christian redemption does not ennoble the natural order but rather renders it of no effect if the biblical standards are met. The entelechy of history is knowable only by revelation; the end, being appointed from above and not upsurging from below, is completely outside the range of ontology and the natural law and is beyond the limits of human reason. Life in the state also becomes a preparation for salvation through Christ and an expectation of eternal reward hereafter. Origen, on the other hand, seems to expect a reflection of the perfection of the Divine Order in the world, and anticipates in the here and now the perfection of the hereafter.

Tertullian leaves one unsettled, plagued with a bad conscience, determined for a life of severe discipline almost as rigorous as that expected of the Jaina ascetic. Origen speaks of *theosis* as the highest end of man. Through the operation of the Holy Spirit, man is given not only the fullness of the knowledge (*gnosis*) which the Gnostics claimed, but also becomes almost fully participator in the divine nature through the mediation of the Incarnate Word. This of course is a very bold claim indeed, but it is paralleled in other cultures, for example by the Taoist claim to the "that which permeates all and from which all proceeds". Man's path, in other words, is set towards the Realm of Glory which the Christ has opened in his resurrection, ascension and union with the Father and the

Holy Spirit. The Way of Perfection, far above the *meden agan*, is opened and it only behooves the true Christian to follow on into it. In short, arguments about human nature stop and discussions of its transformation begin.

Concerning the theme of whether enlightenment is a gift or a human achievement, Origen does not see any discrepancy between enlightenment through the uplifting of *eros* into *agapé* and thus the mystical *theosis* of man, and the perfecting redemption through the Divine *Logos* (the Reason that orders the cosmos) and the descent and indwelling of the Holy Spirit. Origen's *theosis* is closely parallel to the achieving of Buddhahood and the *Bodhisattva* ideal of divine compassion in the *Lotus Sūtra* schools, in contrast to the Hindu Mīmāṁsā sacrificial rigorism or even to the Theravāda practice which is not so romantically ambitious or metaphysically complex. Tertullian runs the risk of simply substituting a new "hammer and nails" practicality without graciousness or harmony, all too like what Mīmāṁsā or Chinese Legalism at its worst could degenerate into. For Origen, judgment and crisis are not so important in the establishment of the eschatological perspective as the confirmation of the Divine Harmony which is above the natural reason but not unavailable to it. Thus he writes:

> For it was not (Jesus') purpose at his first advent to judge men's deeds even before he had taught them and given them an example of the life that they ought to live, nor did he come to punish the wicked and to save the good. He intended to sow the seed of his word by miracles and by a certain divine power among the whole human race, even as the prophets showed.[5]

It is important to note that the theme of the redemption of all beings was a major point of discussion both in the Mediterranean and in popular Mahāyāna. In both Mahāyāna and Patristic Christianity it became a technical theological controversy dividing sects. Origen seemed to believe that even the devil would eventually be saved since Origen put most emphasis on the scriptures about the redemption of all creation and not of man only, much less of Christians only. This caused quite a stir and Origen was later anathematized for it.

With Origen it seems that it is not so much grace as the Holy Spirit as the extension of Plato's Demiurge — which some Gnostics had even claimed was the devil rather than the Holy Spirit— that is operative in the universe and not just in human, let alone Christian-only, affairs. Thus for Origen even more than for the Stoics, cosmology and ethics are not separable. Christianity means for him total transformation of everything no less than in the Mahāyāna traditions of the *Lotus Sūtra* and the *Prajñāpāramitā*. According to Origen, the Holy Spirit governs through immanence both the ordering of the universe and ethical oughtness and accomplishment, briding the gap between theory and practice. Ethics is for such a philosophy as Origen's part of the divine *chorismos*, the unfolding of potentialities, the emergence of new possibilities as well as accomplishment of new feats formerly thought impossible, with eventually the bringing about of the role of man as a cosmic being — in short, destiny and vocation replacing the older Stoic fate. Origen here is somewhat like Sri Aurobindo, Teilhard de Chardin, Vasconcelos, or Bergson in contrast with the various positivists who do not believe in an ethics of harmony but an ethics of arbitrariness, of confrontation, of crisis, of Promethian self-assertion against the natural course of things and hence of violence instead of peace. Tertullian was not quite so bad as some of these latter, but he was headed in that direction.

Origen seeks to make things Christian acceptable to all, adapting where basic principles are not compromised. Tertullian seeks more to wipe away the old order and to get a fresh start on new ground. He vigorously attacks almost everyone and has infected the whole of the cultural history of the West with a dogmatic tendency that will risk intolerance in order to establish the orthodox view. The new ground, of course, is that of faith which is at once the foundation of truth made available by the blood of the martyrs (not by the ink of *les écrivains*) and by the prophetic life, whose source is not just aesthetic vision of the One but the infusion of grace, even irresistible grace, compelling the soul to conform to the Will of God. For Tertullian and most of the Latin Christians after him, therefore, piety assumes almost pathological proportions — *personal* piety, including an overriding responsibility to the established order but also a seeking, through a certain heroic response to the challenge of the revealed law, to turn the world upside down in a puritanical revolution that would be impossible had not God commanded it under pain of an eternal damnation which all will suffer who do not accept the Church's discipline.

Origen is not so rigorous, although he too expects a very high degree of moral perfection to follow upon participation in the Perfection of Christ:

> Both Jesus himself and his disciples did not want people who came to them to believe only in his divine nature and miracles, he did not share in human nature and had not assumed the human flesh which lusts against the Spirit; but as a result of their faith they also saw the power that descended into human nature and human limitations ... or Christians see that with Jesus human and divine nature began to be woven together, so that with divinity human nature might become divine, not only in Jesus, but also in all who believe and go on to undertake the life which leads everyone who lives according to Jesus' commandments to friendship with God and fellowship with Jesus.[6]

This was written by one who was well acquainted not only with the mystery cults of pagan Greece and all the magic and demonology of the Gnostics, but with the whole of Egyptian, most of Persian, and some of Indian philosophizing, and who yet maintained his loyalty to Plato and the Stoics and Epicureans and, of course, the *Bible*, which he interprets with much greater allegorical freedom, after the manner of Philo, than Tertullian. He does not reject all of this heritage but screens it and reinterprets it in order to see it with the tragedy of Jesus' betrayal and crucifixion, resurrection, and ascension. The important point is not just how much of others' views Origen knew, but that awareness of the rest of the world was definitely a part of his consciousness so that in a rough sense he may be called a globalizer in spite of his Faith, or perhaps even the first globalizer of the Christian Faith. Origen might be said to have encompassed in essence the basic viewpoints of almost all of his Mahāyāna contemporaries, Aśvaghoṣa, for example. whose piety towards the Buddha took on a coloring very similar to that of Origen toward the Christ, i.e., both of them heavily loaded with metaphysical concepts and both of them having virtually forgotten the human qualities of their avatars.

The foundation upon which Origen's synthesis is built is his interpretation of the *Logos*. Concerning this he writes :

> There are, as it were, different forms of the Word. For the Word appears to each of those who are led to know him in a form corresponding to the state of the individual whether he is a beginner, or has made a little progress, or is considerably advanced, or has nearly attained to virtue already, or in fact has attained it.[7]

He goes on to argue for a Divine Wisdom (a very close parallel to the Mahāyāna *prajñā-pāramitā*) that is greater than the highest merely human wisdom. Here he and his fellow Alexandrians, as well as his Buddhist and Neo-Taoist contemporaries, are in rather close agreement. The difference between human divine wisdom, sharp enough though it remains in Origen, is bridged by him rather smoothly:

> Human wisdom is what we call "the wisdom of the world", which is "foolishness with God", but the divine wisdom, which is different from the human, ... comes by the Grace of God who gives it to those who prove themselves to be suitable persons to receive it. ... We maintain that human wisdom is a means of education for the soul, divine wisdom being the ultimate end. So the latter is said to be "solid food" for the soul by the writer who says : "But solid food is for full-grown men, who by reason of use have their senses exercised to discern between good and evil".[8]

Origen tends toward a certain qualified monism, and it takes only a little interpretation to make these words explicitly state that the lower human knowledge should be lifted into the divine wisdom and not remain in conflict with it. This problem of the proper linking of the transcendental and the practical was the chief point of controversy in both Christian and Buddhist affairs of this period, especially in China and Byzantium, with an especially wide range of theories as to how the divine and human natures of Christ or of the Buddha were joined (and therefore how the government and the Church should be ordered and uplifted). The controversies over the defining of the relation of the two natures were not just idealizations of the nature of man but existentializations of the relation of Godhood and manhood in the unique Person of Jesus and in his prototypes and saints who were striving for *theosis*. Likewise, controversies about the relation of the eternal divine Buddha or Buddhahood and the historical Śākyamuni ran the full gamut of heresies and orthodoxies. These problems of relations have been thrashed over so much that it is easy to lose the significance of the historical/metaphysical events. Also, the problem of the relation between the *Trikāya* and the *śunya* vexed the Buddhists no less than the problems of the relation of the indescribability and namelessness of God and the necessary proposition of the relatedness of the Supreme to His creation among the Christian Fathers. In the same way, moreover, the relation of the *Trimurti* (Brahmā-Śiva-Viṣṇu, which began to have its formulation in Hinduism about the same time) to *nirguṇa* Brahman became the basis of endless dialectics in the Brahmanical milieu. Later, to a certain extent, the Mutaxalite-Ashirite controversy in Islam takes up the same problems.

The Christians were in a situation analogous to that of the early Buddhists in China who were accused by the Confucianists of inducing people to neglect affairs of the state for the life of renunciation; and Origen's position on this issue is as pertinent now as it was then. For clearly, without sanctioning anything like an overt theocracy, Origen does expect society to be benefited as much or more by those who follow the way of renunciation (not retirement, much less escapism; there is a *vast* difference!) as by those who actively become engaged in public affairs. He is without that radical dualizing of sacred and secular which followed upon the failure of the papacy after only a few centuries of comparative success (under Gregory the Great, for example) in attempting to measure up to the standards set by Augustine's *Civitas Dei*.

Origen's social philosophy must not be called less than that since it is not just political and not just ethical in the individualistic sense; but, by way of a critique of preceding ethical and political ideals and systems, it seems to have a base tone that presupposes the feeling that society under the new Faith must, like the individual Christian, undergo a transformation. One may of course become unduly cynical in the face of the fact that Constantine and his successors — not to mention Pope Gregory later in the Latin West — did not succeed in factualizing this new ideal. But that is not the point. Rather, it might be considered in this way: maybe there is always going to be a gap between the ideal and the actual in public affairs anyway; but when the ideal itself is not sufficiently high to challenge those in authority, what can one expect? The old Stoic *apatheia* had given way, having proved itself inadequate for the times, to a Christian *gnosis* and *Homoiōsis Theō* (likeness to God). The Stoic *apatheia* could be and too often was a pretext for callousness and arrogance on the one hand and neglect on the other. But if radical altruism, mercy, compassion, and humility are demanded of those in public responsibility as well as of the populace, then the whole of society must come into *metanoia* (transformation) quite as much as the individual converts to the Faith. Again the analogies with China under increasing Buddhist influences come to mind.

Origen admittedly did not have much direct influence; but indirectly through the Cappadocians, Basil and Gregory Nazianzus, as well as through John Chrysostom, his ideas did have considerable effect in shaping Byzantine polity. Whether the Byzantine pattern was a better model in theory if not in practice is extremely difficult for us to assess, especially if we have been nurtured completely in that other tradition which insists on a sort of schizophrenic division of church and state, of sacred and secular.

Origen realized that the pagan past could no more be eliminated that it could be ignored. It would be mere fanatical pretense to expect a total superimposition of the Mosaic Code on the Greek civilization, much less to expect that merely from *New Testament* sources, with Paul's confusions and the delusions of the Apocalypse as the only guides besides Jesus' own ambivalence about "things that are God's and things that are Caesar's", could a complete code of laws for a total empire be derived.

The theme of striving and searching for some Principle beyond dialectics which is at once transcendent and therefore universally reliable and yet also operative in the world and in man continues even though such thinkers as Origen, Vasubandhu, and Aśvaghoṣa claim to have already found such a Principle. This searching has now become inclusive of such philosophizing about nature as survived the neglect of research in the natural sciences. Nature has become, not the battleground of opposing forces nor even the eternal ground out of which all things have emerged and back into which in cycles of involution all things ultimately subside, but the manifestation of the Wisdom of God, *Logos*, Buddhahood. Nothing in itself, but everything as the crucible of transformations and an expression of cosmic rationality and divine justice is inseparable. Even matter is so treated. In the Mahāyāna we must remember the dictum that *nirvāṇa* is *saṃsāra* and *saṃsāra* is *nirvāṇa*. It is difficult to deny that a new dimension of existence has opened, different sort of wisdom than mere *jalpa* or even *tarka*, but philosophy in the sense of of *darśan*, a wisdom that is at once compassionate and capable of integration of man, nature and Godhead in one Grand Harmony.

Origen was not a naturalist such as Wang Ch'ung or Lucretius were; nor was he the magic-mongering other-worldly recluse which was common among the Neo-Taoists who cultivated the "dark learning", although Alexandria had its share of these also, especially among such Gnostics as Celsus. And while Origen avoided these extremes, he still did not go to the extremes of religiosity or syncretism that Tertullian and Mani did. Somehow he managed to combine piety and intelligence in a way that is relatively rare in any age.

Such were the times : non-theological philosophizing had virtually disappeared everywhere. But theology was becoming a sort of science, an attempt to bring consistency and system into what had heretofore been left to chaotic cultic religion. As historians we cannot ignore this basic factual shift of attention by the time of Origen, Mani, and their contemporaries.

E. Jainism

Kundakundācārya

The Jaina community has a history quite as rich as that of the Buddhists, Vaiṣṇavas, or Śaivas; but that it has remained so independent throughout the centuries is somewhat remarkable. Much more work is yet to be done in order to explain this and the fact that Jainism survived in India when Buddhism did not. One might conjecture that the Jainas retained their tradition without corruption by virtue of their much more rigorous moral discipline, never allowing corruption from Tantric tradition. On the other hand, one might conjecture that they survived because they were more accommodating to the Hindu social system and, in practice though not in theory, became for all intents and purposes members of the Vaiṣya Caste whereas Buddhism never compromised at all with the caste system.

Even before Aśoka, Bhadrabāhu (fl. cir. 324-300 B.C.) had led a large community of Jaina devotees from the north central area into the south to escape famine. As a result it was claimed that the original canon was lost and had to be restored by such scholar-saint-philosophers as Kundakunda and Umāsvāti who then became the chief authorities. Nevertheless, at least one sect within the Jaina community did not recognize this claim so that we get a rather remarkable parallel to the situation in China with the dispute between the Old Text School and the New Text School. Thus there developed in Jainism the chief division between the Digambaras and the Śvetambaras.

What can specifically be called philosophy before Kundakunda and Umāsvāti is mixed in with the rather amorphous mass of material in the long list of *āgamas* or scriptural compendia which resemble much of the Hindu *Purāṇas* and are not unlike some of the *Old Testament Apocrypha* literature in form if not somewhat in content also. Traditional lore gathered up after the canon was lost served as scripture, and it is to the credit of these two philosophers that they systematized the basic tenets into the sūtra form so familiar to all Indian *darśanas*.

Although the Jainas did retain their identity perhaps more pointedly than the Buddhists, at least the Mahāyāna Buddhists, they were not entirely immune to the general syncretistic trend of the period. However, another trend seems to emerge as we move towards the period from 325 to 625, that being the production of aphoristic, even cryptic, memorizable handbooks and schematic formulae of all sorts, which then become the basis of the later medieval commentaries on commentaries on commentaries. Such, for example, were Aenesidemus' *Tropes*, Nāgārjuna's *Kārikās*, and Epictetus' *Enchiridion* which becomes the model for similar works by virtually all the Christian Fathers of the Church, both Greek and Latin; and such, of course, were the various sūtras of Nyāya, Sāṃkhya, Vaiśeṣika, and Yoga, not to mention the long list of Mahāyāna sūtras.

Kundakunda (probably first century A.D.) may be styled the most dominant personality in South India. Concerning Kundakunda there is, needless to say, a lot of fascinating hagiology, apocryphal stories and semi-apocryphal stories. It seems that in order to trap him some mischief maker left a bottle of wine with him secretly and then reported this breach of discipline to the authorities. The wine, by Kundakunda's magic, was turned into a jar of jasmine, this being the meaning of his Sanskrit name. There are many inscriptions testifying to his capacity to levitate, a common story about yogis everywhere; but the interpretation given in one inscription is significant : he did not touch the dust of the earth because he was untainted by the dust of worldly attachment.

Kundakunda did not follow the usual manner of exposition of Jaina tradition, especially in his *Samayasāra*. Critical examination of this work in comparison with his earlier works, *Pancāstikāya* and *Pravacanasāra*, reveals that he evidently changed his views during the course of his career. His *Pancāstikāya* served as a sort of *vade mecum* compendium or enchiridion and as a semi-popular handy introduction to the fundamentals of his tradition. In the *Pravacanasāra* there is heavier emphasis on epistemology in a technical sense, and more space is given to the philosophy of the emotions and to the nature of the soul, physical elements, etc. But the major difference between these two works is his emphasis in the latter on the Jaina logic of *syādvāda*.

The Jaina concept of matter (*pudgala*) is much more like the hard stuff concept than the notion of a primordial void eliciting the infusion of form such that the combination of this prime matter and form produces finite things as was the view (with some qualifications) of the Aristotelians and the Sāṃkhyans. The Jaina view of matter is more like that of Democritus. What then of souls (*jivas*) ? As with Buddhism there is virtually a total absence of reference to the *ātman* concept. But on the other hand, in contrast with Buddhism, *jivas* are substantial definitive entities. The Buddhists said no-soul, but the early Jainas ran the risk of the opposite extreme of almost making a material entity out of the *jivas*.

Since the Jainas consider karma to be physical while the soul is spiritual, they had to account for the possibility of influence between them, the interaction of two distinct substances being a problem common to any philosophy which is not a complete materialism. According to Kundakunda there is a nonessential relation between the soul and matter, even the very subtle matter of karma, and thus the essence of the soul can be understood without reference to matter. Perhaps this is the Indian philosophy that later influenced Plotinus and that influenced Apollonius of Tyana during Kundakunda's own century. Still Kundakunda was primarily interested in the soul as embodied.

Kundakunda's position is in contrast to the theme in both Mādhyamika and Vijñānavāda, not to mention the *Lotus Sūtra* and a large part of the *Prajñāpāramitā* literature, that from the ultimate point of view there is no difference between *saṃsāra* and *nirvāṇa*. It will be remembered that very early the Christians had to combat a similar teaching among the Gnostics, and Chuang Tzu and the *Huai-nan Tzu* had something very similar. Hence, Kundakunda is an exception to a rather universal trend. In fact, throughout the tracing of our history in the future this is another of those ideas that keeps recurring, like the micromacrocosm doctrine or the coincidence of opposites. It is one of the perennial ideas.

In the *Samayasāra* the distinction between the *pāramārtha* and the *vyavahāra* points of view (even though typically for Jainas expressed in slightly different terms) comes sharply into focus. Contrary to the traditional Jaina view that all perspectives are partially true and partially false (*syādvāda*), Kundakunda emphatically claims that the *vyavahāra* (the empirical, practical, this-worldly point of view) is the standpoint of absolute untruth and that only the *pāramārtha* (transcendental) point of view gives truth. This distinction of viewpoints is especially important since it will be with us for several centuries now and in all of Eurasia it will often become the dominant theme for philosophizing.

Umāsvāti

It can be claimed (probably with some exaggeration) that early Jainism was basically dualistic with a sharp distinction between soul and matter, loosely resembling classical Sāṃkhya. However, Umāsvāti (Umāsvāmi; circa. second century A.D.) recognized a plurality of substantial entities quite aside from *jiva* and *pudgala*, e.g., *dharma, adharma*, space, time. *Jiva* is the soul as vital principle, not the *ātman* as permanent Self in Brahamanical style. *Pudgala* is the Jaina particular term for 'dead' matter. It is claimed that only yogis can perceive clearly what is involved in this pluralism.

The Jaina doctrine of *dharma* and *adharma* is quite different from that of either the Buddhists or the Hindus. They are the milieu of movement and rest in which things are found. The Jainas considered space and time as substantial, but most Buddhists, and certainly almost all Mahāyāna Buddhists, considered them as unreal. Umāsvāti himself affirmed a kind of ultracosmic space in which there is neither matter nor souls; but as far as the finite world is concerned, space and time, *dharma* and *adharma*, are inseparable.

Kundakunda, Umāsvāti, and their fellow Jaina thinkers proposed a theory of substance quite different from and really as a challenge to the emerging Buddhist schools. This theory is based more on common sense than on religious postulates. Actually, the whole Jaina tradition may have been somewhat misrepresented by being treated too much as a religion rather than as a philosophy. Substance, then, is what is permanent and very real even though its attributes of qualities change. However, the Jainas apply their logic of *syādvāda* so that they can say that in some ways a substance and its attributes are alike or even the same and in other ways they are different.

With both Kundakunda and Umâsvâti, although these matters of metaphysics and ontology do have a prominent place, the primary emphasis rests with the doctrine of the karmans, and upon this rests most of the religious discipline. In Umâsvâti there is little variation on the basic Jaina doctrine that all karmans are material howsoever fine the matter concerned. Every karman which lodges in the soul makes it more gross and every karman which is dislodged from the soul leaves it more purified. A new note added by Umâsvâti is that he doubles the series of the six senses of the body with a parallel set of spiritual senses whose function is to know when the soul has been infused by or purified from these influences. Nevertheless, the soul does not depend only on these spiritual senses, nor only on the gross senses, but uses also the other *pramāṇas* familiar to all schools of Indian philosophy. Umâsvâti, however, insisted that all the *pramāṇas* are traceable back to sense perception of the twofold kind.

First in Umâsvâti's *Tattvārthādhigama Sūtra* is the topic of *mokṣa* (salvation, release). Documents are still relatively rare for the previous periods for India and China, but it seems that throughout Eurasia by the first century A.D. salvation — man's ultimate goal, his destiny, his place in the universe both individually and collectively — was everywhere the basic problem. The Stoics in particular were much concerned with fate and destiny. The Epicureans, in a negative way, likewise could not avoid the issue, claiming almost that the world is "just there", meaningless in itself except as an object of curiosity for man to play with in order to derive intellectual pleasure. The Chinese Confucianists were really more concerned with this topic than might be thought. Even the naturalistic minded Wang Ch'ung, debunker that he was, could not discard the concepts of *ming* and *hsing*. The Neo-Taoists were almost obsessed with the search for immortality and for some way to get into contact with supernatural forces. They were beginning to come forth with their doctrine of the transformation of human nature, the very concept upon which the *Gītā* is based. Although the Nyāya-Vaiśeṣika Sūtras along with the Mīmāṁsā and the Sāṃkhya-Yoga

Sūtras may have added this feature at a relatively late date, since most that they offer has little to do with salvation of any sort, nevertheless, they too begin in the same manner as Umāsvāti's *Sūtra*. As for the Theravāda literature and the Mahāyāna literature like the *Lotus Sūtra* and the *Prajñāpāramitā Sūtras* (not to mention the many minor sūtras), all are based either on the attainment of *nirvāṇa* or at least are an elaboration of the *Bodhisattva* vow. Finally, it need not be pointed out that Philo and Justin Martyr are very much concerned with such matters. Hence, once again, it would have been strange if Umāsvāti had not begun his *Sūtra* as he did.

Umāsvāti spends what might seem to be an inordinate amount of space on the *pramāṇas* or epistemology. Again, this seems to be in keeping with the general leaven of scepticism that was characteristic of the whole Han-Hellenistic-Bactrian Period. It must be remembered, however, that scepticism then did not mean an attitude of refusing to believe in the religious sense; rather, it meant thoroughness in analytical method in regard to the nature of knowledge. It seems strange now that more then did not realize that knowledge about knowledge is still just knowledge. It is here that the Yogācāras and the Jainas may have some insights if it be true that yoga meditation does open to some other dimension whereby *vijñāna* and *prajñā* allow one to be free of complete dependency on the reflexivity of *jñāna*. *Jñāna* as distinct from *vijñāna*, could hardly be self-knowledge or immediate, unmediated knowledge of or about knowledge without reflexivity. *Jñāna* leads to *vijñāna* when there is sufficient accumulation of *jñāna* so that one may reflect on the quantity and types of *jñāna*, what effect it has on oneself, on other mortals, and ultimately, though only infinitesimally, on the universe, and whether this *saṃskāra* has become subconsciously habitual, a part of one's nature. Then it would have gone through the stage of reflexivity on the way to *vijñāna*. But the reflexive stage is an awkward, half-way stage, whereas supposedly through meditation (*dhyāna*) immediate 'knowledge' without differentiation between subjective and objective takes place. One becomes, as it were, what one knows, knowledge being then not just an alienation or an effort but a part of what one is. Later, perhaps, even that is inverted:

one no longer assimilates knowledge into oneself but one is immediately assimilated into the field of the unity of knower-knowledge-known.

The Jainas, and Umāsvāti in particular, seem to outshine virtually all the rest in the field of epistemology. One reason is that for them the basic problem is ignorance and the goal is omniscience. All their ascetic discipline is directed towards this goal. According to the Jainas, knowledge, as the essential characteristic of the soul, is real and not a mere superimposition or epiphenomenon on reality. Umāsvāti deals in great detail with the types of knowledge as such even more emphatically than the means of acquiring that knowledge, for the end here naturally should be expected to determine the means. When Umāsvāti deals with the soul, even then he is primarily interested in scientific classification of the phenomena inherent in psychological matters (if we may attempt to return the word "psychological" to its original meaning).

The Jaina cosmology was one of the most scientific of its time, if by scientific one may mean that they had a greater realization of the vastness of the cosmos, a realization quite in contrast to anything of its kind in the Mediterranean or even in China. In short, there are many worlds, which are more and more definitively enumerated. Also, Umāsvāti's *Sūtra* considers how many and what kind of human beings there are among all the other living inhabitants of the earth. Now this would not be remarkable except that such considerations were ruled out in the *Brahma Sūtras* later on as not worthy of consideration for philosophers. Had the Jaina pattern prevailed of what is to be considered philosophy in India, it might have been that science, virtually all of the sciences, would have received a much greater stimulus than they did. It is very difficult at present to discern how much of the Jaina mania for enumeration and classification, which is at least proto-scientific if not a remnant of what was an abortive beginning of real science in India during the first century A.D., stems from the original tradition as formulated by Kundakunda and Umāsvāti and how much is later medieval superstructure.

Plotinus and some of his predecessors, and, for that matter, even Philo, have some panpsychic tendencies, as certainly the

Neo-Taoists do; and the Neo-Pythagoreans (Apollonius, for example) are basically of this type. Being systematically atheists, the Jainas affirmed the existence of both soulless matter and ensouled matter, as well as souls (*jivas*) virtually if not actually free of matter. Kundakunda's and Umāsvāti's introduction of divinities into Jainism may have been like the Hinduization of Mahāyāna Buddhism, with many of the Hindu devas, gods, and demons reappearing either under different names or in full dress. However, the Jainas, still extreme rationalists, attempted a semi-scientific rationale concerning the function of these supra-mundane *jivas*, no longer just believing in them out of unexamined tradition in mythological form but trying to make them fit into a cosmic scheme of things which would be incomplete without them. Like Thomas Aquinas' hierarchy of being, these devas fill the gap between the super-etherial Nothingness of Śūnyavāda and the gross materialistic views of Cārvāka.

But we must not read history backwards. We must not forget what is also not in Lucretius or Wang Ch'ung who also did not completely discard notions about the gods or celestial beings. And for that matter, their doctrines of atoms and/or matter are likewise still pretty crude. All we can claim is that in discipline the Jainas were no less rigorous than the Stoics or Cynics or Taoist monks at their best. They took their vows of nonpossession very seriously, their refusal in the case of the Digambaras to wear clothing being that they did not want to be tempted with the feeling of having even that much of possessions lest they be possessed by them.

Let us risk the hypothesis that the *yin-yang* polarization principle is at work here between Umāsvāti (*yin*) and Kundakunda (*yang*) just as it is between Yang Hsiung and Wang Ch'ung, Philo and Seneca, Aśvaghoṣa and Nāgārjuna. *Yin* is more recessive, more or less idealistic or even esoteric or mystical, dark, intuitive or stressing potentiality and quality. *Yang* is more rationalistic, aggressive or assertive, less questioning than logically systematizing, more argumentative, more realistic, better explicated than full of insights left as such, more emphasizing quantity and actuality.

One senses in Umāsvāti somthing that evidently is just not available in contemporary secularized circles. It is not just mysticism but a scientific psychological discipline designed to lead to the maximum possible facility for learning, understanding and real wisdom. By comparison with Seneca, Epictetus, Aenesidemus, Philo, or Wang Ch'ung, Umāsvāti's subjects and goals are truly amazing. Jindall is right in bewailing the state of present day Jaina pundits who have allowed such Promethian goals to be forgotten, largely because they have compromised with the bourgeois spirit and are no longer willing to undergo the discipline necessary to achieve them. Renaissance? We shall see.

APPENDIX

THE PROBLEM OF PERIODIZATION

with

JAMES M. DOLIN AND PAUL D. MAYS

This study is not intended to offer a final solution to the very perplexing problem of establishing a twentieth century, post-Hegelian, post-Marxist periodization of world history, but rather to issue a challenge toward finding something more accurate and adequate than those periodizations which are currently available.

Throughout the history of mankind, theories of history have been based on mythology, over-speculation, or over-emphasized views of such single historical factors as religion, economics, or politics. But none of the views so far has given us an adequate perspective on the history of mankind as a kaleidescopic whole. The old periodization of history in terms of ancient, medieval and modern, even when applied only to the history of the West, is awkward; and frequent attempts at forcing other civilizations into the traditional framework of the history of Europe have caused many distortions in the entire picture of the history of cultures and civilizations. Even the division of "East" and "West" does not fit the facts at all.

No longer may we propose periodizations which are not inclusive of all historical factors, including art, literature and music; and certainly the importance of transportation and intercultural communications in the developments of all civilizations has been greatly underestimated. Therefore, we hope to stress the need for a *multi-dimensional* approach to the general philosophy of history as well as to world history itself.

The discrepancies between all the current periodizations of world history make it a moot question whether a periodization which is acceptable to all is even possible. But, in the face of the distortions that have become common usage, it is necessary, as a *modus vivendi*, to attempt something more workable than what has thus far been offered, to attempt something that may help deliver future generations from the provincialism, cultural fanaticisms, and ethnocentricities which have plagued mankind thus for.

Our periodization has three main purposes. First, to explore the possibilities of a more workable scheme, as we have just said. Second, to correlate the world history of philosophy more closely with general world history than has heretofore been attempted. Few if any periodizations thus far proposed have taken philosophical developments as even a minor criterion for the forming of historical periods, although it could be asserted that from about 500 B.C. or so to the present the real key to everything else is the periodization of the world history of philosophy in preference to, although not divorced from, all other aspects of culture and civilization. While such a thesis may to some seem too extreme, surely any periodization of world history which does not give the history of philosophy at least as much prominence as, say, the history of religion, economics or politics must, as a comprehensive cultural periodization, be inadequate. Of course, we must not expect that correlations between development of philosophical traditions and systems and general cultural history should hold good at all times and places. Certainly, there are historical sequences (globally) when philosophy *appears* to be in a position subordinate to the other factors which must be considered for a periodization of general world history.

Third, though this periodization may be found to be virtually as inadequate as any other, our study will have succeeded if we have helped clarify those questions, and/or pointed more directly to those confusions which must be considered in any world periodization. We do hope to present the problems involved, and we might say, philosophically involved.

Any periodization may be quite arbitrary and at best only pragmatically or pedagogically useful, not by any means indisputable. Indeed, we are confronted with a sort of Kantian antinomy : Even though any possible periodization runs the risk of arbitrariness or even dogmatism, without periodization we cannot historicize at all.

THE AXIAL PERIOD
(750-250 B.C.)

Introduction

Arnold Toynbee, Karl Jaspers and others are fairly well agreed that a major breakthrough period occurs around 500 B.C. But what of the periods, if any, before that ? After all, we too easily forget that by then civilization in general already had a greater past than the past which we usually take into consideration since the Axial Period.

One of the first problems in attempting a periodization is how to consider "beginnings". The date 5969 B.C. is offered (speculatively, of course) along with several others, largely Byzantine or Alexandrian in origin, as the date of the creation of the world. Of course such notions would hardly meet the approval of Hindus, Buddhists and Jains since they, aside from rejecting anything like the *creatio ex nihilo* concept, had a much more extensive time scale, as may readily be seen from a perusal of such well-known texts as the *Bhāgavata Purāṇa* wherein a *yuga* can extend for more than a million years. One proffered date for the beginning of the Kali yuga is 3102 B.C. Is that any more awkward than Al Birūni's assignment of the date 3760 as the date for Adam, for by then a date of 4077 as reckoned by a cycle of 2700 years had long since been assigned to the beginnings of the Saptarṣi-Kāla era according to Kashmiri sources ?

Not only are non-mythological beginnings difficult to find, but even if we could find them we would still have to know *how* to *move* from there. The date of 2700 B.C. is given as the beginning of the Chinese cycles of 60 years, while contemporary Western practice forces everything into the decimal 100-years system (even though we retain a different system for daily time, i.e., 60 seconds, 60 minutes, etc.). The sense of cyclic time has apparently been much stronger with the Chinese than with the West all through the long history of both civilizations. Indeed, in the total perspective of the history of mankind, the modern Western non-cyclic view may be the inferior. After all, there are cycles in almost everything we know, from astronomical phenomena to psycho-physical biological rhythms. In the traditional Chinese view all of these are perfectly natural, being fluctuations of the yin and yang, as likewise in the Hindu and Jaina cosmologies wharein sparśa and vimarśa (evolution and involution) are considered as the basic pattern of all "created" reality, interspersing the "night of Brahmā" when in Pralaya everything remains for a season in unmanifest potentiality. Thus the rhythms between the basic polarizations of all reality might well predispose us toward the cyclic view of time.

The phenomenon of polarization and the resulting patterns affect our problem of periodization very much since one way of periodizing (which we have not necessarily followed) is that of marking when these polarizations become most pronounced whether or not they would correlate with other factors, although no doubt they would.

The polarization of ancient Assyria and Babylon is not so evident since both together were polarized against Egypt; and further examination might reveal internal polarization in Egypt, Babylon and even Mohenjo-Daro and Harappa. But to mention a few clearer polarizations: within Israel, the Pharisees and Sadducees; within Hinduism, Vaiṣṇavism and Śaivism; within Buddhism, Mahāyāna and Theravāda; within China, first between Confucianism and Taoism and later those together against Buddhism, or else for short periods Buddhism and Taoism together against Confucianism; in Japan, between Buddhism and Shinto; in Christianity, early polarization between Athanasius and Arius as also first between Greek and Latin forms and then between them both more or less together against Nestorianism and/or the Monophysite Coptic tradition, as many centuries later the Latin Church polarized between Catholic and Protestant even as the Greek Church polarized between the Bogomils and the Orthodox.

Nor did Islam escape this seemingly inexorable law of history: Shi'a and Sunni Islam soon began to divide the Ecumene between themselves, and in the meeting-grounds many martyrdoms are to be found on both sides. The mystique of "the enemy" is indeed a matter difficult to understand, profoundly primordial as it seems to be in human affairs. For even human *games* are matters of "we" and "they" or "I" and "my" opponent. Toynbee somewhere reflects that it is almost axiomatic in world history thus far that federations are not likely to be successful except in defense against a common—enemy ! But is nature as a whole like that too ? Yin and yang, yes; but necessarily *conflict* ? Opponent, perhaps yes; but *enemy* ? Must dialectics take that form ? Apparently the heritage of Heracleitus-Hobbes-Marx at present lies more heavily on us than the Taoist Wisdom of Nature. Harmony of opposites : is this not always possible (whether it is actualized or not) without eluding dialectics ? The Diagram of the Supreme Ultimate by Chou Tun-i (1017-1073) schematizes this for universal application, and it may be that in the wisdom of chairman Mao we have an echo of both heritages at last : "One makes two": polarization is as natural and therefore as predictable as bilateral symmetry or bisexuality in mammals. That there should likewise be polarization between Capitalists and Communists, and again between Moscow and Peking — to mention only one instance — should therefore not disturb us. History should have taught us to expect it.

Polarization may be applied in another way, namely, in terms of North-South (as opposed to East-West): in India, Aryan North and Dravidian South; in China, the Northern and Southern Sung dynasties, not to mention the Northern "gradualist" and Southern "sudden" schools of Ch'an Buddhism; in Japan, Buddhist and Shinto religions; in Europe, Latin South and Germanic North; in Russia, between the Kievans (or Ukranians) and the Muscovites, and later between the Slavophiles and the "Westernizers" ; in Indonesia, peaceful Bali and aggressive Java and Sumatra; in Theravāda Buddhism, between Burma and Thailand, and later between Thailand and Cambodia; in the U.S., the Civil War between the "Damn Yankee" North and the "Confederate" South. The division of North and South Korea and North and South Viet Nam in the twentieth century is not entirely out of accord with previous history. The rivalry between Mexico and Argentina for cultural hegemony in Latin America might also be mentioned, but certainly the polarity between Hispano-America and Luso-America (Brazil) cannot be overlooked. These polarizations affect not only political, military and economic factors in history but also philosophies themselves.

The essential point that concerns us in suggesting these problems of "beginning" and how to move from them is that we must have a metaphysics behind any possible science of periodization.

The Pre-Axial Period

We must question whether there was an "Axial Period" sometime around 3500 B.C., for it soon becomes rather evident that there were qualitative leaps (whatever pattern of causation may be ascribed to that "period") in such basic matters as religion, metallurgy, means of production and patterns of social organization, in astronomical or astrological observation, and above all in matters of transportation and communication.

It also seems fairly evident that it was in the time span between approximately 3500 to 1600 B.C. that the basic mythologies that have given meaning to our subconscious cultural heritages in all their richness and variety took on their present forms. True, myths may or may not be reliable as history or even as proto-history; but myths do *make* histories: 'holy' wars, holy places, holy persons, taboos (both positive and negative), genealogies (both factual and fictitious), relics and temple architecture, art, and music — the list becomes exhaustive only slowly. All have mythological origins but very enduring effects; and most of them are still with us. They have set our moral and legal codes, such as those of Hammurabi and Moses and 'Manu', and ultimately even Solon and Shotoku in other eras. They have set equally our aesthetic canons and patterns of poetry and drama; and above all, they have heavily infused our conceptions of time and of man's place in the universe, and indeed of history itself.

Our earliest considerations must not overlook Egypt, for the durée of Egyptian civilization is extremely difficult for us to comprehend. Though we know about such things as Egyptian hieroglyphics (begins about 4000 B.C.) and Sumerian cuneiform libraries of clay tablets, no doubt there are relatively few people who realize their complete significance even today. Indeed, we still have to await the final verdict from specialists as to the independence of, or communication-influence between, the ancient civilizations which did invent different scripts and kept entirely different records, such as China, Mesopotamia, Mohenjo-daro, Harappa, and Phoenicia, as well as Egypt. (It would be fascinating to trace as a pattern of periodization the use of different scripts. Do they parallel other periodizings? Of course we cannot answer that question now, but once the problem of periodization as such is posed then the researches can begin in earnest.)

The next periodizing point or pivotal turn of developments seems to have occurred around 1600 B.C. In addition to the mention of 'Father' Abraham and the Elamites, Amalekites and the Hittites and such Old Testament stories, was there some connection between the famed Trojan wars and the equally famous and equally semi-legendary Mahābhārata war of mutual extermination out of which Ulysses and Krishna emerge as Hero and Avatar? Sagas emerge along with sages, and mythology begins to be sacred literature — sacred, perhaps because of its rarity, but also because it preserves the 'soul' of its peoples. Perhaps behind this there was a world war and a *Volkerwanderung* not unlike that in subsequent cycles of Eurasian history. Otherwise, we would not so easily speak of Indo-European languages and other Indo-European or "Aryan" or "Caucasian" types of men and cultures, with their cattle and horses. Moreover, would we have the ethnocentricities which still bedevil mankind today?

Indeed, several romantics like Kurt Schilling rejoice in this period, most of all glorifying "*vorphilosophische Weisheit*" (pre-philosophical Wisdom) deeming the emergence of science and systematic philosophy with the primitive. We would prefer to use more discretion, the "wisdom of the middle way" between the myth of Progress and the myths of the "Fall" or of the degeneration of men down from the "golden" age of antiquity. Hence again our interest remains focused on cycles, epochs, ages, and periods of history both already made and in the making.

Earlier Axial Period (750-500 B.C.)

One of the most obvious periodizations, because one of the

most dramatic, is that occurring around 500 B.C., with some beginnings even by 750 B.C. or so, and continuing to about 250 B.C. This has been labeled the "Axial Age" by Karl Jaspers, Arnold Toynbee and others. It is in the Axial Period that philosophy in the technical sense emerges.

If we do not overlook the "coincidence" of some relatively simultaneous events — computation of the Olympiads (776), the Era of Nebuchadnezzar (747), the beginnings of the Iron Age in Etruria (labeled the Hallstatt Period by some) (c. 750), the development of feudalism under the Chou dynasty and the transfer of the capital of China to Loyang (c. 722), and similar developments — then a secondary pattern emerges as a prelude to the dramatic developments around 500 B.C., and that (which we call the Earlier Axial Period) deserves more attention than has heretofore been given to it.

Middle Axial Period (500-325 B.C.)

Concerning the Middle Axial Period, what cannot be ignored is the proximity of the dates of the Buddha Śākyamuni (566-486), Vardhamāna Mahāvīra (599-527), Confucius (551-479), Zoroaster (660-583; although according to most datings now, he does come slightly earlier), Socrates (470-399) — who emerged at the zenith of the encounter between Hellenic and Persian civilizations, the possible emergence of Japanese civilization (cf. Jimmu, c. 660), and the witness of the best of the Old Testament prophets.

But perhaps the most significant point of periodization is the date 544 B.C., given as the date of the Buddha's Nirvāṇa, from which the great majority of calendars in Buddhist Asia take their orientation. Parenthetically, why should it be regarded as any less important than A.D. or A.H. datings ? For example, it is just as wrong to periodize Egyptian dynasties and ancient Chinese history in terms of B.C. as it would be to periodize the whole of human history in terms of Egyptian or Chinese dynasties. Actually the date 544 B.C. would serve better, were it possible to get it universally adopted, to punctuate the pivotal importance of the Axial Period. Though the dating B.C. and A.D. has no doubt distorted many of our perspectives, it has become so deeply entrenched that we cannot easily cast it aside for a new method of dating.

Later Axial Period (325-250 B.C.)

This next period, which has received now almost universal attention, is that of Alexander, the prodigal product of Aristotle's pedagogy. It is ironic indeed that it was Plato's intellectual grandson and not Plato himself, or even Socrates, who *moved* history — howbeit not necessarily in the directions idealized either in the *Republic* or the *Laws*. Alexander entered Phoenicia in 333 and Babylon in 350; but the most dramatic date is that of his reaching the Indus River in 324 B.C.

Alexander's career is of "axial" importance. We must remember, for example, that Aristotle sent scientists along with Alexander's army, and we must note that before the Greek influence in India there were no images of the Buddha. It is also very significant that Pyrrho became a sceptic and not a mystic as a result of his trip with Alexander to India. How much influence pre-Alexandrian Greece had received from Iran and India is still a matter for investigation; but the easiest and most plausible inference is that it must have been quite a lot, enough to have given Alexander and Aristotle enough curiosity about India to make the expedition worth the effort. The fact that success in political administration in the satrapies set up after this military conquest was not so great is of far less importance than the fact that it is overtly evident that communications were already open, and remained increasingly so, due to the excellence of the Persian roads and postal service, right down to the ascendency of the Bactrian kingdoms and the opening of the silk routes to and from China.

It was in the milieu of these pan-Eurasian communications that the greatest of the world's religious and philosophical syntheses later arose and flourished — Mahāyāna Buddhism, Nestorian Christianity and Manichaeanism, and eventually Kashmir Shaivism, all of them more or less infused with Neo-Platonism and thoughts found in the Upaniṣads. Thus this period of three-way communication between India, Greece and China (as well as Israel and Iran) yields this next dating of about 325 B.C. Admittedly, given the constellation of dates that are available, the sequence from 325 to 250 could easily be considered as part of the next period rather than as the Later Axial Period, but ending the Axial Period at 250 and then beginning the next period seems to us to be a reasonable possible compromise since the division between any two periods can never be very rigid and a certain amount of overlapping must be expected.

THE HAN-HELLENISTIC-BACTRIAN PERIOD
(250 B.C.—A.D. 325)

Introduction

Concerning periodizations for the sequence, M. Mujeeb in *World History, Our Heritage* designates the time-span from 600 B.C. to A.D. 200 as "The Spiritual Revolution" and A.D. 200 to 900 as "The Religious World-State". However, Mujeeb's divisions cover too long a span for our purposes. William H. McNeil in *The Rise of the West* only slightly improves on this. McNeil usually subdivides his larger periods into more convenient units, and does not insist that the same date-grouping should fit all areas simultaneously even though some of them overlap dramatically. For example, he periodizes the Hellenic between 500 and 146 B.C. and the non-Hellenic civilization of Eurasia between 500 and 100 B.C. This periodization does not refute any implicit ethnocentricity, but rather leaves McNeil open to accusations of preference for the Hellenic over the others, whereas surely this is not his intention. He then designates a period of Rome and Western Europe as subdivided between 336 and 146 B.C., and the high cultural tradition of Eurasia between 100 B.C. and 200 A.D. Such periodizings are certainly closer to the facts; but they are likewise, unfortunately, rather confusing, especially from the pedagogical point of view. But at least, along with Jean Duché (*Histoire du Monde*), he does attempt to find the middle between the two extremes of atomistic meaningless chronology without any characterization and neo-mythologizings such as we have inherited from St Augustine.

One would think perhaps the UNESCO *History of Mankind* would come to our rescue. But it does not; and we suspect some influences of Hegel still obscuring the facts. Or could it be that Eusebius is still our mentor, even though he knew very little of the "non-Hellenic" civilizations of Eurasia — though one could, with even more accuracy perhaps, speak of the non-Chinese civilizations of the same time and the same areas. The UNESCO perspective, like McNeil's, is such that we find that

Greece and Rome still occupy the preferred positions. Moreover, the periodizing between 500 B.C. and 1 A.D. is still rather awkward, as again that between 1 A.D. to 500 A.D. is completely arbitrary if not rather meaningless. The UNESCO *History*, however, does avoid the other fatal error of selecting only one single characteristic of each period as its designation. For every chronological unit both the UNESCO *History* and the Martin and Brunn *Graphic Guide to World History* do take into consideration, with equal emphasis, economic, political, social, religious, artistic, and even philosophical as well as scientific and technological factors.

Therefore, considering the deficiencies of these periodizations, we prefer to label the sequence from 250 B.C. to 325 A.D. as the Han-Hellenistic-Bactrian Period. In cultural history there may be sensed a definite watershed about 250 B.C. which marks the end of the Axial Period, during which the classical canons were set for the fundamental religions/philosophies, and the basic characteristics of each civilization were established, and the beginning of the Han-Hellenistic-Bactrian Period. In the Han-Hellenistic-Bactrian Period, syncretism at best, and eclecticism at worst, were rife in religion, art philosophy and other matters. Fascination with the esoteric and exaggeration of the erotic are prominent characteristics of this "sensate" period.

Culturally, it must be noted that it was during the Han-Hellenistic-Bactrian Period that India and China made major contributions to world civilizations. For example, the "arabic" numerals universally in use in preference to the clumsy Greek and Roman use of letters as numerals originated in India; the calculations with zero and the decimal system also originated in India; and students came from everywhere to Taxila, not to Athens or Alexandria, to study medicine, just as at Nālandā one could find scholar-monks from all of Asia in numbers that were as great as any school could boast in the Mediterranean. Astronomy was advanced enough in China to record the appearance of Haley's comet; and of course many of the things that we take for granted such as paper, "chinaware" or porcelain, silk, construction of canals for purposes of transport as well as for irrigation, windmills and wheelbarrows came into use in China during this period.

Unlike Caesar's Gaul, this long sequence cannot be "divided into three parts"; but all together, it is too big an expanse to manage under a single heading. Therefore, we have subdivided the Han-Hellenistic-Bactrian Period into Earlier Han-Hellenistic-Bactrian and Later Han-Hellenistic-Bactrian, parallel with the division between the Earlier and Later Han dynasties and with the transition from Athens to Alexandria as the chief intellectual center.

Earlier Han-Hellenistic-Bactrian Period (250 B.C.-A.D. 50)

The beginning of the Earlier Han-Hellenistic-Bactrian is marked in the political sphere by Aśoka Maurya (ruled c. 272-c. 232), who unified India and sent ambassadors of peace to Greece, China and elsewhere. Incidentally what seems to be a subconscious notion that India has always been only the receiver of cultural influences needs correction, since Indic civilization has spread, both deliberately and naturally rather widely, certainly beginning with Aśoka if not much earlier, and continuing even down through the period of the British *Raj*. In China, a new cycle of civilization, adumbrated by the Warring States Period, begins with the unification (221 B.C.) under Shih Huang-ti (259-210 B.C.). The Great Wall was completed by 204 B.C., and the Western or Early Han dynasty continues from 202 B.C. to 9 A.D. (According to Jean Duché, the Chinese dragon and the Roman wolf divide the world between themselves around 200 B.C.) It also seems to be during this time that Southeast Asia emerges, and Hellenistic Judaism emerges with the *Septuagint* about 170 B.C.

Even though the trends within the Earlier Han-Hellenistic-Bactrian are by no means homogenous, the polarizations that take place do have an implicit unity within which they occur. Buddhism splits into Mahāyāna and Hīnayāna, with the highly hellenized *Questions of Milinda* (Menander) (c. 155 B.C.) still debatably in between. There is also an increasing polarization between Confucianism and Taoism, with other Chinese schools falling in abeyance (except, perhaps, Legalism, which was often in practice while Confucianism remained nominally in ascendency). Likewise, the polarization between the Herodians and the Zealots in Israel becomes very pronounced, as does that between the Platonists (who themselves became polarized between the Skeptics and the Neo-Platonists) and the Aristotelians, as also between the Stoics and the Epicureans. But such polarizations should be taken as indices of vitality rather than of weakness.

In summary, the Earlier Han-Hellenistic-Bactrian carries the origins of the cultural trends, with the emergence of Mahâyâna Buddhism, Neo-Taoism, and Han-Confucianism, which mark the transition from skepticism through eclecticism and syncretism to fascination with mysticism, esoterics and erotics. As for actual events and eras, it includes the political, military and commercial decline of Greece coupled with the emergence and ascendency of the Roman empire, the full cycle of the Earlier Han dynasty, the decline after Aśoka of the Mauryan empire, and the emergence and ascendency of Bactria and Sogdiana at the pivot between the three civilizations of Rome, China and India.

Later Han-Hellenistic-Bactrian Period (A.D. 50-325)

Concerning dates and events marking the beginning of the Later Han-Hellenistic-Bactrian, we may note, among others, 45 B.C. as the beginning of the Julian calendar; 38 B.C. as the Spanish Era; 31 B.C. as the Actiae Era of Macedonia; 37/36 B.C. as the Era of Cleopatra in Syria; 57 B.C. as the Mālava (Malwa) or Vikramâditya Era. Loyang becomes the capital of China around 25 A.D., while 9 A.D. is the date of Wang Mang's coup d'etat. There are several other critical dates, such as 9 B.C. for the Ethiopian Era and 78 A.D. for the Śaka Era. The Śaka Era coincides very closely with the Adi-Śaka Era in Bali and is very close to the Era of Commagenius (Samosatus), while 7 A.D. or 8 A.D. is considered the beginning of the Hungrvrka calendar of "Ireland".

In philosophy, during the Later Han-Hellenistic-Bactrian, this is the time of Nâgârjuna (c. 100), Philo (20 B.C.-A.D. 50), and Seneca (4 B.C.-A.D. 65); and in China, of Pan Ku (32-92) the historian, as well as of Wang Ch'ung (27-107) the super-skeptic and debunker of hoary tradition, with the Neo-Taoists Wang Pi (226-249), Wei Po-yang (fl. 147-167) and others close after, with their "back to nature" motif (although they had been preceded by the great Tung Chung-shu (c. 179-104 B.C.) who had hypocritically, according to his opponents, made Confucianism into the state religion). But of course likewise not to be ignored are Wang Mang (ruled 9-23 A.D.) who is claimed to have been a socialist dictator, or one of the greatest "failures" of socialism thus far known. Meanwhile Dravidian civilization in South India emerges (or re-emerges) after a temporary subordination to the Aryans. The Later Han-Hellenistic-Bactrian includes the ascendency, as well as the downfall, of "pagan" Rome and the emergence of Iberian civilization. It pivots at its end with Mani (215-276) as the product as much of Nestorian Christianity as of Sassanian Zoroastrianism, not to mention his connections with India also, for Mani was the "supersyncretist" of all times, and therefore typifies the period. To put it at a minimum, we need to add to the glory that was Greece and the grandeur that was Rome, "The Wonder that was India" and "The Splendor and Decadence of China", if we may use Duché's epithet.

Incidentally, the theme of the fullness of time introducing the Christian system of dating needs to be called into question. This period could be considered a "fullness of time" even from the non-Christian point of view, for then trans-Eurasian communications were open in a way that they have seldom been until our own time. However, there is the danger of bigotry or even of ethnocentrism in regard to the doctrinaire interpretation of the "Era of the Incarnation". For as Toynbee has observed, there have been many other "fullnesses of time", both in the first century A.D. and in other "Axial Ages", as well as other Avatars, other Incarnations, other Prophets. Thus for Christian, Muslim, Hindu and other neo-orthodoxies, universality rather than uniqueness should be stressed, especially in this period when *syncretism* dominated the whole of Eurasia, soon followed by fascination with esoterics whether that be an index of "decadence" or of expanding horizons.

THE PATRISTIC-SŪTRA PERIOD

(A.D. 325-800)

Introduction

Whereas most traditional historians of European philosophy ignore the Patristic Period altogether and include the whole stretch from Augustine to the Italian Renaissance as Medieval, Paul Deussen, in his *Allgemeine Geschichte der Philosophie*, while he might well be overlooked because he has not synchronologized, calls the stretch from 500 to 800 the Later Patristic Period. Kurt Schilling follows him very closely in his *Weltgeschichte der Philosophie*; and he and Deussen are much more in line with our perspective. Volume III of the UNESCO *History* has been far too ambitious without adequate periodization, trying to include *everything* between about 400 to 1300 as the "Medieval" period. It is a major disappointment that they follow the traditional European pattern of periodization since that just does not accurately represent the rest of the world at all. *The Columbia History of the World* simply does not meet our needs at all since it not only tries to push together the whole sequence from 500 to 1500, but also treats each of the geographical units separately.

Our designation of Patristic-Sūtra for this period is derived from the basic trends in religion and philosophy, which had become almost completely fused. It was from this point of view a very fruitful period and not a "dark ages" at all, even though admittedly there had been virtually no advance in the applied or theoretical sciences, except perhaps in Byzantium and in North India where Āryabhaṭṭa (fl. 476) had accomplished some new things in mathematics and astronomy.

Since Patristic-Sūtra does not necessarily include the "Barbarians", "Gothic-Gupta" sounds good, but it is not inclusive enough, omitting Byzantium and overriding Persia/Sogdiana, and taking no note of South India, Japan or Southeast Asia. Nevertheless, with the understanding that the word "Patristic" includes the trans-Eurasian spread of Nestorian and Monophysite Christianity as well as the Greek and Latin

"Fathers", and with the understanding that the word "Sūtra" includes the full range of Hindu and Mahâyāna literature which spreads all over Asia from Damascus to Kyoto and from Korea to Bali, we still propose Patristic-Sūtra as the most workable, even though imperfect, designation for the total sequence from 325 to 800.

One of the most prominent characteristics of the Patristic-Sūtra Period is the dominance of theology. This appears to be the age of Avatars, Bodhisattvas, and Trinities, with Buddhology side-by-side with Christology (or even, in the Barlaam and Josephat story, mixed up together). A definite theological system begins to form around the figures of Viṣṇu-Kṛṣṇa and Śiva. The Blessed mother concept spreads all over Eurasia along with the halo. Indeed, the Byzantine *Holy Wisdom* epithet for the Theotokos becomes equally applicable to Kuan Yin in China and Japan, to Saraswati and to Parvati in India. Brahmā, Śiva, Viṣṇu; Father, Son, and Holy Spirit; Dharmakāya, Nirmānakāya, Sambhogakāya — all are "logicalized", while empirical science goes into almost total eclipse. During this time civilizations itself took refuge in, and was diffused from, monasteries from Peking to York, from Mount Hiei in Japan to Kandy in Ceylon, from the plateau of Abyssinia to the fortresses of Andulusia, from the rain-forests of Indonesia to the desert of Mount Sinai. Dark Ages? But all over Eurasia there was cultivation, with a vengeance, of the *Inner* Light.

It was also an age of translations. Not only was Saint Jerome (c. 340-420) translating the Bible into Latin and Boethius (480-524) attempting to translate Greek philosophy into Latin, but the whole canon of Greek civilization as well as the Christian scriptures were translated into Syriac, Edessa being the center of that activity. (As a matter of fact, when Moslems later encountered the Greek heritage and became Hellenized, it was through the Syriac translation that they became aware of the importance of Greek civilization.) But still more importantly, the Sanskrit Buddhist classics began to be transmitted and translated, first into Chinese and then into Tibetan, Korean and Japanese, as also the Pali Canon became adapted to vernacular use in Ceylon, Burma and Southeast Asia in general. Meanwhile, the spread of Christianity throughout Northern Europe, in its Aryan form at first and later in its Irish form, carried with it a remarkable zeal for translating. And no doubt there were other areas of translating, such as the emergence of Coptic translations and literature in Egypt and Ethiopia, and the beginnings of the emergence of Slavonic civilization with Cyril (827-869) and Methodius (815-885).

Another major characteristic of the period, as is evidenced most in art, language, religion and philosophy, is the triumph of mysticism, whether in its Neo-Platonic (both 'pagan' and 'Christian') forms, or in the multiplying versions of Mahāyāna Buddhism as it migrated through Central Asia into China, there to become no longer the philosophy of the intellectual elites but the religion of the masses. In the Gospels of the New Testament (both canonical and apocryphal), as well as in the *Lotus Sūtra*, salvation is equally guaranteed for everyone, and no longer for just a chosen few. These promises of a better future replaced the cultivation of an ideal antiquity, and the idea of the *transformation* of human nature replaced the older philosophizing about human nature as naturally given. It seems that from the eclecticism and syncretism of the previous period there has been a transition to the *via negativa*, fascination with esoterics, and not infrequently authentic disciplines leading towards genuine mystical enlightenment (partly as a desperate, and sometime successful, effort to remove the degeneracy into which all the older civilizations had descended). "Other-worldliness" triumphed, and it is then that we find the "Mystical East" — but extending everywhere, including the "West" !

The world had not come to an end with Mani, who evidently was not the Second Coming of Christ after all; rather, in Central Asia at least, trade and commerce flourished. Capitalists and proletariats — rather international ones at that — not only in Byzantium but also in Edessa, Alexandria, Babylon, Nisibis and other centers along the so-called silk routes, seem to have had their boom-and-bust cycles in a way reminiscent of the other centuries. The Byzantines took to the sea in preference to the more expensive overland routes to China with the result that the Arabs prospered as well as the Persians.

Dravidian South India and Indonesia also got their share of international communications, due in part to improved navigation techniques that allowed harnessing the monsoon winds for human benefit.

Byzantium continues in pomp and splendor, and, as Duché states, "China always renews itself", with "Persia at the crossroads" making a "holy and stupid war" with Byzantium, trying to profit unduly from the silk trade which had to pass through their borders in order to satisfy the luxury-loving Byzantine aristocracy. The "Barbarians" had added all the vices of every civilization to their own, and had themselves become "civilized" and "Christianized"; or rather, as Duché puts it, "the West had become barbarized and Christianized."

We prefer to divide the Patristic-Sūtra Period into two subdivisions, i.e., Earlier Patristic-Sūtra Period (325-625) and Later Patristic-Sūtra Period (625-800).

Earlier Patristic-Sūtra Period (325-625)

The Earlier Patristic-Sūtra Period is often taken as the Early Medieval Period. We could continue to use the term "medieval" giving it a new connotation; however, we prefer not to use the term "medieval" at all except for concessions to current usage in westernized circles. Instead, we prefer to use the term "Scholastic" for the period usually designated as Medieval, but we submit that this does not come into full character until around 800 A.D. The traditional word "medieval", literally and figuratively, really, holds no sense whatsoever for universal or world history.

In support of 325 as the date of division between the Later Han-Hellenistic-Bactrian and the Earlier Patristic-Sūtra, there are, among others, the following evidences: the shift from Loyang (West Chin) to Nanking (East Chin) as the capital of China (c. 317); the beginnings of the Gupta Era in India (320-c. 535); the beginnings of the Maya calendar in Central America (c. 330); the Council of Nicaea marking the triumph of Constantine (325); the *Laṅkāvatāra Sūtra* (c. 333) and the Kojiki in Japan (c. 300).

Heresy and Orthodoxy become the major issues in both Christian and Buddhist worlds — not much being operatively left of the other ancient heritages — and this effects even political and economic affairs. We need not review all the Christian Councils and their results in defining "heresies", nor do we need to catalogue in detail all the Mahāyāna and Hindu Sūtras; but we might stress the global importance of such characters as Buddhaghoṣa (fl. 412-434) and Nestorius (380-451), and we should note the translating activities of Boethius (480-524) in the Latin Christian world as of Kumārajīva (344-413) in the Chinese Buddhist world, were Ch'an (Zen) Buddhism comes into form with Bodhidharma (fl. 429-479). That Proclus (412-485) had been the last of the great 'pagan' philosophers, as Augustine (354-430) had been the first truly seminal Christian philosopher in the Latin West, need not be mentioned as too well known; but that they, along with others of lesser fame, belong to this period is often forgotten.

The Earlier Patristic-Sūtra Period was not a happy time for the inhabitants of the old established civilizations; but it was a happy time for the so-called Barbarians. McNeil refers to the "Barbarian Onslaught and Civilized Response" for the period from 200 to 600 A.D.; and Jean Duché refers to "The End of the Ancient World" (volume I, p. 688) as follows :

> Let us thank the barbarians, they furnished us with a cataclysmic turn of fortune. In China, 311; Rome, 410; and India, 484. The curtain falls on the last act — an act of death which was also an act of birth. In China, Rome, and India, the barbarians struck three blows. (tr. by Plott)

But was it a matter of the "fall" of the ancient civilizations, or the rise of the Northern European and Central Asian civilizations? They had not been recognized as 'civilized', first because of language difficulties, and second because, having swift horses and constructing everything of wood, which was plentiful, they left little permanent evidence of their culture. But they were highly mobile; and above all, they had very good social and political organization. Their mythology, for example, was certainly no more primitive than that of the other civilizations. The mythical Fire Bird, the *Coq d'or*, the Phoenix, cyclically immortal but terrible as well as terribly beautiful; the Valkyrie and Thor and the rest of the Germanic gods — were these "barbarian" any more than the gods of

Greece and Rome? Or were they any less 'real' than Śiva and Viṣṇu? Much research is yet to be done in order to understand the rightful role of these "Barbarians".

But the phenomenon of this *volkerwanderung* was not at all unique; and the close proximity of these 'Barbarian' invasions to the Islamic conquest of the Eurasian Ecumene does, if any sequence does, constitute a period.

Later Patristic-Sūtra Period (625-800)

Needless to say, the date 500 A.D. so commonly used by many as a dividing point we have left behind. It simply does not make sense, whereas 622 A.D. or the year 1 A.H. does. Thus we designate the years 625 A.D. as the transition point between the Earlier and Later Patristic-Sūtra Period.

For support of our designation of 625 we have, among others, the following: the rise of Islam (625); the Era of Yezdegerd (632); the "Second National Era of Japan" (644-45); the Era of Magi in Sogdiana and Khorem (Persia) (652) the beginnings of the T'ang dynasty (618); the repair of the Great Wall (608); Buddhism gets official patronage in China with the thinkers Hui-neng (638-713) and Chi-tsang (546-623); Prince Shotoku (573-622) issues his famous Seventeen Article "Constitution" in Japan; Hsüan-tsang (596-664) and other Buddhist monks make great pilgrimages to India, stopping in Indonesia on return journey; under Harṣavardhana in India, the Mīmāṁsā school of Hindu philosophy splits between Kumārila Bhaṭṭa (fl. 600) and Prabhākara (d. 600); Nestorian Christianity and Manichaeanism receive benefits of official toleration, along with Buddhism, Taoism, etc., in China; Maximus Confessor (580-622) develops Christian Neo-Platonism in Byzantium; the Malaja kingdom flourishes in Sumatra (644); Era of Śrī-Harṣa in India (605-7); the Sakkaraj Era in Burma begins (638), and the Magi-San Era at Chittagong (638); the Synod of Whitby (c. 618) had "settled things" between Rome and the Irish Church (i.e., between Latin and Celtic civilization); Korea, by adopting Chinese culture, also comes on the scene seriously with the Silla dynasty having come into full power (670-780); the reign of Krhi-lde-srong-bcon in Tibet (620-650) marks the Baiduryakarpo cycle as the full emergence of Tibet in the world scene. Many other details could be brought in to establish this century as a very pivotal one, even without the prophetic "explosion" of Islam. Indeed, the Hegria (1 A.H. or 622 A.D.) can well be said to mark another "fullness of time" comparable to that of 1 A.D.

Admittedly, preceding the year 622 (1 A.H.), the Academy at Athens had been closed in 529; the Code of Justinian had been promulgated by 534; and the Cathedral of Hagia Sophia had been completed by 537. But these mark the completion of the previous cycle more than the opening of a new one, and that, moreover, limited to Byzantium. Therefore we still think the year 622 (1 A.H.) is the much more pivotal point between the Earlier and Later Patristic-Sūtra Period.

Our subdivision at 625 is especially in order not to overlook the beginnings of Islam as others have done. For the impact of Islam was too catastrophic to be ignored by any, except perhaps the Japanese. Christianity and Buddhism had also spread over almost all of Eurasia, either in overt or in disguised forms, but they had not had the same total impact on the total order of things. Another "Axial Age", another cycle of civilization, began with the Prophet Muhammad, and Eurasia became unified as scarcely ever before or since. It also appears that it was not until the rise of Islam that revelation became such a prominent theme and scholasticisms began to take on remarkably similar forms all across Eurasia. Bible, Vedas, Qur'an, Confucian Classics, even Kojiki and Nihongi, not to mention the Mahāyāna sūtras, began to be regarded as eternal and divine. Nevertheless, as we have said, religion/philosophy as such should not be taken as the only key to periodization any more than art or technology or economic modes of production or even patterns of transportation and communication. And yet, that is just the point with Islam : it does not allow such fragmentation of the different aspects of life but it is a unifying total order of things.

The era of Islamic expansion — or as Duché calls it, "Paradise under the Shadow of the Swords" with the "*Montée du Croissant*" designated as between 622 and 842 — is closely paralleled by T'ang China (618-907), during which Duché characterizes Japan as "Sinicized, Buddhized, and effeminized", while

"Byzantium is absorbed in the quarrel over images (642-843)". Duché also registers the "Passing of the Mayas" and characterizes Charlemagne's activities as "An Empire by Accident (714-843)" and "An Empire of Piety" in which Europe is born.

Concerning the end of the Later Patristic-Sūtra Period about 800, we have the following: Era of Chola (or Kolamba or Paraśurāma) in Malabar and Travancore (825), as well as the Ganga dynasty about the same time; the Nara Period in Japan (710-794); and the Third Older Empire of the Mayas (731-987), decline having become serious about 830. Just as the previous period included the Hellenization, Sinification and Nipponization of Buddhism, so this period includes the Hellenization, "Iranification" and Indianization of Islam. That these encounters were two-way processes can scarcely be denied.

THE PERIOD OF SCHOLASTICISM

(800-1350)

As to the extent of this period Mujeeb does not help very much since, after designating 200-900 "The Religious World State", he simply calls the sequence 900-1450 "The Middle Ages", acceding to unthinking Euramerican tradition which supposedly thinks of "middle" as inconsequential transition from hoary "antiquity" to "modernity". Duché, who made his previous sequence extend from 616 to 907, allows a little overlap so that his next division is between 850 and 1050, which coincides much more closely with our own findings thus far. Yet in the more technical sense we must question whether he has really periodized at all, for systematically one must distinguish between the typifications of trends and the substance of actual grouping of sequences into meaningful patterns. McNeil unacceptably gives us at one stretch periods within the dates 600-1000 and 1000-1500 without a break; however, we do incline more to McNeil's original insight in *The Rise of the West* that in many if not most respects Latin Europe did not really catch up with the rest of the world until long after Columbus. The Bingham, Conroy and Iklé *A History of Asia* (Vol. I) takes Central Asia all the way through from earliest beginnings to 1600, and then correspondingly India, and then China, and finally Japan in the same one-block sequence. Even though their divisions for each of these areas do make more sense than many others, still they do not help us towards a general periodization of world-history.

As we have noted earlier, the authors-editors of volume three of the UNESCO *History* have scarcely periodized at all, thus rendering their work of lesser value than would have been the case had they made some sort of subdivisions of the grand sweep of developments between 400 and 1300. Also, this volume of the UNESCO *History* has a very strong flavor of European ethnocentricity. Even the objections by the Soviet contributors still seem badly out of focus, writing as though the whole purpose of the Mongol conquests was to facilitate this "birth" (as they say in the preface) of Europe. Over against this the facts are not only obvious but brilliant : the cultural excellence of Baghdad and the cataclysmic destruction of it by the Mongols makes the "fall" of Constantinople look like a mud-pie tea party of children. Arnold Toynbee somewhere makes the remark that if he had had his choice of which place and time to live, it would have been in T'ang or Southern Sung China, for in most respects it was then that mankind was most "civilized" in terms of cultural refinement, even if economic, political, military, and technological achievements were not so stupendous as some North Americans would demand as their definition of being "civilized". And as for India, there is an underestimation of the emergence of Dravidian culture as manifested in such things as art, architecture, literature, and philosophy. This feature is even more important than the overlay conquests of the Muslims, for they were scarcely more than raids sporadically carried out, admittedly defacing a lot of great art and architecture, but really leaving the indigenous tradition virtually unaffected at the village level. This emergence of South India is no less phenomenal than the emergence of Europe, for it was definitely paralleled by the Indianization of Southeast Asia. Even if we neglect the continuing Indianization through Buddhism of the rest of Asia, the fact that Islam itself becomes Indianized very quickly and almost completely it seems, needs more emphasis than the fact that the Muslims 'conquered' India.

Besides such things as pilgrimages, crusades and monk-philosophers wandering on foot and on horseback free of charge, there is evidence of continuing trade along the silk routes plus the presence of Christians of Nestorian and Monophysite persuasion as well as Manichaeans all across Eurasia. (Incidentally, people were not in such a rush in those days as now and, mixing with all-and-sundry enroute, they probably learned much more than modern jet-age "take-a-look and write-a-book" travellers who seldom see anything but airports and bars in Euroamerican style hotels.) The speed and ease of the Muslim, Turkish and Mongol conquests, plus the fact that it is during our centuries that paper, gunpowder, movable type, navigational skills and many other essentials of civilization travelled from China to Europe along with Indian mathematics — these accumulatively reinforce the opinion that communications were remarkably open contributing to the fundamental cultural unity of the Period of Scholasticism all across Eurasia. Even though national prides do emerge soon after, largely in defense against the exaggerated claims and demands of the Western European explorers, pirates, conquistadors, and missionaries, they are scarcely distinguishable between 800 and 1350 or so.

The terms "Medieval", "Scholasticism", "Feudal", and "Mongol", plus the prominence of "Crusades", "Jihads", and "Pilgrimages", have come to characterize the sequence from approximately 800 to 1350 such that we are at a loss to find any one viable, inclusive term. Nevertheless, this being a period in which ideational values throughout Eurasia supposedly dominated over sensate values, we prefer to use the term "Scholasticism" to include all the other factors and variables.

It was during this time that philosophy and theology developed a very highly sophisticated technique of balancing and counter-balancing arguments and refutations and counter-arguments and counter-refutations before coming tentatively to some considered opinion in lieu of a "conclusion", most of these architectonic structurings being in the form of commentaries on basic handbook texts handed down as authoritative scripture from antiquity or at least from the New Testament, the Purāṇas and the Qur'an. For these and many co-ordinate reasons we offer the term "Scholastic" as a general typification of the whole cycle which ranges before and after the trans-Eurasian conquest and overlaying unification by the Mongols. The term applies equally not only to Muslim, Jewish, and Christian developments, but to Hindu, Buddhist, Neo-Confucian Chinese and even Jaina compendia. Not only that, however; these commentaries begin to develop sub-commentaries and even second and third generation commentaries on commentaries on commentaries, right down to the 15th and 16th centuries when individual supposedly original shorter essays replaced these archetectonic theological and philosophical "cathedrals of scholarly exigesis" or "summas" as they are often called.

We have chosen to call this section the Period of Scholasticism in order to stress that the scholastic method, with its emphasis on polarization of thesis, antithesis and its attempt at synthesis, became universal throughout Eurasia. Out of the welter of dates throughout the Period of Scholasticism admittedly nothing definitive emerges as convenient dividing points for the whole of Eurasia — at least in the external world. And yet in the cultural and intellectual sphere it seems to us that a pattern does emerge. The monist trends of the 9th and the 10th centuries extend into exfoliation by the mid-12th, and go into decadence by the time of the Mongol *volkerwanderung's* repetition of the previous cycles of "Barbarian" invasions. We should like to emphasize the view that this cycle of periods from 800 to 1350 does constitute another "Axial Age" and also that the fundamental unity of the "Medieval" world has never been adequately spotlighted in universal history.

In this period, philosophy had a place of honor in the hierarchy of values everywhere, and it seems to manifest the spirit of the period more than any other aspect of things cultural. At least this might be said of the 12th and 13th centuries, these having been preceded by another "pre-socratic" development leading toward syntheses, and after the syntheses, a sort of "Han-Hellenistic-Bactrian" after-glow, until the infusion of new forces introduces some hybrid vigor. We are fully aware that this may be playing too close to the precipice of the Theory of Ideal Types and therefore mention these speculations with a considerable measure of caution. At any rate, from Scotus through Anselm and Abelard to Aquinas and Bonaventura, from al-Kindi to Ibn Rushd (Averroes), from Śaṅkara to Rāmānuja and Madhva and his successors, from Han Yu and Li Ao to Chu Hsi and Lu Hsiang-shan, from Kukai and Saicho to Dogen, Nichiren and Shinran — all of these developments seem to run remarkably parallel. The fact that the Scandinavian, the Slavonic and the Central American civilizations follow the same essential pattern certainly needs further explanation, and a cause of their simultaneous developments, which further penetrate our claim that it was another "Axial Age", must be sought for until it is found. The Amerindian civilization, however, constitutes for the philosopher and the historian, even if not for the archaeologist and anthropologist, a truly remarkable puzzle, especially for this cycle of periods, for they seem to follow the same pattern.

Islam was not only a bridge between East and West during these truly great centuries but constituted a positive unity to Eurasia such as it had never before and has never since known. Indeed, we could almost call it the Period of Islamic Unification rather than the Period of Scholasticism, although of course that would be too much de-emphasizing Chinese, Japanese, Dravidian, and Southeast Asian developments. That fantastic episode of mixed human emotions which was the Crusades of the Latin "Christian" world should be re-examined from the Muslim point of view in order to see such things in the global perspective : Civilized and if anything over-sophisticated and living in considerable luxury, but also patronizing science, the arts and learning, the Muslims of that era must have been curiously amused at first, then alarmed, and then provoked by those uncouth 'Franks' who came wandering into their territory singing barbarian but beautiful tunes based on otherworldly romantic legends which could never be actualized. It must be admitted that *pilgrimages* in East and South Asia were often scarcely less fantastic. This period produced some of the world's greatest *bhaktas* and minstrel singers as well as theologians and philosophers. It was in short, in Sorokin's terms, a supremely *ideational* rather than a *sensate* time. Indeed at its inception and apogée, the ideational prevailed even though sensate qualities began to emerge by the end of the period.

Admittedly we have not been able to find subdivisions for this period which are to our satisfaction. Therefore we have used those subdivisions which seem to fit the history of philosophy. By no means do we propose that periodizing only according to philosophical developments is desirable. We only want to add it, highlight it as significant in the midst of a very richly complex nexus in a cycle of Eurasian civilization. Thus, for the Period of Scholasticism (800-1350), we suggest the following divisions : the Earlier Period of Scholasticism or "Monism in Many Moods" (800-900); the Middle Period of Scholasticism or "Exfoliation and Elaboration" (900-1150);

and the Later Period of Scholasticism or the "Great Summas" (1150-1350).

The most prominent characteristic of the ninth century nexus is a rather remarkable domination of monist philosophies — systematically monist and not merely syncretistic mixtures. Also, what has usually been called the "mysticism of the Orient" is primarily the product of this particular nexus. It is not geographically limited, but rather the product of a definite period in the world history of philosophy. As representative of this period, we have the amazing constellation of the following philosophers : Śaṅkara (788-820), Han Yu (768-824), Li Ao (fl. 798), Kukai (774-835), Saicho (c. 767-822), Ennin (fl. c. 847), al-Kindi (801-873), al-Hallaj (858-922), Bayazid Bisṭami (d. 874), Photius (820-891), Cyril (827-869), and Scotus Erigena (810-877). This was one of the most remarkable times in world history, a time when all of Eurasia manifested very similar trends.

In every civilization during the Earlier Period of Scholasticism the themes of philosophizing were heavily weighted towards theology. Their basic outlines were remarkably parallel, embracing epistemology, ontology, and arguments for transcendence, ascesis for spiritual attainments, ritual practices and the reasons for them and the expected fruits thereof, and eschatology, with an implicit aesthetics couched in the form of emotional piety and a profound sense of Wonder and Mystery. Meanwhile, expertise and techniques of logic increase in sophistication quite parallel with the other trends towards refinement and elaboration. The *via negativa*, inherited from the previous period, also basically prevails; and analogies abound, rather than analyses. Emanational theories generally take precedence over simple creationist theories.

By the close of the 9th century we have at best qualified monisms and often openly dualist and pluralist trends. Out of the unification of Islam in the external world emerged a new metaphysics of unity which was almost monolithic; but as the political and theological unity of Islam became fragmented, so this monist trend was soon lost in proliferation of distinctions and subtleties of scholastic argumentation until we reach the "Great Summas" (1150-1350). This trend from monistic simplicity through elaboration to excessive complexity and ornamentation is remarkably paralleled in architecture in the transition from Romanesque to elaborate Gothic in Europe and in Dravidian India from the solidity of Tanjore to the filigreed fragrance-in-stone of Belur and Halebīd. In Islam likewise we can see essentially the same transition from the early puritanical unadorned mosques to the elaborate and even gaudily ornate mosques of the later centuries (Cordoba being only one case in point). In the Buddhist world the halo begins with the pure simplicity of the early Gupta style, but eventually in China, Japan and India it encompasses the entire universe. Similar developments of the halo motif transpire also in Byzantium and even in Gothic Europe. During the Later Period of Scholasticism the greatest works of Bonaventura and Aquinas, al-Ghazali and Ibn Rushd (Averoees), Rāmānuja and Madhva, Lu Hsiang-shan and Chu Hsi, Dogen and Nichiren emerge systematically out of previous seminal insights and formulations such as the *Sentences* of Peter Lombard, the Brahma Sūtras, and the speculations about the Great Ultimate. They mark without doubt the culmination of that cycle of systematization in a way that has seldom been achieved.

THE PERIOD OF ENCOUNTERS

(1350-1850)

Introduction

The problem of periodization for the whole stretch of time from about 1300 to 1750 has been a disturbing one for all periodizers, including the contributors and compilers of the fourth volume of the UNESCO *History of Mankind.* Indeed in the prefatory "Note on the Preparation and Editing of Volume IV" we find the following discussion (p. xviii) by Professor Roland Mousnier:

> Concerning the composition of the book, we find an analytic plan in which each subject is studied in and of itself ... so that the subdivisions of each chapter look like a juxtaposition of descriptive passages, a series of dictionary articles.. ... But the links between the facts studied in each case and those considered in other categories are rarely shown clearly enough. ... There is lacking a general view of all these human activities, their reciprocal actions and reactions, their relationships as variables and functions. ...
>
> This failure to consider things as a whole has made it impossible, on the one hand, to distinguish types — types of societies, types of civilizations, types of states — and, on the other hand, to distinguish periods, characterized by the predominance of certain types. The period from 1300 to 1775 is too often regarded as a whole with little difference from beginning to end. The movement and flow of time is too often lacking in this study of history. Would it not be possible, at any rate for Europe and possibly for the rest of the world as a whole, to single out a period from 1300 to 1450 (in which Europe was moving towards a scientific and technological capitalist civilization which created the axle rudder with hinged stern-post, borrowed the magnetic needle from the Chinese, disseminated the bill of exchange and capitalism, invented the system of crank-shaft, launched the caravel — a ship suited for long ocean voyages — improved rural tools and the tools of craftsmen and, with the great nominalists, inspired by William of Ockham, Jean Buridan, Albert of Saxony, Nicholas Oresme,

began the great intellectual mutation of mankind, the creation of mathematical physics), a Renaissance period from 1450 to 1650, and an Age of Enlightenment from 1650 to 1775? At the very least, an effort should have been made to determine a period, or periods, allowing for all the factors and all the aspects of civilizations.

Of course Professor Gottschalk and his associates make some reply to this (p. xix) — not necessarily to our satisfaction — pleading that different authorities would not really make different selections; but he does not answer directly the issue of periodization, at least in this context, and the divisions in volume IV of the UNESCO *History* remain basically 1300-1500 and 1500-1775, with only a minor variation in the case of the section on science, which takes the date 1530-1775. We must concede that this division made by the compilers of the UNESCO *History* is about as convenient as any; however, the division is still too arbitrary and does not answer Professor Mousnier's demand — which we poignantly share — for characterization.

Jean Duché's volume three, which bears the caption *L'Age de Raison*, extends from 1500-1660 and thence directly down to 1815, although he makes some very perspicacious observations on subperiods within these 'periods' while walking the tightrope between art and chronology. The brevity of these sub-periods reminds us of the danger of descent into the labryinth of shortsightedness as we come closer to "home" in the twentieth century; for time perception, like the perception of space with our stereo vision, is rather funnel shaped for us human beings, though it would seem that every century should be viewed as of equal length, if not of equal importance also.

Increasing Encounters : Syntheses and Sophistication (1350-1550)

Once again deeming the cultural developments — and especially the patterns of emergence, or lack of emergence, of types of philosophy — of greater importance than the political and economic much less military factors, we have opted to call the division from 1350 to 1550 Syntheses and Sophistication. If any prefer "Renaissance" for this sequence we have only the objection that the designation is easily misread, even though Arnold Toynbee has catalogued a long list of "renaissances" in world history as anything from the transition from ideational to sensate culture (Sorokin) to liberation from "medieval gloom" and the emergence of free-for-all competitional capitalism and commercialism. Among others, Duché has the following suggestive themes during these centuries : "Seigneur Dieu, es-tu là ?"; "La douloureuse danse" ; "La marche turque"; "L'Asie s'endort"; "Le Japon choisit les plaisirs de la guerre"; "A l'Quest : vers les monarchies absolues"; "A l'Est : des monarchies féodales"; "Terre des hommes".

For beginning around 1350 the following dates are of significance: Ming dynasty (1368); Thailand establishes its identity (1350) ; the beginning of the Ashikaga Period in Japan (1336); the Timurid Empire and Uzbek ascendency in Central Asia (c. 1350) ; Casmimi the Great in Poland (1333-1370); end of Mongolian (Genghis Khan) domination of Persia (1334); beginning of Muromachi epoch in Japan (1333); founding of the Vijayanagar empire in India (1336); beginning of the so-called "100 years" war in Europe (1339) ; founding of the Bahmanide dynasty in India (1337) ; St Bridgit of Sweden to Rome (1349); revolt of Southern China against the Mongols (1350) ; Nanking taken away from the Mongols (1356); Mourad first Ottoman Sultan (1359-1389) ; Tamerland begins conquest of Central Asia (1363).

After the Period of Scholasticism instead of creativity or originality or thorough systematizing we get merely a series of commentaries on commentaries in Europe, the Islamic world, India, and China; and even in Japan and Byzantium we do not find much more than further refinement on what had already been achieved. Thus 1350-1550 is an age of over-refinement.

Although indeed Pletho and Bessarion in the Byzantine world could be pointed to as a great apogée in humanist philosophy that was a mainspring for the Italian Renaissance, another aspect of even their work is that it is not so much creative and original as a summing up of the whole heritage of the past, done in very refined (if not indeed over-refined) style. But what one sooner or later learns concerning the reappraised story of the so-called "Fall" of Byzantium to the "Turks" may also be said of their work to a great extent : Entirely too élitist —the cost of sophistication achieved may have been too great. The Muslims were welcomed by the masses as deliverers from the oppression of the aristocrats, the monasteries, and the almost totally corrupt government which was levying exhorbitant taxes on all the under-privileged people.

In Latin Europe, some might claim that the works of Ockham (1280?-1348) and those who have been called the "positivists of Paris", namely John Buridan (d. 1360), William of Autrecourt (1300?-1350?), Nicholas of Cusa (1401-1464), et al., were really great in that they attained an expertise in logic and epistemology seldom achieved before or since — except, of course, in India, as far back as Diṅnāga, Dharmakīrti, Śāntarakṣita and Kamalaśīla in the 5th to 8th centuries, and the Muslims not only between the the time of Avicenna (Ibn Sina) and Averroēs (Ibn Rushd) but also as far back as Ibn Ḥasm or even al-Farabi for that matter. But, on the other hand, brilliant as these achievements were in their own way, when the expertise in technique is deemphasized (as indeed later it was for the most part after Francis Bacon and other beginners of the mordern cycle in the well-known history of Euramerican philosophy), there is very little that is original and genuinely creative. It is all, or virtually all, superstructure. Also, Nicholas of Cusa (1401-1464) can be for the most part reduced to what is aleady in Albert the Great (d. 1280), with just an echo of proto-Renaissance stimulation from his trip to Byzantium, while even Ficino (1433-1499) and Pico Della Mirandola (1468-1533) are more transmitters and translators of Byzantine materials (not to mention their completely decadent fascination with magic and the Caballa) than really creative and original philosophers in their own right.

The Gei an mystics (Eckhardt, Tauler, Suso, et al.) were operating in a tradition that can be traced very far back in old Germanic literature, and they even eventually influenced Luther, at least indirectly; nevertheless, it may be queried whether this refuge in mysticism was completely authentic or whether it was a sort of retreat from genuine philosophy in the systematic sense. In other words it may be that the yin and the yang, the logical expertise and the very opposite in intuitive mysticism, ceased to stimulate and complement each other, and, having gone into separation, soon became decadent and even degenerated into unphilosophical sentimentality.

As to the Islamic world, according to most recent researches the myth of the decadence of Islam has come up short since it came about by the very odd notion that Muslim philosophy had nothing to offer except as it contributed to the devęlopmnet of Latin Scholasticism. Although Ibn Khaldun (d. 1406) was one of the greastest minds in the entire history of philosophy, it seems that most of the other philosophers in the Islamic world during this period were for the most part looking backwards and only attempting further interpretations and adaptations in an overly refined sophisticated way of what had already been achieved. Moreover, just as the yin and the yang seem to have polarized and come apart in Latin and Germanic Europe, so in the Islamic world the Sūfis seem to lose communication with the scholastics, and although they too achieve a great delicacy and grace in their poetry, it is all too often on the border of playing with words and overly ornate and therefore "decadent" by comparison with al-Ḥallaj.

In India, Madhusūdana Saraswatī and Appeya Dikṣita might be brought to the fore as synthesizers who were by no means "sterile", though actually Madhusūdana Saraswati was doing (good) patchwork on the wornout Advaitic tradition trying thereby to strengthen Hinduism enough so that it could purge India of the "Islamic scourge". As for Nanak and the Sikhs, like the German Mystics they achieved a great new revelation, as it were, in religion, but very little that is philosophically significant. Actually, India does not (except for the possible exception of the Navya-Nyāya school of logic) produce another really great thinker until the encounter with the British. Here we may mention the late scholastics of Vallabha and the second and third generation commentaries on commentaries in both the Śaṅkara Advaitin heritage and the Rāmānuja tradition.

Except for the new cycle which seems to begin with Wang Yang Ming (1472-1529), in China for this sequence we mostly have the sterile scholasticism of commentaries on commentaries on Chu Hsi. And finally in Japan, after Dôgen, Nichiren,

Honen and Shinran there is very little new development in Japanese Buddhism, although noteworthy representative of their respective traditions appear in due course. Of course there is the Neo-Shintoism of Kitabatake Chikafusa (1293-1354) and others after him who continue to strive for a reconciliation of nationalism (or Japanese ethnocentricity ?) and Buddhist universalism. But to make a long story short, once again syntheses and sophistication.

Maximum Encounters: *European Expansion, Exploration, and Exploitation* (1550-1750)

The sequence from 1550 to 1750 which includes the Renaissance and Reformation in Europe now reduced to its proper place in the perspective of world history, we have labeled as Maximum Encounters : European Expansion, Exploration and Exploitation. During the rather nondescript period of transition between the Scholastic apogées (1150-1350) and increasing encounters in the 15th and 16th centuries there were evidently few really major developments; but by the time we come to the 1550's we are, traumatically indeed, in a different world. It was not just the voyages of the Portuguese and the Spanish navigators — who were actually using Chinese nautical expertise, only slightly improved by the Muslims — that made the difference. We should and do give much attention to the effect of the European expansion and (supposed) domination of the rest of the world but we too often forget even to investigate the feedback effects on Europe, many of which vividly illustrates the Toynbeesque "law" that military conquerors are very likely to be culturally conquered by their subjects. Another comment that must not pass : How did that barbarian notion of the Europeans that discovery entails possession ever get into the laws ? Who "discovered" what ? — could not those explorers have come as friends instead of as conquistadors, pirates (for many were no less than that), missionaries and slave traders ? To say the least, the caption Age of *Discovery* needs revising.

Jean Duché reinforces our view that beginning with the 16th century the Europeans violated the Americas if not the rest of the world as well. In volume three, he puts the chapter heading in the question: "L'Europe au Centre du Monde?"—he need not ask according to whom for it certainly has never been so for the Chinese, or the Japanese, or for most others (even though some in India and Africa were almost persuaded that it was so).

The African slave trade, the genocide in North and South America were only some of the many exploitations that went along with the European expansion. Needless to say, none of the gold and silver which ended up in Dutch and British Banks ever came back.

To explicate the *cultural* alienation that has transpired would require many volumes. Besides the Spaniards' prohibition of printing of books in the colonies, enough to point to the British policy — which was actually *liberal* by comparison with the Dutch and Portuguese — of setting up educational systems in order to "create little Englishmen" in brown or black or yellow skins. The role of the missionaries is such an emotional topic that one wonders whether an objective appraisal of their work will ever be possible. Even where they were able to counter the mischief done by the conquistadors, perhaps their greatest service was pioneering in translating the classics of the "natives" into European languages, although thereby supplying the myth of the Orient as the mystical counterpart of the materialist West. And even they sometimes spread hatreds rather than Christian charity.

Protestant against Catholic, French against British, Dutch against both, the Europeans, in spite of Christian charity in theory, in practice learned to hate each other by virtue of their rivalry for empires. Not being content with becoming contemptuous of all non-Europeans, European hatred has even wrought, by virtue of the classical dictum of "divide and rule" and ambition for empire, enmity and strife between Japan and China, Hindus and Moslems in India and Pakistan, whites and blacks in most of Africa, and, perhaps worst of all, between China and India, who had lived in peace and amity for many thousands of years. Between Rousseau's innocent and noble savage and Hobbes' "nature red with tooth and claw" the truth was eliminated : the rest of humankind were really *just people* like themselves. But that realization has come too late.

In India, the Court of Akbar (1556-1605) made Queen Elizabeth's entourage look like playhouse imitations of children. In

China, the contemporary of King George was not joking when he replied that China "had no need of the Barbarian king's trinkets", for not only was he not at all impressed but no doubt was genuinely puzzled at the Britons' unwillingness to become vassals of the "Central" kingdom and thereby accepting the benefits of *civilization.* Later, to some extent, in France the tables were turned; the physiocrats and not a few of the "philosophers", Leibniz (1646-1716) included, insisted that the Court of the Louises be modelled after the Chinese pattern—until the pope interfered and put a stop to it. Though Portugal got some cultural feed-back benefits from the 'Oriental' trade, no Europeans penetrated the doors of Japan or Thailand or Iran — at least not for very long, for these civilizations "caught on" soon enough to escape becoming part of European empires owing allegiance to the pope of Rome. They already had their own 'popes'. "Europe at the Center of the World ?" — only according to the Europeans ! So, we must reinvestigate the sequence 1550-1750 which is so often labeled the "Age of Discovery" and "The Age of European Expansion"; and, ironically, it might well be questioned whether the scientific and technological revolutions in Europe could have taken place without the accumulated wealth extorted from the rest of the world. Nevertheless, Toynbeesque *Encounters between Civilizations* can be either positive (as Indian Buddhism in China) or negative (with Islam either the True Faith or the Sword) or both as the British in India.

Also, during this period we may note the following: the Era of Akbar (1556); the little Era of Azarias of Dschulfa in Armenia (1616); the adoption of the Muslim calendar in Java (1633); the Rājyābhiṣeka Śaka Era of Hindu India (1673); beginnings of the Tokugawa Shogunate in Japan (1600), and the 'closing' of Japan to all but Dutch science (1639); Pegu comes under the beginnings of modern Burma (1550); Siam regains independence (1567), and about the same time the Vietnamese for the first time invade the Mekong Delta, which hitherto had belonged to Cambodia; the Sikhs revolt, sealing what might be called the "Post-Muslim" or "Protestant" Reformation in Hindu-Muslim India (1606); the beginnings of the Ch'ing dynasty, or the Manchu dyarchy (1644); the T'ung-lin Academy founded by Ku Hsien Ch'eng (1550-1612); Shah

Abbas of Persia takes Baghdad (1632); the beginnings of the Maratha Empire under Shivaji in India (1662); the Taj Mahal completed (1653); and the Russian expansion over Siberia reaching Lake Baikal (1634). The importance of such dates makes us wonder whether there is not a possible 'subperiod' division naturally emerging sometime around 1660 — even though it was not yet clear which Europeans would gain "possession" of which part of the globe; and, dates or no dates, the importance of the European expansion (which in a way perhaps ought to be compared to the expansion on land of the Hūṇs, the Turks and the Mongols) cannot be minimized.

The Scientific Revolution was bought at a very dear price, and sometimes we wonder whether it was really worth that price. A truly wise man then might have predicted a sort of New Age, but an Age of Uncertainty? With *science*, however, more certainty? Certainly not ! Galileo with his "Copernican Revolution" in science untied the knot of tradition, and even the Angels trembled. Moreover, without the wealth gained from the *other* worlds, how could science flourish?

Withdrawal from Encounters : Nationalism and Naturalism (1750-1850).

After 1750, a reaction began. It was not only the USA that tried to get independence from Europe; no one ever wants to become a colony or be called "the natives". It has taken two whole centuries to begin to rectify that unbalance between (Latin-Germanic) Europe and the other civilizations. The apex of the 18th century saw the counter-currents real beginning, the Withdrawal from Encounters. Even the tolerant Chinese in self-defense had to withdraw the Edicts of Toleration as Japan had done even more rigorously several years before.

It is noteworthy as reinforcement of our characterization of Withdrawal from Encounters that McNeil designates the sequence 1700 to 1850 as "The Tottering World Balance" — partially upset, as Toynbee has remarked, by the fact that the steamship replaced the overland trade routes, lessening communications by land across Eurasia and thereby heightening the myth of the separateness of "East" and "West".

What we mean by Withdrawal from Encounters is very much evident in the fields of religion and philosophy. For example, in India there was, in sharp contrast to the syncretism between Hinduism and Islam with Akbar (1542-1605) and Dārā Śikoh (1615-1659), and Rāmānanda (1299-1411), Kabīr (1440-1518) and Nānak (1469-1538), a "back to the Qur'an" movement especially among the sūfī orders, but also in the anti-Hindu fanaticism of the later Moghul rulers. In the case of Iran, the successors of Mulla Sadra Shīrāzī (1571-1640) tended more and more to retrench from his synthesis and to withdraw into a sort of scholasticism. From things as well as from the relative sterility in philosophy of the Ottomans has arisen the myth of the "decadence" of Islam during the 17th, 18th, and even 19th centuries; but we have increasing evidence that this myth was rather generated by the *lack* of communication between the European Islamicists and the indigenous tradition.

Among Hindus, there was, both under Śivāji and in Vijayanagar, and with Madhusūdana Saraswatī and Appaya Dīkṣita, a "back to the Vedas" anti-Muslim movement. We have already mentioned the "closing" of Japan to the European missionaries, and we could have also mentioned that toleration was rescinded for Buddhism to a very critical degree. Nationalist Shinto became, with a vengeance, the State religion in an overtly chauvinistic way. We have already mentioned the rescinding of the Edicts of Toleration in China; and as even more critical than that we should note the "back to Confucius" sort of "Reformation" with Tai Chen (1723-1777) with its puritanical moralizing which was a reaction against the syncretistic tendencies of Wang Yang Ming. Indeed, the whole of the activities of the Tung-ling Academy was focused in this direction. We need not mention the parallel "back to the Bible" movements in both Catholic and Protestant Christianity; but we should emphasize how the suppression of the Jesuits in the mid-eighteenth century had results everywhere, for they — whatever their vices may have been — had had the policy of encouraging native ways when such were not overtly contrary to the faith.

Nationalism and Naturalism are characteristics which seem to accompany this withdrawal from encounters, not only with Western Europe but also with most of the other areas of the world. These *trends* cannot be mechanically divided into definite year-periods but rather constitute overlaps and undercurrents; nevertheless it may be asserted that they are most evident, or at least have their origins, from about 1750 to 1850 or so. (Mujeeb also notes this calling the division between 1750 and 1850 "A Century of Revolutions".)

Actually the term *nationalism* seems to connote more the phenomenon of Western Europe getting fragmented into smaller units such as we call nations today. Nationalism is often condemned, and rightly so, for it has become a disease of divisiveness, the chief inhibition to global community. For the *myth of national sovereignty* has become the successor to the older ideology of the Divine Right of Kings. Obviously, given modern economic conditions in which no single nation on the planet can be self-sustaining, this myth has very little if any reality behind it; and without the empires which the Europeans acquired, the claim could never have any possibility of acceptance anywhere.

We must moot the question whether this phenomenon of nationalism really applies in the rest of the world, for *nationhood* was not the issue until they become almost completely Europeanized or "Westernized". What was basically at stake was the preservation of the identity of each *total civilization*, over against the conquering or exploiting powers. Indeed, if "nationalism" were carried far enough in the rest of the world, the net result would be what might be called by Europeans the "balkanization of the world". India being much more diversified in languages and general cultural inheritances would have been "balkanized" beyond any possible sense of unity except as a possible geological unit, much less a geographical unity. The same would apply to Central Asia, even to China, and certainly to the Indonesian Archipelago, while the Ottoman remnant of the great unity of the Islamic world itself would have been "balkanized" beyond recognition.

And to an amazing degree, this is just what did transpire. the great exception perhaps being the Spanish "Pax" overlaying Hispanic America. The penetration of Africa by the Europeans in rivalry with themselves as well as with Islam forced a terribly artificial "balkanization" of the whole continent. India's map became so complex under the British that scarcely any expert could accurately count all the principalities and Nawabships and pseudo-autonomous regions. China retained a semblance of unity until the "balkanization" by "sphere of influence" by the rival Europeans, which led into the lowest phase of Chinese history.

The so-called "enclosure" of Japan is easily interpreted as "nationalism", although this needs some qualification since basically it was only a refusal to become a part of any European empire. It was also, however, a continuation of chauvinistic ethnocentricity, stemming as that does at least back to Nichiren; and, with such leading figures as Arai Hakuseki (1657-1725), it was even a rejection of Buddhism as something imported and foreign. By way of strengthening the externalities of this 'nationalism', Neo-Confucianism was freshly imported; but with Kamo Mabuchi (1697-1769) and others even this gave way to what has come to be known as *National* Shinto as distinguished from Shrine Shinto. Shinto had been heretofore more of a high Animism of a frankly polytheistic kind easily adapting in various degrees of syncretism to any-and-all innovations; but with National Shinto by the latter half of the eighteenth century, it became symstematized into a national faith in the emperor cult and the "chosen people" concept, with a sense of divinely appointed destiny to rival England and the other European powers in everything from medicine to nautical technology. Having found out that Europe had gotten ahead of China in such matters, the Japanese during the Rangaku cycle of studies selectively but assiduously learned all they possibly could and adapted it to their own use. To say the least, the "opening" of Japan by Commodore Perry towards the end of this cycle turns out to be little more than a myth.

As for China, the case is not quite so dramatically clear. For example, the Jesuits, who adapted the Christian faith to Chinese culture and customs, were not only tolerated but welcome for quite a time — until the Friars came in and virtually undid all the good. The net result was the withdrawal of the Edicts of Toleration and limiting all foreign trade to Canton. This obviously fits both descriptions of nationalism and withdrawal from encounters. Admittedly it is complicated by the transfer from Ming to the Ch'ing dynasty — the detested Manchu dyarchy being such that many refused to serve this 'foreign' barbarian regime. Though this surely can be taken as evidence of nationalism to a very high degree (even within the dynamics of Chinese civilization itself), admittedly in the case of China our theme does remain more controversial and open as a question for further investigation and discussion. Suffice it then to point to the fact that the trend was there and that it was quite deep-seated, so much so that the so-called Boxer Rebellion and the abortive Taiping Rebellion are only the most obvious outcomes of the trend.

Because of the inadequate research materials currently available, we must skim past the Philippines, what is now Indonesia, and Southeast Asia in general, reminding ourselves nevertheless that Thailand's nationalism was strong enough to play opposing sides against each other and thereby to gain the best from all concerned. To a certain extent this is true of Persia also. Asserting its identity positively, Persia actively sought alliances wherever and whenever possible which would serve her own *national* interest, again, by taking the initiative, especially for instance in seeking for an alliance with France against the Ottomans.

As for Russia, the case is so strong that it scarcely needs mentioning. Dramatized in McNeil's *Rise of the West* by the cartoon of Peter the Great as Janus-faced, looking both East and West, Russia claims to have come out with the very best. The only difference is that her empire was contiguous to the Motherland, and is still becoming a part of that Motherland, so that the charge of colonialism supposedly does not apply as it does to those with overseas empires. Indeed, even if we had no other evidence, the very emergence in earnest of the myth of Moscow as the Third Rome should be sufficient to instantiate our thesis.

Concerning Western Europe and the Americas the facts are so universally known that they need not be dwelled upon. Latin America if anything wanted independence earlier than did the North Americans, but the Spanish autarchy being stronger than the monarchy in London, success did not come as soon. The point which too few still adequately appreciate is that nationalism on the part of every one of that rich and potentially powerful enclave of sovereign nations has continually been so strong that Bolivar's dream of á federation of Latin America without any connections with the United States has thus far not been possible.

Naturalism, another characteristic of this period, is intimately intertwined with the themes of Westernization, modernization, and secularization; but, while it is easily overlooked, it is not so easy to unravel without destroying the total pattern of development.

In the case of the emergence of naturalism in Western Europe between the time of the Renaissance and the present the literature is so copious that we need not mention it. The drama of the emergence of the modern natural sciences, along with even the development of what has come to be called natural theology, is always presented as the chief feature during the last two or three centuries in world history.

It was not only Galileo who met with opposition; indeed, so many of the new ideas were so often challenged that the controversies connected with the later Darwin-Marx-Freud trinity are really mostly previous arguments in different forms. The geology controversy and all the fanciful theories about fossils, for example, were just as traumatic as the Darwinism of the early twentieth century has been. However, no less difficult to reconcile with old established dogma was the impact of the increasing discoveries of the achievements of "the natives" in "the Orient". For example, even the great scientist Cuvier found it difficult to fit into his ethnocentristic scheme of things the realization that the civilization of India reached back behind the antiquities of Greece and Rome; and, aside from upsetting the traditional dating of the creation of the world at about 4000 B.C., he finally hit upon the idea that perhaps somehow some of the great achievements, even in the science of India, if not of other civilizations, were survivals of the superior state of things before the Flood in which Noah was the main figure.

We have only begun to learn of the actual conditions of the sciences in India and China in the eighteenth century, but the following two instances may be taken as representative : The

British banned the Ayurvedic practice of innoculation against smallpox because they thought it was connected with heathen superstition, with the result that there was a fresh epidemic. It was only many years later that the Europeans independently came on to a very similar practice. Likewise British steel was so inferior to Indian steel until relatively late that England was actually importing steel from Sweden until someone learned of the Indian technique and improved on it for mass production. We could mention many other instances of the incredulity of the Europeans concerning the achievements in everything from astronomy to scientific linguistics, not only in the case of India but of China also. Since multiplication of examples would only belabor the fact that European naturalism became more advanced much later than has generally been supposed, we need rather to investigate more carefully the not so well known naturalism of the eighteenth and nineteenth centuries in Japan, China, India, Russia, the Americas, etc.

In the case of China, the claim that Confucian, and especially Neo-Confucian philosophy was *already* naturalistic — so much so that the Jesuits had great difficulty convincing the Chinese intelligentsia concerning their claim to have a "revealed" religion — needs to be checked out with care. Of course Chinese Buddhism did develop some "supernaturalistic" themes, and the theology of grace in the T'ien-t'ai and the Amitābha cults does run remarkably parallel to their Christian counterparts; but these had by the eighteenth century been completely overridden and officially condemned by such leading thinkers as Yen Yüan and Tai Chen. Moreover, over against the idealism of Wang Yang Ming in the sixteenth century there was a reaction, and the realist (or outright *naturalistic*) school of Neo-Confucianism gained the ascendency. Indeed, the cases of Ku Yen-wu and of Chang Hsüeh-ch'eng dramatize the extent to which even empirical naturalism had developed since they often went to the places mentioned in the classical texts and checked their accuracy before writing the history of China for their own generation. In short, one gets the definite impression that although the naturalistic trends had been at least latent since Chu Hsi's insistence on a literal interpretation of *ko wu* as investigation of things, nevertheless this empiricism, pragmatism and naturalism came into fresh flowering in the eighteenth century.

In the case of Japan perhaps it is enough to mention the names of Ishida Baigen, Miura Baien, and Kamo Mabuchi as representative of a very definitely naturalistic trend even in the relatively conservative Shingaku school, quite apart from the naturalism that motivated the Rangaku studies. But more dramatically we have the comparison of Locke and Kaibara Ekiken by Olaf Graf (*Kaibara Ekiken*. E. J. Brill, 1942), which should be sufficiently convincing to offset the strange notion that *only* modern Europe developed a naturalistic outlook on the world.

The case of India, of course, is not so clear, and probably will not be until more research is done in the emerging vernaculars of the eighteenth century. But the career of Ram Mohan Roy (1772-1833) is well enough known that it need not be told here; though he came into his own later than the above mentioned Chinese and Japanese naturalists, he was not without predecessors. To the Indian mind there was little conflict between naturalism and spirituality, for such a Cartesian dualistic dichotomy had never been present with any force in any Hindu, Jaina, Buddhist or Sikh tradition.

Those who look longingly at the pre-revolutionary Russian thinkers and writers for a *lost* spirituality of Mother Russia too easily overlook the work of such as Michael Lomonosov, Nicholai Popovsky and the heritage of the Encyclopedists that Catherine the Great invited from France. Actually, in spite of the tzarist autocracy and censorship, it can be claimed that with Bakunin Marx had a rival who was more revolutionary than himself. It is easily forgotten, for example, that Mendeleyev was not a Western European but completely Russian. Not that the spirituality was not there also; rather we may just as easily point to Skovoroda as a sort of Russian Ram Mohan Roy long before Tolstoi and Dostoyevsky.

As for the Americas, Ben Franklin and Alexander von Humbolt's adventures in Latin America are too well known to need emphasis. But one might also mention Cadwallader Colden in North America; and the thought and researches of José Celéstino Mutis, Francisco Eugenio Espejo and Benito Jerónomo

Feijoo in spite of the Spanish Inquisition, were in full sympathy with the French Enlightenment and the naturalism that went with it. The fact that Tom Paine was extremely popular in both continents should be evidence enough to demonstrate that naturalism was not only present in Latin America but very influential in the eighteenth and early nineteenth century.

As to whether naturalism and nationalism necessarily go hand-in-hand or were only incidentally concomitant we must leave for further investigation.

THE TOTAL ENCOUNTER

The Withdrawal from Encounters continues dialectically even today as the counter-current to the Total Encounter of the present time, as manifested in the continuing movements for complete independence and the cultivation of national and ethic images.

We are *rushed* into the nineteenth and twentieth centuries : acceleration of time,"future shock", begins to be the predominant phenomenon with a profound confusion between modernization, industrialization, secularization, and westernization. This is poignantly dramatized in the Japanese Meiji Restoration, but also in India and many new African countries even today. Everything becomes streamlined into the "instant" generation : electrified, capitalized, socialized, technologized. For Euramerica, empire and exploitation becomes words of approbation, not of accusation.

One begins to wonder : was the war of 1914-18 the first *world* war, or was there not one about 1860 of which the North American civil war was only a part ? But still more critical is the total change in the nature of warfare itself leading to what Raymond Aron has called *The Century of Total War.* War also becomes an *instant* affair — hopefully undergoing a "negation of negation", but the net result is not yet clear. Indeed, how soon the "century of progress" changed its name to the "age of anxiety", the "age of overkill", the "nuclear age", and now may be moving into the Age of Global Guerilla Warfare.

Revolution has become a word of expectancy, a word charged with mystique, so that even Kant conceived of his philosophy as a "Copernican Revolution". Meanwhile, perhaps the greatest revolution of all has been the deliverance of means of communication from means of transportation. Intercontinental telegraph, telephone, radio, and television have altered human dispositions more than any other factor in the history of mankind.

Such has been the acceleration of time within our own lifetime that we no longer measure travel by miles and kilometers, but by the time required for the journey. Moreover, it is no longer organic sun-time or moon-time, but mechanical clock-time that governs our life. The difference between night and day is disappearing, and our biological rhythms are continually being upset or reset so frequently that neurosis has become the major disease. Long since we have lost the sense of astronomical time, geological time, or even historical time. The instant generation has no roots in history, and even the philosophers are depending on computers for instant wisdom.

Unfortunately it takes time to measure time; and the measurement of historical time does need some regularizing and *synchronologizing*. Thus we end with the question we began with: By what measure or measures, or into what periods, may we best divide human time on this spaceship earth? The question by the way is not rhetorical.

NOTES

Rome and China

1. Joseph Needham, *Science and Civilisation in China*, vol. 2, *History of Scientific Thought* (Cambridge : Cambridge University Press, 1956), p. 281 (hereafter cited as *Civilisation in China*).

2. Ibid., pp. 282-83.

3. Wing-Tsit Chan, *A Source Book in Chinese Philosophy* (Princeton: Princeton University Press, 1963), pp. 281-82 (hereafter cited as *Chinese Source Book*).

4. Timotheus Pokora, "Life of Huan T'an" in *Archiv Orientální*, vol. 31 (Czechoslovakia, 1963), p. 565.

5. From an unpublished typescript by Timotheus Pokora, p. 209.

6. Ibid., p. 210.

7. Etienne Balazs, *Chinese Civilisation and Bureaucracy : Variations on a Theme*, H. M. Wright, trans., Arthur F. Wright, ed. (New Haven : Yale University Press, 1964).

8. Iason Xenakis, *Epictetus Philosopher-Therapist* (Nijhoff, 1969), p. 21.

9. Heinrich Busch,. "Hsün Yüeh, ein Denker am Hofe des letzten Hankaisers" in *Monumenta Serica*, vol. 10 (1945), p. 58-90.

10. Ko Hung, *Alchemy, Medicine, and Religion in the China of A.D.* 320: *The Nei P'ien of Ko Hung* (*Pao-p'u tzu*), trans. by James R. Ware (Cambridge, Massachusetts, and London : M. I. T. Press, 1966).

11. Ibid., p. 307.

12. Ibid., p. 169.

13. Ibid., p. 236.

14. L. J. R. Ort, *Mani, A Religio-Historical Description of his Personality* (Leiden : E. J. Brill, 1967), p. 116.

15. Robert Charles Zaehner, *Zurvan, A Zoroastrian Dilemma* (Oxford : Clarendon Press, 1955).

16. A. V. Williams Jackson, *Researches In Manichaeism* (New York : AMS Press, 1965).

17. Ibid., p. 7f.

Scepticism

1. Alain Michel, "La Philosophie en Grèce et à Rome de 130 à 250" in *Encyclopédie de la Pléiade*, vol. 26, *Histoire de la Philosophie*, tome 1 (1969), p. 877ff.

2. Charlotte Stough, *Greek Skepticism* (Berkeley : University of California Press, 1969).

3. Ibid., p. 138f.

4. Ibid., p. 145.

5. Ibid., p. 145.

6. Ibid., p. 146.
7. Needham, *Civilization in China*, p. 365ff.
8. Wang Ch'ung, *Lun Heng*, pt. 2, trans. by Alfred Forke (New York : Paragon Book Gallery, 1962).
9. Ibid., p. 96ff and p. 114ff.

Plotinus and Vasubandhu

1. Bhikshu Sangharakshita, *A Survey of Buddhism* (Bangalore: W.Q. Judge Press, 1957) p. 397 (hereafter cited as *Survey*).
2. Sarvepalli Radhakrishnan, *Indian Philosophy*, vol. I (London : George Allen & Unwin Ltd., 1966), p. 640.
3. Wing-tsit Chan, trans., *Triṃśikā* in *A Source Book in Indian Philosophy*, Sarvepalli Radhakrishnan and Charles A. Moore, eds. (Princeton: Princeton University Press, 1957), p. 337 (hereafter cited as *Indian Source Book*).
4. Edward Conze, *Buddhism : Its Essence and Development* (New York : Harper & Brothers, 1959), p. 166 (hereafter cited as *Buddhism*).
5. Ibid., pp. 168-69.
6. R. T. Wallis, *Neoplatonism* (New York : Charles Scribner's Sons, 1972), p. 66.
7. Emile Bréhier, *The Philosophy of Plotinus*, trans. by Joseph Thomas (Chicago : University of Chicago Press, 1958), p. 93 (hereafter cited as *Plotinus*).
8. D. T. Suzuki, "Philosophy of the Yogācāra" in *Le Muséon*, Vol. V (1904), p. 382.
9. Bréhier, *Plotinus*, p. 59.
10. Ibid., p. 71.
11. S. Das Gupta, "Philosophy of Vasubandhu in Viṃśatikā and Triṃśikā" in *Indian Historical Quarterly*, vol. IV, 1 (Calcutta, 1928), p. 42.
12. Wallis, *Neoplatonism*, p. 74.
13. Clarance H. Hamilton, trans., *Viṁśatikā* in *Indian Source Book*, p. 332.
14. Rakesha Ranjan Sharma, "The Yogācāra Theory of the External World" in *Proceedings and Transactions of the 5th Indian Oriental Conference*, vol. III, November 1928 (Lahore : University of Punjab, 1930), p. 885.
15. Bréhier, *Plotinus*, p. 174.
16. Ibid., p. 116.
17. Ibid., p. 188.
18. *Triṁśikā* in *Indian Source Book*, p. 337.
19. Sangharakshita, *Survey*, pp. 400-401.
20. Conze, *Buddhism*, p. 168.
21. D. T. Suzuki, *Outlines of Mahayana Buddhism* (New York : Schocken Books, 1963), p. 69 (hereafter cited as *Otluines*).
22. Karl Jaspers, *The Great Philosophers*, trans. by Ralph Manheim (New York: Harcourt, Brace & World, 1966), p. 48 (hereafter cited as *Philosophers*).
23. Ibid., p. 47ff.
24. Ibid., pp. 60-61.

25. Ibid., pp. 68-69.
26. Ibid., p. 52.
27. Radoslav A. Tsanoff, *The Great Philosophers*, 2nd ed. (New York : Harper & Row, 1964), p. 132.
28. Bréhier, *Plotinus*, p. 133.
29. Ibid., p. 55.
30. Ibid., p. 195.
31. Jaspers, *Philosophers* p. 70
32. Ibid., p. 54.
33. Suzuki, *Outlines*, p. 72.
34. Bréhier, *Plotinus* p. 195.
35. Ibid., p. 116.

Neo-Taoism

1. Holmes Welch, *Taoism : The Parting of the Way* (Boston : Beacon Press, 1957) p. 126 (hereafter cited as *Taoism*).
2. Chan, *Chinese Source Book*, p. 309.
3. T'ang Yung-t'ung, "Wang Pi's New Interpretation of the I Ching and Lun-yü" in *Harvard Journal of Asiatic Studies*, trans. and notes by Walter Liebenthal, 10 (1947) p. 126n (hereafter cited as "New Interpretation").
4. Fung Yu-lan, *The Spirit of Chinese Philosophy*, trans. by E. R. Hughes (Westport : Greenwood Press, 1970), p. 130 (hereafter cited as *Spirit*).
5. Arthur F. Wright, Review of A. A. Petrov's *Wang Pi* (226-249): *His Place in the History of Chinese Philosophy* in *Harvard Journal of Asiatic Studies*, 10, (1947), p. 80 (hereafter cited as Review).
6. Liebenthal, "New Interpretation", p. 125.
7. Fung Yu-lan, *A History of Chinese Philosophy*. vol. II, trans. by Derk Bodde, *The Period of Classical Learning* (Princeton: Princeton University Press, 1953), p. 180 (hereafter cited as *History*).
8. Ibid., p. 181.
9. T'ang, "New Interpretation", p. 144.
10. Needham, *Civilisation in China*, p. 322.
11. Wright, Review, p. 82.
12. Fung, *History*, p. 187.
13. Ibid., p. 187.
14. Chan, *Chinese Source Book*, p. 323.
15. Ibid., p. 324.
16. Ibid., p. 316.
17. Ibid., p. 324.
18. T'ang, "New Interpretation", p. 148.
19. Chan, *Chinese Source Book*, p. 323.
20. Ibid., p. 326.
21. Fung, *History*, p. 217.
22. Ibid., p. 223.
23. Ibid., p. 233.
24. Ibid., p. 212.

25. Fung, *Spirit*, p. 139.
26. Ibid., p. 143.
27. Welch, *Taoism*, p. 124.
28. Ibid., p. 125.
29. Donald Holzman, "Les Sept Sages de la Forêt des Bambous et la Société de Leur Temps" in *T'oung P'ao*, vol. 43-44 (1954-56).
30. Richard C. Howard, *Hsi Kang's Essays on Nurturing Life* (Columbia University thesis, 1949).

Global Apologetics

1. H. M. Gwatkin and J. P. Whitney, eds., *The Cambridge Medieval History*, vol. I (Cambridge : Cambridge University Press, 1964).
2. Leslie William Barnard, *Justin Martyr: His Life and Thought* (London : Cambridge University Press, 1967), p. 6.
3. Ibid., p. 7.
4. Ibid., pp. 83-84.
5. T. W. Rhys Davids, trans., *The Questions of King Milinda*, pt. II (New York : Dover Publications, Inc., 1963), p. xxvii.
6. Alfred Forke, *Geschichte der mittelalterlichen chinesischen Philosophie* (Hamburg : de Gruyter and Co., 1934), pp. 157-67.

Rise of Mahāyāna

1. Susumu Yamaguchi, "Development of Mahayana Buddhist Beliefs" in *The Path of the Buddha*, Kenneth W. Morgan, ed. (New York : Ronald Press Co., 1956), pp. 180-81.
2. Sangharakshita, *Survey*, p. 462.
3. Ibid., p. 465.
4. Ibid., p. 492ff.
5. Jadunath Sinha, *A History of Indian Philosophy*, vol. II (Calcutta: Central Book Agency, 1952), pp. 347-48.

PERIODIZATION BIBLIOGRAPHY

Anesaki, Masaharu. *History of Japanese Religion.* Rutland, Vermont : Charles E. Tuttle Co., 1966.

Aron, Raymond. *The Century of Total War.* Boston : The Beacon Press, 1954.

———. *World Technology and Human Destiny.* Ann Arbor : University of Michigan Press, 1963.

Artz, Frederick Binkerd. *The Mind of the Middle Ages.* New York : A. A. Knopf, 1966.

Balazs, Étienne *Chinese Civilization and Bureaucracy.* Edited by Arthur F. Wright. Translated by H. M. Wright. New Haven : Yale University Press, 1964.

Basham, A.L. *The Wonder that Was India.* New York: Grove Press, 1959.

Brelvi, Mahmud. *Islam in Africa.* Lahore, Pakistan : Institute of Islamic Culture, 1964.

Berge, François; Buhot, Jean; Levitte, Georges; et al. *Histoire Générale des Religions.* Vol. 2. Paris : Librairie Aristide Quillet, 1960.

Bierck, Harold A. *Latin American Civilization : Readings and Essays*, Boston : Allyn and Bacon, 1967.

Bingham, Woodbridge; Conroy, Hilary; and Iklé, Frank W. *A History of Asia.* 2 vols. Boston : Allyn and Bacon, 1964.

Bleeker, C. Jouco and Widengren, Geo. *Historia Religionum : Handbook for the History of Religions.* 2 vols. Leiden : E. J. Brill, 1969/71.

Bondy, Augusto Salazar. *Historia de las Ideas en el Perú Contemporáneo.* Lima, Peru : Francisco Moncloa, Editores S.A., 1967.

Burns, E. Bradford. *A Documentary History of Brazil.* New York : Alfred A. Knopf, 1966.

Cady, John F. *Southeast Asia : Its Historical Development.* New York : McGraw-Hill, 1964.

Carroll, Jr., Harry J.; Embree, Ainslie T.; Mellon, Jr., Knox; Schrier, Arnold; and Taylor, Alastair M. *The Development of Civilization*. 2 vols. Chicago : Scott Foresman and Co., 1961-62.

Chang, Carson (Chia-sên) *The Development of Neo-Confucian Thought*. New York : Bookman Associates, 1962.

Chang, Chun-shu. *Premodern China : A Bibliographical Introduction*. Ann Arbor : Michigan Papers in Chinese Studies, no. 11, 1971.

Coedès, G. *The Making of South East Asia*. Berkeley : University of California Press, 1969.

Crouzet, Maurice. *Historie Générale des Civilisations*. 7 vols. Paris: Presses Universitaires de France, 1957-65.

Das Gupta, Surendranath. *A History of Indian Philosophy*. 5 vols. Cambridge : Cambridge University Press, 1940-62.

De Bary, Wm. Theodore. *Self and Society in Ming Thought*. New York : Columbia University Press, 1970.

———, ed. *Sources of Chinese Tradition*. New York and London: Columbia University Press, 1961.

———, ed. *Sources of Indian Tradition*. New York and London: Columbia University Press, 1960.

———, ed. *Sources of Japanese Tradition*. New York and London: Columbia University Press, 1965.

Deussen, Paul. *Allgemeine Geschichte der Philosophie*. 5 vols. Leipzig : F. A. Brockhaus, 1920.

Devambes, Pierre and Babelon, Jean, eds. *Histoire de l'Art*. 3 vols. Encyclopédie de la Pléiade. Paris : Librairie Gallimard, 1961/66/65.

Diaz del Castillo, Bernal. *The Discovery and Conquest of Mexico*, 1517-1521. New York : Grove Press, 1956.

Duché, Jean. *Histoire du monde*. 4 vols. Paris : Flammarion, 1958-66.

Easton, Stewart C. *The Rise and Fall of Western Colonialism*. New York : Praeger, 1964.

Elisseeff, Vadime, et al. *Les Grandes civilisations du Moyen Age*. vol. 3. International Commission for a History of the Scientific and Cultural Development of Mankind. Paris : R. Laffont, 1969.

Fanon, Franz. *Towards the African Revolution*. Tr. by Haakon Chevalier. New York : Grove Press, 1968.

Ferrater Mora, José. *Man at the Crossroads.* Tr. by Willard R. Trask. New York : Greenwood Press, 1968.

———. *Philosophy Today.* New York : Columbia University Press, 1960.

Fickett, Lewis P., Jr. *Problems of the Developing Nations : Readings and Case Studies.* New York : Thomas Y. Crowell Co., 1966.

Freyre, Gilberto. *The Masters and Slaves.* New York : A. A. Knopf, 1946.

Gardner, Martin. *The Ambidextrous Universe.* New York : Basic Books, 1964.

Garraty, John A. and Gay, Peter, eds. *The Columbia History of the World.* New York : Harper and Row, 1972.

Gottschalk, Louis; MacKinney, Loren C.; and Pritchard, Earl H. *History of Mankind.* Vol. 4. International Commission for a History of the Scientific and Cultural Development of Mankind. New York : Harper and Row, 1969.

Graf, Olaf. *Kaibara Ekiken.* Leiden : E. J. Brill, 1942.

Grousset, R., and Léonard, E. G., eds. *Hsitoire Universelle.* 3 vols. Encyclopédie de la Pléiade Series. Paris : Gallimard, 1956-58.

Hall, D. G. E. *A History of South East Asia.* London: Macmillan, 1961.

Hawkes, Jacquetta, and Woolley, Sir Leonard. *History of Mankind.* Vol. 1. International Commission for a History of the Scientific and Cultural Development of Mankind. New York : Harper and Row, 1963.

Henríques Ureña, Pedro. *A Concise History of Latin American Culture.* Tr. by Gilbert Chase. New York : Praeger, 1966.

Jairazbhoy, R. A. *Foreign Influence in Ancient India.* Bombay : Asia Publishing House, 1963.

Jaspers, Karl. *The Origin and Goal of History.* Tr. by Michael Bullock. New Haven : Yale University Press, 1953/65.

Keen, Benjamin. *Readings in Latin American Civilization : 1492 to the Present.* New York : Houghton Mifflin Co., 1967.

Kern, Fritz, ed. *Historia Mundi.* 10 vols. Bern : Francke Verlag, 1952-61.

Kincaid, C. A., and Parasnis, Rao Bahadur. *A History of the Maratha People.* New Delhi : S. Chand and Co., 1968.

Kitagawa, Joseph M. *Religion in Japanese History*. New York : Columbia University Press, 1966.

Kohn, Hans. *The Idea of Nationalism, A Study in its Origin and Background*. New York: Macmillan Co., 1944.

———. *Nationalism, its Meaning and History*. Rev. ed. Princeton, N.J. : Van Nostrand, 1965.

———. *Pan-Slavism, its History and Ideology*. 2d. ed., rev. New York : Vintage Books, 1960.

Langer, William L., comp. and ed. *An Encyclopedia of World History*. Boston : Houghton Mifflin Co., 1972.

Latourette, Kenneth Scott. *The Chinese : Their History and Culture*. 4th ed., rev. New York : Macmillan, 1964.

Lee, Shao Chang. *The Development of Chinese Culture*. Honolulu; University of Hawaii Press, 1934.

Leonard, E. G., ed, *Histoire Universelle*. 3 vols. Encyclopédie de la Pléiade Series. Paris : Librairie Gallimard, 1958.

Lerner, Max. *The Age of Overkill*. New York : Simon and Shuster, 1962.

Li, Dun, J. *The Ageless Chinese : A History*. New York : Charles Scribner's Sons, 1965.

Ling, Trevor. *History of Religion East and West*. New York : Harper and Row, 1970.

Madariaga, Salvador de. *The Rise of the Spanish American Empire*. New York : Free Press, 1965.

Majumdar, R. C., gen. ed. *The History and Culture of the Indian People*. 11 vols. Bombay : Bharatiya Vidya Bhavan, 1965-69.

Martin, Michael Rheta, and Bruun, Geoffrey. *A Graphic Guide to World History*. New York: Holt, Rinehart and Wilson, 1959.

McLuhan, Herbert Marshall and Fiore, Quentin. *The Medium is the Message*. New York : Bantam Books, 1967.

McNeill, William H. *The Rise of the West : A History of the Human Community*. Chicago : University of Chicago Press, 1963.

Métraux, Guy S., and Crouzet, François. *The New Asia*. New York : New American Library, 1965.

Morazé, Charles. *Le XIXe Siècle*. Vol. 5. Paris : R. Laffont, 1969.

Mujeeb, M. *World History, Our Heritage.* Bombay : Asia Publishing House, 1960.

Narain, A. K. *The Indo-Greeks.* London : Oxford, the Clarendon Press, 1962.

Needham, Joseph. *Science and Civilisation in China.* 4 vols. Cambridge : Cambridge University Press, 1965-71.

Oliver, Ronald, and Atmore, Anthony. *Africa since* 1800. Cambridge, England: Cambridge University Press, 1972.

Pandey, A. B. *Early Medieval India.* Allahabad, India : Central Book Depot, 1965.

———. *Later Medieval India.* Allahabad, India : Central Book Depot, 1963.

Parain, Brice, ed. *Histoire de la Philosophie.* Vol. I. Encyclopédie de la Pléiade Series. Paris : Gallimard, 1969.

Pareti, Luigi. *History of Mankind.* Vol. 2. International Commision for a History of the Scientific and Cultural Development of Mankind. New York : Harper and Row, 1965.

Picón-Salas, Mariano. *A Cultural History of Spanish America.* Berkeley : University of California Press, 1962.

Plott, John C., and Mays, Paul D. *A Bibliographical Guide to the Global History of Philosophy.* Leiden : E. J. Brill, 1969.

Prescott, W. H. *History of the Conquest of Peru.* 3 vols. Edited by Wilfred H. Munro. New York : AMS Press, 1968.

Puech, d'Henri-Charles, ed. *Histoire des Religions.* 2 vols. Encyclopédie de la Pléiade Series. Paris : Éditions Gallimard, 1970-72.

Quigley, Carrol. *The Evolution of Civilizations.* New York : Macmillan, 1961.

Randall, John Herman. *The Making of the Modern Mind.* rev. ed. Boston : H. Mifflin, 1968.

Riepe, Dale. *The Naturalistic Tradition in Indian Thought.* Seattle : University of Washington Press, 1961.

Riha, Thomas, ed. *Readings in Russian Civilization.* 3 vols. Chicago : University of Chicago Press, 1964.

Rippy, J. Fred. *Latin America : A Modern History.* Ann Arbor : University of Michigan Press, 1958.

Robertson, William Spence. *Rise of the Spanish-American Republics.* New York : The Free Press, 1965.

Romein, Jan Marius. *The Asian Century : A History of Modern Nationalism in Asia.* Tr. by R. T. Clark. Berkeley : University of California Press, 1962.

Rybakov, Boris Aleksandrovich. *Early Centuries of Russian History.* Moscow : Progress Publishers, 1965.

Samaran, Charles, ed. *L'Histoire et ses Méthodes.* Encyclopédie de la Pléiade Series. Paris : Librairie Gallimard, 1961.

Sansom, George. *A History of Japan.* 4 vols. Stanford, California : Stanford University Press, 1958-73.

Sanyal, J. M. tr. *The Srimad-Bhagavatam of Krishna Dwaipayana Vyasa.* 5 vols. Calcutta : Oriental Publishing Co., cir. 1952.

Sastri, K. A. Nilakanta. *A History of South India.* Madras : Oxford University Press, 1966.

Schilling, Kurt. *Weltgeschichte der Philosophie.* Berlin : Duncker and Humblot, 1964.

Segal, Judah Benzion. *Edessa 'The Blessed City'.* London : Oxford, the Clarendon Press, 1970.

Shinoda, Minoru. *The Founding of the Kamakura Shogunate.* New York : Columbia University Press, 1960.

Sigmund, Paul E., Jr., ed. *The Ideologies of the Developing Nations.* New York : Praeger, 1967.

Sinha, Jadunath. *A History of Indian Philosophy.* 2 vols. Calcutta : Sinha Publishing House, 1952-56.

Sorokin, Pitirim A. *The Basic Trends of Our Times.* New Haven, Conn. : College and University Press, 1964.

———. *Social and Cultural Dynamics : A Study of Change in Major Systems of Art, Truth, Ethics, Law and Social Relationships.* Boston : Extending Horizons Books, 1957.

Ssŭ-ma, Ch'ien. *Records of the Grand Historian of China.* 2 vols. Tr. by Burton, Watson. New York : Columbia University Press, 1961.

Stavrianos, Leften S. *Man's Past and Present : A Global History.* Englewood Cliffs, N. J. : Prentice-Hall, Inc., 1971.

———, ed. *Readings in World History.* Boston : Allyn and Bacon, 1970.

Taylor, Henry Osborn. *The Mediaeval Mind.* 4th ed. Cambridge : Harvard University Press, 1949.

Toynbee, Arnold. *Change and Habit*. N.Y. and London : Oxford University Press, 1966.

———. *A Study of History*. 12 vols. New York : Oxford University Press, A Galaxy Book, 1962-64.

Van der Pot, J. H. J. "La Division de l'Histoire en Périodes" in *L'Homme el l'Histoire, Actes du VIe Congrès des Sociétés de Langue Française*. Paris : Presses Universitaires de France, 1952.

Valjavec, Fritz. *Weltgeschichter der Gegenwart*. 2 vols. Bern and München : Francke Verlag, 1962—.

Vasiliev, A. A. *History of the Byzantine Empire*. 2 vols. Madison : University of Wisconsin Press, 1964.

Ware, Caroline F., Panikkar, K. M.; and Romein, J. M. *History of Mankind*. Vol. 6. International Commission for a History of the Scientific and Cultural Development of Mankind. New York : Harper and Row, 1966.

Whitaker, Urgan G., ed. and comp. *Nationalism and International Progress*. San Francisco : Chandler Publishing Co., 1961.

Wilgus, Alva Curtis, and d'Eca, Raul. *Latin American History*. 5th ed. New York : Barnes and Noble, 1963.

BIOGRAPHICAL SKETCHES

Apollonius of Tyana (d. 97): Syncretistic, charismatic religious thinker of Roman Empire of whom incredible miracles were reported; travelled widely, probably including India

Arjuna: Warrior in the *Bhagavadgītā* to whom Kṛṣṇa, as his chariot driver, addresses the book's teachings

Asaṅga (c.350/480): Disciple of Maitreyanātha, the founder of the Yogācāra school of Mahāyāna Buddhism; author of the *Mahāyāna Saṃgraha*; brother of Vasubandhu

Aśoka (ruled c. 272-c. 232): Unified India under his rule; known for peacefully spreading Buddhism

Aśvaghoṣa (c. 50): Poet and dramatist; systematizer and popularizer of Mahāyāna Buddhism

Boethius (c. 480-524): Roman philosopher and statesman; translator of and commentator on Aristotle's *Organon* and Porphyry's *Isagoge*; author of famous *Consolation of Philosophy*

Carneades (219-129 B.C.): A Greek Sceptic; snake and rope metaphor indicates probable Indian influence

Chrysippus (280-209 B.C.): Systematizer of early Stoic school of Hellenistic philosophy

Chuang Tzu (c. 369-c. 286 B.C.): After Lao Tzu foremost of the Taoists; author of the *Chuang Tzu*

Cleanthes (310-230 B.C.): Successor to Zeno in history of Stoic school of philosophy; author of famous *Hymn to Zeus*

Clement of Alexandria (150-216): One of Christianity's first full-fledged theologians; precursor of Origen, who also lived and wrote in Alexandria; perhaps first Christian theologian to have some knowledge of Indian philosohpy

Epictetus (50-125): Stoic, slave; teacher of Marcus Aurelius, who became Rome's emperor; known for his *Enneads* ("The Nine")

Hsi K'ang (223-262); Neo-Taoist; executed for refusing a high government position; member of the *Seven Sages of the Bamboo Grove*; cultivated hedonist intuitive metaphysics

Hsü Kan (171-218): Confucian; later cited as a key authority during the Neo-Confucian revival c. 800 A.D.

Hsün Tzu (c. 320-c. 238 B.C.): Prominent early Confucian; served as a government magistrate; noted for his theory that human nature not naturally good; opposed Mencius

Hsün Yüeh (148-209): Confucian of the Later Han period; allied with the liberal Old Text School

Huan T'an (33 B.C.-39 A.D.); Reforming thinker, speaker and activist associated with the liberal Old Text School of Confucianism

Jaimini (fl. c. 400 B.C.): Founder of the Mīmāṁsā school of Hinduism; reputed author of the *Mīmāṁsā-sūtras*

Justin Martyr (100?-165?): Early Christian apologist martyred under Marcus Aurelius

Kautilya (c. 300 B.C./300 A.D.): Hindu political scientist of Machiavellian persuasion

Ko Hung (253-333 A.D.): Neo-Taoist mystic who tended to use Confucian terminology; affirmed radical simplicity

Kuo Hsiang (d. 312): Neo-Taoist; the foremost of commentators on the *Chuang Tzu*

Lucretius (99-54 B.C.): Roman Epicurean; author of the famous philosophical poem *De Natura Rerum*

Ma Jung (79-166 A.D.): Scholar who left service in the Later Han court to write a commentary on all the Chinese classics

Maitreya Buddha: The Buddha to come; Buddhist "Messiah"

Mani (215-276): Eclectic Persian religious teacher; after his execution by Bahram I, his teachings formed the basis of Manichaeanism

Manu (c. 500? B.C.): Traditional author of the Code of Manu of Hinduism

Marcus Aurelius (121-180): Stoic, disciple of Epictetus; became emperor of Rome; known for his *Meditations*

Mou Tzu (b.165): Chinese Buddhist who first popularized Buddhism in China, writing in dialogue form

Kundakundācārya (fl. c. 25): Authoritative Digambara Jaina philosopher; author of *Pañcāstikāyasamayasāra*

Milinda (Menander) (d. cir. 150 B.C.): Bactrian king who held dialogue with Buddhist monk Nāgasena in the famous Theravāda text under the title *Questions of Milinda*

Musonius Rufus (c. 50): Stoic; the teacher of Epictetus, who in turn taught Marcus Aurelius

Nāgārjuna (c. 100-200): Author of the first systematic exposition of Mādhyamika Buddhism, the *Mūla-Mādhyamika-kārikā*; see also Śūnyavāda Buddhism in the Glossary

Numenius of Apameia (c. 175): A syncretizing Platonist in the grand, exalted, idealist manner; forerunner of Plotinus

Origen (185-254): Alexandrian Christian theologian who, like his model Clement, drew on Philo and the Greek Classics; not always doctrinal by later Church standards

Parmenides (564-456 B.C.): Outstanding expounder of the early Eleatic school of Pre-Socratic Greek philosophy; emphasis on ontology: monistic trend

Philo of Alexandria (20 B.C. 50 A.D.): Jewish theologian and Neo-Platonist philosopher; early attempt at synthesis of Mosaic and Greek Traditions

Plotinus (204-261): Foremost of the Neo-Platonists; an extreme idealist, he considered 'matter' virtually synonymous with evil, 'spirit' with good

Plutarch (50-125): Popular biographer of the Greek and Roman world; wrote in Greek but greatly influenced Rome

Pyrrho (365-275 B.C.): Early Greek Sceptic; went to India in the army of Alexander the Great

Rāmānuja (d. cir. 1137): Vaiṣṇava Hindu commentator on the *Bhagavadgitā* and the *Brahmasūtras*; founder of Viśiṣṭādvaita school of philosophy

Śabara: Exhaustive compiler of the rituals of Mīmāṁsā Hinduism

Saint Augustine(354-430): Convert to Christianity from Manichaeanism who became Bishop of Hippo in North Africa; perhaps the most influential of the Latin Church Fathers

Seneca (4 B.C.-65 A.D.): Stoic of Spanish extraction; tutor to Nero; influential on Christian ethical theory

Sextus Empiricus (c. 200-250): Chief Hellenistic sceptic philosopher and scientist following Pyrrho and Carneades; emphasized suspended judgment (*epoché*) and detachment

Tertullian (155-235): One of the first full-fledged Christian philosophers; puritanical and suspicious of non-Christian terminology and traditions

Tung Chung-shu (179-104 B.C.): Founder of Confucianism's

conservative New Text school; adapted Confucius' humanism into a Chinese state religion

Umāsvāti (Umāsvāmi)(fl. c. 25): One of the earliest Śvetāmbara Jaina philosophers; author of *Tattvarthādhigamasūtra*

Upatissa Thera (fl. 66-129): The very level-headed, unpresupposing author of the *Vimutimagga* of Theravāda Buddhism; wrote in Pali; predecessor of Buddhaghoṣa

Vasubandhu (c. 280-400): A key thinker of Vijñānavāda (or Yogācāra) Buddhism; highly idealist, his thought bears great similarity to that of his contemporary Plotinus

Wang Ch'ung (27-c. 100): Liberal Confucian; debunker, sceptic, naturalist, rational reformer; associated with the liberal Old Text School

Wang Fu (90-165): Liberal Confucian with Taoist tendencies; outspoken critic of corruption in the Civil Service

Wang Mang (ruled 9-23 A.D.): Radical reforming dictator whose reign interrupted the Han Dynasty; Former Han preceded him, Later Han followed him

Wang Pi (226-249): Neo-Taoist, famous for his commentaries on Lao Tzu, *I-Ching*, etc.

Yang Hsiung (53 B.C.- 18 A.D.): Syncretistic Taoist who propounded Confucianist ethics; author of *The Great Mystery*; taught that human nature is a mixture of good and evil

Zeno the Eleatic (c. 490 B.C.): Zeno and the other Eleatics held that Being was the only reality, and that change, motion and plurality were illusions; the school was named for Elea, a Greek colony in Italy

Zeno the Stoic (340-265 B.C): Greek thinker; founder of Stoicism

GLOSSARY

Advaita Vedânta: an Upaniṣadic-based school developed by Gauḍapāda and flowering in the 9th century philosopher Śaṅkara

Advaitin: a non-dualist; a Vedāntin Hindu

agapé: (Greek) spiritual love

ākāśa: (Sanskrit) space, ether

Ālaya (or *Ālayavijñāna*): (Sanskrit) the cosmic mind, self-evolving thought, great storehouse of consciousness; similar to Jung's 'collective unconscious'

ānanda: (Sanskrit) supreme joy, bliss

anātman: (Sanskrit) 'no soul' or 'no Self'; a Buddhist concept (Pali: *anatta*)

apatheia: (Greek) detachment, indifference to feelings

Arhat: (Sanskrit) the ideal saint of Theravāda Buddhism

asatkāryavāda: (Sanskrit) a theory of causation which holds that the effect does not pre-exist in the cause

ascesis: (Greek) pattern of discipline for an achievement of spiritual refinement

ataxaria: (Greek and Latin) non-action

ātman: (Sanskrit) soul, spirit, Self; or the 'selfless Self'

avatār: (Sanskrit) an incarnation of deity

avidyā: (Sanskrit) ignorance, not seeing; from the root *vid*, meaning 'to see'

Axial Period: the period of philosophy's origins, approximately 750-250 B.C.; the subject of Volume One of the present series

Bactria, land of : a country centered at the crossroads of ancient trade routes, where northeastern Afghanistan now lies

Bhagavadgitā: one of the most popular Hindu sacred texts, rather eclectic, dated from between 200 B.C. and 200 A.D.

bhakti: (Sanskrit) devotion, active service

bikkhus: (Sanskrit) monk

Bodhisattva (Sanskrit) the ideal saint of the Mahāyāna Buddhism

Brahman: (Sanskrit) Ultimate Reality; God

buddhi: (Sanskrit) mind or intellect in its natural, psycho-physical function

Cārvāka Hinduism : early materialistic Hindu school, often equated with Lokāyata

ch'i: (Chinese) vital force, breath, air, ether not to be confused with other ideograms also transcribed as *ch'i*

chidākāsha : (Sanskrit) an element resulting from the trans-mergence of the other four elements with ether

contemptus mundi: (Latin) contempt for the world

contemptus populi: (Latin) contempt for the common people

Cyrenaics: extreme philosophical hedonists of the Greco-Roman world

dharma: (Sanskrit) law, duty, virtue, merit, order; body of teachings; element; motion (Pāli: *dhamma*)

dhyāna: (Sanskrit) intensive meditation

eclecticism: the unsystematic selection of ideas from various systems, doctrines or sources

epistémé: (Greek and Latin) certain knowledge or knowledge with certainty; science of life

epoché: (Greek and Latin) suspension of judgement

geist: (German) spirit, ghost

gnosis: (Greek) knowledge; often with the implication of esoteric knowledge, as in Gnosticism

guṇa: (Sanskrit) quality, attribute; the three constituents of *prakṛti*: *sattva*, *rajas* and *tamas*

Hassidism: mystical movement among the ghettoized Jews of eastern Europe, 17th century to present but roots stemming back to Babylonian Talmud

Hīnayāna Buddhism: literally 'Little vehicle'; the Mahāyāna Buddhists often thus refer to Theravāda Buddhism; see Theravāda Buddhism

hormé: (Greek) attraction, desire

hsing: (Chinese) human nature; punishment; form

hsüan (Chinese) dark, profound, secret intuitive mysteriousness

i: (Chinese) righteousness, justice; one of the four Confucian fundamentals of the moral life

jeu des systèmes: (French) play of the systems

jīva: (Sanskrit) soul, in the sense of vital principle; distinct from *ātman jivanmukta*: (Sanskrit) one who attains emancipation while still living

jñāna: (Sanskrit) pure knowledge, thought, consciousness, wisdom, idea

Kali Yuga: in Hindu mythology, the age of greatest conflict and darkness; several thousand years in duration; last age in cycle of civilization in which dharma becomes degenerate and culture becomes decadent; many contend we are in it currently

Kalki Yuga: in Hindu mythology, the age of the final triumph

karma: (Sanskrit) action; deeds; the results of good or bad deeds

karuṇā: (Sanskrit) compassion, mercy, pity

kṣaṇavāda: (Sanskrit) Buddhist doctrine of momentariness

Legalism: conservative movement during the Han Dynasty; favored literal enforcement of legally prescribed punishments

li: (Chinese) law, rational principle; good form; ritual ceremony; reason; decorum

logos (Greek) reason, word, principle; as used by the Stoics, the rational order of the universe

Mādhyamika Buddhism: see Sūnyavāda Buddhism

Mahābhārata: great Sanskrit epic containing the *Bhagavadgītā*

mahākaruṇā: (Sanskrit) the great compassion of the Buddha and/or Bodhisattvas

Mahāyāna Buddhism: literally 'Great Vehicle'; Buddhist systems, centered in northern India, which migrated to China and, eventually, to Japan

manas: (Sanskrit) mind, understanding; the unifying principle which analyzes and synthesizes sensation

māyā: (Sanskrit) ultimately unreal; illusion

metempsychosis: the passing of a soul at death into another body, either human or animal; the transmigration of souls

Mimāṁsā Hinduism: a school closely associated with Vedānta; founded by Jaimini, author of the *Mimāṁsā-sūtras* (c. 400 B.C.) and primarily concerned with the *Brāhmaṇas*, the first part of the *Vedas* (Vedānta being concerned with the last part of the *Vedas*, the *Upaniṣads*)

ming: (Chinese) destiny, fate; the decree of Heaven

Mohism: a philosophy of universal love and social equality founded by Mo Tzu (c. 470-c. 391 B.C.); initially influential, but functionally extinct after 300 B.C.

mokṣa: (Sanskrit) emancipation, liberation, salvation

natur-mensch: (German) nature people

neti neti: (Sanskrit) not this, not that

New Text School of Confucianism: conservative, idealist wing of Confucianism during the Han Dynasty, founded by Tung Chung-shu

nihil ex nihilo: (Latin) nothing comes from nothing

nirguṇa (Sanskrit) without attributes, qualities or qualifications; indescribable

nirvāṇa: (Sanskrit) the emancipated state, salvation, (heaven); non-finite existence (Pāli: *nibbāna*)

niṣkāma: (Sanskrit) desireless

nous: (Greek) mind, intelligence, reason

Nyāya: literally, (right) argumentation; Hinduism's first school of logic, founded by one Gautama (c. 400 B.C.), not the Buddha; closely associated with the Vaiśeṣika school of metaphysics

Old Text School of Confucianism: liberal, realist wing of Confucianism during the Han Dynasty; also known as the Kuwen party

parousia: (Greek) presence, in the sense of the essence

Peripatetics: another name for the Aristotelians

phronēsis (Greek) worldly wisdom, practical understanding, right judgement

pneuma: (Greek) vital breath

prajña: (Sanskrit) wisdom, knowledge, insight, intuition (Pāli: *panna*)

Prajñāpāramitā: (Sanskrit) in Buddhism, the perfection of knowledge or intuition; the name given to seminal *sūtras* of Mahāyāna Buddhism dating from circa 100 A.D.

prakṛti: (Sanskrit) original, uncreated matter or substance consisting of the three *guṇas* (in Sāṃkhya); see above, *guṇa*

pralaya: (Sanskrit) periodic dissolution of the world; cosmic involution

pramāṇa: (Sanskrit) means of acquiring valid knowledge; mean of cognition; measure

prāṇa: (Sanskrit) vital breath, life, vitality

Pratyekabuddha: (Sanskrit) a person on the way to *nirvāṇa* who has not necessarily taken the *Bodhisattva* vow

psyché (Greek) soul; World Soul; spirit

Purāṇas: (Sanskrit) 'ancient stories'; literature which develops the Hindu trinity of Brahmā, Śiva and Viṣṇu

puruṣa: (Sanskrit) a term used primarily in the Sāṃkhya-Yoga school of Hinduism; the 'person' in the sense of observer-consciousness

Rāmāyaṇa : great Sanskrit epic traditionally ascribed, as also the *Mahābhārata*, to the authorship of Valmiki

ratio: (Latin) Reason; in Stoicism conformity to natural law and harmony of the universe

sādhana: (Sanskrit) means to an end; spiritual discipline or exercise; accomplishment

Śaivism: a post-Buddhist form of theistic Hinduism

samādhi: (Sanskrit) concentration, trance; highest stage in yogic meditation

saṅgha: (Sanskrit) Buddhist (and sometimes Jaina) monastic community; brotherhood

Sāṃkhya Hinduism: a school of 'right knowledge' founded, according to tradition, by Kapila, and forming the theoredical background of yóga

saṃsāra: (Sanskrit) cycle of death and rebirth; the continuing transmigratory rounds through mundane existences and deaths

saṃskāras: (Sanskrit) old habits from past experiences; potencies resulting from past lives

sannyāsa: (Sanskrit) one of the four Hindu *āśramas*, or stages of life; the stage of renunciation, mendicancy

śaraṇagati: (Sanskrit) positive and complete surrender

Sarvāstivāda Buddhism (also Vaibhāṣika): a major school of Indian Buddhism from about 100 B.C. to ascendency of Vijñānavāda about 350 A.D.; its original Sanskrit texts are lost, but Chinese translations have survived

satkāryavāda: (Sanskrit) a theory of causation holding that the cause is inherent in the effect

Sautrāntika Buddhism: relatively early school of Theravāda

Buddhism; philosophically associated with the 'indirect realism' (or 'representationism') doctrine

Septuagint: the Greek *Old Testament*; translated by Hellenized Jews in Alexandria about 250 B.C.

sophia: (Greek) wisdom, not practical but theoredical, or even esoteric

sophrosynê: (Greek) wisdom derived from rational thought; understanding

śruti: (Sanskrit) holy scripture, primarily the *Vedas*

śūnya: (Sanskrit) empty, void

Śūnyavâda Buddhism (also called the Mâdhyamika school): a branch of Mahâyâna first systematically expounded by Nâgârjuna in the second century A.D.; emphasizes the Buddha's teachings on the inability of intellect to comprehend Reality and the inability of language to express Reality

sūtras: (Sanskrit) aphorisms expressing the essense of the teachings of a school of philosophy

sva-dharma: (Sanskrit) one's own *dharma*, or duty, with the implication that everyone has his or her own *dharma*

syâdvâda: (Sanskrit) the Jaina doctrine that all knowledge is relative syncretism: the attempt to combine or reconcile differing ideas or beliefs

Tamil Saṅgam: a center in the extreme south of India beginning about 100 A.D. concerned with aesthetics and with the formalization of Tamil grammar and poetry

Tao: (Chinese) Way; cosmic order, Nature; the moral order; ineffable Reality

Tao Teh Ching: short, aphoristic work attributed to Lao Tzu containing the earliest formulation of Taoism

Tathatā: (Sanskrit) 'thatness' 'suchness', ultimate Reality

teh: (also *te*) (Chinese) power, virtue; Tao as manifested; Tao particularized; character

theosis: (Greek)identification with, or Ultimate absorption into, the Deity, or the transcendent Reality

Theravâda Buddhism: also known as Hīnayâna, which means literally 'Little Vehicle' originally emerged from Sthaviravâda Buddhism; with Mahâyâna it remains today one of the two main branches of Buddhism extant

T'ien: (Chinese) sky; Heaven, Supreme Power; Nature

Tīrthaṅkara: in Jainism, the special qualities of the twenty-four 'ford-finders' or enlightened one; "Avatar"

Upaniṣads: the last part of the *Vedas*, containing monastic speculations and providing the basis for the Vedāntic philosophies

vade mecum: (Latin) a handbook or manual carried on one's person for frequent use

Vaiśeṣika Hinduism: a realist but not materialist school of metaphysics, founded by Kaṇāda; associated with the Nyāya school of logic

Vaiṣṇava Hinduism: sect treating Viṣṇu as the personal deity while advocating absolutism

vāsanā: (Sanskrit) seeds from past experiences; dispositions; unconscious impressions; potentialities resulting from *karma*

Vedānta Hinduism: literally 'the end of the *Veda*' (*i.e.*, the *Upaniṣads*) but also implying the goal or meaning of the *Veda*; applied to philosophies based on the *Upaniṣads* or Brahma Sūtras of Bādarāyaṇa

via negativa (Latin) method of philosophical and theological argument based on first determining what is not the case

vijñāna: (Sanskrit) consciousness, cognition, thought; mental act or process; mind

Vijñānavāda Buddhism (also called the Yogācāra school): generally considered founded by Maitreyanātha (c. 270/350 A.D.) a Mahāyāna philosophy of 'objective idealism' much concerned with the Buddha's psychology of consciousness; died out in India about 800 A.D., continuing in China as the Wei-shih ('Consciousness Only') school

Vijñaptimātra: (Sanskrit) pure consciousness, pure subject, the Universal Self

Viśvarūpa: (Sanskrit) manifestation of a deity to a devotee, particularly Kṛṣṇa's revelation of his cosmic form to Arjuna in the *Bhagavadgītā*

wu: (Chinese) Eternal Non-Being, or non-manifestation, the first principle of the *Tao*; also matter, things, creatures; opposite of *yu*

wu wei: (Chinese) non-assertion, spontaneity, naturalness; accomplishment without effort *yin-yang*: (Chinese) passive (*yin*) and active (*yang*) cosmic principles, contrasting yet complementary

yoga: (Sanskrit) union; the use of controlled breathing, prescribed postures, mental concentration, etc. in pursuit of union with the Ultimate Reality

Yogācāra Buddhism: see Vijñānavāda Buddhism

yu: (Chinese) Being; 'the mother of all things'; also space; also desire; opposite of *wu*

yüan: (Chinese) origin, beginning, cosmic source of all things

zeitgeist: (German) world spirit

Zoroastrianism: Persian religion founded by Zoroaster (Zarathustra) about the 6th century B.C.; dualistic, in that emphasis is on cosmic struggle between good and evil; survives today among Iran's Gabars and the Parsis of Bombay

Zurvanism: a cult, with probable roots in Zoroastrianism, which taught that Time was the supreme, all-inclusive Deity, with primacy over the good and evil deities of Zoroastrianism

TO THE READER

The reader of this volume is referred to the Appendices, Glossaries and Indices of other volumes in the series. In addition, Volume One of the series contains a chart tracing the development of the various schools of Hinduism and Buddhism, as well as three synchronological charts providing dates for over 1000 philosophers of all periods and areas.

INDEX OF PERSONAL NAMES

SUBJECT INDEX